Exploring Lost Borders

WESTERN LITERATURE SERIES

Exploring Lost Borders

CRITICAL ESSAYS ON MARY AUSTIN

Edited by
Melody Graulich and
Elizabeth Klimasmith

University of Nevada Press
Reno Las Vegas

WESTERN LITERATURE SERIES

University of Nevada Press, Reno, Nevada 89557 USA
Copyright © 1999 by University of Nevada Press
All rights reserved
Manufactured in the United States of America
Designer: Susan Walsh

Library of Congress Cataloging-in-Publication Data

Exploring lost borders : critical essays on Mary Austin / edited by
Melody Graulich and Elizabeth Klimasmith.
p.   cm. — (Western literature series)
Includes bibliographical references and index.
ISBN 0-87417-335-3 (alk. paper)
1. Austin, Mary Hunter, 1868-1934 — Criticism and interpretation.
2. Women and literature—Southwestern states—History—20th century.
3. Western stories—History and criticism.
4. West (U.S.)—In literature.
I. Graulich, Melody, 1951- . II. Klimasmith, Elizabeth, 1969- . III. Series.
PS3501.U8Z584   1999
818'.5209—dc21   99-10485
                            CIP

The paper used in this book meets the requirements of American
National Standard for Information Sciences—Permanence of Paper for
Printed Library Materials, ANSI Z39.48-1984. Binding materials were
selected for strength and durability.

First Printing
08 07 06 05 04 03 02 01 00 99   5 4 3 2 1

To Brock Dethier and Bayard Klimasmith

Contents

Contents   VIII

Acknowledgments

We thank The Huntington Library, San Marino, California, for permission to print unpublished materials from their Austin collection.

We would also like to thank Christine Ransom and Heather Robbins of the English Department at the University of New Hampshire and Sabine Barcatta, Managing Editor of *Western American Literature* at Utah State University, for their expert computer help.

The contributors acknowledge the following institutions for the use of material in this collection, as follows: In "Between Worlds, Crossing Borders: Mary Austin, Liminality, and the Dilemma of Women's Creativity" by Anna Carew-Miller, the author quotes from letters Mary Austin wrote to Mabel Dodge Luhan, which are housed in The Yale Collection of American Literature, Beinecke Rare Book and Manuscript Library, Yale University. In "Singing Like the Indians Do: Mary Austin's Poetry" by Dale Metcalfe, the author reproduces (1) in its entirety the poem "Home Thoughts in the City" by Mary Austin from the journal issue *Folksay IV: The Land is Ours*, edited by B. A. Botkin and reprinted by permission of the University of Oklahoma Press, copyright © 1932; (2) in its entirety the poem "Not to You Only, O Pythian" by Mary Austin from the journal *The Nation* (Dec. 1, 1926); (3) excerpts from the poem "Cassandra" from *H. D. Collected Poems 1912-1944*, copyright © 1982 by The Estate of Hilda Doolittle and reprinted by permission of New Directions Publishing Corp.; (4) in its entirety the poem "Caller of Buffalo" by Mary Austin from the journal *Poetry* (June 1928); (5) in its entirety the poem "The Flower-Fed Buffaloes" by Mary Austin, which appeared in *Going-to-the-Stars* by Vachel Lindsay (New York: D. Appleton and Co., 1927).

Introduction

MELODY GRAULICH

I.

In 1968, Ansel Adams, who had worked with Mary Austin on a book called *Taos Pueblo* (1930), offered this tribute: "Seldom have I met and known anyone of such intellectual and spiritual power and discipline. . . . She is a 'future' person—one who will, a century from now, appear as a writer of major stature in the complex matrix of our American culture."[1] When Adams wrote those words, only one of Austin's works, *The Land of Little Rain,* was in print, and the contemporary feminist movement was just beginning. Adams set a prudent deadline; but today, only thirty years after he wrote, Austin is fast achieving that "major stature" in American cultural studies. At this writing, nine Austin works are in print: *The Land of Little Rain* (1903); *Lost Borders* (1909), in *Country of the Lost Borders; A Woman of Genius* (1912); *The Ford* (1918); *Land of Journey's Ending* (1924); *Earth Horizon* (1932); *Western Trails: A Collection of Stories by Mary Austin* (1987), which includes previously unpublished and uncollected stories; *Cactus Thorn* (1988); and *Beyond Borders: The Selected Essays of Mary Austin* (1996). New editions of *The Basket Woman* (1904), *Isidro* (1905), *The Flock* (1906), and *The Trail Book* (1918) are under way.

Austin's "rediscovery," largely the result of the contemporary feminist and environmental movements, has brought her new and more varied critical attention, reflected in *Exploring Lost Borders,* the first collection of critical essays on her work. In making our selections from the many fine essays our call for papers generated, the editors tried to put together an assortment offering a variety of critical perspectives. Some of our writers extend such established approaches to Austin's work as ecocriticism (Anne Raine, Mark Schlenz), feminist criticism (Anna Carew-Miller, Tara Hart), and Native American studies (Mark Hoyer, Dale Metcalfe). Others rethink and redefine the roles in which Austin has usually been cast: as nature writer (Michelle Campbell Toohey), as western American writer (Melody Graulich), and as social critic (Nicole Tonkovich, Barney Nelson). Others read Austin within new theoretical frameworks such as consumer studies (Elizabeth Klimasmith), postcolonial studies (Kathryn DeZur), composition studies (Linda K. Karell), and autobiographical literary criticism (Judy Nolte Temple). As a whole, *Exploring Lost Borders* demonstrates the importance of placing Austin's writings within a richly described historical and cultural web, yet many of the essays offer readings informed by poststructuralist and postmodern theorists: Bakhtin, Foucault, Barthes, Lacan, Kristeva, Cixous. Several essayists present Austin as challenging hierarchical thinking, a challenge fundamental to contemporary theoretical models from ecofeminism to deep ecology. In showing how Austin anticipates poststructuralist, feminist, environmentalist, and postcolonial theory, the essayists in this volume establish her "future" thinking.

Perhaps partly because Austin herself so resists categorization, most of her critics position her at the intersection of a variety of perspectives, corresponding, perhaps, to Adams's "matrix of our American culture" or to one of Austin's own water holes. Describing one of her stories in *The Flock* (1906), Austin said, "One finds tales like this at every point of contact with the Tejon [region], raying out fanwise like thin, white runways of rabbits from any waterhole in a rainless land."[2] Austin leads readers along particularly fertile and exciting trails into contemporary critical landscapes; the essayists in *Exploring Lost Borders* show us how her interests ray out into various political concerns.

Austin was once largely overlooked because she wrote in undefinable genres about borderless subjects; ironically, the range and variety of her work led critics to dismiss her as an eccentric dilettante. As Adams implied by calling her a "future" person, Austin's first insightful readers recognized that her work would become visible only when the proper critical vocabulary and context had been put in place. While contemporary theory has taught us how to read her, as the essays in this collection demonstrate, she also teaches us how to read the emerging map of a multicultural "America," a country of diffuse borders and intersecting histories, a country she herself surveyed for us. In 1932, Austin wrote in "Regionalism in American Fiction" that American critics have "flinch[ed] from the task of competently knowing, not one vast, pale figure of America, but several Americas, in many subtle and significant characterizations."[3] Austin has led the contributors to *Exploring Lost Borders* in search of many Americas.

Her autobiography, *Earth Horizon* (1932), describes how important it was to Austin to find the patterns in her own life. In one passage she locates the "matrix" of her own creativity: "In the Rain Song of the Sia, Earth Horizon is the incalculable blue ring of sky meeting earth, which is the source of experience. It is pictured as felt, rays of earth energy running together from the horizon to the middle place where the heart of man, the recipient of experience, is established, and there treasured" (33).[4] In images like this one, again and again throughout her career, Austin established a relationship between individual experience and vision and communal stories, cultural histories. Like the rabbit trails leading toward the water hole, the "rays of earth energy" lead toward the "middle place," the creative source. Like those trails, the essays in this volume ray out from Mary Austin, the fertile "matrix," providing tracks for future critics.

Austin's descriptions of the natural world often instruct her readers *how* to read the desert landscape of the "country of the lost borders," which looks lifeless to the uninitiated but is actually filled with complex patterns: "The earth is no wanton to give up all her best to every comer, but keeps a sweet, separate intimacy for each."[5] We who have come to Austin know that sweet intimacy. We offer paths to it, but we also know that readers will find their own way.

II.

Ansel Adams was not alone among Austin's contemporaries in recognizing her stature. Such influential critics of American culture as Charlotte Perkins Gilman, Van Wyck Brooks, Carl Van Doren, Constance Rourke, and Carey McWilliams praised her work, offering insightful responses that anticipate many of the current critical approaches. Rourke's review of *Earth Horizon* describes Austin as a critic who provides "large perspectives" on American cultural practices; McWilliams calls her an "incisive and illuminating" "social historian" and recognizes her contributions to women's history.[6] At Austin's death in 1934, Elizabeth Shepley Sargent called her one of the most important American women writers. Henry Smith's exploration of Austin as a cultural "trail marker," published in 1932 in the first issue of *New Mexico Quarterly,*[7] is one of the most perceptive essays ever written about her.

Even after her death Austin had devoted followers. She continued to receive sporadic attention as a nature writer, and *The Land of Little Rain* remained consistently in print. Yet most of her other work went unread. Edward Abbey, for instance, declared that she wrote only "one living book," then added in characteristic fashion that he hadn't read any of her others.[8] Little substantive attention was paid to Austin's work until the period of feminist recovery. Working from library copies and photocopies, a number of powerful critics wrote about Austin in the 1980s: Elaine Showalter, Lois Rudnick, Blanche Gelfant, Vera Norwood, Elizabeth Ammons, Karen Langlois. Three biographies appeared: Augusta Fink's *I-Mary,* Peggy Pond Church's *Wind's Trail,* and Esther Lanigan Stineman's *Mary Austin: The Song of a Maverick.* Austin's reprinted works include substantial critical introductions or afterwords by Nancy Porter, Marjorie Pryse, and myself. While Austin continued to receive some attention as a nature writer, most readings during this period were feminist. Critics were excited and intrigued by Austin's portrayals of powerful, unconventional women; her connections between women and nature; her critiques of marriage; her exploration of women artists; her role as a feminist theorist; her portrayals of relations between women; her re-vision of male themes and myths, particularly of the American West; her depictions of American Indian women; and her strong, original, often defiant voice. In largely feminist readings, critics discussed Austin's place in American culture; her political activities; her relationships with other cultural icons such as Mabel Dodge Luhan, Charlotte Perkins Gilman, Lincoln Steffens, and Jack London; as well as the formal concerns in her work, her interest in storytelling, her theories about the relationship between landscape and art, her analyses of regional cultures, and her stylistic experimentation.

Critical debates in the 1980s centered largely on two issues: Austin's personality and her style. Some critics and biographers admired Austin's achievement but found her egotistic, pretentious, and male-identified; others—I was among them—celebrated her sympathetic portrayals of women of all races and classes and her connections to women's literary traditions.[9] Some valued Austin's ideas despite what they perceived as an arcane, convoluted style. Others noted the variety of the styles in which she wrote and found her original and provocative. They explored in detail what she learned from Native Americans and began the close readings of her stylistic innovations and narrative techniques that characterize many of the essays in this volume. Particularly insightful readings of Austin's style were offered by David Wyatt; Marjorie Pryse; Carl Bredahl, who found a term, "divided narrative," to describe Austin's unconventional merger of fiction and nonfiction; and Esther Stineman.[10]

Critics also read Austin within a variety of feminist frameworks that have been debated since the 1980s. Familiar approaches and metaphors appeared in Austin scholarship: how did she develop her "voice," "negotiate" an independent self, "resist" male narrative structure? Do such works as *A Woman of Genius, The Arrow-Maker,* and "The Coyote-Spirit and the Weaving Woman" recapitulate the old dichotomy between love and work, marriage and career, so prevalent in nineteenth-century women's literature? Or did Austin offer new models for the woman artist in stories such as "Frustrate," in *Earth Horizon,* and in her portrayals of nonconforming women? Are her characters victims of cultural definitions of womanhood, or do they, like the Walking Woman, "walk off all sense of society-made values"? Are they culturally handicapped by unequal opportunities or enriched by women's culture? Is Austin's connection of women to landscape radical or essentialist? The appearance of *Cactus Thorn* in 1988, with its threatening, unnerving message and original style, drew immediate comparisons to such feminist classics as "The Yellow Wallpaper" and "A Jury of Her Peers."

Those of us who used the work of women writers in our literature courses in the 1980s often had to teach from photocopies, and the works of Austin were no exception. I remember with pleasure the amazed and delighted response of my young women students to "The Walking Woman" and "The Coyote-Spirit and the Weaving Woman" in the class on nature writing that I taught in 1980. Majoring in forestry, outdoor education, and environmental studies, working summers for Outward Bound and the Appalachian Mountain Club, they had never encountered a woman writer who spoke so directly to their own feelings about the land. The reprints have made Austin available to a new generation of "common readers"; some of the most perceptive reviews of *Western Trails,* for instance, are from the *Kansas City Star* and the *Los Angeles Times.* The reprints have also allowed scholars to begin teaching Austin to a new generation of students who read her work with enthusiasm and in the context of new theoretical and critical approaches—students who have built on the scholarly work described above and have begun to publish their own work in journals.

Many of those critics are contributors to this volume.[11] Feminist critics helped us to recognize the range of Austin's achievement, yet our contributors simply assume that gender is a crucial category in understanding
human identity and branch out into racial, ethnic, regional, religious, and
class territories. Ecocritics range beyond familiar texts, often using new
theoretical maps. In making an argument for the richness in such under-
valued Austin works as *Isidro, The Flock,* the Indian plays, and the poetry,
many critics are still implicitly doing recovery work, but they present so-
phisticated readings that engage with larger cultural issues. The essays in
Exploring Lost Borders show Austin to be central to rereading some of the
key paradigms in American studies scholarship: the construction of gender,
the representation of ethnic minorities, multiculturalism, the fluidity of
race and gender in the borderlands, genre crossings, modernism, the West
and its "geography of hope." They suggest that Austin will be a central figure in the theoretical debates in the emerging field of ecocriticism. And
they show how she can help us in our ongoing reexamination of what
constitutes our American literary and cultural legacies.

Our essayists continue to examine Austin's multidimensional analysis of
gender, but their approaches reflect more recent critical insights: Judith
Butler's concept of "the performance of gender," Hélène Cixous's theories
of writing from the female body, Sidonie Smith's work on representation
in women's autobiography, Gail Bederman's analysis of the social construction of masculinity. A number now bring Austin into relationship
with male nature writers, suggesting that she borrowed from some, such as
John Wesley Powell; disagreed with others, such as John Muir; and defied
the assumptions of others, such as John Burroughs. Much of the conversation in this collection might be seen as a response to Elizabeth Ammons's
assessment of the dilemmas facing turn-of-the-century women writers,
whom she sees as refusing the category of "woman writer" and claiming
instead the role of "artist":

> Paradoxically, this claim both liberated and confined women. On the
> one hand, they found themselves free from many of the limited de-
> finitions that had constricted women aspiring to be artists in earlier
> periods.... On the other hand, turn-of-the-century women writers
> found themselves, often in deep, subtle ways, emotionally stranded
> between worlds. They floated between a past they wished to leave
> (sometimes ambivalently, sometimes defiantly) and a future they had

not yet gained. They were full members neither of their mothers' world, at the one extreme, nor of that of the privileged white male artist, at the other. Further, the ways of living and types of writing associated with "art" had by and large been shaped by men; they were not necessarily compatible with the kinds of lives and types of stories that women writers wished to express. Tension between the tradition they aspired to enter and the lives and fictions they sought to create as women was inevitable.[12]

The first wave of Austin critics saw her, like Georgia O'Keeffe, as escaping some of these conflicts in the relative freedom of the southwestern landscape. The writers represented in this volume discover a number of other spaces where binary oppositions can be challenged. As she anticipated many theoretical and critical perspectives, Austin herself recognized the usefulness of the borderland trope so central in contemporary multicultural criticism, and so much in evidence in this volume. Nicole Tonkovich, for instance, sees Austin's use of cross-dressing as a way to challenge rigid gender boundaries, and Mark Hoyer conceptualizes her "syncretism" as an effort to bring together on the dramatic stage religious beliefs from various cultures. Our critics generate a series of metaphors to explore Austin's creative territories: Tara Hart envisions "suspended spaces" to understand Austin's sentences; Anna Carew-Miller borrows Victor Turner's concept of liminal spaces to discuss "the dilemma of female creativity"; Elizabeth Klimasmith proposes the stage as a place for Austin to play with scripted female roles; and Linda Karell reads *Earth Horizon* as a collaborative space. The writers represented in this volume generally do not see Austin as invading a territory defined by others, and they generally believe she succeeded in finding a style that allowed her to tell the kinds of stories she wanted to tell. Dale Metcalfe argues, for instance, that Austin abandoned virtually all attachment to "Western poetical traditions" by 1923, learning from Native American cultures how to develop her own original, assertive poetic style. The essayists also agree that Austin redefined the concept of "high art" on her own terms and in a variety of genres, that she was a strikingly original writer.

Yet like Metcalfe, most of the writers in this volume emphasize that Austin crafted her theories of art from her understanding of the multiplicities of American culture. Like some of the best earlier work on Austin, the essays in *Exploring Lost Borders* present complex, multilayered readings informed by the close historical analysis of cultural studies; they demonstrate that Ansel Adams was right in predicting that Austin would reveal to future readers "the complex matrix of our American culture."

While readers have always noted Austin's use of American Indian materials, critics now approach the ways American Indian cultural practices and spirituality informed Austin's art in a more precise and knowledgeable way, exploring tribal differences and referring to particular tribal myths, stories, and political realities. Unlike some earlier critics who sometimes used postcolonial studies to critique Austin—to represent her as appropriating, or "colonizing," American Indian beliefs and stories, presenting stereotypical or even racist portrayals of Native Americans—most of the writers in this volume use both Native American studies *and* postcolonial theory to emphasize Austin's knowledge of and respect for cultural difference.[13] In "Mary Austin's Disfigurement of the Southwest in *The Land of Little Rain*" (1992), for example, Scheick argues that Austin uses "the language of subjective appropriation" and "annexes the landscape through a verbal act akin to proprietary naming by colonizers. She seizes metaphorically what has been resistant to her metaphysically. The language of anthropomorphism and autobiography confiscates the land through a rhetorical figuration that amounts to a disfigurement of what is Other. She accordingly idealizes Native Americans, who seem to her to be like the desert plants and animals."[14]

In contrast, Dale Metcalfe suggests that "[b]ecause she knew individual Native Americans, Austin could not perpetuate romantic fictions about them, nor could she write them out of existence." Michelle Campbell Toohey argues that Austin "shows her readers the possibilities of working, as Patrick Murphy suggests, 'from a concept of relational differences and *anotherness* rather than Otherness.'" And Kathryn DeZur uses Eric Cheyfitz's discussion of the imperializing nature of "unproblematized metaphor" in *The Poetics of Imperialism* to suggest that Austin shows her readers "how imperialist ideology views land [and] also how imperialism concerns itself with the 'natives' who live on it." These essays demonstrate that although Austin sometimes accepted the racial assumptions of her time, her works provide critics with ways to understand the role of American Indian cultures in the complex matrix of "our" American culture.

Austin's United States was peopled with a variety of groups with particular cultural histories, many of them intersecting. In exploring her concern with the multiple facets of American culture, the essays in this volume examine her portrayals of California mission history and Catholicism, midwestern small towns and Protestantism, Hispanic water use, and urban life. Critics will have much more to say about these themes when more Austin works are republished. Perhaps most strikingly, the contributors to this collection examine Austin's underexplored attention to class in America. Works such as *A Woman of Genius, No. 26 Jayne Street, The Ford,* and *Earth Horizon* all attend to the cultural dominance of America's middle class and its values. Barney Nelson takes a particularly original approach in using Richard White's essay "'Are You an Environmentalist or Do You Work for a Living?': Work and Nature" to frame her reading of the differences between Mary Austin's respect for the rural working class and John Muir's understanding of wilderness as a playground for the elite.

Austin focused her vision on the American West, and other essays in this volume suggest that she saw class and racial conflicts as central to western history. Austin was a "new" western historian by 1900. Several essayists explore issues of landownership and water politics in the West. The attention to water that flows through this volume, reflecting Austin's own focus on water and water rights, suggests that Austin in many ways anticipated Wallace Stegner's now famous definition of the West in *The Sound of Mountain Water:* "The West's ultimate unity is its aridity."[15] Indeed, the present volume is flooded with imagery associated with water: fords, fountains, thirst, wells, water holes, and water trails. As this example implies, Austin will prove to be a major theorist of the meaning of the West. She paid close attention, for instance, not only to American Indians but also to cultural exchanges with Mexico and to Hispanic cultural traditions. The essays in *Exploring Lost Borders* make clear why Austin's representations of the American West and its multicultural history encourage revisionist readings.[16]

Several contributors suggest that Austin's West offers a redemptive and healing modernist vision. Words such as *regenerative* and *utopian* appear throughout this collection. Her work thus also encourages a revisionist reading of modernism. While Tara Hart and Kathryn DeZur emphasize Austin's ties to modernist stylistic innovations in the composition of her sentences, the construction of her collections, and her use of narrators, and while familiar distinctions between male and female modernists as developed by Sandra Gilbert, Susan Gubar, and Elaine Showalter are much in evidence throughout *Exploring Lost Borders,* most of the essays address what we might think of as "regional" modernism, as opposed to "international" or "European-sited" modernism.[17] Many writers in this volume suggest that Austin, with her focus on the richness of regional cultures and the sustaining force of the land, offers a less despairing understanding of modernism, a point Dale Metcalfe explicitly makes in exploring Austin's critique of modernism's "maimed voices" and the differences between her poetic voice and H.D.'s.

Lois Rudnick's *Utopian Vistas: The Mabel Dodge Luhan House and the American Counterculture* provides a context for Austin's version of modernism. Rudnick examines a group of Anglo artists she refers to as "transcendental modernists," borrowing a term from music historian Judith Tick. Believing that "non-Anglo, nonwhite cultures had laid the groundwork for a revitalized American civilization," the "transcendental modernists who came to New Mexico were seeking to heal what T. S. Eliot called *the* disease of modernity: 'the dissociation of sensibility.'"[18] They sought "a coherent worldview that [would] sanctify the human community, provide meaning and order in the universe, and maximize individual consciousness."[19]

Rudnick suggests that Austin "searched for alternative models of community in the village socialism that [she] associated with Pueblo, and with certain aspects of Hispanic, culture."[20] She quotes Austin's sometime friend and associate John Collier as summing up best "the millennial promise these Anglo expatriates from mainstream America constructed from the Native American cultures of the Southwest": "If our modern world should be able to recapture this power, the earth's natural resources and web of life would not be irrevocably wasted within the twentieth century. . . . True democracy founded in neighborhoods and reaching over the world would become the realized heaven on earth. And living peace, not just an interlude between wars, would be born and would last through the ages."[21] Austin herself "stated that the 'apostles of a new social order' should not go to 'the cafés of Prague or the cellars of Leningrad,' but to New Mexico to discover 'the most interesting possibility of social evolution that the world scene at present affords.'"[22]

Of course, this worldview is replete with assumptions and dangers, as Rudnick goes on to point out: "The Anglo expatriates' hunger for spiritual and psychic renewal often blinded them to the more unpleasant social, political, and economic realities that surrounded them," particularly the exploitation of racial minorities.[23] At its worst, this viewpoint is cultural manifest destiny. And although it is profoundly multicultural, its rejection of European-based and urban modernism perhaps reflects a kind of potentially irresponsible nationalism, yet another version of an isolationist New World. It is interesting to note that in Elizabeth Klimasmith's reading of *A Woman of Genius,* which was written in 1912 while Austin was living in New York, Olivia Lattimore makes peace with the modernist city and emerging consumer culture by negotiating various compromises, while in *Cactus Thorn,* written around 1927, Dulcie Adelaid Vallodón, like her creator, flees the corrupt and corrupting city for a more life-affirming landscape.

The essayists in this volume recognize that Austin developed a coherent social vision, that she attempted in her politics and her art to put her theory into practice. Although she focused her cultural studies on the borderlands of the United States, she recognized intersections between various new and old worlds, over time and space, between "island" cultures, as a quotation from "Aboriginal American Literature" demonstrates: "It is still easier to know more of Beowulf than of the Red Score of the Delaware, more of Homer than of the Creation Myth of the Zuni, more of Icelandic sagas than of the hero myths of the Iroquois and Navajo. Here in the United States, the first-born literature of our native land, such as becomes among all other peoples a proud and universally accepted literary heritage, is still unmediated by the application of creative literary intelligence."[24]

In placing Austin at the center of the "complex matrix of our American culture," Ansel Adams testifies to the fertility and generative capacity of her vision. Paralleling the discussions of whether Austin emphasized the liberation or the constrictions of turn-of-the-century women, many essays in this collection question whether she was disappointed in the trajectory of American civilization or continued to believe in the "American grain." Although she repeatedly pointed out America's failure to live up to its vision, she held onto the possibility that the nation could achieve its promise, in her view defined by a recognition of community and commonality, by mutual respect and enrichment between races and classes, by fluid and flexible racial and gender identities, by the importance of satisfying work and creative expression for all people, by the understanding that the landscape is not property to be used but a spiritual resource, and by the discovery of sustaining cultural traditions from diverse sources. While this vision of America certainly has not come to pass, I believe that it is still a powerful shared dream.

And so we return to Adams's assessment that Austin was a "future person" with much to say to later generations. In *Exploring Lost Borders,* turn-of-the-new-century critics, many of them just beginning their careers, find connections between Austin's politics and her writing and suggest that her exploration of ecology, race, culture, gender, and creativity still resonates with contemporary concerns. Their exciting and original readings of works often dismissed as quaint period pieces show us new ways to understand the hybrid genres Austin employed in such works as *Isidro* and *The Flock,* new ways to understand Austin's strategies to introduce audiences to unfamiliar subject matter and perspectives. They reveal the variety of Austin's work and its coherence. While showing how past attempts to categorize Austin beckon like mirages in the lost borders, they map many new directions for Austin scholarship. In *Earth Horizon,* Austin wrote that she "wanted to write books that you could walk around in" (73); *Exploring Lost Borders* affirms her success, and we hope it will also be a book readers can walk around in, discovering other connecting trails leading to various water holes. We look forward to the essays that will branch off from these initial explorations.

One of Austin's most beloved stories, "The Walking Woman," offers a neat parable for the relationship between Austin and her critics. The story's narrator, the critic, seeks the Walking Woman, the writer whose text is nature. The desert folks don't really understand the Walking Woman; they think she is crazy. But the narrator wants to hear the woman's story and believes she is just the one to understand her. They meet at a desert spring and share their stories and experiences, and the narrator recognizes the Walking Woman's wisdom. She initially admires the Walking Woman for what she has learned, for having recognized and "walked off" society's values, but then she questions whether the Walking Woman is right, whether her knowledge is as free and complete as it appears. In conversation with the Walking Woman she develops her own perspective, a congruent but different understanding of the meaning of life. Yet the story's final image suggests how the narrator has been transformed by her encounter with the Walking Woman: "recollecting suddenly that people called [the Walking Woman] lame," the narrator runs down to the "open space" and finds in "the bare, hot sand the track of her two feet bore evenly and white." Austin always provokes us to think independently as we follow her trail into the lost borders.

NOTES

1. Ansel Adams, "Notes on Mary Austin," in *Mary Hunter Austin: A Centennial Booklet Published by the Mary Austin Home* (Independence, Calif., 1968), 7.

2. Mary Austin, *The Flock* (Boston: Houghton Mifflin, 1906), 221.

3. Mary Austin, "Regionalism in American Fiction," in *Beyond Borders: The Selected Essays of Mary Austin*, ed. and intro. Reuben J. Ellis (Carbondale: Southern Illinois University Press, 1996), 131.

4. Mary Austin, *Earth Horizon* (1932; reprint, Albuquerque: University of New Mexico Press, 1991), 33.

5. Mary Austin, *The Land of Little Rain* (1903; reprint, Albuquerque: University of New Mexico Press, 1974), xvi.

6. Constance Rourke, "The Unfolding Earth," *New Republic*, 21 December 1932, 166-67; Carey McWilliams, "Mary Austin's Autobiography," *Saturday Night*, 19 November 1932.

7. Henry Smith, "The Feel of the Purposeful Earth: Mary Austin's Prophecy," *New Mexico Quarterly* 1.1 (1932): 17-33.

8. Edward Abbey, introduction to *The Land of Little Rain*, by Mary Austin (New York: Penguin Books, 1988), viii.

9. For instance, in *Mary Austin: Song of a Maverick* (New Haven: Yale University Press, 1989), Esther Lanigan Stineman suggests that "although [Austin] embraced the theory underpinning the cause of women's rights, she preferred to identify intellectually with men" (3), and that "[a]ny analysis of Austin must consider her personality in its formidable and inescapable aspects, some of which are not altogether pleasant" (5). See my afterword to *Earth Horizon*, "A Book You Could Walk Around In," for a different view (Albuquerque: University of New Mexico Press, 1991).

10. David Wyatt, *The Fall into Eden: Landscape and Imagination in California* (New York: Cambridge University Press, 1986); Marjorie Pryse, introduction to *Stories from the Country of the Lost Borders*, by Mary Austin (New Brunswick: Rutgers University Press, 1987); Carl Bredahl, *New Ground: Western American Narrative and the Literary Canon* (Chapel Hill: University of North Carolina Press, 1989); and Stineman, *Song*.

11. Authors of recent works on Austin include Mark Hoyer, Mark Schlenz, Linda Karell, Barney Nelson, and Elizabeth Klimasmith. See the Works Cited for more information. Nicole Tonkovich, Mark Schlenz, Barney Nelson, and I are now editing reprints of Austin works.

12. Elizabeth Ammons, *Conflicting Stories: American Women Writers at the Turn into the Twentieth Century* (New York: Oxford University Press, 1991), 10.

13. Ammons, for instance, says that Austin is racist but generally reads her sympathetically, offering readers a conditional affirmation: "If it is possible for a member of the dominant group honestly to cross cultural boundaries, then Mary Austin may have succeeded better than most" (102).

14. William Scheick, "Mary Austin's Disfigurement of the Southwest in *The Land of Little Rain*," *Western American Literature* 27.1 (1992): 43, 40.

15. Wallace Stegner, "Introduction: Some Geography, Some History," in *The Sound of Mountain Water: The Changing of the American West* (New York: Dutton, 1980), 15.

16. Unfortunately we received no essays on Austin's most sustained multicultural history of the West, *The Trail Book* (1918), soon to be reissued by the University of Nevada Press.

17. See Sandra Gilbert and Susan Gubar, *No Man's Land: The Place of the Woman Writer in the Twentieth Century*, especially vol. 1, *The War of the Words* (New Haven: Yale University Press, 1988); and Elaine Showalter, "The Other Lost Generation," in *Sister's Choice* (Oxford:

Clarendon Press, 1991): 104–26.

18. Lois Rudnick, *Utopian Vistas: The Mabel Dodge Luhan House and the American Counterculture* (Albuquerque: University of New Mexico Press, 1996), 22, 27. Of course, Austin developed her views of the importance of native peoples and regional cultures long before she—or the others—moved to New Mexico.

19. Ibid., 26.

20. Ibid., 29.

21. For a reading of Austin's relationship to Collier that stresses the "paternalistic" nature of Anglo assumptions about "native" art, see Stineman, *Mary Austin*, especially 173–79.

22. Rudnick, *Utopian Vistas*, 29.

23. Ibid., 35.

24. Mary Austin, "Aboriginal Indian Literature" (no date or page number), contained in Box 25 of the Mary Austin Collection at the Huntington Library, San Marino, California.

CHAPTER ONE
At Cross Purposes
Church, State, and Sex in Mary Austin's *Isidro*

NICOLE TONKOVICH

*In "At Cross Purposes" Nicole Tonkovich demonstrates why Austin's first novel,
generally critically dismissed, so fascinated contemporary readers. By exploring what
she establishes as its central trope, border crossings, Tonkovich argues that* Isidro's
*convoluted "dime-novel" plot allows Austin to trace the tangled lines of church and
state in California in the 1830s, the book's setting. Tonkovich shows how* Isidro
*reveals the social and political controversies about Catholicism, gender, race, and
feminism that concerned the United States in 1905. In Tonkovich's reading,
Austin's narrative "double crosses" allow her to explore the instability of politics,
gender, and property, and to reinscribe and challenge attitudes about Catholicism
and religion in American society. Tonkovich also draws on current political and
scholarly debates to suggest that* Isidro *resonates with contemporary concerns about
religion, gender performance, and national identity. Her perceptive criticism both explains the book's early popularity and argues for the novel's reassessment by current
readers.*

*Tonkovich's essay opens up several patterns that recur throughout this volume.
As our title—borrowed, of course, from Austin—suggests, other critics will consider
the various borders Austin and her characters transgress. While Tonkovich recognizes
the ways in which Austin accepted stereotypical views of Catholicism, she, like
Mark Hoyer, believes that Austin often crossed religious boundaries and borrowed
freely from religions whose institutional practices she sometimes criticized.
Tonkovich also establishes Austin's interest in the Mexican presence in the borderlands and her knowledge of Spanish and Mexican history, a theme taken up again
in subsequent essays; introduces the importance of property and class in Austin's
writing; and oVers a complex reading of Austin's recognition that gendered behavior
is often a performance. She introduces the idea that Austin braids together various*

I

narrative approaches, combining, in this case, melodrama and romance with politics, historical fiction with cultural criticism of contemporary times. Perhaps most significantly, by presenting the way the apparently unsophisticated Isidro *reveals Austin's concerns with social issues, Tonkovich establishes a pattern followed by subsequent essayists, who see larger meanings beneath the exotic surfaces of Austin's local landscapes.*

When critics notice Mary Austin's first novel at all, they generally slight it. Recently it has been called a book with a "prosaic setting" wherein a "conventional hero" is saved by a "chum" in classic dime-novel style. The only "new twist" *Isidro* gives to the dime novel is to make the chum a "woman in disguise who accomplishes heroic feats."[1] An early Austin biographer, T. M. Pearce, considers *Isidro* to be "one of [her] fine achievements in the long narrative form";[2] nevertheless he faults the novel because it only hints at the social and political stakes at issue in the secularization of the California missions. Thus, Pearce dismisses it as a novel with "only an inkling of social consciousness."[3]

Regrettably, such dismissive evaluations have consigned *Isidro* to the status of mere biographical curiosity—a precursor, at best, to Austin's later narratives that show a mature feminism, a grounded and textured sense of locale and history. Yet the intricacies of *Isidro*'s plot conceal a profound and complex social consciousness. In fact, the seemingly gratuitous or formulaic plot elements find coherence in Austin's pervasive use of the figure of crossing,[4] a trope that indicates the overlapping interests of church and state in 1830s colonial California, where *Isidro* is set; in the early twentieth century, when it was written; and in the present moment. Moreover, such a reading suggests new dimensions to Austin's work. Scholars already appreciate Austin as a regionalist who explored the mystic potential of the southwestern landscape. *Isidro* establishes her as a novelist aware of wider national, social, and political issues as well.

A novel set in the exotic world of the Southwest missions, remote to eastern readers in space and time, that includes murder, romance, intrigue, several chase scenes, robbery, two kidnappings, an Indian uprising, an incipient revolution, and a forest fire in its 425 pages may justly be said to have a dime-novel plot. It is likely, in fact, that these elements are precisely what made the novel attractive to its first readers, easterners who had shown a great appetite for "historical novels set in picturesque locales," Helen Hunt Jackson's *Ramona* (1884) chief among them.[5] *Isidro* was, in fact, one of Austin's most widely circulated novels. First serialized in the

Atlantic Monthly, this "fascinating Old California romance" found instant approval among that magazine's readers.[6] In 1905, Houghton Mifflin printed 11,770 copies of the novel's first edition, nearly twice as many copies as it published of any other Austin work.[7]

Yet plot is not the book's central concern, if plot be understood as merely how the novel comes out. In fact, the denouement is revealed in the first sentence: "It was the year of our Lord 18—, and the spring coming on lustily, when the younger son of Antonio Escobar rode out to seek his fortune, . . . as if it were no great matter for a man with good Castilian blood in him, and his youth at high tide, to become a priest; rode merrily, in fact, as if he already saw the end of all that coil of mischief and murder and love, as if he saw Padre Saavedra appeased, Mascado dead, and himself happy in his own chimney corner, no priest, but the head of a great house."[8] This sentence deflects the reader's attention from *whether* Isidro will become a priest to *how* he escapes the obligation and *why* his path to the priesthood will be crisscrossed with four hundred pages of distractions. It also summarizes the substance of those distractions—"mischief and murder and love." These three "coiled" elements name the categories of crossings the book contains. "Mischief," an element grammatically equated with "Padre Saavedra appeased" in the following clause, signals the thematic treatments of the double-dealings of and with the church in the face of imminent seizure of its lands and monies by the new Mexican republic. "Murder," or "Mascado dead," introduces the theme of patricide, a sin that results from cross-breeding, mistaken parenthood, and parental default, whether of families, churches, or nations.[9] Nor does "love," which eventually enshrines Isidro in a domestic rather than a Catholic "house," proceed in a straightforward fashion, for it begins in the affection of a patrician gentleman for a "slim, dark lad" (33). The book's plot is driven by the necessity of sorting out these and similar double crosses, which produce convoluted chases across religious, political, and sexual boundaries—differences just beginning to be erased in colonial California, and so completely effaced by Austin's day that California had indeed become a "country of lost borders."

"A Priest Is a Shepherd in Some Sort": Religion in Colonial California

Isidro is a novel written under the sign of the cross. The first edition bears the image of the Mission San Carlos Borromeo at Carmel on its cover, and the novel opens: "It was the year *of our Lord*" (1; emphasis added). The first two chapters introduce a trope of shepherding and immediately establish a rough equivalence between the crosier of the cleric and the crook of his secular counterpart, the shepherd. Before events intervene to keep him from his priestly obligations, Isidro Escobar proves that he need not be a priest in order to be a good shepherd when he rescues two dumb creatures—a fox and an Indian—from predators ("Priest's work," he tells himself [6, 12]) and, aided by a young shepherd lad, tries to restore a flock of sheep to its owner.

As the novel progresses, it becomes evident that Isidro represents the future of both church and state in post-1830 Mexico. His secular shepherding proves far superior to the church's. Isidro protects his adopted flock from predators; by contrast, the padres of Carmel *are* predators, punishing their neophyte Indian slaves for stealing food to keep from starving. Whereas Isidro tries to return lost sheep to their owner and takes care to ensure that the flock does not become dispersed nor intermingle promiscuously with others' sheep, the padres lose track of their flock. Most seriously, they have lost a lamb of pure lineage and the best breeding stock. Their attempts to recover this lost lamb set in motion a plot whose resolution demonstrates the stakes in power, land, and inheritance incipient in the realignment of church and state in the new Mexican republic. The new state, heady with rhetoric and posturing, proves to be as ephemeral as Valentin Delgado's fashionable clothing. The church's interests will best be served by pure-blooded gentlemen like Isidro who father secular dynasties and practice their religion independent of the promises rendered to—and the supervision of—the Mother Church.

The action begins when Valentin Delgado, a foppish fortune hunter sympathetic to the new republic, is given the task of identifying and locating sixteen-year-old Jacinta Concepcion Castro, daughter of the comandante of the Presidio of Carmel. Jacinta stands to inherit "a considerable estate," and if Delgado succeeds in finding her, he will win her hand in marriage. If he fails, or if Jacinta's pure bloodline cannot be established, her fortune "reverts to the church" (52). One of the reasons this particular ewe cannot be found is that she is dressed in wolves' clothing, as it were. Delgado is looking for a young woman, but he is doomed to fail because the young woman he seeks is dressed as and behaving like a young man. In fact, she is Zarzo/the Briar, the "lad" who has helped Isidro rescue the flocks of the murdered shepherd Ruiz.

In *Isidro,* cross-dressing is not simply a sensationalistic or dime-novel device. Rather, the gender instability manifest in cross-dressing suggests an accompanying political instability. Like other families of pure blood and privilege in the novel, the Castro and Ramirez families stand to lose their patrimony because their lines of genealogical inheritance, which depend on documentable heterosexual reproduction, are crossed. Jacinta has been abandoned by her mother and father and left to the care of an Indian woman who dresses her as a boy because "she fancied [the child] was safer so" (232). Isidro, potentially a fine breeder himself, has been promised to the church, where he will be expected to dress in skirts and obey laws of sexual abstinence. That this will not happen is reinforced in an early conversation between Isidro and Zarzo. Trying to discover the state of his new friend's soul, Isidro asks whether Zarzo has ever seen a priest. Zarzo replies, "One. He was fat, and had small hair, and wore a dress like a woman's. You look not like such a one" (77).

The friars' "dresses" echo Zarzo's improper attire and suggest political, rather than familial, instability. Their robes, and the clothing of most of the novel's supporting cast, are "essentially uniforms: garments denoting the one form or single shape to which each individual's life [is] confined by birth, by circumstance, by custom, by decree."[10] The priests' feminized attire is a source of amusement to the soldiers of the Mexican state and to renegade Indians, whose uniforms and ceremonial garb signify manly bravery. Both groups believe that a colony ruled by men who wear women's clothing, but who own all the arable land and control all the cheap labor, is a world upside down, a world ripe for revolution.

Confusion and mayhem dominate this world of petticoat government and bad shepherding. It is a world of double crosses and substitutions. Isidro is on his way to become a priest not of his own volition, but because his mother, who "had vowed herself to Holy Church and the Sisterhood of the Sacred Heart," had been drawn back from her novitiate to become the bride of the "hot-hearted" Antonio Escobar, Isidro's father. Her family was thus "obliged to surrender a good lump of her dowry to Holy Church, with the further promise, not certified to, but spiritually binding, to give back of her issue as much as in herself [the family] had taken away" (3). Like his maternal grandparents, Isidro double-crosses the church—doubly. He repeats his mother's defection, and for the same carnal reasons. Worse, he easily locates and promptly marries Jacinta Concepcion, thus cheating the church of both the Escobar and Ramirez fortunes.

In a world ruled by men who dress like women, where novices desert the church for passionate love, where wives run away from their husbands and heiresses dress like men, the lines of power and inheritance become crossed. The novel is generally populated by mongrels, "men of no blood" (14), whose faculties of reason are poor, who can sign their legal papers only with "a cross" (161). These crossbreeds, although would-be rebels, are not, the narrator assures us, "the stuff of which new civilizations are made" (336). They "wished not to live always in one place, wear clothes, marry one wife and stay by her. . . . They missed the excitement of tribal feasts and dances, feuds and border wars" (336, 337). Nomadism, improper dress, and impure breeding, this declaration implies, inevitably produce fathers who are not fathers, sons who are not loyal sons.

In such a topsy-turvy world, revolution and patricide go hand in hand. *Isidro*'s first murder is committed by a drunken shepherd who, hearing his mother's reputation sullied, unwittingly murders the man who is his father. Patricide is in turn a figure for other social and political disruptions that result when genealogical inheritance and fraternal obligation are disregarded. Indians who run away from the missions foment rebellion against the father-priests—an act again associated with a form of atavistic cross-dressing. When Isidro expresses doubt that Indians who had been raised in the missions, "made Christians, [and] taught to save their souls from hell," would turn against the church, his guide ironically replies, "Manuel . . . was a Christian. I remember an Easter when he served the mass. That was he you saw last night, with the rattle of ram's horn and a bear's teeth grinning on his shoulders" (284, 285). Manuel's reversion is doubly dangerous: not only does he dance "out of season"—suggesting that he has become estranged from his indigenous tribal culture—but he is also engaged in the "Devil's work," participating in a war dance preparatory to raiding the mission (275–76).

Most seriously, in rebelling against Spain, Mexico is attempting patricide. The revolutionary ideas on which the rebellion is based are laid at the feet of unruly and unfaithful women who have exceeded appropriate social roles. For its part, Spain blames Mexico's insurrection on the church. As the narrator ironically remarks, "Liberty in the figure of a female finds easy worship among a people who count a woman chief among the Holy Family" (123). The implication here is that loyalty and respect to the state are undermined by the church's inappropriate Mariolatry. Similarly, however, the church, which stands to lose its real estate if the Mexican rebellion succeeds, figures Mexico as "the strumpet Republic [contriving] evil against the Brothers of St. Francis" (45).

The dime-novel plot of *Isidro,* then, entails a number of different crossings: cross-dressing implies the confusion of apparently unproblematic sexual identity; chases and pursuits involve the physical crossing of territory; disputed state boundaries are soon to be obscured by other modes of political organization, whether because of the impending revolt of the Indian tribes or because of revolution in the south. Padres and shepherds exchange functions: the best shepherds are generally also the best fathers; careless shepherds are also impotent, disposable, absent, or despicable fathers. Highbred women and their sons renege on their promises to the Holy Church. Daughters forsake proper reticence to dress as men, ride horses, herd sheep, and pursue lovers. Parents are unwilling to stay put to raise their children; mothers abandon or are abandoned by their children's fathers, leaving their mongrel children with no natural loyalty to family or nation. All these unruly subjects threaten the authority of the church, the spiritual and political center of colonial California. Only by extricating Isidro from his vow to this doomed system can an orderly line of familial inheritance be maintained. Thus the novel's purpose, of showing how and why Isidro breaks his promise, is closely related to its social, political, temporal, and geographic settings.

"I Wish to Do a Man's Work More": Isidro's Resonances in Fin-de-Siècle America

Although T. M. Pearce faults *Isidro* for lacking consciousness of the social issues confronting colonial California, at least his evaluation indicates his thoughtful measure of the novel. Virtually no Austin scholar, however, has considered how *Isidro* spoke to the social and political issues of Austin's own day.[11] Yet its success in the *Atlantic* and Houghton Mifflin's large press run suggest that it was positively received. Certainly this success was the result of the novel's treatment of issues still coiled around church, state, and sex, exacerbated by pressures of immigration, labor unrest, and women's increasing agitation for a more liberal share in the intellectual and political issues current in the first decade of the twentieth century.

Isidro joined a flood of other nostalgic works about the romantic West and Southwest. Eastern editors, publishers, writers, and readers had had their appetites for this material whetted by such popular tales as Jackson's *Ramona* and Wister's *The Virginian,* as well as by the illustrations of Russell and Remington that appeared regularly in the periodical press. In southern California, antiquarians, artists, and writers actively courted the interest of eastern readers, both by contributing to eastern periodicals and by seeking to establish their own version of an authentic regional culture. According to Kevin Starr, a "consolidated myth of Southern California" emerged beginning in the 1880s, using the nostalgic appeal of mission times as the myth around which to tout the restorative benefits of Southwest living.[12] Chief among the promoters of this myth was Austin's friend and mentor Charles Lummis. Lummis, a former editor of the *Los Angeles Times,* housed the Museum of the Southwest at El Alisal, his Los Angeles estate. Devoted to saving the California missions, Lummis used funds from the Landmarks Club to begin "reroofing California missions and preserving other historical landmarks."[13] During his years of acquaintance with Austin, he took over the editorship of *Land of Sunshine,* a magazine promoting regional interests, and fashioned it into an important venue for literature of the Southwest. Austin herself shared these interests, seeking with her writing to insist that "American" history and literature recognize the importance of the southwestern Indian and Hispanic cultures.[14]

Isidro's mission-days setting, characters, and theme exceed the period's fascination with things southwestern, however. Austin's chronicling of church history in *Isidro* also speaks to the uneasy truce between church and state in turn-of-the-century United States. The novel measures quite accurately the paradoxical fascination of contemporary Protestant readers with things Catholic.[15] The United States had only recently emerged from an era of rabid anti-Catholicism marked by the formation, in 1887, of the American Protective Association, a secret anti-Catholic order whose prejudices were fueled by a second wave of immigration from Catholic Europe; by rumors that major American cities—San Francisco among them—were under Catholic control; and by the church's support of labor union agitators.[16] Membership in the APA peaked in 1893, but declined rapidly thereafter. By the 1896 presidential election, both major political parties had turned their attention to other issues—notably free silver. By 1899, H. D. Sedgwick Jr. could write in the *Atlantic Monthly:* "old feuds between Protestant and Catholic have ceased to be as important as their united battles against moral decay."[17]

Isidro captures the essence of the nation's fascination—both negative and positive—with Catholicism. In its detailing of the moral laxity, economic opportunism, racial oppression, and ineffective civic leadership of the friars of San Carlos Borromeo, the book virtually endorses what many Americans thought they already knew about the church. In Isidro, however, readers found a hero who could be a model of acceptable Catholic American citizenship. Isidro respects the Mother Church while resisting the "unnatural" chastity of the priesthood; he demonstrates a characteristic American independence of thought and action by refusing to honor earlier generations' thralldom to the church; he chooses to be "a man": to father children and pursue economic opportunity and political independence; and, above all, he knows how to handle his woman, allowing her independent ways—indeed, even finding them attractive—but also harnessing her independence to the ends of pure breeding.

By "The End of the Trail," the novel's final chapter, turn-of-the-century readers would have had any lingering doubts about the Catholic threat completely assuaged. Isidro's assertion that he will not be bound by a promise made before he was born, and "therefore hardly within [his] power of agreeing or disagreeing" (411), is an effective assurance that second-generation Catholic immigrants might naturally reject their parents' unquestioning support of and obedience to church policy. The perception of monastic life as unnatural and demeaning to men, depriving them of their inherent masculinity as expressed in the qualities of action and sexuality, is simultaneously endorsed and forestalled in Isidro's reply to Father Saavedra's query about whether he wishes "not to do the work of Our Father Christ?" Isidro answers: "It is not that I do not wish it, but I wish to do a man's work more" (412). By the novel's end, readers are informed that Isidro has fathered children, taken over the Ramirez estates, and obtained "political preferment" (422). In an implicit address to readers convinced that the power of monastic politics had not declined over the intervening fifty years,[18] Isidro confesses an enlightened doubt "in regard to the foundation of the Franciscans—the Missions" (413), a doubt engendered, the narrator claims, by "all that Jacintha [*sic*] had taught him, all that he had learned from Mascado in the hills, all the eager young straining after ideals of liberty which fomented in the heart of Mexico" (414). In fine, Isidro embodies the ideal new turn-of-the-century American Catholic: respectful of the church and its traditions, aware of its failings, and independent of its dictates. In the best (Pan-) American tradition, he and his wife leave a land where religion has become corrupt to establish a "great house" in a new land of liberty (1).

For readers not embroiled in anti–Catholic sentiment, the book addresses, at least by implication, a number of other political and social issues. Southern Californians certainly would have been aware of Austin's implicit comparison of the "strumpet Republic's" wish to dismantle the mission system as an obstacle to economic development to the then-current arguments from developers in the Los Angeles area who saw the water claims of Owens Valley farmers as hindering the city's economic growth. Readers across the United States could not have overlooked the similarities between the Mexican struggle for independence from Spain in 1830 and the currently escalating border tensions under Mexican president Díaz, the recently resolved Spanish-American War, the ongoing negotiations over the Panama Canal, and the debates over Philippine independence. As Austin's fiction repeatedly demonstrates, "knowing the real estate history is one way of tracing the trail of a particular piece of land."[19]

The entanglement of politics with gender is foundational to the personal tensions Austin and other intellectual women like her suffered during the period in which *Isidro* was written. In the novel, the genealogy of real estate is paralleled by a concern over the personal genealogical entitlement manifested in heritable physical traits, as well as in more overtly political matters such as property inheritance and political enfranchisement. Here, family—like race and gender—is a mutable concept, one whose meaning far exceeds the "natural" bonds between parents and children. *Isidro* has no mothers, a theme that echoes Austin's own distance from her mother, a troubled relationship that remained unresolved at her mother's death in 1896, as well as the distance of this generation of New Women from their mothers. In 1905–6, as *Isidro* was reaching publication, Austin made the difficult decision to institutionalize her handicapped daughter, Ruth, an act she saw as effectively reproducing the maternal abandonment she herself had suffered and that she figured as "losing" her daughter.[20] By placing Jacinta/Zarzo under the foster care of a half-breed Indian woman and her French sheepherder common-law husband, Austin fictionally explores what might happen to a child bereft of her natural family. Both the artificial family of *Isidro* and the institution into which Ruth was placed are marginal to the dominant social/class system and are therefore more forgiving of deviance from the norm. Jacinta is allowed to grow and dress as a young man because it is natural and proper within her environment. Austin can thus believe that Ruth's institutional family will tailor her care to the child's "natural" behaviors as well. Austin, then, would be free to attend to supporting herself and pursuing her artistic dream in a society unforgiving of such unnatural maternal decisions.

Just before the novel was published, Austin received information that led her to attribute Ruth's mental deficiencies to heritable characteristics from her husband's side of the family.[21] Her attention in the novel to the supposed links between pure blood, miscegenation, and "natural" (or genetically linked) traits are evidence of her struggle with this issue. *Isidro* seems to assert that mixed blood leads almost inevitably to subaltern status. For example, the novel's villains are invariably characterized as being of mixed race. Mascado is "comely in a dark, low-browed sort, and look[s] to have some foreign blood in him" (12).[22] Mariano is a "man of no blood" (14), while his murderer, Ruiz, who is also his illegitimate and unacknowledged son, is "a mongrel as to breed" (15). The perquisites of "pure blood," on the other hand, cannot be denied. The novel emphasizes Isidro's "white" lineage: he is "of good Castilian blood" (1), with a "touch of Saxon ruddiness that he had from some far-off strain of his mother's" (9). And while Zarzo initially appears to be an ill-bred and wild young man, the narrator also stresses that "he" possesses inward traits of grace and inherent privilege: "The lad had seen only Indians, vaqueros, and some such wayfarer as Escobar. It had been a rough life, but he showed no roughness; he had been servilely bred, but used no servility" (88).

Austin's concerns over this issue were entirely consistent with those of her contemporaries. In the wake of Reconstruction and with floods of immigrants entering the country from both coasts, white Americans had become obsessed with the purity of their Anglo-Saxon heritage, seeking to equate whiteness with American-ness. When, by century's end, it had become apparent that race could not be guaranteed by surface signifiers of skin color, shape of skull, or alignment of facial features, white Americans sought to prove their entitlement by other means. Genealogy, earlier used to establish class privilege, now was pursued to document racial purity.[23] Genealogically based societies such as the Daughters of the American Revolution effected a rapprochement between whites North and South through establishing their common patriotic identity in ancestral Revolutionary patriotism, at the same time effectively barring recent immigrants from a claim to that identity. In California, the Native Sons of the Golden West echoed those policies on a local scale. Founded in 1875, the group was created to "function as a living, self-perpetuating monument in memory of [the pioneer] forebears of the gold rush era."[24] Membership was "limited to white males born in California on or after July 7, 1846," a date selected "because it marked the raising by Commodore Sloat of the Stars and Stripes at Monterey and proclaimed California under American rule."[25]

Such organizations reinforced gender roles as well, usually by designat-

ing the men's group as the main organization and then establishing
women's "auxiliary" organizations. (The Native Daughters of the Golden
West was founded in 1886.) The popular press urged women of Austin's
generation to trace the heritable traits of their children through regular
photographs, measurements, and written estimations of their health, accomplishments, and talents. Thus personal and nostalgic artifacts collected
in albums and baby books, buttressed by documentary records, became ad
hoc claims to citizenship and its entitlements.[26]

Despite her exacerbated personal concerns over these troubling and di-
visive issues of genetic inheritance, however, Austin also demonstrated a
passionate commitment to challenging the dangerous race hatred such ob-
sessions could fuel. Her obvious admiration for the Indian and Hispanic
women with whom she associated led her to resist actively the deplorable
practice of "*mahala* chasing," sexual violence against and abduction of
women of color in Austin's own community.[27] (This practice offers an interesting parallel to Austin's decision to explain how Jacinta's assumption
of masculine disguise has kept her safe in a dangerous world.) And while
Isidro's mixed-breed men are more or less amiable and amoral weaklings,
all the novel's women, regardless of racial descent, are admirable, strong,
principled, affectionate, self-reliant, intelligent, and brave.

"The Whole Art of Putting Yourself into Your Appearance":
Isidro'*s Relevance to the Twentieth-Century Reader*

Clearly the crossings of *Isidro* have social relevance to the circumstances,
personal and political, under which it was composed. The book's address
to social issues of our own time centers on the novel's resolution, which
might be seen as problematic for readers eager to establish Austin's feminism. In her afterword to *A Woman of Genius,* Nancy Porter calls Austin an
"overlooked classic of feminism" and a "significant contributor to feminist
analysis."[28] While such evaluations may be true of *A Woman of Genius,* they
are harder to see as relevant to *Isidro,* especially to the novel's ending, in
which Jacinta is properly married and reproducing children who will receive and pass on the Escobar and Ramirez inheritances. Sadly, it would
seem, Jacinta Concepcion, who is much more interesting to contemporary
readers—as well as to her would-be lover—when she is dressed as a man,
is exposed. She is dressed in women's clothing and given a married woman
as a dueña to teach her "the mysteries of the toilet and needlework, of

which she knew nothing at all" (318). Worse, because she dressed in men's clothing, accompanied Isidro and slept by his side, and was kidnapped by a renegade Indian, it is assumed that "hands have been laid on her" (268), and Isidro must marry her to save her honor.

The novel's obsession with crossings "saves" this star-crossed marriage for feminism, however. The first, improperly contracted, marriage of Isidro and Jacinta/Zarzito stands not at the end of the novel but at its midpoint (237), suggesting that it is yet another double cross. It does not produce a comedic, happily-ever-after resolution because the couple was married for the wrong reasons: he has no romantic interest in her, nor she in him. Having rushed Jacinta to the altar to save her reputation, Isidro immediately abandons her to return to his father and defend himself against charges that he besmirched her virtue. Jacinta, for her part, is left to mull over this unforeseen and thoroughly unpleasant change in her circumstances. Thus their initial alliance threatens to reproduce the loveless marriage of Jacinta's parents (and Austin's own marriage as well). Only after Isidro is kidnapped by Mascado and Jacinta resumes mannish garb to search for him do they realize their love for each other. The narrator insists that "[a]s often as he thought of the Briar his heart warmed toward the lad,—always the lad,— never the cold, still girl" (267).

The novel's narration provides both a puzzle and a clue to an interpretation more comfortable to contemporary feminism. The puzzle is that even after it has been revealed that Jacinta is a woman, the narrator on occasion refers to her as Zarzo. This duplicity suggests that the narrator does not insist on Jacinta/Zarzo's essential identity as either woman or man, but seeks to emphasize the connection of gendered behavior to social and political context. Demonstrating in small how contingent the seemingly self-evident matter of dress may be is this short interchange between Jacinta and Marta, one of her surrogate mothers. Having again donned masculine clothing so that she can pursue her husband, Jacinta confesses to Marta, "I doubt I shall ever grow to like skirts." Marta replies, "I see no use in them myself. . . . It was not so in my mother's time, but is a custom of the Missions. No doubt it is an offense to God to look on a priest or a woman and know that they have two legs" (354). The answer to the puzzling inconsistency in narration lies in this interchange. When constrained by mission society, Jacinta dresses and acts as a woman; in the borderlands, as well as in the private sexually charged interchanges, dressed in trousers and doing men's deeds, she becomes Zarzo.

When abducted by Mascado, Zarzo foils the half-breed's sexual designs simply by refusing to play the woman: "Mascado saw he had still to deal with Peter Lebecque's graceless boy. Many a time in the last year at the hut of the Grapevine he had tried to betray her into some consciousness of himself as a lover through her consciousness of herself as a maid, and had been beaten back by the incorrigible boyishness of her behavior" (182). Yet he persists in his fantasy, imagining her as womanly against all odds. In the novel's climactic scene, as Zarzo enters the rebel compound, Mascado looks at her "in her boy's dress" and sees "the same slim lad . . . rounded and ripened to the woman of his dreams" (365). (Admittedly, at the time Mascado is suffering some delirium from a serious wound.)

Only moments later, Isidro, who is "thinking homesickly of El Zarzo," sees an entirely different person: "She stood beyond him in the shadow. . . the *erect* young figure and the level, unfrightened gaze. . . . 'Lad, lad,' he whispered. 'Señor,' she breathed" (372, emphasis added). In fact, the novel emphasizes that "lad" "was always after a word of supreme endearment between them" (402). This term implies that even after their marriage, Isidro considers Zarzo his companion rather than his property. That Doña Jacinta, who is, the novel assures us, "kept at home with her young children" (422), will retain a measure of independence is forecast by her choice to ride to the couple's second, church-sanctioned wedding "as the custom was . . . not [on] her father's splendid mount as would any girl in her senses, but [on] the same kicking pinto" she had ridden when in the mountains with Isidro (420). She dominates the willful animal conventionally associated with male sexuality, effectively incorporating and reversing the symbolism of this custom. Thus marriage affords the best of all possible worlds for Jacinta/Zarzito and Isidro. She need not be a conventional woman within her home, since her husband (who was once satisfied to enter a celibate fraternity) still prefers to think of her as a lad. Just as important, Zarzo need not be merely a serving boy or an asexual companion to Isidro. Rather, s/he assumes, to use Sandra Gilbert's terms, a "third sex beyond gender,"[29] an identity that places her outside the traditional subordination of women. Because Jacinta has name, blood, and inheritance but lacks social conditioning as a woman, she knows that masculine as well as feminine behavior can be taught and learned, and, like clothing, may be assumed and discarded as the situation warrants.

Furthermore, a refusal to have Isidro and Jacinta marry would not only violate dime-novel sensibilities, but also would be unthinkably false to history and politics. Throughout the novel, Austin foregrounds her determination to keep her characters' actions and perceptions consistent with historical fact, frequently prefacing descriptions and actions with the explanatory phrase "as any one of that time must have done" (292). She occasionally addresses the reader overtly as well:

These are the pipes of history, the breadth of whose diapason sets many small figures going to various measures like midges in the sun. They go merrily or strenuously, with no notion of how they are blown upon; but let the great note of history be stilled, and they fall flat and flaccid out of the tune of time. If you would know how . . . Isidro and Mascado, Peter Lebecque and his foster child, called the Briar, played out their measure, you must know so much of the note of their time. (288)

Emphasizing historical accuracy, Austin thus withholds her own judgment of her characters' actions. *Isidro*'s historical and geographical setting offers no alternative model for Jacinta's life; its women are either respectable señoras; déclassé mixed-breed unmarried mothers, such as Marta; or promiscuous and slightly ridiculous public gossips such as Delfina. Equally important, marriage keeps Jacinta's inheritance, Isidro's good character, and the Escobar money from the grasp of a compromised and doomed Catholicism. Other alternatives are unthinkable. If Jacinta and Isidro do not marry, she and her money will become the property of the fortune-hunting revolutionary gigolo, Valentin Delgado. If her true identity is not revealed, her fortune will revert to the church.

The contemporary reader wishing to claim Mary Austin as a feminist foremother must bear in mind the novel's contexts. Not only is the novel true to the gendered norms for behavior predominant in colonial California, it also respects a code of reality for Austin's own day. Although Austin and others of her generation of "New Women" successfully challenged many of the norms that hindered the fictional Jacinta, they were nevertheless not entirely free of stereotypical presumptions about their own behavior. Like her friend Charlotte Perkins Gilman, Austin left her husband and child, but not without consequences. Both Gilman and Austin may have explored new ways of thinking and writing, and may even have pushed at the boundaries of acceptable sexual behavior, but their success was limited to their immediately personal behavior and had limited effect on the masculine enclaves of art, religion, and politics. An example from Austin's life illustrates this contention. After separating from her husband, she bought land in Carmel and began to associate with the artists' colony there. The homosexual dalliances among several of this mostly male group—notably George Sterling, Jack London, and Ambrose Bierce—as well as their disdain for the formalities of marriage vows led Austin to assume that she, too, was free to explore her own desires. She soon discovered, however, that "the official logic of the Carmelites claimed grand passions necessary to the poetic inspiration of the male" but not the female.[30]

In her short story "Frustrate" (1912), Austin comments directly on the double standard that prevailed even among the supposedly enlightened intelligentsia in the early twentieth century, granting men a degree of sexual license while presuming that women's sexuality was—and should be—containable. In this autobiographical fiction, a gifted woman learns that men, despite their bohemian pretensions, prefer women who are attractive, self-effacing, and charming; these same men read the writer's own eagerness as unattractive aggression. A woman friend comforts her with these words: "It is the whole art . . . of putting yourself into your appearance . . . . I have too much waist for that sort of thing. I have my own game."[31] "Frustrate" appeared in *Century* magazine in January 1912 but, according to Melody Graulich, was never reprinted because Austin "may well have felt the story was too autobiographical, revealing too much about her own disappointments."[32] Thus Austin's biography and autobiographical fictions are echoed in *Isidro*. The novel works because most of the male characters persist in not seeing what is in front of them. Assuming that men dress and act in predetermined ways, they eat, sleep, ride, work, and travel with Zarzo for weeks on end, never suspecting the truth. Yet Delfina, who does not share these limited perceptions, discovers the Briar's secret within moments. Delfina plays such a minor part in the novel, in fact, that one suspects she has been inserted into the plot at this moment precisely to emphasize Austin's ironic point about the differential privileges of gender.

Although many readers may be interested in finding a place for *Isidro* in a feminist tradition of U.S. fiction, others may assume this to be a nonissue in a scholarly world supposedly enlightened by a quarter century of feminist politics. Regrettably, however, binary thinking and gendered language persist, even in the most careful scholarship. For example, Eldon G. Ernst summarizes the Spanish/Catholic impact on colonial California in these words: "At best some Indians benefited from Franciscan spirituality and

European technology; at worst many Indians died from imported diseases; overall, much of the Indians' cultural heritage was *emasculated*."[33] While some might argue that this is merely a figure of speech, it seems clear that the traditional associations of religion with feminized weakness still pervade the thinking about this period. Ernst's language is a symptom of a larger problem facing scholars wishing to account for religion's role in U.S. history as well, particularly in the matter of racial politics. Just as gender is presumed to be binary and stable, so is it apparent that church, state, and ethnicity are separate concerns, at least in popular histories. For example, a scholar wishing to learn about the history of Catholicism in California will discover a relative paucity of survey sources that consider religion after the secularization of the missions in the 1830s. One seeking such information must consult specialized regional and religious histories.

Literary history repeats the assumption that church and state remain separate concerns in scholarship and in biography. Scholars, for example, agree on the importance of understanding Austin's immersion in and devotion to Native American mystical, spiritual, and religious practices; yet her biographers only briefly acknowledge her fascination with the mystical practices of Catholicism. Nancy Porter is relatively straightforward in asserting that Austin "credited" "Catholic mystical practices" "with her recovery from the cancer she was certain she had developed back in Carmel,"[34] although her short essay does not allow Porter space to elaborate on Austin's experience. Only Augusta Fink treats Austin's friendship with Cardinal Merry del Val, who had an interest in the mission at Carmel and its pivotal role in Austin's novel. In turn, del Val introduced Austin to other scholarly practicing Catholics who instructed her in church history and in the practice of prayer. Yet Fink, whose biographical intent is to emphasize mysticism, devotes only a page to Austin's experiences in Rome while giving an entire fifteen-page chapter to the writer's first contact with Native American mysticism in the Owens Valley days. As well, Fink deflects attention from Austin's contact with Catholicism by asserting that she was interested in how the "rites of the early Christian church resembled the approach she had learned from the Paiute Indians."[35] Esther Stineman, otherwise an impeccable source, scants Austin's Italian sojourn, only summarizing her transcendent experience in conquering breast cancer: "In Italy, even with 'pronounced' symptoms of breast cancer, Austin 'evaded' it by praying, by which she did 'not mean the practice of petition, but the studied attitude of the spirit of transaction with the creative attitude working within.'"[36] Admittedly, Austin's account of her association with Catholicism in *Earth Horizon* is also brief, but neither Fink nor Steinman honors the tone of awe that pervades her account of the experience;[37] nor do they probe for the details of mysticism, details that cannot be subsumed to Austin's interest in the supposedly quaint practices of ethnic groups.

Thus *Isidro* emerges as a novel of great potential interest to a generation of scholars who study performances of gender as well as those interested in Austin and the West. Those pursuing gender studies, particularly of transvestism and the performance of gendered identity,[38] should find in Austin a fascinating use of the trope of cross-dressing to address not only the politics of gender and race, but also the relationship of church and state, a political alliance rarely considered in scholarly discourse. Scholars whose interests center on Austin's corpus and its development will see in *Isidro* a breadth of social concern, present even in her earliest works, that exceeds the regionalism by which she is most traditionally classified. A literary community interested in the political issues surrounding national and postnational identities will find that the novel makes clear the links between crossing land and crossing gender, and between crossing gender and crossing national identities.[39] Finally, a political society still convulsed with the issues of gender hierarchies and racial/ethnic identities will be challenged by a novel that demonstrates that identities are fluid, existing within a network of roles proffered by church and state, family and peers, and are always able to be crossed.

NOTES

1. Shelley Armitage, "Mary Austin: Writing Nature," in *Wind's Trail: The Early Life of Mary Austin*, by Peggy Pond Church, ed. Shelley Armitage (Santa Fe: Museum of New Mexico Press, 1990), 28.

2. T. M. Pearce, *Mary Hunter Austin* (New York: Twayne, 1956), 89.

3. Ibid., 91.

4. I am indebted to Ona Russell for several discussions in which our mutual understandings of this figure have been clarified. Her dissertation, "Discourses of Crossing: Reconceptualizing Representation in the Nineteenth-Century United States, 1840–1890" (Ph.D. diss., University of California, San Diego, 1998), offers a study of the trope of crossing in U.S. literatures in figures ranging from Henry David Thoreau to Calamity Jane.

5. Karen S. Langlois, "Mary Austin and Houghton Mifflin Company: A Case Study in the Marketing of a Western Writer," *Western American Literature* 23.1 (1988): 34.

6. *Atlantic Monthly,* January 1905.

7. Langlois, "Mary Austin," 41.

8. Mary Austin, *Isidro* (Boston: Houghton Mifflin, 1905), 1. All subsequent parenthetical

citations in the text refer to this edition.

9. Francis F. Guest presents a valuable analysis of the theological bases of the Franciscans' treatment of the Indian populations of California. According to Guest, under Spanish law, priests became "legal guardians" of their converts, which gave them binding responsibilities as parents (Francis F. Guest, "The Franciscan World View," in *New Directions in California History: A Book of Readings,* ed. James J. Rawls [New York: McGraw-Hill, 1988], 27, 30). Father Junípero Serra, for example, wrote to the military commander of the Alta California presidios: "I state to you that those wayward sheep [fugitive neophytes] are my burden, and I am responsible for them not at the treasury in Mexico but at a much higher tribunal than that" (qtd. in Guest, 31).

10. Sandra M. Gilbert, "Costumes of the Mind: Transvestism as Metaphor in Modern Literature," *Critical Inquiry* 7.2 (1980): 392.

11. Esther Lanigan Stineman suggests that *Isidro*'s plot offers parallels to Austin's biography, but she does not relate the novel to a larger cultural and historical context. See Stineman, *Mary Austin: Song of a Maverick* (New Haven: Yale University Press, 1989), 68.

12. Kevin Starr, "A Myth for Southern California," in Rawls, ed., *New Directions in California History,* 205.

13. Stineman, *Song,* 63.

14. Vera Norwood, "Mary Austin 1868-1934," in *Heath Anthology of American Literature,* 2d ed., ed. Paul Lauter et al. (Lexington, Mass.: D. C. Heath), 2:917.

15. For the interest of southern California Protestants in mission-period Catholicism, see Kevin Starr's *Inventing the Dream: California through the Progressive Era* (New York: Oxford University Press, 1985), 86-89. Starr characterizes northern California at the turn of the century as predominantly populated by "foreign-born Roman Catholics," while in southern California "the dominant population was Midwestern native-born Protestant" (238). According to Starr, "the mission myth was an essentially Protestant creation for an essentially Protestant Southern California. . . . For all its luxuriant imagery, the mission myth fundamentally celebrated the Protestant virtues of order, acquisition, and the work ethic" (89).

16. In San Francisco, for example, the church appointed Peter C. Yorke as a priest in 1891. In 1894, Yorke, an impressive rhetor, took on the de facto assignment of defending the church's interests against attacks from the American Protective Association. Father Yorke so successfully mobilized Catholic voters that, according to Mary E. Lyons, "in the [San Francisco] city elections of 1896 even the mere suggestion that a candidate shared some allegiance with the APA could and did sway the large Catholic vote" (Lyons, "Peter C. Yorke: Advocate of the Irish from the Pulpit to the Podium," in *Religion and Society in the American West: Historical Essays,* ed. Carl Guarneri and David Alvarez [Lanham, Md.: University Press of America, 1987], 402–3). Encouraged by this success, Yorke went on to support Irish dock workers in their waterfront strike in 1901, invoking the 1891 papal encyclical *Rerum novarum* as the basis for his position (Lyons, 404; Eldon G. Ernst, "American Religious History from a Pacific Coast Perspective," in Guarneri and Alvarez, 17).

17. Arthur M. Schlesinger Sr., "A Critical Period in American Religion, 1875-1900," in *Religion in American History: Interpretive Essays,* ed. John M. Mulder and John F. Wilson (Englewood Cliffs, N.J.: Prentice-Hall, 1978), 314, 317 n. 48.

18. For example, in 1893, rumors circulated concerning a spurious papal encyclical "ordering the faithful to 'exterminate all heretics' at the time of the feast of Ignatius Loyola"

and of Catholics stockpiling weapons in the basements of church buildings (Schlesinger, "A Critical Period," 313).

19. Marjorie Pryse, introduction to *Stories from the Country of Lost Borders,* by Mary Austin, ed. Marjorie Pryse (New Brunswick: Rutgers University Press, 1987), xxvi.

20. Stineman, *Song,* 54.

21. Ibid., 227 n. 43.

22. In this case, the implication is that Mascado's comeliness is the result of foreign blood, Indian breeding being considered the lowest of the low in colonial California.

23. By 1900, at least seventy organizations in the United States based their membership on hereditary privilege. Thirty-five of them were founded in the 1890s. See Donald K. Pickens, *Eugenics and the Progressives* (Nashville: Vanderbilt University Press, 1968), 16.

24. Peter Thomas Conmy, *The Origin and Purposes of the Native Sons and Native Daughters of the Golden West* (San Francisco: Dolores Press, 1956), 5.

25. Ibid., 9.

26. Shawn Smith's "Superficial Depths: Visions of Identity in the Age of Mechanical Reproduction" (Ph.D. diss., University of California, San Diego, 1994) offers a brilliant analysis of the relation of technologies of photography, genealogy, and domestic documentation to the discourses of white supremacy in the United States in the late nineteenth century.

27. Augusta Fink, *I-Mary: A Biography of Mary Austin* (Tucson: University of Arizona Press, 1983), 84.

28. Nancy Porter, afterword to *A Woman of Genius,* by Mary Austin (Old Westbury, N.Y.: Feminist Press, 1985), 297.

29. Gilbert, "Costumes," 416.

30. Porter, afterword, 301.

31. Austin, "Frustrate," in *Western Trails: A Collection of Short Stories by Mary Austin,* ed. Melody Graulich (Reno: University of Nevada Press, 1987), 234.

32. Ibid., 228.

33. Eldon G. Ernst, "American Religious History from a Pacific Coast Perspective," in Guarneri and Alvarez, eds., *Religion and Society in the American West,* 4; emphasis added.

34. Porter, afterword, 302.

35. Fink, *I-Mary,* 144.

36. Stineman, *Song,* 105.

37. Mary Austin, *Earth Horizon: An Autobiography* (New York: Literary Guild, 1932), 103.

38. Marjorie Garber, *Vested Interests: Cross-Dressing and Cultural Anxiety* (New York: Routledge, 1992); Judith Butler, *Gender Trouble: Feminism and the Subversion of Identity* (New York: Routledge, 1990).

39. George L. Mosse, *Nationalism and Sexuality: Respectability and Abnormal Sexuality in Modern Europe* (New York: H. Fertig, 1985); Andrew Parker et al., eds., *Nationalisms and Sexualities* (New York: Routledge, 1992).

CHAPTER TWO

Approaching the Imperialist Mirage
Mary Austin's *Lost Borders*

KATHRYN DEZUR

Like Nicole Tonkovich, Kathryn DeZur, in "Approaching the Imperialist Mirage,"
also explores the prevalence of "crossing" imagery in Austin's work, drawing on re-
cent postcolonial theory and feminist geography to argue that Austin's narrative
structure exposes the artificiality of social, territorial, and racial boundaries. While
Nicole Tonkovich focuses on Austin's "double crossing" of religious, political, and
sexual borders, however, DeZur discusses how Austin resists translating land, "na-
tive" bodies, and narrative into "property," suggesting that Austin's work has much
to teach about how to escape the property lines of imperialism, capitalism, and civi-
lization. For Austin, DeZur claims, narrative itself can be complicit in establishing
boundaries; in DeZur's reading, Lost Borders *exposes the "pitfalls of creating nar-*
ratives in an imperial culture" and attempts to destabilize oppressive hierarchies.
The conclusions DeZur draws from Lost Borders *are placed in fuller historical*
context in several of the essays that follow.

When Mary Hunter Austin moved to the California desert as a young
woman, she began complicated relationships with both the land and the
people who inhabited it. She followed her older brother, who supported
the family and had come to the West to homestead public land; she later
married a man who would take the job of registrar of the Desert Land
Office at Independence.[1] Thus she was undeniably tied to the colonizing
network of American expansionism in the late nineteenth and early twentieth centuries. Much of Austin's earlier writing, however, including the
stories collected in *Lost Borders,* encompasses her endeavor to distance herself from that imperial network—and in fact, to write against it. In *Lost
Borders,* Austin seeks to demystify imperialist ideology by crossing territorial, biological, and narrative "borders." Austin challenges the idea of bio-

logical and territorial borders by disrupting the interdependence of property and identity. Her playfulness with the short story form, as well as her direct commentaries on making meaning, show narrative, too, to be inflected with imperialist ideology. In her border crossings, Austin forces the recognition of property, bodies, and conventional narrative as constructs that limit, and as such, destroy, but she does not stop there. Her work suggests that there are "synthesizing" or "hybridizing" modes of both reading and living. *Lost Borders* emphasizes connection to the land, to racial "others," and to myriad stories (as opposed to a monolithic narrative of identity and history). In this essay, I trace Austin's border crossings in order to determine the effectiveness of her strategies of resistance to imperialism.

By 1909, the year she published *Lost Borders,* Austin was heavily enmeshed in what Mary Louise Pratt terms the "contact zone" of imperialism, defined as "social spaces where disparate cultures meet, clash, and grapple with each other, often in highly asymmetrical relations of domination and subordination."[2] *Lost Borders* represents Austin's attempt to enter the contact zone and upset the asymmetrical balance of power between the dominant (the imperialists) and the subordinate (the colonized). The extent to which she succeeds—and fails—has important implications for postcolonial theorists trying to discover how interpolation into and resistance to imperialism occur, particularly for those of the colonizing culture.

Perhaps the degree of Austin's success in disrupting imperial paradigms can be measured by the level of discomfort experienced by even some recent readers of her text. For instance, critic John O'Grady writes that Austin "is most profoundly aware of the 'shadow side' of the wild—its dark, brooding, and indeed, threatening aspects, those that undermine the foundations of society and even the integrity of the individual self."[3] O'Grady is quite correct in his observation that Austin understands nature as contesting the border between self and other (whether that other is the land or a Native American); she tries to create a kind of borderland where crossover is possible. The "foundations of society" undermined in Austin's *Lost Borders* rely on social, territorial, and racial boundaries. It is not the annihilation of social foundations that wreaks havoc on the land and its inhabitants; rather it is the imposition of these foundations that is ruinous. However, the language O'Grady uses to characterize the wild in Austin's work ("dark," "brooding," and, even more revealing, "threatening") is distinctly negative in tone and betrays a certain investment in imperial notions of self and society. But the crossing of the imperial boundaries confining and defining society and self that O'Grady seems to fear is, for Austin, a profoundly positive act. It is not a danger; it is a necessity. It is her means of approaching the imperialist mirage, of more closely examining an ideological structure that seems a solid oasis but when approached from the "shadow side" of the wilderness becomes increasingly diffuse.

This is not to say that Austin manages to stand in the center of the mirage and fully dissipate its power, however; while she resists imperialist ideology, she is also circumscribed by it. Her resistance is not an unqualified success; as a member of the colonizing culture, she constantly runs the risk of slipping from "connection" into "appropriation." Sometimes she negotiates this risk well; at other times she is less successful.[4]

Imperialism is a slippery structure to get a critical hand on. As postcolonial critics have made clear, imperialism extends beyond the control and exploitation of physical resources and into the realm of ideology. For instance, in *The Poetics of Imperialism,* Eric Cheyfitz focuses on the processes of an unproblematized use of metaphor—violently turning the foreign into the familiar.[5] Perhaps the quintessential (or at least fundamental) example of this process is the translation of "land" into "property" in the English, Spanish, French, and later American expansions into the "new world."[6] It is in this ideological and specifically European cultural act of translation that the basis for physical exploitation lies. The translation of "land" into "property" endows that land with alienable value. Property has value because it can provide resources and materials for cultural processes.[7] Once value has been assigned to it, land becomes property and is interpolated into the cultural systems of dominance, possession, and imperialism.[8] Austin's *Lost Borders* critiques the way land is given value through its translation into property. She suggests that the relationship to land should be formulated on the basis of its inalienable value, its personal or spiritual significance.

Austin enters the debate about land value with "The Land," in which the desert resists the texts of culture. Unlike the texts Cheyfitz examines, in which "certain figures of place in the West . . . are contained, not always obviously, within the figure of place as alienable land, or property, or conquerable territory that can be claimed (typically through colonies)," in this story, place as property is always a construct.[9] Austin writes of the desert: "Out there, a week's journey from everywhere, the land was not worth parcelling off, and the boundaries which should logically have been contrived until they met the cañon of the Colorado ran out in foolish wastes

of sand and inextricable disordered ranges."[10] Here, the connection between value and drawing boundaries is clear; imperialism (combined with
capitalism) is the overarching narrative that creates borders and owners.
Land is categorized by use value, but the desert's very lack of use value
makes it uncategorizable. The desert is, furthermore, beyond even the concept of place—it is "a week's journey from everywhere," which leaves it
precisely nowhere. The narrator cautions us, "first and last, accept no man's
statement that he knows this Country of Lost Borders well," for "the best
part of it remains locked, inviolate," known to a very few "whose account
of it does not get into the reports of the Geological Survey."[11] There is no
official knowledge on which to draw to delineate place as property.

If the desert escapes a definition of place as property, it escapes culture
too, "[f]or law runs with the boundary, not beyond it."[12] The narrator states
that men do not make law because the land demands it; rather, "men make
law for the comfortable feel of it, defining them to themselves."[13] Law ostensibly categorizes land but actually serves as a means of self-determina-
tion and differentiation for the men who make it. The law creates bounded
property because men wish to identify themselves as possessors. Possession
of land as property becomes an expression of possession of a self as property.[14] Landownership becomes a means to determine subjectivity and status. Land's use value not only is material, but it is also psychological and
social. In the imperial paradigm, the cultural practices of property and
identity are interdependent and inextricable.

This leads us to consider not only how imperialist ideology views land,
but also how imperialism concerns itself with the "natives" who live on it.
Imperialism requires the construction of categories of identity that distinguish colonizer from colonized. Often, the colonizer's identity is defined
negatively; the colonizer is "not native."[15] In order for this negation to take
place, however, any sense of connection between colonizer and colonized
must be severed. Therefore imperial acts depend not only on the translation of land into property, but also on the translation of natives into "others." The categories "self" and "other" are structured not only by the obvious cultural binary of "civilized" and "savage," but in a fundamental way
are based on what appear to be natural—but are in fact ideological—notions of the body.[16] There is a restriction of "nativeness" to an "other
body" that allows the colonizer a sense of control over the colonized.

The translation of land into property and of natives into "other bodies"
depends on the tracing or mapping of boundaries. Mary Austin's threat to

the project of transláation through mapping should be immediately apparent in the very title of her collection: *Lost Borders*. Bodies, in Austin's work, transcend their biological boundaries at the same time that they cross borders traced on land. Throughout *Lost Borders*, Austin shows the destructive consequences of imperialist ideology's attempt to naturalize constructed boundaries.

Austin first erases the line between land and body in a passage often quoted by critics, in which she represents the desert as a woman:

> If the desert were a woman, I know well what like she would be: deep-breasted, broad in the hips, tawny, with tawny hair, great masses of it lying smooth along her perfect curves, full lipped like a sphinx, but not heavy-lidded like one, eyes sane and steady as the polished jewel of her skies, such a countenance as should make men serve without desiring her, such a largeness to her mind as should make their sins of no account, passionate, but not necessitous, patient—and you could not move her, no, not if you had all the earth to give, so much as one tawny hair's breadth beyond her own desires.[17]

This conflation of land and body has repercussions not only for visualizing landscape, but also for conceptualizing the (female) body. Austin has already described the desert as a place without borders—vast and, for the most part, unknown. Her desert body has the same qualities. It has a "largeness of mind" that extends beyond and above the petty acts of men. Nor is this body limited to the land itself; in her representation of the desert body's eyes, the land and sky are united. The desert body is, furthermore, a mysterious figure—a sphinx—that is both terrifying and alluring. The imagery becomes even more significant when we consider the sphinx's form—half human, half lion. Unclassifiable as either human or beast, it is both at once. It crosses species boundaries. The image of the hybrid becomes a metaphor for the connection with the environment Austin seeks.[18]

William Scheick has criticized the conflation of land and body in Austin's *The Land of Little Rain* as perpetuating an imperial act. He objects to the anthropomorphizing of the landscape, calling it "an act of appropriation by means of perspective."[19] I would like to qualify Scheick's observation in relation to the passage quoted above. Here, the metaphor of the desert woman is conditional (the passage begins with "if"), and Austin's

anthropomorphizing of the land works in opposition to common contemporary paradigms of perceiving the frontier as "virgin territory" to be
sexually desired and conquered by men.[20] Alison Blunt and Gillian Rose
note that "the construction of a 'sexual space' [in imperialist ideology par-
allels] the construction of space to be colonized, and the desire for colonial control [is] often expressed in terms of sexual control."[21] Austin's
desert body does not serve men; rather, men serve it, *without desire.* The female land's desire displaces the erotic economy of imperialism. Moreover,
men cannot give the land anything—the desert already has "all the
earth"—they cannot add value to the land. Rather, men use the land to
define their self-worth by imposing property laws.

Feminist critics may also find this passage problematic in its equation of
a female body and land. Catherine Nash notes that "feminist use of ideas
of place and landscape ... avoids the biologism and essentialism of the idea
of natural, organic, and intuitive closeness to nature" in women.[22] I would
like to suggest, however, that Austin resorts to racial or sexual essentialism
in *Lost Borders* only when she is attempting to reverse conventional paradigms,[23] and in so doing she forces a reexamination of predominant binaries. Yet it must be noted that while Austin privileges the "subordinate" element of the binaries she represents, she does not offer an alternative to
the binary structure itself. She merely reverses the terms.

If Austin begins *Lost Borders* with what seems to be a fairly simple reversal of the conventional relationship between men and the land, she
moves toward a more complex understanding of imperialist desire in "The
Hoodoo of the Minnietta." Here, imperialist desire (by which I mean simply the desire to own and control property and resources) escapes the
boundaries of the body and inhabits a landscape until it is impossible to
separate desirer from desired. If the land is shaped into "the casting of a
man's soul" through imperialist desire, the land also shapes the destinies of
men through its "hoodoo," or curse.[24] The narrator traces the consequences of the curse on the men who mine the Minnietta. Hogan curses
the land when he loses ownership of a mine to the company he created.
The uninitiated suppose that this curse began the hoodoo, "but, in fact, it
began in the fake assay" Hogan gave to Antone, the first and rightful owner
of the mine.[25] The original imperialist impulse created the curse; Hogan's
words merely confirm it. Betrayal follows betrayal, and imperialist desire
continues to be imprinted on the land by greedy owners, each of whom
receives his due. McKenna loses his wife to another man. Jordan, in an at-

tempt to exploit workers in unsafe working conditions, ventures down into the tunnels and is killed by falling rock. The mine passes to Jordan's heirs, "who knew nothing of silver mines except that they were supposed to be eminently desirable."[26] The heirs' mistaken belief that the mine is desirable because it is valuable ensures that the hoodoo will remain in place. The land both is twisted by men and twists men into "the shape of hate and rage" when imbued with imperialist desire, and the effects are devastating.[27]

Austin continues to pursue her theme of imperialist desire's destructive potential in "The Pocket-Hunter's Story," in which murderous imperialist desire transfers not from body to land, but from body to body. In this story, however, the object of imperial desire is an Indian woman, and she serves as a point of entrance for my discussion of race relations and racial boundaries in imperialist ideology and in Austin's text.[28] The story begins by introducing two enemies. Mac and Creelman were once good friends and partners in the mining camps; their animosity began over their desire to possess an Indian woman: "She was Mac's woman; though, except as being his, he was not thought to set particular store by her."[29] Mac does not care for this woman except in terms of his proprietary interest in her. He owns her. But Creelman "steals" her, and "the tacit admission of an Indian woman as no fit subject for white men to fight over forbade [Mac's] being put to the ordinary provocation on account of her."[30] Both men and white culture view the woman as alienable property endowed with use value because of her race, but her race simultaneously makes her not worth fighting over. Her status as object is reflected in the fact that she is never given a name in the narrative. Her race is the defining factor of her identity. The imperialist desire to own her as property drives Mac beyond death, beyond his own body and into another's, in order to murder Creelman. Austin repeats a variation on the destructiveness of the hoodoo here; she shows it to be a short step from objectification and delineation of a body based on race and the resulting imperialist desire, to the ultimate antisocial act: murder. The imperialistic construction of boundaries, whether traced on land or on bodies, destroys social relations.

"A Case of Conscience" also exposes the problem of race and/as imperial property. It begins with Saunders, "an average Englishman with a lung complaint,"[31] who moves to the desert in order to cure his affliction. He clearly participates in the male erotic economy of imperialism when he decides to settle near Ubehebe ("Maiden's Breast"). Saunders is attracted to the land because it is "lovely and alluring, soft with promise and austerely virgin."[32] The virgin land is literalized in a virgin Shoshone named Turwhasé, whom Saunders sexually "conquers" and who then bears his child. When Saunders fully recovers, he decides to leave Ubehebe. He feels no regret at leaving Turwhasé behind; she is simply part of the land that no longer has any use value for him. However, when the desire for "civilization" invades him, "the old, obstinate Anglo-Saxon prejudice that makes a man responsible for his offspring" accompanies it.[33] He takes his daughter with him, not because she has any intrinsic value to him, but simply because he can then reassure himself that he is "civil." His daughter is merely a means to reinforce his self-conception as a "man of conscience."

On his return to the urban center of Lone Pine, Saunders realizes that "there was something more than mere irresponsibility in the way of desert-faring men who formed relations such as this and left them off with the land, as they left the clothes they wore there and its tricks of speech."[34] He comes close to realizing the dynamics of the imperialist desire for both the land and the Indian woman; however, his recognition of the cultural difference between whites and Indians does nothing more than convince him that his child would be better off dead. Saunders is relieved when Turwhasé arrives to take back their daughter. Her insistence on ownership ("'Mine!' she said, fiercely. 'Mine, not yours!'") is not based in economics; she laughs at Saunders when he tries to pay her.[35] Her daughter holds no alienable value for Turwhasé; she merely speaks in terms with which Saunders will be familiar.

At this point, the narrator essentializes Turwhasé's race: "You could see by the slope of the shoulders under the blanket and the swing of her hips, as [Turwhasé] went, that she was all Indian."[36] Here, we seem to have race engendered on the level of biology—the shoulders and the hips. Of course, the phrase "all Indian" can be read as highly ironic when considering the common contemporary binary Indian/white, often translated into savage/civilized. Saunders is, if anything, "all white"; the narrator emphasizes his Englishness and his Anglo-Saxon heritage. He should, then, be "all civilized." But here the binary is reversed—it is Turwhasé in her Indianness who is ultimately civilized. She takes responsibility for her offspring, the mark of Anglo-Saxon civility; and furthermore, she does so out of love for her child rather than out of an empty sense of duty.

The child incorporates both parents' lineages and cultures; she becomes a figure of the hybrid, much like the sphinx in "The Land." She is "gold-colored" like her mother, and "grey-eyed" like Saunders's mother.[37] Linking Turwhasé's daughter back to the image of the sphinx may seem problematic because she would then symbolically become half human and half beast. This could be seen as fitting into contemporary racist discourses that represented Indians as bestial. However, Saunders is so heavily ironized in this story that the status of white culture cannot be said to necessarily occupy the privileged (i.e., human) position. Which half is which comes into question. Furthermore, it becomes obvious that Saunders does not sufficiently appreciate his daughter or what she symbolizes in terms of the hybridization of cultures. Austin seems to suggest that a true "man of conscience" would value Indian culture and the products of its intersection with white culture.

Austin not only questions the socially created boundaries between self and other (whether an Indian or the land) through the figure of the hybrid, but she also interrogates the imperially inflected narratives through which those borders are represented and reproduced. Bill Ashcroft, Gareth Griffiths, and Helen Tiffin comment in their introduction to *The Postcolonial Studies Reader* that "the most formidable ally of economic and political control had long been the business of 'knowing' other peoples because this 'knowing' underpinned imperial dominance and became the mode by which they were persuaded to know themselves: that is, as subordinate."[38] For Austin, this imperial "knowing" of borders distinguishing self from other and one's own property from others' property is often constructed through narrative. Austin reveals how these narratives are constructed in her attempt to dispel the imperial mirage.

Before considering the characters' relationships to narrative within the text, we must establish Austin's relationship to her narrator and text. The narrator is clearly an author figure; she searches out and creates stories. She moves through the desert landscape and attempts to represent it meaningfully, much as Austin did. However, the narrator is not reducible to a purely autobiographical representation of Austin; her similarities to Austin exist in tension with her status as a fictional character.[39] This tension, springing from the overlap of fiction and history, allows for a self-reflexive commentary on making meaning through narrative. Austin's "hybrid" narrator, who is simultaneously Austin and more than Austin, becomes a means to interrogate some of the pitfalls of creating narratives in an imperialist culture. The narrator not only represents the ways other characters deploy narrative for imperialist ends, but also becomes implicated in the process of creating imperial "knowing" through narrative.

Austin's critique of how narrative is used to buttress imperialism begins in "The Land." Here, the narrator reveals the imperial process by which historical narrative is transformed or translated. Long Tom Bassit tells the narrator about an incident related to him by an eyewitness, "the Man-who-saw." As an emigrant caravan crossed a salt pit, trusting the crust to hold, several people fell through the surface; some were never recovered. The Man-who-saw went back several years later and found the body of a woman dressed in red, encased in salt crystal. The narrator tells us that "Long Tom wished me to make a story of it."[40] It is, of course, already a story, narrated first by the Man-who-saw and then by Long Tom. However, the story's commentary on historical narrative becomes complicated when the narrator tries to retell the tale. She cannot finish it because "there, about the time the candles began to burn their shades and red track of the light on the wine-glasses barred the cloth, with the white, disdainful shoulders and politely incredulous faces leaning through the smoke of cigarettes, it had a garish sound."[41] This story that preserves the consequences of imperialist desire (death through the attempt to settle the West)—just as the salt preserves the silent testimony of the woman in red and the emigrants' records preserve the incident—is not appropriate to the setting of an upper-class dinner party.[42] Context, then, determines the narrative of history, and furthermore determines which narratives of history are told and heard. The narrator escapes this dilemma, however, by preserving the story in the text at hand. She manages to insert the "inappropriate" narrative and question its status as inappropriate.

If, in the dynamics of imperial "knowing," history can be relegated to the realm of fiction, so, too, can fiction be turned into history via imperialist desire. "Curiously," the narrator states, "in that country, you can get anybody to believe any sort of tale that has gold in it."[43] When a character named Woodin brings the narrator a potsherd and suggests she find a story about it, she replies, "I will do better than that, I will *make* a story."[44] The two create a tale that includes an Indian woman, an earthenware pot, and "a lost river bedded with precious sand," and then go their separate ways, agreeing to spread the fiction whenever they have the opportunity.[45] Eventually the story comes back to the narrator as a well-known truth. Miners take the trouble to correct her published version of the tale, and one of her friends, Tennessee, claims to know the Indian woman in the story. The metanarrative that drives the dissemination of the story and its conversion into "truth" is imperialism. The imperialist possibility of creating property out of land makes the story attractive as "truth." Tennessee, for instance, believes the story because he desperately wants to discover the lost river and exploit its wealth. The desire for the lost river is the desire to transform a nonplace (it is "lost") into a place that can then become alienable property. Tennessee's name, a place-name, is surely no coincidence. He represents the imperialist expansion of named country into "undiscovered" territory. The implication is that even though Tennessee will not find the lost river (he can't, as it is a fictional creation), he will find land and turn it into property in his search for the gold in the story. The imperialist fiction creates an imperialist history.

The narrator also reveals the arbitrary and incomplete nature of imperial "knowing" when she says, "I should get no credit with you if I were to tell what really became of Loring, and what happened to the man who went down into the meaning pit of Sand Mountain."[46] We never discover who Loring is or what happened in the meaning pit. By refusing to share these tales with an appeal to credibility, the narrator forces us to recognize not only that the believable is not always real, as shown in the potsherd story, but also that the real is not always believable. The status of the "real" is always in question. Furthermore, the narrator's reference to the "credit" it takes to gain "purchase," the trust it takes to gain influence, also ironically refers to capitalism and economies of ownership. This brings the status of narratives as property into question. Whose story is whose? Who has the "rights" to which story?

Austin examines these questions in greater detail in "The Woman at the Eighteen-Mile," in which the narrator perceives a chance to "write a story of Death Valley that should be its final word."[47] But there is no final, single, definitive, or monolithic word; there are only many words told in many voices. Characters vie for the chance to tell the "authoritative" version of the dead man Lang's story. Almost no one, however, can tell the whole tale from beginning to end. First, "it was a teamster who told it," though "he called the dead man Long, and failed to remember who was supposed to have killed him, and what about."[48] Although the narrator has lived in the area for seven years, she has not yet found anybody who can give her the whole story. "I went about asking for it, and got sticks and straws."[49] Information floats in from various sources—a barkeep in Tio Juan, a Mexican, a man in San Francisco—but a coherent narrative does not form. It remains fragmented and therefore untellable in a comprehensive way; "the story glimmered like a summer island in a mist."[50]

Austin's use of this simile, a "story" like an "island," solidifies the connection between narrative, property, and imperialism. The island and the story are shrouded in mist, making it difficult to distinguish borders. The narrator's drive to "have" the whole story becomes a kind of imperial desire for narrative, for clearly defining the parameters of the tale. Only the Woman at Eighteen-Mile can connect all the elements—the mine, the murder, the mystery, the sacrifice, the Shoshones, lonely water holes, deserted camps, and a woman—and make their boundaries clear. The narrator confuses the story with property and property rights; she speaks of "the heart of my story. Mine!"[51] She puts her imperialist impulse to possess the narrative into perspective by her later reflection that "I called it [mine] by that time, but hers was the right."[52] But the woman resists the narrator's attempts to make the story into alienable property: she makes the narrator promise not to tell it. The story, however, is valuable only in its telling. Without the telling, the story drops out of circulation and the processes of exchange; it is no longer on the market. The narrator says, "I sat within the shallow shadow of the eaves experiencing the full-throated satisfaction of prospectors over the feel of pay dirt, rubbing it between the thumb and palm, swearing over it softly below the breath. It was as good as that. And I was never to have it!"[53] She becomes a prospector of narrative who fails to make her "claim" on the story as a "final word" about the West. She can tell part of the story, linking events and characters through inference, but the details of motive and action remain missing.

Furthermore, the narrator can only loosely sew the parts of the narrative together with the thread of imperialism. Whitmark, a "business man with an obsession for accomplishing results," had, after almost two years, obtained possession of "the property."[54] The story of Whitmark's imperialist guilt, as sketchily outlined as it is, threatens to destroy not only his reputation but the possibility of an imperialistically innocent "final word" of the West. Whitmark becomes a figure for the narrator. Whitmark's implied criminality in his attempt to gain control over property parallels the narrator's implied criminality in her attempt to "steal" the story, suppressing its many voices and offering only her own. Yet, the narrator is also differentiated from Whitmark. Based on what the narrator knows, Whitmark "ought to have been hung."[55] The narrator, on the other hand, keeps her promise not to tell the story (although the promise is qualified by her plan to tell the story after the Woman at Eighteen-Mile is dead). The narrative criminal act has not taken place. Instead, the narrator tells the story of the woman telling the story, a technique that allows for the presence of a multiplicity of voices in the text.

Finally, the story cannot represent life in the West, for "[l]ife . . . cannot yet square with Respectability, with the Church and Property. Threading through these, Love weaves the fascinating intricacies of story, but here in the Borders, where the warp runs loose and wide, the pattern has not that richness it should show in the close fabric of civilization."[56] Life that escapes the boundaries of property and institutions escapes the boundaries of narrative. Here Austin recognizes that her stories do not reflect the brilliant, rich, and closely woven aesthetic patterns found in "civilized" society. It is, in fact, her aim to "de-civilize" narratives by violating commonly accepted criteria for short fiction.

When Brander Matthews set out the "required elements" of a short story in 1884, he included unity and compression: "A short story deals with a single character, a single event, a single emotion, or the series of emotions called forth by a single situation . . . no digression is tolerable."[57] Austin rarely focuses on the singular in her work, instead preferring to explore the possibilities of multiplicity. The very form of her stories and the structure of *Lost Borders* as a whole reinforce the theme of permeability between self and other, and between self and land. Indeed, Austin tends to digress at the ends of her stories as a means to connect them to other stories. For example, the narrator ends "The Last Antelope" with the following sentence: "When one has to think of death in connection with strange tiptoeing men felicitating themselves on millinery effects, with the suggestion of what was to be charged for it lurking under the discreetly dropped lids, and all the obvious mechanism of modern burial, one can understand that what happened at Agua Dulce is quite another matter."[58]

The reader knows that Agua Dulce represents death in an entirely different manner from the "mechanism of modern burial," which is, finally, concerned with "what was to be charged for it," or capitalist interests. However, we do not know what actually happened at Agua Dulce—who was involved, who died or how, or how that death was dealt with—until we read the story "Agua Dulce." The narrator also uses this strategy in "The Hoodoo of the Minnietta," "A Case of Conscience," and "The Fakir." Such endings force Austin's reader to realize that narratives always lead to other narratives, and that the endpoint of any narrative is a matter of formal convention that limits through its attempts to confine and bound.

This bridging technique also emphasizes the form of the work as a collection (as opposed to the linear movement of a premodernist novel, for instance), a grouping together of disparate items or ideas—or in this case, narratives—that are connected associationally rather than hierarchically.[59]

Although the stories relate to one another, one story never serves as the "key" to another. And yet, each story, to be fully understood, must be read in the context of the entire collection. In order to understand the part, one must be familiar with the whole. This process, however, does not work in reverse: to know a part is not to know the whole.

According to Austin, the artificial boundaries between narratives, properties, and bodies created by imperialist ideology obscure knowledge of the whole. These borders create the mirage of societal and individual integrity, which is based on imperial economies of ownership and possession. As Austin approaches that mirage, she finds that it begins to vanish into the "foolish wastes of sand and inextricable disordered ranges" of the desert landscape.[60] And while she doesn't manage to completely dissipate imperialism's power, she at least alerts us to the fact that imperialist ideology is a mirage.

NOTES

My thanks are due to several readers who looked over this essay in its numerous incarnations: Rochelle Johnson, Maureen Woodard, Carol Carney, Nancy Gamer, Melody Graulich, and Betsy Klimasmith.

1. Marjorie Pryse, introduction to *Stories from the Country of Lost Borders*, by Mary Austin (New Brunswick: Rutgers University Press, 1987), xi-xiii.

2. Mary Louise Pratt, *Imperial Eyes: Travel Writing and Transculturation* (New York: Routledge, 1992), 4.

3. John P. O'Grady, *Pilgrims to the Wild: Everett Ruess, Henry David Thoreau, John Muir, Clarence King, Mary Austin* (Salt Lake City: University of Utah Press, 1993), 125.

4. According to Abdul Janmohamed's distinctions between types of colonial litterateurs, Austin's text can be categorized as a "symbolic" text, one that uses a native culture to reflect on the efficacy of the dominant culture's values, assumptions, and habits, as opposed to an "imaginary" text, which is structured by objectification, aggression, and a fixed opposition between self and other (Abdul Janmohamed, "The Economy of Manichean Allegory," in *The Post-Colonial Studies Reader,* ed. Bill Ashcroft, Gareth Griffiths, and Helen Tiffin [New York: Routledge, 1995], 19). Yet it must be noted that just because a text is "symbolic" rather than "imaginary" does not mean it is not liable to the problems of appropriation. For instance, in *American Rhythm,* Austin makes the problematic statement, "[W]hen I say that I am not, have never been, nor offered myself, as an authority on things Amerindian, I do not wish to have it understood that I may not, at times, have succeeded in being an Indian" (Mary Austin, *American Rhythm: Studies and Reexpressions of Amerindian Songs* [Boston: Houghton Mifflin, 1930], quoted in Michael Castro, *Interpreting the Indian: Twentieth-Century Poets and the Native American* [Albuquerque: University of New Mexico Press, 1983], 3).

5. Eric Cheyfitz, *The Poetics of Imperialism: Translation and Colonization from* The Tempest *to Tarzan* (New York: Oxford University Press, 1991), 35-37.

6. Cheyfitz illustrates this transaction of forcible translation with a 1832 Supreme Court ruling (*Johnson and Graham's Lessee v. M'Intosh*) that "translated Indian notions of native peoples' relation to their lands into the language of Anglo-American property law—the language where 'title' is the supreme term—not so that Indians could be empowered in that language, but so that ultimate power over their lands, the historical inalienability of which constituted their cultures, could be 'legally' transferred to the federal government" (Eric Cheyfitz, "Savage Law: The Plot against American Indians in *Johnson and Graham's Lessee v. M'Intosh* and *The Pioneers*," in *Cultures of United States Imperialism,* ed. Amy Kaplan and Donald E. Pease [Durham: Duke University Press, 1993], 110).

7. Howard Horwitz defines *value* as "a narrative principle of differentiation distinguishing human artifact from alien nature (mere matter)" (Horwitz, *By the Law of Nature: Form and Value in Nineteenth-Century America* [New York: Oxford University Press, 1991], 7).

8. It is perhaps best to mention here that this paradigm of imperialism and the one at work in Austin's *Lost Borders* are based in the context of capitalism. Capitalism and imperialism are not, of course, the same thing. Other economic-political systems attempt to conquer and control territory; yet in colonial and postcolonial American history, capitalism has served (and still serves) as the engine of American imperialism.

9. Cheyfitz, *Poetics,* 45.

10. Mary Austin, *Lost Borders,* in *Stories from the Country of Lost Borders,* 155–56.

11. Ibid., 159.

12. Ibid., 156.

13. Ibid.

14. The idea of possessing a "self" as one possesses property can be found in Locke's *Essay on Human Understanding* (1690). The relationship between property, identity, and agency may be traced to the even older practice of basing voting privileges on property holdings.

15. Richard Dyer points out that "[t]rying to think about the representation of whiteness as an ethnic category . . . is difficult, partly because white power secures its dominance by seeming not to be anything in particular, but also because, when whiteness *qua* whiteness does come into focus, it is often revealed as emptiness, absence, denial or even a kind of death" (Dyer, "White," *Screen* 29.4 [1988]: 44). Whiteness becomes that which is not colored, just as colonizer becomes that which is not native.

16. My understanding of the biological as ideological comes in large part from recent work on sex in feminist theory. Judith Butler, for instance, comments that biological sex is the result of cultural processes of identification. She is quite right to ask, "[W]hat is 'sex' anyway? Is it natural, anatomical, chromosomal, or hormonal? . . . Does sex have a history? . . . Are the ostensibly natural facts of sex discursively produced by various scientific discourses in the service of other political and social interests?" (Butler, *Gender Trouble: Feminism and the Subversion of Identity* [New York: Routledge, 1990], 6–7). Even biologically speaking, that which we consider a body's boundary, the skin, is an incredibly permeable membrane.

17. Austin, *Lost Borders,* 160.

18. The relationship between women and the land depicted in this passage is echoed in Austin's novella *Cactus Thorn,* in which a woman becomes a figure of the desert (as opposed to the desert being figured as a woman). Dulcie, when Arliss meets her, seems to be a part of the desert landscape. Although the isolated location of their first meeting suggests the proper setting for seduction, Arliss finds that his attraction to her is not an erotic one (al-

though this later changes). See Mary Austin, *Cactus Thorn* (Reno: University of Nevada Press, 1988).

19. William J. Scheick, "Mary Austin's Disfigurement of the Southwest in *The Land of Little Rain," Western American Literature* 27.1 (1992): 42–43.

20. Annette Kolodny traces this paradigm in much of her work. See, for instance, *The Lay of the Land: Metaphor as Experience and History in American Life and Letters* (Chapel Hill: University of North Carolina Press, 1975); and *The Land before Her: Fantasy and Experience of the American Frontiers, 1630-1860* (Chapel Hill: University of North Carolina Press, 1984).

21. Alison Blunt and Gillian Rose, "Introduction: Women's Colonial and Postcolonial Geographies," in *Writing Women and Space: Colonial and Postcolonial Geographies* (New York: Guilford Press, 1994), 10.

22. Catherine Nash, "Remapping the Body/Land: New Cartographies of Identity, Gender and Landscape in Ireland," in Blunt and Rose, eds., *Writing Women and Space,* 229.

23. Linda Karell sees Austin's representation of the desert as a female body as a case of what Diana Fuss ("Reading Like a Feminist," *Differences* 1 (Summer 1998): 77-92) terms "strategic essentialism"—"a method of resistance [that] can grant authority to speak." Karell perceives Austin's "spiritual authority" derived from her essentialism as performing cultural critiques structured by an understanding of "difference from the universal" (Linda Karell, *"Lost Borders* and Blurred Boundaries: Mary Austin as Storyteller," in *American Women Short Story Writers: A Collection of Critical Essays,* ed. Julie Brown [New York: Garland, 1995], 165).

24. Austin, *Lost Borders,* 167.

25. Ibid., 163.

26. Ibid., 166.

27. Ibid., 167.

28. Austin's stories also create a space for discussions about ideologies of the body and gender. I have chosen to focus on race here because of its obvious connection to colonizing practices. It is interesting to note, however, that most of the Indian figures in the text are female. The connection between native culture and femininity in *Lost Borders* has yet to be explored.

29. Austin, *Lost Borders,* 223.

30. Ibid.

31. Ibid., 168.

32. Ibid., 169.

33. Ibid., 171.

34. Ibid., 173.

35. Ibid.

36. Ibid.

37. Ibid., 171.

38. Bill Ascroft, Gareth Griffiths, and Helen Tiffin, introduction to *The Postcolonial Studies Reader* (New York: Routledge, 1995), 1.

39. This seems to function in a way similar to Austin's narrator in her autobiography, *Earth Horizon.* In that text, Austin refers to herself in the third person. This technique creates a gap between the Austin narrating the autobiography and the Austin represented within it. See Mary Austin, *Earth Horizon* (Boston: Houghton Mifflin, 1932).

40. Austin, *Lost Borders,* 157.

41. Ibid.

42. Karell also discusses this scene; see "*Lost Borders* and Blurred Boundaries," 162–63.

43. Austin, *Lost Borders,* 157.

44. Ibid., 158; original emphasis.

45. Ibid.

46. Ibid., 157.

47. Ibid., 203.

48. Ibid.

49. Ibid., 204.

50. Ibid.

51. Ibid., 205.

52. Ibid.

53. Ibid., 207.

54. Ibid., 206, 208.

55. Ibid., 209.

56. Ibid., 210.

57. Quoted in Fred Lewis Patee, *The Development of the American Short Story: An Historical Survey* (New York: Harper and Brothers, 1923), 294.

58. Austin, *Lost Borders,* 196.

59. For a discussion of Austin's nonlinear form in her book *The Land of Little Rain,* see Elizabeth Ammons, *Conflicting Stories: American Women Writers at the Turn into the Twentieth Century* (New York: Oxford University Press, 1991), 86–104.

60. Austin, *Lost Borders,* 156.

CHAPTER THREE

Ritual Drama/Dramatic Ritual

Austin's "Indian Plays"

MARK HOYER

Mary Austin's portrayal of American Indian characters and myths has been challenged and debated by numerous scholars. In "Ritual Drama/Dramatic Ritual,"
Mark Hoyer reveals how Austin's rich and particular knowledge of native California cultures and history informs her Indian dramas, an approach Dale Metcalfe
applies to Austin's poetics in "Singing Like the Indians Do" as well. While others
read Austin as appropriating Indian lives and materials and as "colonizing"
through her use of metaphors, Hoyer identifies a syncretic vision of historical
adaptation and regeneration in her work, showing how she explores key intersections between peoples. As he does in his broader study of Austin's use of religious
syncretism, Dancing Ghosts, Hoyer presents Austin as ethnologically sophisti-
cated, as aware of and learning from the ongoing presence and influence of a
variety of native cultures and their myths.

Hoyer's essay is characterized by his understanding of historical context, what
anthropologist Clifford Geertz might call "thick description." He focuses on some
of the least explored Austin works, her three Indian plays: The Arrow-Maker,
"The Coyote Doctor," and Fire. Instead of dismissing these works as dated allegories, Hoyer discovers in them complex treatments of race and gender. In Hoyer's
explication of the connections between the Christian and Native American
mythologies that inform the dramas, Austin's familiar chisera figure becomes a link
between differing worldviews. Hoyer's essay provides a new perspective on the feminist exploration of the woman artist by showing that these staged performances
both warn against oppression and offer the woman artist a chance to transform
private ritual into public ceremony, as character and as author. His discussion of
Austin's understanding of ritual and performance implicitly engages with Judith
Butler's concept of "gender as performance," as explored by Nicole Tonkovich;

later in this collection Elizabeth Klimasmith and Judy Temple will return to the
theme of performance in Austin's works.

The style of the mythological tales combines narrative form with
dramatic art; the characters ought rather to be called actors.[1]

[R]itual dramas are . . . the collective or communal counterpart of
the mystical and sacred experience of an individual. . . . [They] differ
from theatre as pure entertainment because they are performed
out of necessity.[2]

In the process of creating ritual, the shaman acts as theatrical manager—playwright and performer of sacred history.[3]

Readers of Mary Austin's *The Land of Little Rain* may recall several juxta-
positions of a character or story from Owens Valley Paiute or Shoshone
cultures with one from the Bible: Austin compares Seyavi to the prophet
Deborah, for instance, and Winnenap's beloved Shoshone Land to a kind
of Eden. She alludes to the culture hero Winnedumah after framing "My
Neighbor's Field" with the story of Naboth's vineyard; and she claims in
the first chapter that she has drunk from Hassaympa, a spring foretold in
native lore, during her "twice seven years' wandering," the same time span
as the cycle of famine and plenty that, according to Joseph's prophecy,
would befall Egypt.[4] I argue elsewhere that Austin's juxtaposition of
stories from two cultures in conflict demonstrates her interest in and
experimentation with religious syncretism. It was an interest that continued throughout her life and drew inspiration from the Northern Paiute
Ghost Dance, a syncretic revitalization movement that began in an area of
western Nevada directly adjacent to California's Owens Valley (where
Austin lived from 1892 to 1906). The religion's prophet, Wovoka, declared
a vision of interracial harmony after "dying" and "talking to God."[5]

Austin makes the same kind of move—bringing into contact biblical
and native oral tales—in three "Indian dramas" she wrote between 1911
and 1915, after she had left the Owens Valley for good. That she should find
drama a congenial medium for spiritual expression comes as no surprise.
At the age of ten she began what she later called her first "serious" piece of
writing, "A Play to Be Sung," which seems to have been precipitated by
her discovery that she possessed "a language which the elders actually did
not understand[,] . . . the language spoken by talking animals in dreams."[6]

At the same time, she was learning a very public language and role, which she performed within her family. As part of a contest initiated by her Grandpa Graham, she read the Bible all the way through, in the process learning "whole chapters by heart, to recite to him" (67). All this occurred during a period in her life when she reacted with such revulsion to the biblical Heaven depicted in Revelation, Grandpa Graham's favorite book, that she was staging elaborate private rituals with friends—such as attempting to recite the Lord's Prayer backward—to avoid going there (54). The struggles between her public and private selves formed part of the fabric of the dual identity that Austin later dramatized in her autobiography with the names "I-Mary" and "Mary-by-herself." Indeed, nowhere is her own sense of the dramatic quality of her life more apparent than in *Earth Horizon,* in which her language is shot through with the vocabulary of the stage, and *A Woman of Genius,* whose semiautobiographical protagonist is a stage actress.[7]

Austin's belief in the possibilities of drama was forged, however, as much in the Indian villages of the Owens Valley as in the theater. Her interest in Paiute ritual led her once to "lay out all one cold night on the mountains at the risk of her life to watch the Piutes dance their Dance of Death." The stories she collected from her Paiute contacts in the Owens Valley show the same tendency toward syncretic expression as stories later collected by anthropologists doing fieldwork there in the mid-1930s.[8]

Syncretic expressions of faith were of intense personal interest to Austin in the years immediately following her move from Bakersfield to the Owens Valley in 1892, for at this point in her life she was experiencing both a growing frustration with conventional Protestantism and a budding interest in Paiute forms of prayer, which she was learning under the tutelage of the shaman Tinnemaha. One passage from her autobiography is particularly instructive in showing how she tended to link the theater and Indians with the spiritual drama unfolding in her life. Referring to the "parts" she was playing in Independence, Austin writes of being read out of the Methodist church for teaching the Higher Criticism and for organizing a community theater, and then continues:

> There was a part for her in the Indian life. . . . She entered into their lives, the life of the campoody, the strange secret life of the tribe, the struggle of Whiteness with Darkness, the struggle of the individual soul with the Friend-of-the-Soul-of-Man. She learned what it

meant; how to prevail; how to measure her strength against it. Learning that, she learned to write.

There is a thing called the Friend-of-the-Soul-of-Man, a reality, an influence which you can call up around you. You wrap yourself in it. You are effective through it. You make use of it through rhythm; the beating of the medicine drum; the pound of feet in the medicine dance. You give way to it through rhythmic utterance. You find it expressing itself in rhythmic movement, the running of quail, the creaking of the twenty-mule team, the sweep of motion in a life-history, in a dance, a chant.[9]

The same sentiments about the possibilities of drama as a medium for spiritual expression are revealed in a 1911 short story, "The Song-Makers." Here Austin's narrator manifests an attitude toward "rhythmic utterance" that would later be developed fully in *The American Rhythm*.[10] Drifting away mentally from a conversation among "intellectuals" about Wagner's operas, her narrator has been dreaming of a conversation between Kern River Jim and Tinnemaha about Indian song making. After hearing Tinnemaha sing, the narrator privately muses: "Good Medicine! There I had the whole business of song-makers; painted songs, printed songs, or whatever; not to preach, not to please merely, but to make a short road to the mood of power, to touch the Friend. But you had by Tinnemaha's account to touch him yourself first, to swing up by the skirts of the Great Moment and to let down a hand to stumbling men." When her musing is interrupted by a companion's query about her having said nothing for almost an hour, she responds, "I was thinking ... that I should like to write a song like this"—the irony being, of course, that her companions assume she is referring to Wagner's operas.[11]

This passage reveals not only Austin's sensitivity to the spiritual dimensions of dramatic expression, but also, through the image of "swing[ing] up by the skirts of the Great Moment," her conviction that women—and, in particular, women artists such as herself—are and should be participants in accessing that sacred dimension, leading the way for the general public and thus transforming private ritual into communal ceremony. Austin's three Indian dramas—*The Arrow-Maker,* "The Coyote Doctor" (which remains unpublished), and *Fire*—represent attempts "to write a song" like the one she heard from Tinnemaha, to dramatize a spiritual journey that begins as personal illumination but must (according to the author) extend to the community as well.[12] Syncretism between Native American and Christian forms, beliefs, and stories plays a fundamental role in this journey, and an examination of her Indian dramas that considers this overlooked feature of Austin's work reveals these plays to be far richer and more complex than critics have heretofore acknowledged.

"The Sweep of Motion in a Life History": The Chisera *and* The Arrow-Maker

First the Indians fed and then the *Chisera* danced. She leaped before the gods of Rain as David before the Ark of the Lord when it came up from Kirjath-jearim; she stamped and shuffled and swung to the roll of the hollow skins and rattles of rams' horns; three days she danced, and the Indians sat about her singing with their eyes upon the ground. Day and night they sustained her with the whisper and beat of their moaning voices. Is there in fact a vibration in nature which struck into rhythm precipitates rain, as a random chord on the organ brings a rush of tears? At any rate it rained, *and* it rained, and it *rained!* The barley quickened in the field, a thousand acres of mesa flung up suddenly a million sprouting things. Rain fell three weeks. The barley and the wheat lay over heavily, the cattle left off feeding, the budding mesa was too wet to bloom. "For another steer," said the *Chisera,* "I will make it stop." So the toll of food, and cloth, and beads was paid again, and in three days the sun broke gloriously on a succulent green world.[13]

Thus does Austin first introduce us to the figure that would become the central character of her first Indian drama, *The Arrow-Maker.* In this passage from *The Flock,* a book describing the life of sheep and shepherds in the southern San Joaquin and Owens Valleys and the Sierra Nevada of California, Austin tells us that the Chisera is a witch and a rainmaker. It is a dry year at Rancho Tejon, and the Chisera has been called on to perform her medicine.

Both by comparing her to David and by having General Beale declare, "'Let her be proven,' like Elijah to the prophets of Baal," Austin molds our first impression of the Chisera in the light of myth, framing her account as a revision of the biblical story about Elijah and the prophets of Baal, who were proven to have no such power as that possessed by the Chisera.[14] The biblical allusions as well as the lack of physical detail in regard to her appearance here serve to naturalize the foreignness of the Chisera and the god(s) she worships. Into the world of *The Flock,* a world peopled by shepherds, Austin introduces the alien god of an Indian people dependent on the fertility of the land. Although she casts the Chisera as the prophet of a pagan and inferior god, she simultaneously, by invoking the comparison with David, transforms her rhetorically into a prophet of Yahweh, the One True Lord of ancient Hebrew belief (a move which, in the prophetic tradition established in the Bible, has an analogue in the Book of Hosea).[15]

These stories are part of the mythological context Austin imports into *The Arrow-Maker* via the preface to the 1915 edition. By providing a glossary entry that refers readers to the Chisera as depicted in *The Flock,* Austin invites us to read into her play the entire mythological context of the Chisera as presented in that earlier work.[16] The glossary was added to the second edition, which was revised, Austin writes, to more nearly conform "to the author's original conception of the drama, [and] to the conditions of the life it presents." The original preface, reprinted in the later edition, simultaneously points toward a context seemingly far removed from both ancient Near Eastern and Native American cultures, and it thus encourages us to see her characters as multirepresentational. In that preface, Austin insists that, in order to read the play "profitably," the reader must bear in mind the contemporary situation of "the enormous and stupid [waste] of the gifts of women." This situation is embodied in the story of the Chisera, whom Austin identifies as "the Genius, one of those singular and powerful characters whom we are still, with all our learning, unable to account for without falling back on the primitive conception of gift as arising from direct communication with the gods" (x–xiii).

The turning of the word *primitive* back on the audience highlights the strategy that undergirds the presentation of Indian characters and mythological themes. Austin sees something fundamentally dramatic in the "struggle of Femininity to recapture its right to serve, and still to serve with whatever powers and possessions it finds itself endowed. But a dramatic presentation of it is hardly possible outside of primitive conditions where no tradition intervenes to prevent society from accepting the logic of events" (xii). These qualifications make clear that Austin's exoticizing of the Indian is a tactical move to confront the audience with its own "primitive" prejudices against women.

While in one sense, then, the "Indian" in *The Arrow-Maker* is but a mirror reflecting "Woman," in another important sense the Indian also represents the Indian. Thus, to read the play strictly as allegory, as the few critics who have thought the play worthy of comment have tended to do, wholly effaces the Indian by focusing on only one strand of its elaborate network of signification. Austin emphasizes the play's dual focus by elaborating, in the first part of the preface, on the difficulties of dramatically presenting Indians to an audience whose conception of them is stereotyped and overgeneralized, thus making clear the (at least) double inflection of *The Arrow-Maker*—it is both about Indians and about women. The glossary entry on the Chisera, who is the central figure in the play's mythological complex, multiplies these inflections in the direction of spiritual orientation.

The blending of biblical religions with "pagan" ones, and the biblical revisionism that Austin performs in *The Flock* when she validates the "pagan" religion by depicting the Chisera's success, is a familiar move for her. As in other Austin works, the Indian doctor, the woman artist, and the biblical prophet are closely linked, and the blending of characters concurs with a syncretism of religious mythologies. As constructed in the play, however, this syncretism represents a negotiation not only between biblical and traditional native mythologies, but also between various native mythologies of the Owens Valley and south-central California.

The play, set in a Paiute village, is based on a conflict arising from two disputes: the first is between the Paiutes and the Castacs, who are depicted as traditional allies; the second is between the Paiutes and the Tecuyas, traditional enemies. History explains why Austin brought these cultures together in the play. In the early 1860s, the army drove the Indians of the Owens Valley to the Tejon area and forced them to live on rancherias already inhabited by other native peoples, including Interior Chumash such as the Tecuyas and the Castacs, who lived on three rancherias in the immediate vicinity of Rancho Tejon (and were thus well within the radius of Austin's forays into the surrounding countryside): Sasau, on the north shore of Castac (now Castaic) Lake; Lapau, at the mouth of Canada de las Uvas; and Takuyo, in Tecuya Canyon.[17] Since it is unlikely that the Paiutes would be allies of the Castacs and enemies of the Tecuyas—both groups were Interior Chumash—the conflict on which the plot is based seems an inaccurate reflection of cultural alliances.

Despite the seeming inaccuracy, however, the play does seem to accurately represent the blending of the mythological contexts that had occurred and was still (in Austin's day) occurring in the area. Even in precontact times, the area was culturally diverse because of its location at the nexus of north-south and east-west axes of trade and travel; thus boundaries dividing people and cultural elements tended to blur and shift rather than being rigid and static. For that reason it is not surprising that the myths of the Indians of south-central California share many similarities with those of their adjacent Great Basin neighbors, the Northern Paiute.

Austin's dramas reflect a familiarity with the myths of both cultural areas. Drawing on the sacred number found in Chumash myth, for example, Austin (in *The Flock*) has the Chisera dance for *three* days in order to bring the rain; the rain initially lasts for *three* weeks and subsequently for an additional *three* days after she has been paid to make it stop; and the result of the Chisera's power is expressed in a sentence that repeats three times that "it rained." The mythological context of the Paiutes, on the other hand, is highlighted by the mythological names Austin chooses for her characters, names that, significantly, multiply during the drafting of the play: Padahoon, the Sparrow Hawk; Tavwots, the Cottontail Rabbit; Haiwai, the Mourning Dove; Pamaquash, the brother of the culture hero Hinono; and Winnedumah, the culture hero whom Austin mythologizes in both *The Land of Little Rain* and *The Basket Woman*.[18]

These mythic themes and motifs—drawn both from several native traditions and from the Christian Bible—provide much of the dramatic framework undergirding *The Arrow-Maker*. In the play's climactic scene, as in *The Flock,* the Chisera dances, and her dance presents an image of fertility that provides the nexus around which the disparate mythological elements in the play come into clearest focus. Using the image of a world transformed from a dry, almost lifeless desert into "a succulent green world," Austin makes these traditions intersect in a figure reminiscent not only of the dying god figure of native south-central California cultures and the Baal of biblical cultures, but also of the native prophet who foretells the earth's cyclic destruction and regeneration (e.g., Wovoka of the Ghost Dance).

Since *The Arrow-Maker* is little known and not widely available, I offer a brief plot summary, which will take us up to that final scene in which the Chisera dances. A Paiute band living in the Sierra foothills is engaged in a dispute with a neighboring Castac band that is a traditional ally. The question is how to respond. Chief Rain Wind, now old, needs to choose a new war leader from two candidates. Padahoon, the Sparrow Hawk, is older and more experienced, and his plan is to preserve the Castacs as allies. His rival is Simwa, the arrow-maker, younger and more brash, who would ignore the historic ties between the two groups and attempt to humiliate his opponents in battle. The Chisera is called to the council to help decide the matter. Since she and Simwa have been carrying on a clandestine affair, and she has been "making medicine" to ensure that Simwa is elected war leader, the conclusion is foregone. Three months after the council decision appointing Simwa and the ensuing defeat of their Castac enemies, Simwa consolidates his power by wedding the chief's daughter, Bright Water. The Chisera, who is unaware of the wedding, comes on the villagers preparing for the festivities. She confronts Simwa, who denies her. Claiming that all his considerable fortune is due to his own merit rather than the favor of the gods, he publicly humiliates her. Unable to supply proof that she was Simwa's lover, the Chisera, who was never granted the power to curse (her father thought it a skill inappropriate for a woman), can only retract her blessing from Simwa, leaving him to succeed or fail as he will through his own wit and skill. A year later, the Paiutes have been driven from their home by another enemy, the Tecuyas. Simwa has not been able to provide for his wife or the tribe, and Bright Water is wasting away with neglect and hunger. When the capture of the village seems imminent, a council is called, Padahoon is elected war leader in place of Simwa, and the Chisera is summoned to make medicine for their success in battle.

Thus far there are broad similarities of plot and theme between this story and Owens Valley Paiute tales.[19] It is in the final scene, however, that Austin most clearly attempts to place her story within a mythological matrix of native tales—first by manipulating the gambling and magical arrow motifs (common to both Paiute and south-central myth) to serve the play's feminist subtext, and second by invoking the myth of the dying god (a theme unique to native south-central myth and discussed in more detail later), thus linking the Chisera with the mythic Earth-Mother figure and serving the play's mythological context.

After the leadership passes to Padahoon, there is an outcry for Simwa's death, and he asks his wife for his quiver, which, unknown to her, contains the magic black arrow. The chief demands that Simwa admit his wrong and entreat the Chisera on the tribe's behalf; the penalty for refusal is death. The Chisera tells the chief that she cannot make medicine and would not even if she were able, and enlarges the circle of blame to include the tribe, who in her estimation allowed Simwa to do evil to her by segregating her from the rest of the tribe, especially from the companionship and counsel of the other women. Into this stalemated situation steps Bright Water, who convinces the Chisera to act by comparing her own griefs with the Chisera's. By so doing, Bright Water takes on the role of the gambler of myth, a role usually (although not exclusively) reserved in native California myths for men. The stake for which they gamble is the tribe, in particular the women and children, those hardest hit by the ravages of war.[20]

Once the nature of the stake is made clear to her, the Chisera's resolve not to help the people melts. But she feels that her power has left her; she claims that she has "danced until the earth under [her] is beaten to dust, and [her] heart is as dry as the dust." She remains unable to call on her power *until* she realizes that all that is left to her now is "the grief of women," precisely that for which she has been yearning (156). She has become one of them, and the realization "heals" her. In this game Bright Water has "bet" with her words instead of money, reminding the Chisera that the "good medicine" *she* can offer the tribe is contained in nothing less than the sacred words she carries in her memory. Words are thus equated with magic and "good medicine," just as they are in the narrator's response to Tinnemaha's song in Austin's short story "The Song-Makers."

The ability or inability to use that magic is one of the play's central themes, manifested in this scene in the struggle over speaking—that is, over the production and dissemination of meaning, a theme that has been developing throughout the play. In order to bring the Indian and feminist contexts of the play together, however, the issue of the authority to use the magic of words must be settled not only in the context of speech, and thus of oral cultures, but also in the context of reading and writing. Ironically, Austin has introduced this latter context through one of the very elements by which she places her tale in a native context—the magic arrow. When she presents the arrow to Simwa, the Chisera tells him to remark "how the blood drain is cut in a medicine writing round and round the shaft."[21] The medicine writing provides the mirror image of words on a page: white on black instead of the reverse. The arrow was given to the Chisera in compensation for the denial of an oral ability (to curse, or, in Indian terms, to poison or to witch) her father did not think it appropriate for a woman to possess. Throughout the play, the arrow is linked with writing.

But it is not only arrows that are read. So, too, are the Chisera's magic sticks. In fact, the Chisera's "reading" of—or failure to read—these sticks leads directly to the crisis that the tribe later faces. When the council first consults the Chisera about whom the gods favor for the war leadership, they agree that she should decide the matter by consulting her sacred sticks, which are thrown on the ground and then read as an augury. She throws the sticks, which (she says) indicate that Simwa is to be the war leader. We later find out, however, that the Chisera, who by her own account had been making medicine for the preceding week so that the gods would decide in Simwa's favor, failed to look at the sticks at all—failed to "read" them—for the matter had in her mind already been decided. That failure to read the sticks leads ultimately to the arrow's being used as the instrument of the Chisera's death, and the progression seems to enact the ultimate defeat of the oral at the hands of the crushing authority of the written word.

Words, which at least partially control meaning, are chosen by the individual within certain socially determined parameters and then circulated for others to interpret. Thus the issue of authority over language's production and dissemination highlights the related tension between the spheres of the personal and private, on one hand, and the communal and public, on the other.[22] This tension is enacted in the play in the parallelism between personal conflicts and community conflicts: Simwa's turning against the Chisera, the one who had been—and should be—an ally, is paralleled in the tribe's war with its allies, the Castacs. The breaking of traditional alliances precipitates the war that ultimately results in the tribe's destruction at the hands of the Tecuyas, just as, on the personal level, it precipitates the "war" between Simwa and the Chisera that leads to her destruction. Ironically, Simwa's apparent victory in this personal war ensures the tribe's defeat in the communal war. Austin's ethnographic "mistake" of confusing allies with enemies (the Castacs and Tecuyas would in fact usually be allies) only reinforces the theme.

The resulting irony encourages us to read the victory of the written over the oral as illusory, a point reinforced by having the Tecuyas, who are associated with the oral through the magic words of their medicine man, heard (but not seen) at the end as they approach the already defeated Paiutes. In native cultures, as Carobeth Laird points out, the presence in myth of a particular behavior often is meant not to encourage or condone that behavior, but rather to warn against it and to impose a form of social restraint or coercion.[23] The particular behavior warned against in this tale is oppression in any of its various guises as deployed against specific targets—namely women, Indians, and the oral and performative arts generally.

Despite our desire to see the Chisera as the embodiment of these three targets, however—a representation implying that the opposition is composed of men, whites, and the written word—the play does not allow such clear-cut categorical oppositions. Austin specifies in her preface that the Chisera should be seen as representative of Genius, and the Chisera's genius is in her ability to negotiate the struggle between these categories. The Chisera's link with the prophets of Baal constructs her before us as neither "purely" Woman nor "purely" Indian, and the fact that the magic arrow is initially hers to give constructs her as a bearer of written as well as of oral culture. Moreover, these links are forged via the instrument of the myths from both Indian/oral and Euro-American/written cultures. The Chisera thus embodies the negotiation between these poles—a negotiation that, in the context of the religious myths deployed, is a form of syncretism—and the tale thus serves to warn against the fundamentalism, on the one hand (e.g., Elijah), and the unbelief, on the other (e.g., Simwa), that would quash such syncretism.

This point becomes clearest in the moment just after Bright Water has convinced the Chisera to act and before Simwa kills her with the magic arrow. She begins to dance and sing, making medicine for the tribe.

> Come, O my power,
> Indwelling spirit!
> It is I that call.
> Childless, unmated—
>
> Nay, I shall mate with the gods,
> And the tribesmen shall be my children.
> Rise up in me, O, my power,
> On the wings of eagles!
>
> Return on me as the rain
> The earth renewing,
> Make my heart fruitful
> To nourish my children.[24]

In the image of the power "risi[ng] up . . . on the wings of eagles," the chief and most powerful of the mythological creatures in Yokut and many other native south-central California cultures, Austin aligns the Chisera with *both* the biblical prophet *and* the Earth-Mother figure of native myth, who is "mated" to the Sky-Father figure. Their union makes the Earth-Mother "fruitful," and the children are thereby "nourish[ed]." In the Old

Testament we find the wings of the eagle linked with Moses' escape from Egypt (Exodus 19:4) and, more notably in the context of the Chisera's situation, in Isaiah, in which it is declared, "But they that wait upon the Lord shall renew their strength; they shall mount up with wings as eagles" (40:31). Also notable is the figure's use in the Book of Revelation's apocalyptic visions, in which it is associated with a figure Susan Bratton calls "the woman with eagle's wings." The woman is given these wings so that she can escape the serpent and find refuge and nourishment in the wilderness. But the serpent, pursuing, "cast[s] out of his mouth water as a flood after the woman, that he might cause her to be carried away of the flood. And the earth helped the woman, and the earth opened her mouth, and swallowed up the flood" (Revelation 12:14-16).[25] The image of the earth swallowing the flood implies that, as in *The Flock,* "a green and succulent world" will emerge, just as it does in the apocalyptic imagery of the Northern Paiute Ghost Dance. In Austin's play the Chisera's medicine transforms the earth from drought-ridden desolation into green succulence, although the transformation is accomplished in image only. And it is during this earth-renewing act that this prophet of Baal, as in the Bible, is put to death, Simwa taking her life with the magic arrow, the medicine given her by her father.[26]

Dancing with the Old Ones: Bill Bodry and "The Coyote Doctor"

The possibility that the earth (and human cultures along with it) might be renewed, and that humans' tendency to cling to accustomed ways might cause them to miss the chance of realizing that possibility, is a theme Austin takes up in her next drama, "The Coyote Doctor," which she began drafting with Elmer Harris in Carmel in 1911, the year *The Arrow-Maker* was published.

Syncretism both secular and sacred—and Austin, like native Californians of the period, would resist hard distinctions between these two categories—is again put forward as a model, a point that becomes apparent when we look more closely at the sources for this drama. In the foreword to the play, Austin says that what follows is the story of Sina (a name she retains in the drama) and is based on "the story of the daughter of Kern River Jim marrying the Coyote doctor." Austin first heard of Sina from Isabel Watterson of Bishop, the wife of a white rancher or farmer who had several Indians in his employ, and her notes indicate that this tale is the source for both the drama and a later short story, "The Divorcing of Sina."[27]

The letter from Isabel Watterson, dated 2 June 1907, tells of Isabel's brother, Pete, a ranch owner and shepherd who had married a "half-breed" woman with whom he was very much in love. The woman seems not to have been accepted by the Paiutes of the area, and when Pete was away for long stretches, taking his flocks to summer pasture in the Sierra and then driving them down south to market in the fall, she lived alone. Pete and Sina had two children, with another on the way. He apparently had some money worries but, to Isabel's eyes, was doing reasonably well financially. In fact, he was becoming "respectable" enough that people were beginning to take notice of and make comments about his wife and kids. Either his financial problems or the psychological tension caused by the realization that his family, whom he loved and would not leave, might bar him from achieving a more elevated social standing was too much for him, and he committed suicide by shooting himself in the temple. The letter closes with a reference suggesting that Austin had previously heard (or heard about) the story and had indicated an interest in possibly "working it up" for publication.[28]

In 1911 Austin began work on "The Coyote Doctor," transforming the outcome described in Isabel Watterson's letter—Pete's suicide—and modifying it in a direction that reinforces its thematic affinities with *The Arrow-Maker.* Emphasizing her belief that a rigid adherence to tradition—in art, in religion, in any cultural enterprise—is detrimental to *all* people, Native Americans no less than Euro-Americans, and that such fundamentalism is incompatible with successful coadaptation and progress, Austin again employs allusions that imply the need for mutual accommodation by both cultures, and in particular point to the syncretism practiced in native cultures.

Again I begin with a brief summary. In the village of Tunawai live Kern River Jim; his wife, Catameneda; and their daughter, Sina. When Jim is struck by an illness that neither the local native healer nor the white doctor from Maverick can cure, Bill Bodry, a hired hand at the Watterman ranch, hires Tinnemaha, the medicine man from Fish Springs, to treat him. Jim is healed, and, having no money with which to repay Bill, feels it necessary to grant Bill's request to have Sina as his wife, over the protests of Sina and her mother. Bill takes his new wife to his home, which lies between the ranch and the village. There, Bill's mother treats Sina like a slave and subjects her to constant verbal abuse, although Bill treats her with what others consider remarkable restraint in light of the fact that she will not even cook his dinner. Despite Bill's solicitousness, Sina is miserable; her youth and health are wasting away. Back at Tunawai, a council is called, during which enough money is donated to pay off Jim's debt to Bill and thus "buy back" Sina. Sina returns to live with her parents, but her condition continues to deteriorate. Bill has been trying to win her affections by pointing to all the comforts he can provide with the wages he earns from working on the white-owned ranch, but nothing persuades her until he says that he will burn all his possessions rather than find another wife. In that moment Sina first begins to look on Bill as a husband. Later, when Black Rock Maggie, who has always had her eye on Bill but was again rebuffed by him after Sina left, accuses Bill of "coyote-ing" (witching) the girl, Sina comes to Bill's defense. Before the tribe can decide whether or not Bill should be put to death as a witch, he decides to leave and go into the desert. He calls to Sina to accompany him, vowing that they will begin their own tribe. Bill folds his blanket—now his sole material possession—around Sina, and they walk off together into the desert.

Like *The Arrow-Maker*, "The Coyote Doctor" contains multiple levels of signification and is simultaneously about women and Indians. The feminist message is most forcefully delivered in the figure of Sina. When Jim agrees, albeit reluctantly, to give his daughter to Bill in payment for his debt, Sina cries out, "My father, am I no more to you than a pony, that you give me in payment of a debt?" Turning to Bill, she asks, "Am I no more to you than a blanket, that you buy me to keep you warm?" Sina's response to the situation in which she has been placed embodies her own form of cultural blending. Whereas her overtly feminist stance toward marriage, specifically in her insistence on her right to choose a husband, aligns her with white women, her response to Bill after he offers to burn his possessions most clearly represents her "Indian" side.

The theme of cultural blending is seen most clearly in the medicine man, Tinnemaha, and in Bill. It is somewhat surprising that Austin should choose these two characters to represent the adapting Indian. Tinnemaha, *as* medicine man, would generally be thought to represent the "traditional" Indian way of life. And when he appears on the scene, dressed as a healer, he looks the part. He is dressed in a kilt of feathers, probably eagle feathers, which are sacred to the Paiute. A long string of beads and bears' teeth hangs around his neck, the bear thought to be among the most powerful of doctors. His limbs are streaked with white paint; his face is striped with red and white, the sacred colors of healing; and he wears a headdress of woodpeckers' feathers and carries a fetish of rabbit skin and a ram's-horn rattle. The "traditional" native healer, however, as Lowell John Bean points out, has always borrowed freely the ideas, stories, and rituals of other cultures and incorporated them into his or her own cultural framework. Austin reminds us of this tendency by drawing a connection between Tinnemaha and the fictional syncretic figure who is his counterpart in *The Land of Little Rain,* Winnenap: when the healing ritual begins, Tinnemaha's thought is said to "swing out towards Shoshone Land." After he goes through the healing ceremony—accepting offerings of food and silver coin, dancing and singing, then falling into a trance, followed by another round of dancing—he commands Jim, "Arise and walk!"—the same words Jesus used in healing a paralyzed man (Matthew 9:5-6).

Bill, on the other hand, is a surprising figure of cultural blending in that he is a not wholly sympathetic character. Yet he is the character most closely associated with the syncretic figure Tinnemaha, and indeed, Bill and Sina are but secular analogues to Tinnemaha's sacred syncretism. This is apparent in their amalgamation of "white" and "Indian" ways. Bill, for instance, does not live in the Indian village, nor does he board at the ranch's bunkhouse. Instead he lives on the edge of the ranch, between the center of the ranch (as symbolized by the white house) and the Indian village; and his work on the ranch supports both him and his mother. His main attraction to Sina, so he thinks, will be his ability to buy material comforts for her with the wages he earns at the ranch. His materialistic bent and his demand to have Sina for his wife against her will cast him initially in a negative light. Ironically, what ends up making Sina think of him as a husband is not his ability to provide material comforts for her, but his willingness to give up all those comforts in an act symbolic of a "traditionally Indian" response when Sina will not have him. I put "traditionally Indian" in quotes because I do not know if any Indian in Bill's circumstances would consider burning all his possessions, which seems more a romantic gesture than anything else. Nevertheless, because that was the act Paiutes and other Basin Indians performed at the ceremony mourning their dead—a ceremony often discussed among white settlers—Austin's intended audience would have recognized the burning as a "traditional" act. Such manipulation of tradition is dictated by that same potential audience, which, Austin says in her introduction, "deriv[es] its notions of Indian psychology from the high-nosed, knock-kneed Tobacco-store type, . . . the survival of the Pilgrim Fathers' conception of the aboriginal, emotionless, taciturn, bloody and relentless." Bill's offer to burn his possessions, then, signals either his own death to the possibility offered by Sina's love or Sina's symbolic death to him—her unavailability—a mark in either case of the impossibility of their union.

Austin depicts Bill's attempts at cultural blending as worthy by counterpoising them with Black Rock Maggie's attempts to "become white." Maggie is consistently portrayed as trying to live like a white person: she dresses like one, takes a white man as a husband, is schooled by whites. These things in themselves Austin does not see as questionable—Bill was also educated at the white school. But whereas Maggie tries to *imitate* the whites, Bill accepts the gifts that white education and wage work bring but adapts them to his "Indian" values and way of life.

The final scene in the play highlights the need for such a process to continue. Bill has been accused of being a witch, and the punishment for that crime is death. He decides that, rather than allow the tribe to decide his fate for him, he will remove himself and go into the desert to live. As he is about to leave, he has an exchange with Chief Left Hand during which he indicates his yearning not to be bound by "the ways of the ancients." He then responds to the chief's questions about whether he "despise[s] the ways of [his] fathers" by comparing the traditions as the tribe now practices them to "heel ropes which are rotten with lying long in the weather," and adds: "Into the desert I go; not stoned like a dog from camp, but as a free man seeking freedom."

If it were not for Bill's final words, this exchange might seem to signal an "Indianized" version of the escapist myth of the white man leaving civilization for the wilderness. But then Bill adds, "Into the desert I go but I would not go alone, for I am of the best blood of my tribe and would have others to come after me." Thus, despite his seeming "escape" from all societal norms, he retains a social conscience, a conscience he feels is akin to that which his forefathers must have had. In fact, as they head into the desert, his comment to Sina—"Aye, wife, we are become as one with the old peoples"—paradoxically registers that their "escape" from "tradition" is actually a return to the old ways.

Bill, Sina, and Tinnemaha, then, highlight the notion that an unthinking cultural traditionalism (in whatever cultural context) is an inappropriate and inadequate response to a changed and changing historical situation. The phrase "become as one with the old peoples" signals a return to the "tradition" of the native doctor as Bean describes it—that is, a tradition of incorporation and adaptation. Recall here that it was the seeming im-possibility of adaptation that drove Bill's real-life counterpart, Pete Watter-son, to commit suicide: he could not reconcile the "Indian" elements of his life (wife and children) with the "white" elements (desire for success in business).

But Bill Bodry also has *mythological* counterparts in native myth, in-cluding Ghost Dance lore. In 1904, before she wrote "The Coyote Doc-tor," Austin collected from Owens Valley Paiute George Symmes a story that links a "coyote doctor" to the Paiute Ghost Dance prophets Wodzi-wob and Wovoka, leaders, respectively, of the 1870 and 1890 Ghost Dance movements. Wodziwob was originally from Fish Lake Valley, the home of the syncretic figure Tinnemaha, with whom Bill is closely linked and who himself has possible connections to the Ghost Dance.[29] In light of these connections to the Ghost Dance, Bill and Sina's "escape" into the desert reads less like Pete's death or a biblical fleeing into the refuge of wilderness than it does a shamanic reentry into the mythical time before the great change of nature, a time when all boundaries were fluid. As in a Ghost Dance vision, Bill and Sina travel to a place where they can rejoin the old people, paving the trail for those who wish to follow. The place to which they go is less a place separated from *this* place (i.e., the earth) than a state of mind and being that allows the here and the hereafter to be realized to-gether. That is, as in Indian paradisiacal visions, it is an idealized copy of *this* place. Thus, as at the end of *The Arrow-Maker,* the possibility of a regener-ated world, discovered through artistic and religious syncretism, is accepted by a few, but rejected by most.

Through Indian and white characters, as well as through those who are literally mixed-bloods and those whose race is deliberately made indeter-minable, Austin enacts such an ending time and again in her works from this period, mirroring her own desire to get back to the roots of culture—her own as well as that of the Indians. Her enactments of myth are the means by which she fulfills what Bean describes as a central function of the shaman: "As a [person] of knowledge and . . . creativ[ity], . . . the shaman perceives contemporary society and indicates how the knowledge of the past can help define the present, so new adaptive modes can be devel-oped."[30] It is through such gestures that Austin discovers or invents the basis of cultural commonality, blending the best of both cultures' stories and traditions.

Chanting the Coyote-Song: *Evind and* Fire

Austin's third Indian drama, *Fire,* is the most straightforward of the three in manifesting a perspective of religious syncretism.[31] This play, begun in 1912, is a genealogical descendant of Austin's earlier dramas. Its lineage is suggested not only by the sequence of the plays' compositions but also by the fact, which we learn early in the play, that the hero, Evind, was born of a woman who had been cast out of the tribe and had gone to live in the wilderness. Recall also that in *The Arrow-Maker* several of the women who appealed to the Chisera for her help in alleviating the suffering of the women and children expressed the wish that the Chisera had had a child so that she would understand what they were experiencing. Thus Evind stands as the child the Chisera might have had but never did, or the offspring that Bill Bodry (the Coyote Doctor) and Sina will create after finding a home in the desert. Born of an Indian doctor who possesses special powers, Evind becomes an Indian Messiah, the title by which Wovoka was most widely known.

Austin's foreword to *Fire,* like that to *The Arrow-Maker,* shows her awareness of her manipulation and distortion of these myths. She points out that she has taken liberties with the style, manner of presentation, and ritual character of the tale, thus admitting that her presentation is not meant to be a literal translation but is rather a poetic and dramatic rendering of the ritual aspect of Indian life. Acknowledging that she has distorted the "true" character of Indian sacred forms, she then indicates one of the more serious limitations of this adaptation: in order to promote her audience's understanding of the rituals, she has excised the "Indian humor," a critical part of such rituals that often carries with it a "profound mystical quality." Again, as in *The Arrow-Maker,* she cuts her audience down to size, here by indicating that white Americans' ability to understand tribal rituals is so underdeveloped that they have lost any sense that laughter is a natural and appropriate response in the face of the mysterious. She has retained only "the outlines of mystical solemnity which it is proper that the recitation of such a legend should have."[32] These disclaimers, pointing as they do toward a broader (and far different) cultural context, confront the audience with its tendency to consider Indian ritual forms as dead and dying artifacts from lost cultures. In effect, Austin is suggesting that even if one sees a native ritual as it is being performed in a native context (a popular tourist attraction during the early twentieth century, especially in the

Southwest), one will be seeing *not* an "authentic" Indian ritual but rather a *performance* staged for whites' benefit.

The first act of *Fire* is a rather straightforward rendering of the Owens Valley Paiute tale of how fire came to the valley, with one significant difference: Austin portrays human beings as already present instead of featuring only animal-people, the predecessors to humans. Although perhaps one of her "concessions" to the character of her audience, that decision allows her to comment on the nature of human faith in the divine and to suggest the possibility of interspecies communication, something in which she clearly believed.[33]

Evind is the only human with enough "faith" to cooperate with his brother, Coyote, to steal the fire from the fire spirits, who jealously guard their treasure. The other tribe members play the role that animals play in the Indian myth, assisting by participating as relay racers to pass the fire along. After the fire is secured, Evind asks to be made part of the tribe, for he wishes to marry Laela. Laela's father will only consent to the marriage, however, if Evind gives up his companionship with his beast brother, a condition to which he reluctantly agrees. Soon, the people begin to treat the firebrand with exaggerated deference—sacred rites are performed, offerings are brought—and Evind is entrusted with its keeping. In the minds of the people he has attained the status of a Messiah, as attested to by the words of his friend Niko, which echo the sentiments of Jesus' disciples:

> That is the word we young men ask ourselves.
> He has stirred up our minds by his great thought
> To bring the gods to serve our daily need;
> But when we look to him to bring to fruit
> This crop of new sown purpose,
> He leaves us groping while he walks apart
> And seeks out strange behavior for himself,
> Which brings remark on those who follow him.

And Evind, like Jesus, tries to combat his disciples' misinterpretation that the purpose of his mission is to establish a kingdom on earth.[34]

At the end of the second act, as Evind is tending the Sacred Brand, he calls in his despair to Coyote; while Evind draws apart to grieve, the Coyote replenishes the sacred fire. This part of the scene enacts a revision of Jesus' plea to his disciples in the Garden of Gethsemane to remain awake with him while he draws apart to pray, a request that falls on sleeping ears. Just as the Coyote touches the fire, Laela wakes, sees Evind and the Coyote, and yells, "Sacrilege." The rest of the tribe is alerted, and Evind is bound over to the chief.

In the final act, the analogue to the Gospel story—established up to this point by parallels in plot and theme—is made explicit through imagery. The act opens with an image of "Evind with his arms outstretched and bound to a broken tree."[35] The scene that follows reenacts the questioning of Jesus by Pontius Pilate, complete with Peter's (Niko's) three denials of his friend. In the climactic scene, Evind calls to the Beast, who bites through his ropes, knocking over the Sacred Brand in the process. Evind takes up the firebrand, and the two walk together up the Fire Mountain, through the flames, Evind calling to Laela to come with them.

Tales of the world's destruction by fire are common in the native traditions of south-central California, and in that sense this tale follows tradition. The ending is both reminiscent of Bill and Sina's turn toward the desert in "The Coyote Doctor," where they will beget a new tribe of people who are not bound to tradition by formula, and Austin's "Indianization" of the Christ story.[36]

Fire was staged in 1921 in Palm Springs, in what was once Cahuilla territory. Directed by Garnet Holme, the play was performed "on the natural stage, the desert itself," specifically on a point of "rising ground at the entrance to Tahquitz Cañon."[37] Because Tahquitz Canyon is featured in Cahuilla myth, and because Austin appears to have had Indian informants with firsthand knowledge of Cahuilla culture, I should like in closing to use Cahuilla myth to examine two elements that play a central role in the dramas I have been discussing: the water of the earth's beginning and the fire of its destruction.

In the myths of the Cahuilla and the other Yuman and southern Shoshonean peoples, fire and water are associated with the story of the dying god, whose heart Coyote is called on to steal and eat. According to ethnographic analysis, this sequence, and particularly the two elements fire and water, is linked with the destruction and regeneration of the earth—and specifically of the food plants on which the Cahuillas depended.[38] After succeeding in his quest, Coyote has to cross a "Great Dry Desert." In

a later age, the culture hero Evon-ga-net, like Coyote, also crosses a desert
as he is exploring new territory, "mark[ing] more boundary lines for his
new tribes to come."[39] Interestingly, Austin's Evind faintly echoes this culture hero's name, and her Bill Bodry embarks on a Coyote-like journey
that fulfills the same purpose as Evon-ga-net's journey. In the course of his
travels Evon-ga-net gives the name "Kakwawit" to the mouth of Tahquitz
Canyon, the place where *Fire* was performed in 1921.[40] Even if it had been
spring, and even if the audience could faintly hear in the distance the
sound of the waterfall up-canyon, most would not have recognized that
the elements of the earth's cyclic destruction and regeneration were being
reunited in the performance occurring in their presence.

Derived in part from native myth, Mary Austin's tales operate on a cyclic
model in which the world's re-creation is constantly being performed.
Thus her dramas' endings, tragic though they may seem, cannot be seen as
representing ultimate defeat. By dramatizing the end to the messiahs, the
prophets, and the culture heroes she depicts, Austin pictures an end that, as
in the Christian Bible, traditional native myths, and Ghost Dance traditions, is also a beginning.

NOTES

This essay is a revised version of chapter 5 of my book *Dancing Ghosts: Native American and
Christian Syncretism in Mary Austin's Work* (Reno: University of Nevada Press, 1998). I delivered a shortened version of it at a session on Mary Austin organized by Melody Graulich
at the Western Literature Conference in Vancouver, British Columbia, in October 1995.
My thanks to Professor Graulich for that opportunity and for her helpful editorial
guidance.

1. Sven Liljeblad, "Oral Tradition: Content and Style of Verbal Arts," in *Great Basin,* ed.
Warren L. d'Azevedo, vol. 11 of *Handbook of the North American Indians,* ed. William C.
Sturtevant (Washington, D.C.: Smithsonian Institution Press, 1986), 641–59.

2. Peggy Beck, Anna Walters, and Nia Francisco, *The Sacred: Ways of Knowledge, Sources of
Life,* redesigned ed. (Tsaile, Ariz.: Navajo CC Press, 1992), 37. Emphasis in original.

3. Lowell John Bean, "The Artist and the Shamanic Tradition," in *Ethnology of the Alta
California Indians II: Postcontact,* ed. Lowell J. Bean and Sylvia B. Vane (New York: Garland,
1991), 964.

4. Mary Austin, *Stories from the Country of Lost Borders,* ed. Marjorie Pryse (New
Brunswick: Rutgers University Press, 1987), 98, 57–61, 76–77, 17.

5. See Mark T. Hoyer, "Prophecy in a New West: Mary Austin and the Ghost Dance Religion," *Western American Literature* 30.3 (1995): 237–57; Hoyer, "'To Bring the World into Divine
Focus': *The Land of Little Rain* as Syncretic Prophecy," *Western American Literature* 31.1
(1996): 3–31; and Hoyer, "Weaving the Story: Northern Paiute Myth and Mary Austin's *The*

Basket Woman," *American Indian Culture and Research Journal* 19.1 (1995): 33–51; Michael Hittman, *Wovoka and the Ghost Dance* (Carson City, Nev.: Grace Dangberg Foundation, 1990), 63–64.

6. Mary Austin, *Earth Horizon* (New York: Literary Guild, 1932), 74–77.

7. Mary Austin, *A Woman of Genius* (New York: Arno, 1977).

8. Mary Austin, "How I Would Sell My Book 'Rhythm,'" *Bookseller and Stationer,* 1 May 1923, 7; Mary (Hunter) Austin Collection, Henry F. Huntington Library, San Marino, California, item 755 (subsequent references to material from the Austin Collection are abbreviated AU and followed by the item number); Frederick T. Hulse, SERA-Inyo: Owens Valley Fieldnotes, Bancroft Library, University of California, Berkeley, 1935, CU-23.1/90.1. The "Dance of Death" is most probably what is often called the "Cry Dance" or "Mourning Dance," a mourning ceremony for those who died during the previous year.

9. Austin, *Earth Horizon,* 289.

10. Mary Austin, *The American Rhythm,* rev. ed. (New York: AMS, 1970).

11. Mary Austin, "The Song-Makers," *North American Review* 194 (August 1911): 239–47.

12. Mary Austin, *The Arrow-Maker,* rev. ed. (Boston: Houghton, 1915); "The Coyote Doctor," AU 93–96; *Fire: A Drama in Three Acts,* published serially in *Play-book* [of the Wisconsin Dramatic Society] 2 (October 1914): 3–25; 2 (November 1914): 11–26; 2 (December 1914): 18–30.

13. Mary Austin, *The Flock* (Boston: Houghton, 1905), 232–33. In light of my contention about the influence of the Ghost Dance on Austin (see Hoyer, "Prophecy," and "To Bring the World"), it is interesting to note here that the comparison to David dancing before the Ark of the Lord is the very one used by James Mooney in 1896 in his monumental study of the Ghost Dance to explain the power of dancing in native traditions. Austin's notes indicate that she had read Mooney's work. See James P. Mooney, *The Ghost Dance of 1890 and the Sioux Outbreak of 1890* (Washington, D.C.: GPO, 1896), 930; AU 754–55.

The Southern (San Joaquin Valley) Yokuts interviewed by Marjorie Cummins confirmed that the event Austin describes in this passage took place, and described the Chisera as wearing "a fancy combination of Indian and white-style clothing and souvenirs she had collected in trade or pay from Indians of the desert and seashore" (Cummins, *The Tache-Yokuts: Indians of the San Joaquin Valley* [Fresno: Pioneer, 1978], 32–33).

14. Austin, *The Flock,* 231.

15. In the Bible the prophet Hosea gives Yahweh, the God of shepherds and laws who is thought of as a father, a makeover using images associated with the local god, Baal, the god of farmers and fertility who is thought of as husband and lover. My thanks to David Robertson, a professor of English at the University of California, Davis, from whom I derive my understanding of this substitution.

16. Austin, *The Arrow-Maker,* 161–62.

17. Campbell Grant, "Interior Chumash," in *California,* ed. Robert F. Heizer, vol. 8 of *Handbook of the North American Indians* (Washington, D.C.: Smithsonian Institution Press, 1978), 533. It is Lapau that Austin is apparently describing in *The Flock* (224).

18. AU 19–22; Mary Austin, *The Basket Woman: A Book of Indian Tales for Children* (Boston: Houghton, 1910).

19. Although to develop the point fully is beyond the scope of this paper, Austin's drama may have been based on an Owens Valley myth that appears in some accounts as "Coyote,

Magpie, and Dove." See, e.g., Hulse, 90.1. For elaboration on this point, see chapter 5 in Hoyer, *Dancing Ghosts.*

20. Austin, *The Arrow-Maker,* 154-55.

21. Ibid., 43. Later, another arrow is shot by the Paiutes back into their own camp to carry a message of "[d]efeat and flight," thus reinforcing the arrow's connection with writing (132).

22. It is interesting to note that Austin later developed this issue as it relates to Christianity's vitality as a religion and as an agent of social and economic justice. See, e.g., Mary Austin, "Religion in the United States," *Century* 104 (August 1922): 527-38; and Austin, "Do We Need a New Religion?" *Century* 100 (September 1923): 756-64.

23. Carobeth Laird, "Behavioral Patterns in Chemehuevi Myths," in *Flowers of the Wind: Papers on Ritual, Myth, and Symbolism in California and the Southwest,* ed. Thomas C. Blackburn (Socorro, N.Mex.: Ballena Press, 1977), 97-103.

24. Austin, *The Arrow-Maker,* 156-57.

25. Cited in Susan P. Bratton, *Christianity, Wilderness, and Wildlife: The Original Desert Solitaire* (Scranton: University of Scranton Press; London: Associated University Presses, 1993), 152-53. In this and the preceding passages, I use the wording of the King James version, as it is the one that Austin, raised as an Illinois Methodist, probably knew best.

26. This ending is the most dramatic difference between the 1911 and the 1915 editions. The ending of the original has the Chisera making medicine, then leading her people into battle against their enemy.

27. AU 96, "An Introduction," II, "Preface" [to "The Coyote Doctor], I; AU 391; "The Divorcing of Sina," *Sunset* 40 (January-June 1918). The drama remains unpublished; the only published version of Sina's story is the short story, which has a significantly different ending.

28. Isabel Watterson, letter to Mary Austin, 2 June 1907 (AU 5171).

29. AU 755; Hulse, 91.9; Hoyer, "To Bring the World," 9.

30. Bean, "Artist," 964.

31. Like *The Arrow-Maker, Fire* was performed at the Forest Theatre in Carmel in 1912. Two years later it was published serially in *Play-book* [of the Wisconsin Dramatic Society]. Although Austin was not involved, *Fire* was also performed in Palm Springs in 1921. See Smeaton Chase, *Our Araby: Palm Springs and the Garden of the Sun* (New York: Little, Brown, 1923), 51. The "coyote-song," according to Austin in *One-Smoke Stories,* is that song which belongs to you and no one else. The name is derived from the notion that Coyote, the world's co-creator in many Paiute creation myths, has given you this song, and no one else is capable of singing it (Austin, *One-Smoke Stories* [Boston: Houghton, 1934], 38).

32. Austin, *Fire* (October 1914): 7-8.

33. See, for example, the chapter "Scavengers" in *The Land of Little Rain,* as well as Austin's essay "The Folk Story in America," *South Atlantic Quarterly* 33 (January 1934): 10-19.

34. Austin, *Fire* (November 1914): 15-16, 18.

35. Austin, *Fire* (December 1914): 18.

36. In *The Green Bough,* which was published in 1913 and later became the last section of a psycho-biography titled *The Man Jesus,* Austin pictures the ascension in much the same terms, sans the fire, with Jesus "pass[ing] up the hill trail toward his chosen place and the mountain mists receiv[ing] him" (Austin, *The Green Bough: A Tale of the Resurrection* [Garden City, N.Y.: Doubleday, 1913], n.p.; *The Man Jesus* [New York: Harper, 1915]).

37. Chase, *Our Araby*, 51.

38. Patrick C. Morris, "Heart and Feces: Symbols of Mortality in the Dying God Myth," in Blackburn, ed., *Flowers of the Wind*, 41-57.

39. Francisco Patencio, *Stories and Legends of the Palm Springs Indians,* as told to Margaret Boynton, 2d ed. (Palm Springs: Desert Museum, 1970), 26, 52; Lowell John Bean, Sylvia Brakke Vane, and Jackson Young, *The Cahuilla Landscape: The Santa Rosa and San Jacinto Mountains* (Menlo Park: Ballena Press, 1991), 11.

40. Bean et al., *The Cahuilla Landscape,* 54.

CHAPTER FOUR

Singing Like the Indians Do
Mary Austin's Poetry

DALE METCALFE

*Like Mark Hoyer, Dale Metcalfe challenges the idea that Austin can be dismissed
as an "Indian wannabe," showing through careful and imaginative reading how
Austin's poetry and poetic theory are enriched by her concrete knowledge of Native
American cultural practices. In "Singing Like the Indians Do" Metcalfe distinguishes Austin from white imitators of Native Americans by exploring her understanding of artistic ritual as connecting individuals to larger communities, or
"tribes." Also like Hoyer, Metcalfe sees Austin's use of Native American materials
as influenced by her awareness of a largely ignorant audience that accepted a
"noble" romanticized past and a doomed future for Native American populations.
Both Hoyer and Metcalfe, colleagues in graduate school and fellow students of
David Robertson at the University of California at Davis, bring to their scholarship a concrete knowledge of tribal differences and history that has sometimes been
lacking in generalizations about Austin's work.*

*Hoyer and Metcalfe both place Austin at the intersection of cultural traditions, a
view shared by other writers in this collection. While Hoyer shows Austin bringing
together religious myths from Christianity and various Native American tribes,
Metcalfe sees her as uniting some of the well-known myths from Western culture
with Native American mythology. In Metcalfe's reading of such poems as "Not to
You Only, O Pythian," Austin anticipates some of the modern culture wars,
adapting Greek myths to her own multicultural and feminist purposes. By placing
Austin's poetry in the context of early twentieth-century poetic movements such as
imagism and comparing Austin's work with poems by better-known poets such as
H.D. and Vachel Lindsay, Metcalfe shows how Austin drew passion and power
from the American landscape and from regional cultures to counter the cynicism
and despair of her modernist contemporaries. By using Austin's poetry to expose*

*the "maimed voices" of European-sited modernism, Metcalfe suggests that
Austin's faith in "the Word" might offer us a new, more regenerative view of
modernism.*

> This is one of the places where our literature is alive, unfixed, on
> the move, defying definition. What is this stuff? Is it spoken or writ-
> ten? Both. Is it narrative or ritual? Both. Is it poetry or is it prose?
> Both. That's the sort of stuff I want to be able to compose myself.
> —Ursula K. LeGuin on translating alien texts

Decrying the "maimed voices" that characterized the poetry of her day,
Mary Austin had abandoned virtually all attachment to Western poetical
traditions by the time *The American Rhythm* was published in 1923.[1] From
her first forays into the Paiute camps near Bishop and Lone Pine, California, in the late 1880s, Austin's creative work was profoundly influenced by
Native Americans. Her poetry especially resonated to Indian ways of looking at the world. Meantime, literary critics embraced what came to be
called modernism and were only mildly interested in Austin's theories
about the processes by which Native American chants worked. Distracted
by superficial similarities between her re-creations of Indian songs and
imagism, many of her contemporaries imitated Indian "poems" while dismissing their connections to the lands from which they derived.[2]

Celebrating what she called "Allness," and adapting Indian chants' assumptions of the spiritual in the mundane, Austin's poems of the 1920s and
1930s reject the notion of the poetical object in isolation and counterpoint
the cynicism and despair in the poetry of some of her modernist peers. A
realist with a tendency to mysticism, Austin never resorted to romantic eu-
phemisms as did her better-known and more widely appreciated poet contemporary, Vachel Lindsay. And her brand of feminism, unlike H.D.'s, met
male detractors head-on and with a vengeance. Poetry became, for Austin,
a means to draw readers into ritual connections to the land and to what
she called "The Friend of the Soul of Man." Her poems in the Native
American "manner" in the first edition of *The American Rhythm* (1923) and
her collaborative poems with children in *The Children Sing in the Far West*
(1928) are the only collections of her poetry ever published, although a fascinating group might be gathered from the poetry that appeared in magazines from the 1920s until her death in 1934.[3]

She claimed hers was not a "gift for song," but Austin had written
poems even as a girl. Before her first poems appeared in print, Austin and

the children in the English class she taught in Mountain View, California, wrote verses about local wildlife.[4] She later recalled how the youngest children preferred rhymed to unrhymed verse, as well as "good singable vowel tunes, with repetitive and incremental consonances" and the "subtle dissonances" she named "chromatic rhymes" (e.g., drink, drank, drunk).[5] These poems were driven by keenly observant appraisals of life in the wild, as in the following excerpt from "Elf Owl."

> Elf owl, elf owl, what do you do
> When all of us are sleeping?
>
> I go down to the water hole to wait
> Where the frisk-tailed things come creeping.
> And the little gray mice by the grass stalks climb
> To the moon of the mesa, and bide my time
> To mark the blind mole's furrow.
> And I strike my kill,
> And I eat my fill,
> And get me back to my burrow.[6]

Used as the subjects of verses, the creatures the children saw around them in nature served as "pegs upon which to hang the emotional reactions" that the poems generated. This observation may have led to Austin's assertion in *The American Rhythm* that the "landscape lines" in Indian chants carry the emotional meanings. She was beginning to see other similarities, too, between the verse children created and "aboriginal song making," especially their speakers' propensities to actively participate in, rather than simply observe, nature. She made increasing use of these "natural" coincidences in her own poetry.[7]

One of Austin's first published poems, "Night Wind, Wake!" appeared in the April 1904 issue of *Out West,* one year after the publication of *The Land of Little Rain,* a critically acclaimed collection of vignettes about desert California. The poem's shifting, recurring rhythms and its speaker's fearlessness about roaming outdoors at night depart from the strong, British-based tradition of poetry that employs nature as mere backdrop for human reverie. In the last stanza, Austin's speaker invokes the wind:

> Night Wind wake! I am coming up the trail to you, (15)
> Up and past the gullies where the midnight shadows lair

Past the tangle by the creek
Where the trail is all to seek,
To the damp and dusky meadows,
To the willow-skirted meadows, (20)
To go walking in the meadows with the pleasant
Night Wind there.[8]

The poem's lyrical roots are evident, and "Night Wind" does resemble Keatsian verse's apostrophized subjects, but the speaker here might also be calling on natural spirit power in the manner of the Paiutes. Austin employs internal rhyme and repetitions of consonants—as in "willow," "walking," "meadow" (lines 20-21)[9]—in a merger of sound and motion that correlates to the "smooth-flowing wonder of words" Paiute medicine man Tinnemaha had told Austin were essential to the effective magical chant.[10] Her Shoshonean Yokuts–Western Mono neighbors did, in fact, regard Night as a powerful entity one could appeal to for solace or aid, and to them Wind was the movement of spirit in the world.[11] So the poem's recurring "oh" sounds, like breaths, mimic and reinforce the speaker's call on Night Wind, even as the three stanzas correlate to the Paiute medicine man's magical three-part chant.

The brief poems enclosing the essays in *Lost Borders* (1909), another book about the hills and deserts of central California, invoke a kind of power in the landscape that "Night Wind, Wake!" only suggests. The introductory poem, for example, introduces the concept of the elusive "Word" and connects it to the land:

There's a little creek in Inyo, singing by beyond the town,
Through the pink wild-almond tangle and the birches slim and
brown,
Where all night we'll watch the star-beams in the shallow, open rills,
And the hot, bright moons of August skulking low along the hills;
And the Word shall wake in Inyo—never printed on a page— (5)
With the wind that wakes the morning on a thousand miles of sage.

The fact that the Word is borne by the spirit/wind rather than by the printed page proposes that its meaning lies beyond the context and restrictions of human culture, and that one "wakens" to it only while being in nature. The essays that follow this poem move from scenes of thinly pop-

ulated wild lands to cities and back again, divulging a series of secrets about
the land's people, its animals, and its moods that serve as guides for living
in the wilderness. After their travels, speaker and friend return to their
starting place in the poem that closes the collection:

> There's a word we've lost between us we shall never hear again
> In the mindless clang of engines where they bray the hearts of
> men ... (10)
>
> . . . .
>
> And the Word—I cannot name it, but we'll learn its sweetest use (17)
> In the moonlit sandy reaches when the desert wind is loose.[12]

Back home in nature the speaker and her friend will learn how to "use"
the Word, which will not be "named" (17), for it is only by participating
with the natural world—on *its* terms—that one comes to understand its
secrets, a theme developed in the preceding essays. By conflating the
speaker and beloved friend as "we," Austin also draws the reader into this
almost holy rite of outdoors initiation. The poem's rhymed couplets, like
paired footsteps, move across the terrain of the poem in an exuberant jog,
nimbly negotiating its contours, and the seekers return to where the desert
wind, like the spirit-imbued Night Wind, still blows. The speaker cannot
"name" the Word because it is more than a signifier—it is the thing itself,
and it has practical, actualizing power, like the power of words in the Paiute
shaman's chants. Austin's poetry often hints at, then conceals these "un-
speakable" driving forces, and here the unrevealed Word, like some mysterious absence, corresponds to that part of a magical chant intentionally
omitted in the presence of the uninitiated. The mystery, however, is accessible to those who will allow the desert/spirit wind to "inspire" them.

Austin's play *The Arrow-Maker*, produced in New York in 1911, also
draws heavily on her observations of the Paiutes. The protagonist is the
Chisera, a medicine woman—a not uncommon phenomenon among
local Yokuts and Mono people—who at the play's climax contacts the
spirit force that is both part of herself and part of the world around her:

> Come, O my power,
> Indwelling spirit!
> It is I that call.
> Childless, unmated—
> This is my song that I make.[13]

The Chisera's call for power is not supplicative but collegial (as Austin later pointed out, the "ritualistic refrain is not 'Lord have mercy upon us,' but 'Work with us, work with us!'"). Her song, eliciting the aid of the "Friend-of-the-Soul-of-Man" to protect the men in battle, works for the good of the tribe, a motive Austin felt had dropped out of the poetry of her own culture.[14] "The Amerind makes poetry because . . . he believes it a contribution to the well-being of his group. He makes it to put himself in sympathy with the *wokonda,* the *orenda* or god-stuff which he conceives to be to some degree in every created thing."[15] Despite *The Arrow-Maker's* disappointing reception, Austin continued to explore Indian materials, and she wrote the introduction to George Cronyn's collection of Native American songs in *The Path on the Rainbow* in 1918.[16] She saw red when Louis Untermeyer spoke of the Indian poem as "a crude reduction to Imagist verse form" in a review of the book in the *Dial,* and she rebutted in the 23 August 1919 issue: "Indian verse form *is* Imagism. It was not 're-duced' to that form, it was made that way originally. . . . [U]nless Mr. Un-termeyer knew something of the genius of the aboriginal Indian language, unless he knew something of Imagism besides what it looks like on paper, he had no right to review this book. Certainly he had no right to condemn it because it doesn't come within his notion of what poetry is in New York today."[17]

What she felt was lacking in the poetry of her day later became the subject of a review of *The American Rhythm* written by Mark Van Doren for *The Nation.* Seeing Austin's theories on American poetics as a "challenge which will make every honest American poet stop to examine himself," Van Doren quotes from Austin's poem "Fig Leaves" in the section "Songs in the American Manner":[18]

> No guts . . .
> Perhaps that's why we have no poets now
> Can grip the people with creative pain;
> But star cold music such as Sterling[19] makes,
> Or the free versifier's choice, eviscerated phrases, (5)
> Or braying of maimed voices,
> Hybrids of art and sociology,
> Blaming the world and us for their lost potency . . .
>
> What else is music but the pang—
> Wrung from the entrails of some poor, dead beastie— (10)

God, when He first began to make Him creatures,
Fashioned them of guts . . .
Brain, motion, and the serviceable hand,
So many figures of the dance
Of the red-gutted microcosms,
Throbbing to rhythms long rehearsed— (20)
The soul—a song our viscera makes to God.[20]

Focusing on the rhythms of the land and of the blood, on the unaccented "dub-dub-dub" of the heart that she claims in *The American Rhythm* drove the first poetry,[21] Austin drew from a gutsier source than the modernists' "hybrids of art and sociology," although she, too, disdained tradition's restrictive formulas. In the post–World War I angst that generated what Gilbert and Gubar have identified as the territorial fears male poets felt as women poets came into their own,[22] Austin rejected poets who wrote with "maimed voices" (6), "blaming the world and us for their lost potency" (8).

Austin's relation to her poet contemporaries shows up in sharp relief when her poetry is compared with H.D.'s. H.D., "Imagiste," as Ezra Pound dubbed her, employs classical Greek speakers—women such as Helen of Troy and Cassandra whose beauty precipitated their ruin—and demonstrates technical independence from a male indebtedness to Greek poetics by creating her own variations on Sappho's poems.[23] In "Cassandra," originally published in *Heliodora* in 1924, Apollo, taken with Cassandra's beauty, bestows the gift of prophecy and then, when she resists his attempts at seduction, destroys her credibility, a trope for the strategy many male critics of the 1920s adopted in their assessments of contemporary women's poetry. Here Cassandra begs Hymen, god of marriage, for the love of a supportive man:

[M]y trance frightens them,
. . . .
if I but pass they fall
back, frantically;
must people always mock?
. . . .
is there none left
can bear with me
the kiss of your white fire?

is there not one . . .
. . . .
one meet to take from me
this bitter power of song.[24]

Cassandra, abducted, raped, and murdered, is both powerful and powerless, and she articulates H.D.'s sense of herself as a poet and as a woman. Gifted but cruelly used, mocked by the men she most admired, Cassandra yearns for a mate to share her prophetic burden, her pain, and her passion.

Austin makes different use of Greek sources. "Not to You Only, O Pythian," published in 1926 in *The Nation*, is an aggressive, feminist revision of the Delphic myth, a retelling strongly influenced by Pueblo Indian sources. Austin's Pythia stands at the edge of the Grand Canyon in the bright glare of day, and the poem advances in what Austin calls "glyphs," or word pictures:

Not to you only, O Pythian,
Out of rock crevices,
Out of earth's sacred middle
Where the ancient spore of the Sun
Still works in her, (5)
Comes madness.

Here, out of Arroyos Hondos,
Between the prevailing
Stiff stems of the junipers,
Dream shaping vapors set back the moonlight. (10)
Here, from the wine red rift of the rim-rock,
Out of the Grand Canyon's motionless unreality,
Visions prophetic.

Not to you only, the wish-colored (15)
Word Hieratic,
Not solely at Delos, O Pythian,
But here at the desert's fire new edges,
Inebriate of the earth, to the Sun corybantic,
The god with my voice declaring (20)
What I discern not.[25]

In Delphic lore, Apollo overcame the dragon, Pytho, guarding the Cretan earth goddess Gê's cave, and claimed the oracle and its priestess, called the Pythia, as his own. Breathing hallucinogenic vapors rising from a small crevice in the cave floor, the Pythia was inspired by Apollo. Swooning from his power, she uttered the prophetic words that her male priest assistants interpreted for questioners.[26] Alluding to Apollo's merger with, rather than his destruction of, the chthonic goddess who had originally ruled from Delphi, Austin's poem carries the myth forward in time and place to the Grand Canyon, where "the ancient spore of the Sun / still works in her" (4-5). While H.D. defines her speaker according to classical Greek myth, Austin's Pythia derives her power from the American landscape. And whereas Cassandra bewails her loss of credibility and begs for a mate, Austin's Pythia embraces her "madness" and her loneliness.

The site of Austin's oracle, the "sacred middle" (3), can be traced to Pueblo origin stories in which The People, living in an earth "below," climb up to the present world through a dark lake, emerging through an opening the Hopi call Sipapu, guided by their gods. In *The Land of Journey's Ending* (1926), Austin locates the Hopis' geographical "place of emergence" near the confluence of the Little Colorado and Colorado Rivers in the Grand Canyon, "the Hole in the Ground, out of which, in the Days of the New, the Hopi came."[27] The allusion sheds light on Austin's understanding of Hopi origin stories and mirrors the underlying tenet of all her fiction and poetry—place is imbued with sacredness. "Arroyos Hondos" then situates the prophetic place anywhere rivers run through canyons, as at Arroyo Hondo, near Taos Pueblo in New Mexico, centuries-old dwelling place of the Tigua, as well as at the pueblos of the Tewa, Jemez, and Keresan peoples alongside the Rio Grande and its tributaries.

Austin's seer stands at the edge of an immense, sun-drenched red canyon, where "vapors" rise up through the "prevailing / Stiff stems of the junipers" (8-9). On the upper levels of the south rim of the canyon, piñon and juniper forest thrive; "prevailing" alludes to the respect local native peoples accorded these trees as important resources. But "prevailing" also suggests metaphorical readings. Priests surrounding the Pythia "interpreted" her words, so cryptic as to demand exegesis or so inchoate they could hardly be characterized as language at all.[28] The prevalence and career-making power of men in publishing had long distressed Austin, and it is likely that the "prevailing / Stiff stems of the junipers" equate to the men who surrounded and interpreted the woman writer, the men who put words in the Pythias' mouths. These vapors rising between the junipers carry prophetic visions to the woman on the edge, truthful visions that "set back" mere moonlight and its fanciful, lunatic illusions.

The visions that emerge out of the Grand Canyon's "motionless unreality" (13) may also allude to Hopi, Navajo, Zuni, and New Mexico Pueblo peoples' concepts of "sacred" time. Dennis Tedlock says this realm "is hard to talk about in ordinary language. . . . The Hopis refer to it as *'a'ne himu,* 'Mighty Something.'"[29] Austin's "motionless unreality" draws attention to Western culture's antipathy to the nonlinear nature of this sacred time and articulates the extra-real essence of the moment preceding divine inspiration, when the priestess/shaman, emptied of thought, invites the "Mighty Something" to speak through her. And Tedlock reports that the shaman on his vision quest "speaks of the journey as carrying him to 'the edge of the Deep Canyon.'"[30]

Austin's odelike opening line, "Not to you only, O Pythian," pays homage to the Pythian verse, or dactylic hexameter, into which priests translated the Greek Pythia's words—that is, one stressed syllable followed by two unstressed in a line of six feet. Then, the irregular rhythms of the American poet-prophetess take over. "Here, from the wine red rift of the rim-rock" (11), with its two- and three-syllable feet, leads to the more heavily stressed "Weighting the eyelids" (12) and then to the ponderous "Out of the Grand Canyon's motionless unreality" (13), culminating in the cryptic "Visions prophetic" (14). The rhythmic effect is disorienting; the lines stagger to the brink of the chasm. Drunken, ecstatic, the speaker says, "I discern not" (21), perhaps anticipating critics' claims that she is too bold in her ascendancy or that she misuses either classical Greek or Native American themes.

Austin claims in *The American Rhythm,* "It was not until I found my own unpremeditated songs taking the Amerind mold that I realized what I had stumbled upon."[31] Her poetry draws on her observations of Indian people and is enriched by her mimicry of them. "I have naturally a mimetic temperament which drives me toward the understanding of life by living it. . . . I made singing medicine as I was taught, and surprised the Friend-of-the-Soul-of-Man between the rattles and the drums. . . . So that when I say that I am not, have never been, nor offered myself, as an authority on things Amerindian, I do not wish to have it understood that I may not, at times, have succeeded in being an Indian."[32] Today, non-Indian scholars assiduously avoid language implying that they have co-opted Native Americans' rituals, but Austin was not so reluctant. And although she was among the émigrés lured to the Southwest in the 1920s by Mabel Dodge Luhan, Austin was not simply another in that group Rayna Green calls the cult of "Indian wannabees."[33] Green rightly surmises that "playing Indian" offered white women opportunities to escape cultural and gender-driven restrictions, and Austin's Indian-like fictional female characters do enjoy relative freedom, but "being an Indian" was a life's work for Austin. Creating efficacious songs seemed to her the common mission of poet and shaman, and she took her Native American teachers' instructions quite seriously, whether she was creating song "prayers" for power in her own life or writing poetry.

Vachel Lindsay, Austin's contemporary, often wrote about Native Americans as well, and Austin no doubt read the Lindsay poem reprinted in a 1927 review in *The New Republic,* in which one of her own essays also appeared. The poem deals with the destruction of the buffalo herds, and reviewer Hazelton Spench rhapsodizes over Lindsay's "sheer lyric genius," as represented in this excerpt from *Going-to-the-Stars:*[34]

> The tossing, blooming, perfumed grass (5)
> Is swept away by the wheat,
> Wheels and wheels and wheels spin by
> In the spring that still is sweet.
> But the flower-fed buffaloes of the spring
> Left us, long ago . . . (10)
> With the Blackfeet, lying low.
> With the Pawnees, lying low,
> Lying low.[35] (15)

In a poignant look at the past, Lindsay's train rolls over the plains. But Austin's memory is not so short, nor is her vision obscured by nostalgia. Compare her "Caller of Buffalo," published less than a year later in *Poetry*:

> Whenever the summer-singed plains,
> Past my car window,
> Heave and fall like the flanks of trail-weary cattle,
> When the round-backed hills go shouldering down
> To drink of the western rivers, (5)
> And dust, like ceremonial smoke,

Goes up from the long-dried wallows,
Then I remember the Caller of Buffalo.

Then I think I see him,
Head-feathers slant in the wind, (10)
Shaking his medicine robe
From the buttes of Republican River,
At Pawnee bluffs
Offering sacred smoke to the Great White Buffalo.
Then, at dawn, between jiggling curtains, I wake (15)
To the star-keen note of his deer-shin whistle.

O Caller of Buffalo!
Hunt no more on the ancient traces
Pale and emptied of going as a cast snake skin.
Come into my mind and hunt the herding thoughts, (20)
The White Buffalo
Of the much desired places.
Come with your medicine making,
O Caller of Buffalo![36]

Lindsay's naming of the Blackfoot and the Pawnee, who served as scouts for the U.S. Cavalry and guarded railroad crews from the attacks of hostile Cheyenne and Sioux, suggests that all Indians, friendly to whites or not, are doomed. Here, the buffalo roamed in some mythic "long ago," when scarcely fifty years had passed since their wholesale slaughter for East Coast markets. Insulating the reader from any identification with the scene, Lindsay's train rolls over the irretrievable past, through High Plains wheat fields.

What Austin regards from her train "car" window, however, is much less verdant; she sees the landscape of the dust bowl. The hills remind her of parched cattle, and the dust the cattle kick up calls to mind the ceremonial smoke made by the medicine man who invokes the *wakan* Great White Buffalo. Austin had very likely read James Willard Schultz's interviews with the Blackfoot (Piegan) medicine man in *Apauk, Caller of Buffalo* (1916), and she calls him by name in the poem.[37] The valley of the Republican River in Colorado and Wyoming had been home to buffalo numbering in the millions in the 1860s; by the 1880s they had been almost completely wiped out. Wakened from the forgetfulness of sleep by a train whistle that

is like the Caller of Buffalo's deer-shin whistle and its "star-keen note" (16),
Austin's speaker internalizes his ritual call on the Great White Buffalo. Not
content to allow the "medicine making" (23) power of the Plains tribes to
lie low, Austin retrieves this eminently usable Indian past as a source of sustenance, power, and inspiration.

The dusty land speaks, too, in "Campo Santo at San Juan." Named for
the graveyard at San Juan Pueblo, the largest of six modern Tewa villages,
Austin's poem celebrates life and its cycles, and operates within the all-im-
portant landscape. She gives readers the long view first:

> A bow shot nearer the mesa's edge,
> Pale huts drink the sun.
> Long after dark their walls give back warm tones,
> The wine of light.[38] (4)

In pueblo country, distances measured by bow shots allude to what Austin
elsewhere calls the "Twin War Gods," which actually signify the male spirits the Tewa call *T'owa e,* "who were sent out to explore the world before
emergence." They are beings who watch over the pueblo from the surrounding sacred mesas, hills, and mountains.[39] Austin's Pythia stood at the
edge of the canyon, "inebriate of the earth," but in this poem human
dwellings "drink the sun," and the effect is calming rather than intoxicat-
ing. Glowing from within, the pueblo's "wine of light" (4) is almost sacra-
mental.

> Five centuries and more these walls
> Have been drawn out of dust by women's hands.

Smoothing the newly finished wall of the pueblos was, by long tradition,
the women's responsibility. Austin writes in *The Land of Journey's Ending*
that "so far back as the plastic adobe clay became the medium of construction, excavators are perpetually turning up fine, feminine finger-
marks, and the modulation of small, shallow palms, as you can see to-day,
in any pueblo before the fiesta, the house-mothers patting new plaster on
the walls."[40] Woman here is flesh-and-blood builder and creator, not a vision in some lost past or a character in a cultural myth, and the reader is
invited into the pueblo to meet her, to identify with her, and to share her
connectedness to the land:

Sit here by the Cacique's house
And watch Lupita plastering a wall
With dust that was some mother's son,
Mixed with the rain that fell, how many times! (10)
As women's tears,
This was their life;
A wind that rose and struggled with the dust
and stilled to dust again.[41]

Lupita plasters with "dust that was some mother's son," and Austin writes in "Can Prayer Be Answered?" that the virtuous in life were often buried, in death, within the pueblo walls.[42] Lines between people and their dwellings blend and blur, humans resolving from earth as the spirit wind enlivens them, and then falling back to dust again. The woman's tears correspond to the rain that moistens and sustains the crops and makes the earth soft for shaping; rain is sacred and so are tears, as is evident in "Mixed with the rain that fell . . . / As women's tears" (10-11). Readers are invited into this scene whose elements—sun, light, mother, son, dust, tears, rain, wind—all merge in and out of each other. "Campo Santo" flows along its connections, from the larger picture of the huts drinking the sun, to the community that thrives within those walls, to the women who plaster those walls, to succeeding generations, to tears of joy and sadness. Having taken the lessons regarding the movement of Native American chants and songs along the "landscape line" to heart, Austin here creates her own version of that phenomenon.[43] Far from anthropomorphizing nature, Austin is actually "naturalizing" humans, connecting them to all that is "earthly," including that spiritual motive toward manifestation she calls "It," "Friend-of-the-Soul-of-Man," "Earth-Will," and "Wakonda."

Austin, like her contemporaries the imagists, felt that the poetical object disdains metaphorical comparison, abstraction, or ornamentation. She, too, saw the value of representing the object directly, but imagism's hard, clear edges seemed to make its objects stand out in sharp relief from their backgrounds, harbingers of modernism's dictum that literary works might be understood in and of themselves, in isolation. Austin's work did not move in this direction, for she strove to present the poetical object as contiguous with its surroundings, part of a larger design in which the sacred infuses the mundane. She would have understood Lame Deer, as quoted by Paula Gunn Allen: "We Indians live in a world of symbols and images where the spiritual and the commonplace are one. To you [non-Indians] symbols are just words, spoken or written in a book. To us they are a part of nature, part of ourselves."[44] In her assessment of Native American poetics in *The American Rhythm,* Austin claims that the singer merges with the subject in ritual song, and she strove for the same effect in her own poetry, drawing the reader into the scene as tribal ritual might have done.

Austin dared to do "interpretations" rather than translations of Indian chants because her readers required an explicit cultural context that Indian audiences did not need. Nevertheless, she admired the "holophrastic genius" of Indian speech and its ability to express complex operations or ideas in a word, and she suggested that "the translator's problem, then, is not one of simplification, but of achieving a deeply imbricated wholeness."[45] She employs such compression in "Rio Abajo," a poem-trip along the Rio Grande in north-central New Mexico's Pueblo country:

> In October the Valle del Rio Grande
> Is a spate of copper, molten
> Under bright scums of aspen gold,
> Green gold the frost refines
> Till the beholder checks midway his gasp (5)
> Lest the force of an indrawn breath loose round him
> The flood of exquisite disaster.
>
> At Aldogones the orchards
> Shoulder like cows at the milking pen,
> Patient but fain of the hand that strips them. (10)
> At Los Lunas
> The vineyards are prone to the cruising flocks,
> At Isleta the Rio
> Thins finely to a gleam
> Of harness metal on a roan stallion's flanks, (15)
> And all the glimmering ghosts
> Of summer's bright empetalled hosts
> Drift on the moveless air between its banks.[46]

"Rio Abajo" is, like all of Austin's work, place-specific. Flowing past settlements whose Native American and Hispanic origins blend, blur, and reassert themselves, the poem uses the river as its vehicle and the turning leaves as its illustration. Here, the mundane world is imbued with spirituality. "Glyphs" coalesce to signify the transformative movement of summer to fall, life to death, and the stillness that accompanies understanding. "[B]right scums of aspen gold" (3), tinged with the frost, inspire awe; and the "beholder" (5) is very much in this scene if his "gasp" pulls the leaves, so lightly attached now, from their trees in a "flood of exquisite disaster" (7).

The Rio Abajo, or "lower river," flows past the small Hispanic settlement just south of San Felipe Pueblo named after the *aldogón,* or "cotton," that falls from the cottonwoods in this region once known for its fertile fields and peach orchards. Echoing the earlier phrase "round-backed hills go shouldering down to the western rivers," orchards "[s]houlder like cows at the milking pen / Patient but fain of the hand that strips them" (9–10), phrasing that suggests their willing connection to humans. At Los Lunas, the ranchero granted to the Lunas family by the Mexican government in the first half of the nineteenth century, sheep graze about the vineyards after the grape harvest. Its neighbor is Isleta, southernmost of the Rio Grande pueblos and home to the Tigua. The river narrows to a slender stream, like "harness metal on a roan stallion's flanks" (15), as smooth and undulant as the reddish hills through which the river flows.

Occurring between summer's growth and winter's death, autumn occupies a temporal space the Tewa might call "the middle place," where transformations occur. The "glimmering ghosts / Of summer's bright empetalled hosts"—once energy-producing leaves—have dried out and drift from the trees. "Hosts" also signify the Eucharistic bread and suggest the communion-like nature of this scene in which the "beholder" partakes. The "exquisite disaster" prophesied in the first stanza occurs after the journey by quiet settlements engaged in the business of life, when golden leaves "[d]rift on the moveless air" (18) as if arrested by volition. The natural and the metaphysical are one here, and the Mighty Something infuses all.

Finally, just as the train's whistle mimics the whistle of the Caller of Buffalo, skyscraper and mesa waver and merge in this rhymed reverie in a 1932 edition of *Folksay IV*:

> Was it a steam ratchet that I heard,
> Or did my parrot shriek?
> Stale gust of gullied street,
> Or mesa wind that stirred

The sharp-edged yucca shadows (5)
That like drowned weed along the smooth adobe wall
Swim in the heat's high tide of moving jade,
While like a crab the green and scarlet bird
Slides from deep to deep of tawny shade?

When the mind wills, how thin a blade of sound (10)
Lets through the fragile lisp of bougainvillea leaves,
Or ripe fruit dropping on the grassless ground!
How brief an instant turns
The traffic's slithering stream
To the acequia madre's slow ensilvered gleam! (15)

Outside the Zaguan's arch the foothill trail
Winds up to seek
Blue altar-lifted mesa and remote cowled peak,
Through spined and brittle chaparral, where frail,
Bright trumpets of the mimulus (20)
Answer contented pipings of sleek quail.
And where the woodman with his burrow pack
Trudges between chamisa and choyital,
Rises a pagan wind and casts
The dust of imprecation on his track.[47] (25)

The city scene may be "real," but the place the parrot calls to mind has priority. The city's "stale gust" is mistaken for "mesa wind" (3-4); and sharp-edged shadows, perhaps those cast by tall buildings into the "gullied street" (3), seem like yucca shadows. Cool against the hot glare, these shadows swim, miragelike, against adobe walls. The parrot scuttles deeper in, as do we.

Willing her return to nature, the speaker opens her mind and "[l]ets through" the slight but clearly remembered "lisp of bougainvillea leaves," evoking the garden surrounding Austin's adobe home in Santa Fe. The soft thud of falling fruit, perhaps a fig, follows easily. Eyes join in the act of will, looking down on the gleam of moving cars first as if they were a slithering snake, and then as the sparklings of sunlight on the winding irrigation channel yonder. Re-creating herself, she accentuates her transportation to this better place with exclamation points that call to mind the shaman's affirmation of his fait accompli in the Cherokee love chant that Austin cites in *The American Rhythm,* "It is accomplished! / Yuh!"[48]

If the zaguan of the southwestern-style adobe house is the arched opening through which one passes into the interior patio, the Zaguan is also a Portal. Moving deeper into the interior of her mind, into her own "sacred middle," Austin's speaker imagines stepping into the high desert country that could be Zuni land or Hopi or Navajo. Beside a sacred mesa like those near Acoma or toward Taos, the speaker climbs upward to the blue altar that spirits visit, past the showy monkey flower, past quail undisturbed by her presence. And then the woodman appears amid the cactus, on his way to gather firewood at the feet of pines or junipers still out of sight. Or is he on a journey to collect wood or dried yucca stems as prayer sticks for an upcoming ceremony? Might he be Old Prayer-Stick Man himself? The dust puffs up as he trudges, reminiscent of the "dust, like ceremonial smoke" stirred by the shuffling feet of the Caller of Buffalo singing his power song. This "dust of imprecation" (25) is rich, too, with magical connotations, "imprecation" suggesting the invoking of evil or of cursing. The word's root, *imprecari,* however, means something more akin to "pray." But it is a "pagan wind" (24) that stirs the dust here, where praying takes Native American forms. Here, whether it be curse or prayer, the traveler/speaker/voyeur/reader is reminded of Campo Santo and of the spirit-"wind that rose and struggled with the dust and stilled to dust again."

The Word that would reveal the poem's meaning is once again unvoiced. The speaker provides only occasional trail markers; the journey's ultimate destination she leaves to the reader. Enigmatic in ways that schooling in Western civilization cannot elucidate, Austin's poems usually refer to stories and land lore non-Indians can initially appreciate only superficially. But many of the "glyphs," places and histories lying just under the surfaces of Austin's late southwestern poems, may be found in *The Land of Journey's Ending,* a virtual lexicon for her Native American and Spanish imagery.

Most of the creative writers and critics of Austin's day who were interested in her work contented themselves with imitating or admiring the exotic elements in Native American lore; few passed through the zaguan into the cosmological and philosophical terrain inhabited by the indigene. Austin, who dared to go in, teased readers with the only partially revealed Word, her reticence about telling all resembling the Hopis' desire to keep some rituals a mystery. Imparting the principles of prayer and songs and giving glimpses of the lands out of which they materialize, Austin shares visions only with those who, like her, are willing to do the necessary preparatory work.

Because she knew individual Native Americans, Austin could not perpetuate romantic fictions about them, nor could she write them out of existence. At the same time, she disdained the American Indian "craze" of the 1930s and expressed increasing hostility toward other whites' overly facile translations and ignorant borrowings from Indian sources. Criticized by ethnologists for her tendency to explain cultural phenomena intuitively rather than by accepted field methodology, Austin neither rationalized nor apologized for telling stories and making "songs" as the Indians had taught her. Daring finally to speak as the "other," in *One Smoke Stories* (1932), her last "Indian" work, Austin returns to the personal tale shared with listeners she had first heard in the Paiute campoodies.[49]

She admits in *The American Rhythm* that her inquiries into Native American life had given her literary style "its best thing, a selective economy of phrase, and its worst, a habit of doubling an idea back into its verbal envelope so that only the two ends of it stick out, which to this day I labor in vain to eradicate."[50] The reader must pull Austin's ideas out of their "verbal envelopes" and decipher the allusions behind her odd turns of phrase. A hint at how to do that appears in Austin's introduction to George W. Cronyn's *American Indian Poetry,* in which Austin claims the Native American singer's chant is "but a shorthand note to his emotions, a sentence or two, a phrase out of the heart of the situation. It is the 'inside song' alone which is important."[51] Perhaps as literary scholars seek out her nearly forgotten poems and read them alongside studies of the Native American cultures that inspired them, we might all finally hear the glories of Austin's own "inside song."

NOTES

1. Mary Austin, *The American Rhythm,* 2d ed. (1930; reprint, New York: Cooper Square, 1970). Interestingly, in this second edition Austin expanded on her theory of Native American poetics but deleted her "Songs in the American Manner," which appears in the first, 1923, edition.

2. D. H. Lawrence, Santa Fe poet Witter Bynner, and imagist Amy Lowell all tinkered with Pueblo Indian themes in poetry but did not immerse themselves, as did Austin, in Pueblo culture.

3. Mary Austin, *The Children Sing in the Far West* (Boston: Houghton Mifflin, 1928).

4. Austin, *Earth Horizon: An Autobiography* (1932; reprint, Albuquerque: University of

New Mexico Press, 1991), 215.

5. Austin, "Poetry in the Education of Children," *Bookman* (November 1928): 271.

6. Austin, *Children Sing,* 68–69.

7. Austin, "Poetry," 271.

8. Austin, "Night Wind, Wake!" *Out West* (April 1904): 318.

9. Parenthetical references in the text from this point forward indicate poem line numbers.

10. Austin, *Rhythm,* 2d ed., 21.

11. Richard B. Applegate, *Atishwin* (Socorro, N.Mex.: Ballena Press, 1978), 43, 64.

12. Austin, *Lost Borders* (1909), reprinted in *Stories from the Country of Lost Borders,* ed. Marjorie Pryse (New Brunswick: Rutgers University Press, 1987), 154, 263.

13. Austin, *The Arrow-Maker,* produced at the New Theatre, New York, 1911 (New York: Duffield, 1911), 125–26.

14. Austin, *Rhythm,* 2d ed., 169.

15. Ibid., 35.

16. Austin, introduction to *The Path on the Rainbow,* a collection of Native American chants and songs edited by George W. Cronyn (1918; reprint, New York: Liveright, 1934).

17. Austin, "Imagism: Original and Aboriginal," *Dial,* 23 August 1919, 163.

18. Mark Van Doren, review of *The American Rhythm,* by Mary Austin, *Nation,* 18 April 1923, 472.

19. George Sterling, poet and friend of Austin's and Jack London's in Carmel, California.

20. Mary Austin, *The American Rhythm* (New York: Harcourt, Brace, 1923), 140–41.

21. Austin, *Rhythm,* 2d ed., 11.

22. Sandra M. Gilbert and Susan Gubar, *No Man's Land: The Place of the Woman Writer in the Twentieth Century,* vol. 1: *War of the Words* (New Haven: Yale University Press, 1988), ch. 3.

23. Ibid., vol. 2: *Sexchanges* (New Haven: Yale University Press, 1989), 232.

24. H.D. [Hilda Doolittle], "Cassandra," from *Selected Poems,* ed. Louis L. Martz (New York: New Directions, 1988), 52–53.

25. Austin, "Not to You Only, O Pythian," *Nation,* 1 December 1926, 601.

26. Robert Flaceliere, *Greek Oracles,* trans. Douglas Garman (New York: Norton, 1965), 41.

27. Austin, *The Land of Journeys' Ending* (1924; reprint, Tucson: University of Arizona Press, 1985), 416.

28. Flaceliere, *Greek Oracles,* 50.

29. Dennis Tedlock and Barbara Tedlock, eds., *Teachings from the American Earth* (New York: Liveright, 1975), xiii.

30. Ibid., xx.

31. Austin, *Rhythm,* 2d ed., 40.

32. Ibid., 39, 41.

33. Rayna Green, "The Tribe Called Wannabee," *Folklore* 99 (1988): 43.

34. Hazelton Spench, review of *Going-to-the-Stars,* by Vachel Lindsay, *New Republic,* 31 August 1927, 52.

35. Vachel Lindsay, *Going-to-the-Stars* (New York: D. Appleton, 1927), 39.

36. Mary Austin, "Caller of Buffalo," *Poetry* 32 (June 1928): 124.

37. James Willard Schultz, *Apauk, Caller of Buffalo* (Boston: Houghton Mifflin, 1916). Austin read voraciously on Indians, and it is quite likely that she drew directly from this,

one of Schultz's best-known Plains Indians books.

38. Mary Austin, "Campo Santo at San Juan," in *Mary Austin: Woman of Genius,* by Helen M. Doyle (New York: Gotham House, 1939), 228–29.

39. Alphonso Ortiz, *The Tewa World* (Chicago: University of Chicago Press, 1969), 183.

40. Austin, *Land of Journeys' Ending,* 73.

41. Austin, "Campo Santo," 229.

42. Austin, "Can Prayer Be Answered?" *Forum* 91 (1934): 271.

43. James Ruppert's explication of Austin's "landscape line" remains the clearest of all to date. See Ruppert, "Mary Austin's Landscape Line in Native American Literature," *Southwest Review* 68 (1983): 376–90.

44. Paula Gunn Allen, "Meanings," in *Symposium of the Whole,* ed. Jerome Rothenberg (Berkeley: University of California Press, 1983), 184.

45. Austin, *Rhythm,* 2d ed., 60.

46. Austin, "Rio Abajo," *Saturday Review of Literature,* 12 April 1930, 1.

47. Austin, "Home Thoughts in the City," *Folksay IV* (1932): 91.

48. Austin, *Rhythm,* 2d ed., 39.

49. Austin, *One Smoke Stories* (New York: Houghton Mifflin, 1934).

50. Austin, *Rhythm,* 2d ed., 39.

51. Austin, introduction to *American Indian Poetry: An Anthology of Songs and Chants,* ed. George W. Cronyn (1918; reprint, New York: Ballantine Books, 1991), xxxiv.

CHAPTER FIVE
Serving Suspended Sentences
Mary Austin's Compositions and Explanations

TARA HART

Tara Hart's "Serving Suspended Sentences" presents a significant theme in Austin studies: how Austin was influenced by modernism and how she, in turn, can help scholars redefine modernism. While Dale Metcalfe presents Austin as escaping, indeed challenging, modernist alienation and despair—as mocking modernist "maimed voices"—Hart links Austin's aesthetics of "composition" with the work of other women modernists such as Gertrude Stein and Georgia O'Keeffe, women who used stylistic innovations to create a "space" for themselves and their unconventional choices and to "compose" their responses to conflicting cultural demands.

Hart and Metcalfe, however, share a respect for Austin's style and show how close attention to her sentence structure, imagery, and rhythms richly repays the reader; through their own imagery, both connect her style to the body, to breathing. In the past, critics have disagreed considerably over Austin's style: some disparage it as pretentious, overly self-conscious, and abstract; others have been fascinated by her elliptical, ambiguous sentences. Although Austin has no single style and wrote in a variety of genres and voices, modern critics such as Hart and Metcalfe are now describing the characteristics of her writing more precisely. Like Kathryn DeZur, for instance, Hart notes Austin's use of conditional sentences; and her exploration of how Austin's style breaks down borders and boundaries supports the thematic readings by Nicole Tonkovich and DeZur.

Hart argues that Austin's style in Lost Borders *stems from her "conditional female occupation of a suspended space," which she uses to confront and evade dichotomies and to suggest that "the nature of desire is that it is not satisfied." Hart's discussion of how Austin's sentence structure "defers" meaning and the satisfaction of desire and conceptualizes absence, loss, and lack is clearly informed by postmodern theorists, especially Lacan. Yet she, like other writers in this volume, implies that Austin herself was a theorist anticipating the insights of later writers and visual artists.*

A print of Georgia O'Keeffe's *Red Canna* (1924) hangs like a flame on the wall of my small Baltimore kitchen, above the table where I write about Mary Austin and Gertrude Stein. When I can see nothing new (or sometimes nothing at all) in the book beside me or the words on my computer screen, I look up at that flower, severed from context, an image magnified and "suspended," in Linda Nochlin's words, "in a suggestive void."[1] O'Keeffe, like Austin and Stein, deliberately disorients us with an enlarged and timeless perspective and startles the eye into taking its time. The audiences of these three women revisit their sites again and again—as they did—to encounter the familiar and the strange at once, to share the shiver of the uncanny.[2] O'Keeffe's landscape fragments, bare of human bodies yet "continually . . . reminiscent of the female body," do indeed "invite us to see anew and to read anew what we see, to reconsider the language we have used to name the reality we experience."[3] It is in the repeated contemplation of that suspended space framed on my kitchen wall that I began to make connections between language and landscape, the narrative rhythms of encounter and visitation, and what it all has to do with the desire that compels us to represent experience and frame meaning.

What is it about the American landscape that invites a conditional female occupation of a suspended space? In "'Til Death Do Us Part: Impossible Spaces in *Thelma and Louise*," Lynda Hart describes the two women in the 1991 film as "uniquely female outlaws" who elude their pursuers at the end but are yet metaphorically "arrested":

> [T]he camera's eye caress[es] the women as their Thunderbird gently floats above the canyon, then is arrested in mid-air, forever poised to penetrate the space that they are visually barred from entering. . . . The detective running after the car in slow motion continuously approaches an object (the women) that maintains a constant distance. Shot in slow motion, this sequence is suggestive of a fantasy space where the satisfaction of desire is impossible because it is an activity that never reaches an endpoint.[4]

Like the final freeze frame of *Butch Cassidy and the Sundance Kid,* Louise and Thelma's ending is eternally deferred. However, the meaning of their final positions is different. Butch and Sundance, wounded and weary, muster the energy to repeat an old escape routine, unaware that an army awaits them outside and that escape is impossible. The women choose, too, to "keep going," but into a true "fantasy space." The fact that they remain "poised to penetrate" the grand fissure suggests and recalls the gendered circumstances, the "rapes," that led to this moment. The silence that surrounds Louise's "rape," and the interruption of Thelma's, metaphorically anticipate the final scene, in which the women re-create and, some argue, take control of their journey into unexplored territory. Roaring together toward the unknown, Thelma and Louise are fully aware that they are about to enter an "impossible space." The film leaves us there, to contemplate what it means to imagine women in a place that avoids consummation as well as paralysis and keeps possibility alive.

Such space has been charted before—at the turn of the century—by at least two American women writers for whom composition held the key to sustenance and effective representation: Mary Austin and Gertrude Stein. *Composition* means, literally, "arrangement"; and in the ways that a writer arranges words, controls the breath, holds the body, and maps the consciousness, Austin is a composition theorist who implicitly illuminates, particularly in *Lost Borders,* the principles of the female occupation of a suspended space, principles that Stein later espoused explicitly in "Composition as Explanation" (1926). Austin serves us suspended sentences of the desert landscape to explore and identify the nature of a space in which the female self can balance conflicting forces of maternity and artistry, where she can sustain herself while still saying "no" to those who would absorb or use her. The nature, definition, and composition of "suspension" become as well a means of self-definition and self-sustenance within female relationships, between mothers and selves.[5] Through composition, Austin teaches us to transfigure loss, survive severance, and avoid absorption: all through the means of making sentences that balance radical economy, repetition, and the use of the continuous present to maintain the deeply desired still point between movement and arrest.

Austin's style pieces together fragments of what we can know and see until they finally become something larger than their sum: felicitous spaces, to use Judith Fryer's phrase, or spaces to walk around in, to echo Melody Graulich. "Desire, in works of art, must be concentrated within form," says Fryer. "Form is the envelope, the sheath, of the precious element itself—the ancient pottery, for Indian women, in which life-giving water is carried from the stream; the vessel for Thea Kronborg, that can be made of one's throat and nostrils and held on one's breath."[6] Like Willa Cather's female artist in *The Song of the Lark,* Austin makes vessels of her own sentences to sustain us through the desert landscape. In her autobiographical novel, *A Woman of Genius* (often compared with *The Song of the Lark*), Austin envisions Olivia's genius as a sea, and as a *sei-zure,* that shaped her life in the most physical terms:

> [I]f I know anything of genius it is wholly extraneous, derived, impersonal, flowing through and by. I cannot tell you what it is, but I hope to show you a little of how I was seized of it, shaped; what resistances opposed to it; what surrenders. I mean to put as plainly as possible how I felt it fumbling at my earlier life like the sea at the foot of a tidal wall, and by what rifts in the structure of living, its inundation rose upon me; by what practices and passions I was enlarged to it, and by what well meaning of my friends I was cramped and hardened.[7]

The sea that seizes is a familiar and often darkly maternal image in American literature; it is both lure and threat; it identifies Austin's recognition of a force at once ubiquitous, pervasive, nourishing, and dangerous. Liquid metaphors run throughout her desert literature. Like *genus,* meaning those marked as and linked together in kind and kin, as well as birth source, *genius* also signifies production. According to ancient Roman belief, however, a genius was also a guardian spirit assigned to a person at birth: a tutelary deity, a person considered to have strong influence over another. Thus both genus and genius, maternity and artistry, evoke a powerfully influential figure that seizes and shapes us. How do we then develop and sustain a sense of self? Attachment involves the loss of control; detachment, a paralyzing sense of loss. How to occupy the impossible space in between? Such survival, according to Austin, depends on two artful means: on learning to read, and on composition.

In the sketch "The Land of Little Rain," Austin writes of the "tragedy of desert deaths": "Properly equipped it is possible to go safely across that ghastly sink, yet every year it takes its toll of death. . . . To underestimate one's thirst, to pass a given landmark to the right or left, to find a dry spring where one looked for running water—there is no help for any of these things. . . . Most species have well defined areas of growth, the best index the voiceless land can give the traveler of his whereabouts."[8] Austin's prose maps the connections between physical and narrative negotiations of the land, a land forever figured as feminine. The knowing voice charts the possibilities open to the traveler trained to see patterns and landmarks, to gauge the intensity and duration of physical needs, even as it regrets the inevitable mistakes that are made in a place where knowing voices cannot be heard. Learning to read the index of the land means, simultaneously, coming to know and depend on oneself within that land, and we are warned that the underestimation of a woman's desire will take its toll.

In the first sketch of *Lost Borders,* "The Land," Austin introduces us to a literary and emotional landscape of "known trails" that is characterized by lack. In a passage at the end of "The Land," perhaps the one most frequently quoted in discussions of Austin's identification of woman with the natural landscape, she says, "If the desert were a woman, I know well what she would be," and then goes on to describe a powerfully desirable figure.[9] Yet the "woman" at the beginning of the story offers very little to love: "Riding through by the known trails, the senses are obsessed by the coil of a huge and senseless monotony; straight, white, blinding, alkali flats, forsaken mesas; skimpy shrubs growing little and less, starved knees of hills sticking out above them; black clots of pines high upon rubbishy mountain-heads—days and days of this, as if Nature herself had obscured the medium to escape you in her secret operations."[10] With her "starved knees . . . sticking out," forsaken surfaces, and the "black clots" on mountaintops recalling the same sort of deliberate degradation as the "black wires" on the head of Shakespeare's mistress,[11] the she-desert lies on her back in a posture that suggests and yet eradicates desire. She cannot prevent the penetration, but she makes the senses recoil in the representation of the senseless. An invaded self splits open in its own protection; an overzealous autoimmunity can attack its own tissues in self-defense. Nature escapes the "rider" through ceaseless scarcity and self-negation.

> One might travel weeks on end and not come on any piece or occasion whereby men may live, and drop suddenly into close hives of them digging, jostling, drinking, lusting, and rejoicing. Every story of that country is colored by the fashion of the life, there, breaking up in swift, passionate intervals between long, dun stretches, like the land that out of hot sinks of desolation heaves up great bulks of granite ranges with opal shadows playing in their shining, snow-piled curves. Out there beyond the borders are the Shivering Dunes, heaps upon

heaps of blinding sand all acrawl in the wind, drifting and reforming
with a faint, stridulent rustle, and black, wall-sided box-cañons that
give the stars at midday, scored over with picture-writings of a forgotten race.[12]

Again the land blinds and obscures. The active, passionate intervals that
break up the longer "dun" stretches figure certain kinds of narratives, and
that figure is offered up in one of Austin's suspended sentences. The sharp
and jostling contrast between a colorful, fashionable Bret Harte sort of
story and the almost silent, faintly stridulent rustle of palimpsest inscribed
within the female landscape is reinscribed here in three violent severing
movements: a sudden drop, a breaking up, a heaving. The hearty interac-
tions within the close hives seem diminutive in scope and significance
compared with the vast and various discontents manifest in the surrounding landscape, the heaving and shivering laboring to produce beautiful but
unseen shadows, the constant reformation and rustling of "heaps and
heaps" in agonies of misguided housekeeping.

Within this vast and secretive land, the story itself first emerges in the
form of a gleaming fragment, the red flag of a frozen woman's dress: "[H]e
saw the gleam of red in the woman's dress, and found her at last, lying on
her side, sealed in the crystal, rising as ice rises to the surface of choked
streams."[13] This vitally colored piece, the storyteller finds, cannot be dis-
arranged, for when she tried to tell the tale at a formal dinner, "it had a
garish sound." The immersion in salt seals and suspends meaning. Like
many of Austin's narratives that center on the desire to slake thirst, in this
story the evocation of water occurs through a comparison that emphasizes
its absence; the woman is frozen forever, "choked" and silent, like Lot's
wife, in a strangely transfigured baptism, "rising *as* ice rises to the surface
of choked streams."[14] The gerund keeps her moving even as she eternally
resists narration ("I never tried telling it again"). What little does get told,
to us, a more intimate, less "disdainful" and "politely incredulous" audience, shows us how Austin infuses the metonymic with imaginative power,
with the potency of the potsherd to recall more than the whole. Picasso,
showing a visitor his collection of Egyptian sculptures, pointed out a broken piece, "a very striking foot," and explained that he had no need of the
rest of the statue: "There's all of Egypt in that foot."[15]

Small pieces can be used to recall larger frameworks of meaning;
Austin's style deploys many such economical methods. This economy is

often gendered, as in her description of a woman's story, with its emotional omissions: "A man's story like that is always so much more satisfactory because he tells you all the story there is, what happened to him, and how he felt about it, supposing his feelings are any part of the facts in the case; but with a woman it is not so. She never knows much about her feelings, unless they are pertinent to the story, and then she leaves them out."[16] The power of absence is also affirmed in the way Austin defers physical encounters, particularly in "The Walking Woman," in which she restages the meeting between the narrator and her subject, beginning again and again in tidal rhythms of surge and withdrawal that slowly work toward mutual awareness of loss. Instead of a very "satisfactory" man's story, the story of the women reads as an investigation of the desire for reciprocity and satisfaction. As in *Thelma and Louise,* the pursuit occurs and seems to end within a timeless space marked only by the boundaries of its own emptiness, and defined by the implied possibilities for filling it with narrative and meaning.

Austin's stories encode empty spaces with conditional invitations for the reader's own landmarks. "The Hopi experiences space with his entire body, with his senses of touch, smell, and hearing; he knows how long the trail is because he has felt it under his feet. For him, space is also a matter of memory, personal and cultural."[17] If body and memory define space, then no two journeys or readings are the same: there is always the rider's physical awareness and memory of time and space (am I returning? am I arriving? have I been here before? what do I remember?) to mark the landscape with inner meaning. In *Earth Horizon,* Austin offers a vision of women suspended in the timeless space of the desert, a space marked with physical, gendered rhythms and cultural significance:

[I]t was the timeless space that held [the men]. With the women it was not so; they felt, as they hung there suspended between hopes that refused to eventuate, life slipping away from them. For women have "times"; the short recurrent rhythm of well-being, the not-to-be evaded times of birth, the climaxes of their racial function, the effacing hand of Time across their charm, which points inescapably the periods within which experience is available. Herein I am persuaded is rooted their special gift of foresight; time anticipated to account for their primary contribution to society of organization, times unfulfilled to reckon for their restlessness.[18]

The radical economies of Austin's compositions defy the charge of "blank pages," however, for her codes dictate the rules of access and inscription. The repetition of "if, then" sentence constructions, for example, emphasizes the conditional nature of both Austin's landscapes and her tales, as well as their dependence on the reader's imagination or persistence or degree of susceptibility. "If you cut very deeply into any soul that has the mark of the land upon it, you find such qualities as these"; and "you will look long without finding the places where things happened in them unless you are susceptible to those influences that contribute to the fixed belief of the mining countries," she says in *Lost Borders*.[19] But it is in "The Land of Little Rain" (from the book of the same title) that she explicitly connects the persistence of dwelling in the desert, and its land glyphs, with composition: "In all the Western desert edges there are essays in miniature at the famed, terrible Grand Canon, to which, if you keep on long enough in this country, you will come at last."[20] Here, the term *essays* retains both meanings— "trial" and "composition"—and Austin's long sentences, with their repetitions, submergence of the multiple subjects, and deferment of action, re-create the "lotus charm" of the desert: "They trick the sense of time, so that once inhabiting there you always mean to go away without quite realizing that you have not done it."[21]

The rhythms of her writing, like the land, invite revisiting and often mimic the ebb and flow of waves on the shore. "Here . . ." the voice says, again and again. The repeated declaratives deposit images at the same time that they pull back to show what isn't there.[22]

Here you find the hot sink of Desert Valley, or high rolling districts where the air has always a tang of frost. Here are the long heavy winds and breathless calms on the tilted mesas where dust devils dance, whirling up into a wide, pale sky. Here you have no rain when all the earth cries for it, or quick downpours called cloud-bursts for violence. A land of lost rivers, with little in it to love; yet a land that once visited must be come back to inevitably.[23]

What satisfies, in terms of rhythm and production, land and text, is "to pass and repass" through space in a complex and balanced pattern of giving and taking, and to take pleasure in the vastness of the traversed territory: "In that country . . . it is possible to live with great zest, to have red blood and delicate joys, to pass and repass about one's daily performance an area that would make an Atlantic seaboard State."[24] The passings also suggest a different kind of crossing. In *Earth Horizon,* she says, "There is something in Mary which comes out of the land; something in its rhythms, its living compulsions."[25] That autobiography writes itself as a coming out; in that "country" of the text it is possible to "have red blood *and* delicate joys": to move and speak from within masculine and feminine positions, voices, and metaphors. Her landscape descriptions do not paint a picture of how the land looks to an observer; she shows us *how* the land *looks,* as an observer. She fashions her inner self repeatedly as a "roving [and androgynous] mind's eye" that takes its rhythmic cues from the land.[26] Her first glimpse of Kansas, for example, turns that sight into an intimate ride, thrilling in its "vastness" and its quality of suspension:"the vast roll of the prairies like the suspended breathing of a huge earth creature . . . the rhythmic . . . movement."[27] Her tales re-cover ground to emphasize the pleasure of the process, to make economic use of language and energy, to re-present her visions with a difference, and to reveal the nature of the subject through the rhythms of its existence in her sentences.

Austin's prose takes its rhythms from what is heard as well as what is seen. "The Woman at the Eighteen-Mile" conveys the power of audition to structure a space: "Consider how still it was . . . not a leaf to rustle, not a bough to creak. No grass to whisper in the wind, only stiff, scant shrubs and the sandy hills like shoals at the bottom of a lake of light."[28] "*Not* a leaf to rustle, *not* a bough to creak. *No* grass to whisper" conjures both the image and the sound at the same time that it obscures them. What *is* there is "stiff, scant . . . sandy" and submerged, and her alliteration literally hushes us with her *sshh* even as it invites us to make sounds. And the most valuable elements, like springs, are always in some way buried within or figure as final destinations.

The narrator of "The Woman at the Eighteen-Mile" speaks of tracking a much-desired story like a water source; even her own presence ebbs and flows between "waking and sleeping" as she follows the trail of talk:

> Then I heard of the story again between Red Rock and Coyote Holes, about moon-set, when the stage labored up the long gorge, waking to hear the voices of the passengers run on steadily with the girding of the sand and the rattle of harness chains, run on and break and eddy around Dead Man's Springs, and back up in turgid pools of comment and speculation, falling in shallows of miner's talk, lost at

last in a waste of ledges and contracts and forgotten strikes. Waking
and falling asleep again, the story shaped itself of the largeness of the
night.[29]

The babbling brook spawns the story that is woven even as the Woman at
the Eighteen-Mile literally lets down her hair. Her confidences, however,
give us only glimpses of the ostensible story in her ellipses: "I said . . . and
he did . . . the Indian went . . ."[30] But, like the narrator, we invest ourselves
instead in *her* story.

Through layers of retrospect, repetition, and deferment, Austin sustains
a precarious control over vast and intimate spaces. There are four levels
within the woman's reiteration—the romance, the parting, the man's
death, and his wife's letter. The connections between the woman and the
man are forged through repetition and distance: the dailiness of working
side by side, without touching. In an hour that should have been one of
fulfillment, he consummates the relationship instead with "the strangest
good-bye." The woman hears of his death a week later, in a letter sent by
his wife.

As the Woman at Eighteen-Mile re-presents the experience, we "hear"
it for the first time with her listener, but curiously, the story is composed
as a retrospective that insists on our participation in a remembrance. The
woman's repetition of the man's words, in which she repeats the key phrase
with a meaningful difference, emphasizes the presence of the awareness of
loss: a moment that is known to be gone even as it occurs.

> "He took my hand and held it against his breast so—and said—Oh,
> I am perfectly sure of the words; he said, 'I have *missed* you so.' Just
> that, not good-bye, and not shall miss you, but 'I *have* missed you *so.*'
> Like that," she said, her hands still clasped above her wasted bosom,
> the quick spirit glowing through it like wine in a turgid glass—"like
> that," she said.[31]

The woman alters the emphasis from the verb to its auxiliary and modi-
fier, to those elements surrounding the act of lacking, to include herself,
perhaps, in the retrospective awareness, and, with the new emphasis on
"so," heightening the emotional intensity of the loss for both of them. We
look with the narrator's eyes through the woman, past the wasted bosom
to the glowing spirit within; and the desired connection, between the

woman and the man, is desired again, through the storytelling itself. As Marilynne Robinson says in her novel *Housekeeping,* "And here again is a foreshadowing—the world will be made whole. For to wish for a hand on one's hair is all but to feel it. So whatever we may lose, very craving gives it back to us again."[32]

The woman scorns the summative letter that contains the thrice-removed report of the man's final words ("[I]t was a very nice letter; she said he told her I had been kind to him"), for she knows that the nature of desire is that it is not satisfied.[33] This was no "vulgar adventure of satiety and desertion,"[34] for the story in itself continually nourishes her against the backdrop of desert nothingness: "The story was all she had, absolutely all of heart-stretching, of enlargement and sustenance."[35] The marked figure of the woman is striking in its incongruous vitality; her body remembers and transforms the blank space:

> Curiously, long before I learned of her connection with the story, I had known and liked her for a certain effect she had of being warmed and nourished from within . . . a vitality that had nothing, absolutely nothing, but the blank occasionless life of the desert to sustain it. . . . She had the desert mark upon her—lean figure, wasted bosom, the sharp, upright furrow between her eyes, the burned, tawny skin, with the pallid streak of the dropped eyelids. . . . And still the Woman's soul was palpitant and enkindled.[36]

Like "The Woman at the Eighteen-Mile," "The Walking Woman" begins with a tale heard. A study herself in the nature and meanings of suspension, the Walking Woman reveals the explicit attachments that allow her to move about freely just below sight lines; her position suggests a temporary cessation or abeyance of service. Access to the land and to the woman occurs only by traveling/reading across great stretches of space and time, and Austin carefully emphasizes the maddening, tantalizing elusiveness of the Walking Woman herself:

> The first time of my hearing of her was at Temblor. We had come all one day between blunt, whitish bluffs rising from mirage water, with a thick, pale wake of dust billowing from the wheels, all the dead wall of the foothills sliding and shimmering with heat, to learn that the Walking Woman had passed us somewhere in the dizzying dimness,

going down to Tulares on her own feet. We heard of her again in the Carrisal, and again at Adobe Station, where she had passed a week before the shearing, and at last I had a glimpse of her at the Eighteen-Mile House as I went hurriedly northward on the Mojave stage.[37]

Again, the story must wait, and the deferment and repetition of the story become the story, the vital aesthetic and pleasurable elements of its composition. "Getting a glimpse" and an interview, finding "a time of leisure and isolation," are the ostensible goals of the pursuit, but what finally occurs complicates the narrator's and our vision of both composition and time sense. The story and figure of the Walking Woman are composed with conventional elements of western narrative formula, according to Faith Jaycox—with the classic tension between the "noble outlaw" and the community.[38] But Austin unbalances the conventional formula by mediating the tension between the pursuers and the pursued, qualifying our access to the Walking Woman until we are unsure who is moving away from whom. The Walking Woman was "lifted out of white, hot desertness" and put down "at the crossing of unnamed ways"—the construction curiously lacks agency—and the narrator qualifies every reference to her much in the way an investigator documents sources of evidence: the testimony of witnesses, hearsay, alibis, and physical clues.[39] Her behavior and reputation are evaluated within the estimates of particular audiences, "immediate" audiences, and certain "canons" or codes, and the narrator does not hesitate to enumerate the contradictions she encounters.

The reports sketch an ambiguous picture of a woman constantly on the move, intriguingly difficult to find yet not fugitive. Her wandering ways are constructed not as a retreat but as a trail too tantalizing not to follow—a curious *cherchez la femme* format in which the woman has "short hair and a man's boots, and . . . a fine down all over her face from exposure to weather."[40] The description of the narrator's desire to spend time with the woman becomes a story about the nature of desire itself. As in music, the suspension or holding back creates a temporary dissonance. The staccato sentences that interrogate and interrupt themselves, that twist, hitch, and limp, become smoother, more sustained, as they reveal evidence of the subject's and the narrator's insight:

She had a twist to her face, some said; a hitch to one shoulder; they averred she limped as she walked. But by the distance she covered she should have been straight and young. As to sanity, equal incertitude. On the mere evidence of her way of life she was cracked; not quite broken, but unserviceable. Yet in her talk there was both wisdom and information, and the word she brought about trails and water-holes was as reliable as an Indian's.[41]

The narrative voice values the "talk" that weaves the story, as in "The Woman at the Eighteen-Mile." "Like Twain," Melody Graulich says, "Austin learned to imitate oral storytelling, to let stories wander, to tie them together by letting the narrator draw the conclusion about the story told. In early collections like *The Land of Little Rain* and *Lost Borders,* she developed her voice as a writer by acknowledging her role as a storyteller, by not trying to disappear, by emphasizing her relationship to her material."[42] The writer, the narrator, and the subject occupy a space that may at first seem to be neutral, a nexus or crossing of contradictions, an in-betweenness that may be considered at once androgynous, acultural, raceless, and therefore "unserviceable"—not to be located or used. The women do not try to disappear; their absences are not sustained; and the relationships between the women and the material function both to reveal and to protect their stories and their landscape.

The long-awaited interview with the Walking Woman occurs within a landscape and language of contradiction that use images of fluidity to negotiate these crossings of meaning. "It was a Warm Spring in the Little Antelope I came upon her in the heart of a clear forenoon," the narrator says. The landscape of decay, waste, lamentation, and lameness in which the narrator finds the object of her quest contrasts sharply with the "genius of talk [that] flows as smoothly as the rivers of mirage" during the interview. "First you come upon a pool of waste full of weeds of a poisonous dark green, every reed ringed about the water-level with a muddy white incrustation. Then the three oaks appear staggering on the slope, and the spring sobs and blubbers below them in ashy-colored mud."[43] The narrator explains the meaning of this contrast when she says, "You are not to suppose that in my report of a Borderer I give you the words only, but the full meaning of the speech. Very often the words are merely the punctuation of thought; rather, the crests of the long waves of inter-communicative silences."[44] Naming the Walking Woman as a Borderer for the first time, and herself as reporter, she informs us of the discrepant space between self-expression and its mediation through the perceptions of another: the "inter-communicative"—the crossing—allows "the full meaning" for the vision larger than one original source.

The narrative subject begins to narrate, the composer becomes the composition, and both women become walking women; both are story, title, and subject. The text diffuses its attention between speaker and the one spoken of, and alters convention to speak with a doubled perspective. The reported "twist" in the Walking Woman's face, "a sort of natural warp or skew into which it fell when it was worn merely as a countenance, but which disappeared the moment it became the vehicle of thought or feeling," metonymically evokes the concept of cultural masks—those constructed effects we come to wear "naturally"—and also the power of narrative to create and destroy.[45] Picasso erased the face of Gertrude Stein in his famous portrait of her and replaced it with an image reminiscent of an African tribal mask. When told that the new face looked nothing like Stein, he replied, "It will." "The Walking Woman" becomes a countertext about seizing the means by which women are represented, and then about walking and even wandering around in the space between the myths of what it has come to mean to be a Woman.

Seizing and occupying this space requires the syntactical suspension of traditional boundaries of time and space: in order to dwell on the nature and beauty of the transient and temporary, that which comes and goes, Austin creates a continuous present through constant recurrence, beginning again and again, restaging the meeting between the two women over and over, continually deferring the desired moment.

A sandstorm in "a dateless spring" is the obscure setting for the telling of "the first of the experiences the Walking Woman had found most worth while."[46] In this largely nonverbal episode of violent winds, in which all words are "broken and small,"[47] the Walking Woman narrates the wordless connection between herself and the shepherd as she simultaneously forms an increasingly intimate connection with the narrator-turned-listener, until her companion, too, is reduced to a wordless cry:

"And we had saved the flock together. We felt that. There was something that said together, in the slope of his shoulders toward me. It was around his mouth and on the cheek high up under the shine of his eyes. And under the shine the look—the look that said, 'We are of one sort and one mind'—his eyes that were the color of the flat water in the toulares—do you know that look?"

"I know it."

"The wind had stopped and all the earth smelled of dust, and Filon understood very well that what I had done with him I could not have done so well with another. And the look—the look in the eyes—"

"Ah-ah—!"

I have always said, I will say again, I do not know why at this point the Walking Woman touched me.[48]

The woman's story mirrors the wordless connections between the subjects of her tale (Filon and herself) and the subjects of Austin's tale (the walking women), and with that connection, time becomes not only suspended but "encompassing." In "some flash of forward vision, encompassing the unimpassioned years, the stir, the movement of tenderness were for *me*."[49] The fluid boundaries between narration, mediacy, and representation are further articulated through the landscape itself when the Walking Woman expresses desired things: to work together, to love together, and to have a child. In the silent pause that follows, Austin repeats liquid metaphors: "There ensued a pause of fullest understanding, while the land before us *swam* in the noon, and a dove in the oaks behind the spring began to call. A little red fox came out of the hills and lapped delicately at the pool."[50] Water and movement are linked in a narrative about transience: the love that did not last, the baby who "had not stayed long enough." The story also celebrates the importance of valuing those temporary intimacies that form the very nature of desire: "taken as it came, not picked over and rejected if it carried no obligation of permanency . . . not to wait upon a proper concurrence of so many decorations that the event may not come at all."[51] Austin manages to articulate and embody this slippery space between what is considered naturally good and culturally right for women through this representation of women temporarily released from such constructions.

Today, at the end of the twentieth century, we are still haunted by the image of two women suspended within the desert landscape. The canyon of timeless space has become one of the central preoccupations of modern literature, as an excerpt from T. S. Eliot's "Burnt Norton" (1943) illustrates:

At the still point of the turning world, Neither flesh nor fleshless; Neither from nor towards; at the still point, there the dance is, but neither arrest nor movement.[52]

The space between the "neithers" and "nors" is defined solely by its own nothingness, and the proliferation of prepositions seeks to locate the timeless space through links with what surrounds it. This, too, is writing from the country of lost borders. "I had long wished to write a story of Death Valley that should be its final word," writes Austin, "so charged with the still ferocity of its moods that I should at length be quit of its obsession, free to concern myself about other affairs."[53] Charging the landscape with the language of suspension, Austin writes our way toward alternative narratives that confront the tremendous potential of blank and unhoused spaces with her own still ferocity and that track sentences in the direction of the burnished and tender horizon.

NOTES

1. Linda Nochlin, *Women, Art and Power: And Other Essays* (New York: Harper and Row, 1988), 93.

2. Austin "deliberately disorients her readers and gets us lost. . . . The cues that help us find our way in conventional narrative appear to be missing" (Marjorie Pryse, introduction to *Stories from the Country of Lost Borders* [New Brunswick: Rutgers University Press, 1987], xxi).

3. Elizabeth Duvert, "With Stone, Star and Earth: The Presence of the Archaic in the Landscape: Visions of Georgia O'Keeffe, Nancy Holt, and Michelle Stuart," in *The Desert Is No Lady: Southwestern Landscapes in Women's Writing and Art,* ed. Vera Norwood and Janice Monk (New Haven: Yale University Press, 1987), 199.

4. Lynda Hart, "'Til Death Do Us Part: Impossible Spaces in *Thelma and Louise*," *Journal of the History of Sexuality* 4.3 (1994): 430-31.

5. The vexing question of the missing or reluctant mother, whose power becomes magnified in absentia, and the daughter's paradoxical and often self-destructive quest to sever and reestablish their connection is more specifically addressed in Tara Jeanne Hart, *Tender Horizons: The American Landscapes of Austin and Stein* (Ann Arbor: UMI Microform, 1996). Late twentieth-century writers such as Cynthia Ozick, Marilynne Robinson, Kathryn Harrison, Susanna Kaysen, and Jane Smiley indicate that American women are still composing answers to the question and that this investigation of the suspended space continues.

6. Judith Fryer, "Desert, Rock, Shelter, Legend: Willa Cather's Novels of the Southwest," in Norwood and Monk, eds., *The Desert Is No Lady,* 29.

7. Mary Austin, *A Woman of Genius* (1912; reprint, New York: Arno, 1977), 4-5.

8. Mary Austin, *Stories from the Country of Lost Borders,* ed. Marjorie Pryse (New Brunswick: Rutgers University Press, 1987), 11-12.

9. Ibid., 160.

10. Ibid., 156.

11. "My mistress' eyes are nothing like the sun; / Coral is far more red than her lips' red; / If snow be white, why then her breasts are dun; / If hairs be wires, black wires grow on her head" (Sonnet 130).

12. Austin, *Lost Borders,* 156-57.

13. Ibid., 157.

14. Ibid., 157, emphasis mine.

15. Françoise Gilot and Carlton Lake, *Life with Picasso* (New York: Anchor Books, 1989), 22.

16. Austin, *Lost Borders,* 202.

17. Fryer, "Desert, Rock, Shelter," 28.

18. Mary Austin, *Earth Horizon* (New York: Houghton Mifflin, 1932), 284–85.

19. Austin, *Lost Borders,* 160–61.

20. Ibid., 10.

21. Ibid., 15.

22. Stein, on the other hand, is not "here," but points at the American landscape from afar. "There is no there there," she says.

23. Ibid., 10–11.

24. Ibid., 16.

25. Austin, *Earth Horizon,* 15.

26. Ibid.

27. Ibid., 95.

28. Austin, *Lost Borders,* 206.

29. Ibid., 204.

30. Ibid., 207.

31. Ibid., 209.

32. Marilynne Robinson, *Housekeeping* (New York: Farrar, Straus and Giroux, 1980), 152.

33. Austin, *Lost Borders,* 209.

34. Ibid., 200.

35. Ibid., 210.

36. Ibid., 205.

37. Ibid., 255.

38. Faith Jaycox, "Regeneration through Liberation: Mary Austin's 'The Walking Woman' and Western Narrative Formula," *Legacy: A Journal of Nineteenth-Century American Women Writers* 6.1 (1989): 5–12.

39. Austin, *Lost Borders,* 256.

40. Ibid., 257.

41. Ibid.

42. Melody Graulich, ed., *Western Trails: A Collection of Short Stories by Mary Austin* (Reno: University of Nevada Press, 1987), 22.

43. Austin, *Lost Borders,* 257.

44. Ibid., 258.

45. Ibid.

46. Ibid.

47. Ibid., 259.

48. Ibid., 260.

49. Ibid., 260–61.

50. Ibid., 261.

51. Ibid., 261–62.

52. T. S. Eliot, "Burnt Norton," in *Four Quartets: The Centenary Edition* (San Diego: Harcourt Brace Jovanovich, 1988), 15–16.

53. Austin, *Lost Borders,* 203.

CHAPTER SIX

Between Worlds, Crossing Borders

Mary Austin, Liminality, and the Dilemma of Women's Creativity

ANNA CAREW-MILLER

Like the previous essayists, in "Between Worlds, Crossing Borders," Anna Carew-Miller explores Austin's engagement with modernism, analyzing her efforts to "enter modernity as an artist" in a woman's body, a woman unwilling to suspend or defer her desires and sexuality. Carew-Miller's use of anthropologist Victor Turner's concept of liminal territory provides her with another way of theorizing Austin's border crossings, a trope explored from different vantage points by Tonkovich and DeZur. Carew-Miller brings together the border trope with the spatial metaphors of Tara Hart, arguing that "Austin invokes the potential power as well as dangers of liminality," but ultimately presents the artist figure as "escaping fixity and definition by remaining in a gray area of the border."

Carew-Miller defines Austin's modernist borders through the work of Elizabeth Ammons, who sees turn-of-the-century writers as struggling between identifying themselves with women "writers" or with male "artists." Like Gilbert and Gubar, Carew-Miller wonders how women can "construct a female discursive subjectivity that can successfully counter the power of male narrative authority." While Carew-Miller believes that Austin explores "the space between genders," or androgyny (a border crossing similar to the one described by Tonkovich), as one solution, she finally sees Austin as reconciling her conflicting notions of identity as an artist and a woman. Like Hart, who ultimately believes Austin's suspended sentences reflect her female body by deferring desire, Carew-Miller finally cannot present Austin as rising to Hélène Cixous's challenge—"Your body is yours, take it"—and leaves the reader with questions about how an artist can write from her body without compromising her womanhood.

In the preface to her play *The Arrow-Maker,* Mary Austin claims that she wants to protest "the waste, the enormous and stupid waste, of the gifts of women."[1] Much of the vast body of her work can be read as protesting the struggles creative women faced in being heard, in having a voice in early twentieth-century American culture. This protest motivated her idiosyncratic feminism, her theories about women's creativity, and her exploration of the difficult situation of the woman artist in her autobiographical novel, *A Woman of Genius* (1912); in her play *The Arrow-Maker* (1911); and in her autobiography, *Earth Horizon* (1932). Austin merges the identities of the female genius, artist, and visionary into a single figure or type, the chisera, who struggles with a difficult choice: to live as a woman and be limited to that submissive social role or to live as an androgynous being whose voice has prophetic authority. Austin herself felt a conflict between her roles as woman and artist, a conflict she creatively resolved in her writing. By developing a variety of chisera figures in a number of her works, she attempted to find alternatives to this duality by redefining the status of the artist as an outsider.

Austin understood her own life as marginal because she was a woman writer and because she believed that an artist needed to be different from ordinary people and separate from society in order to be creative.[2] She was certain that a degree of social isolation accompanied the discovery of truth, while conformity limited vision but ensured a place in the community. The very truths the artist had special access to, via her visionary abilities, were those that excited her rejection from the community. These almost mystical powers marked the artist as different. And that, as Austin observes in *Everyman's Genius,* can be a tremendous stigma: "From the early Christian conviction that a work of genius was evidence of your having sold your soul to the devil, down to the present Mainstreetian notion of its being an evidence of your thinking yourself smarter than other people, inhibiting notions have always obstructed the path of genius."[3] Austin used her experience of being cast out from "Main Street" to formulate her notion of the artist's social position as marginal while simultaneously privileging artistic nonconformity and her prophetic abilities. In much of her writing she attempts to transform the artist into a powerful outsider who is not disowned.

Austin transforms marginality into liminality in order to envision a way for her roles as woman and artist to coexist.[4] By placing the artist in a space at the border, Austin invokes the potential power as well as the dangers of *liminality,* which Victor Turner defines as a condition that allows one to "elude or slip through the network of classifications that normally locate positions in cultural space."[5] Western culture often casts artists as liminal figures, and Austin does nothing unusual when she inverts the outcast status of the artist and grants her a position of authority as community prophet. But she interprets the artist figure as liminal not only in terms of her relation to the community but also in terms of her self-construction. In her work, the "network of classifications" that define gender can also become ambiguous in such a space, allowing a woman to elude the social impediments that would silence or diminish her voice.

Thus, Austin chooses to construct the position of the artist as liminal, escaping fixity and definition by remaining in a gray area of the border, between (or across) genders, between visionary and ordinary life. Virginia Woolf shared Austin's belief in the powers of liminality in terms of gender. In *A Room of One's Own,* Woolf states "that it is fatal for anyone who writes to think of their sex. It is fatal to be a man or a woman pure and simple; one must be woman-manly or man-womanly."[6] As a liminal figure, Austin's artist flirts with a kind of bisexuality that allows access to both masculinity and femininity. This is, at times, a liberating strategy for Austin; it frees her voice from the burdens of gender, from the social inhibitions that limit her creativity. By situating artists in this space between genders, Austin eliminates the barriers that prevented her from claiming her authority as a writer.

Liminality also works to remove male artists from social constructions of masculinity. In a rather odd little passage in the manuscript of her book *Christ in Italy* (1912), Austin muses on the instability of gender in artists as she tries to understand the powerful connection she feels with the paintings of several male artists from Renaissance Italy: "I wanted to ask them if my understanding was because I was myself so much more a man, having Made Good, or they being artists were so much the more women."[7] Austin links artists and women in their liminal status as both outcasts and figures of power. By moving all artists into a liminal space and making gender ambiguous, Austin gives herself the potential to acquire male narrative authority.

By placing herself as an artist in a liminal position, however, Austin also risks losing her woman's body and the experiential subjectivity that empowers her work. Unwilling to ignore the woman's body from which she writes, and unwilling to forgo (male) narrative authority, Austin faces the woman writer's dilemma: how to construct a female discursive subjectivity that can successfully counter the power of male narrative authority.[8] For Austin, narrative authority meant success as a writer in the form of public recognition of the value of her work. As she complains in a letter to a friend, however, her most publishable work was often her least satisfying, and she was concerned about producing a "thin, glittering kind of intellectual essay."[9] This concern about superficiality echoes the modernist desire for authenticity shared by men *and* women. However, Austin felt that men could reproduce an authentic version of themselves in their work because their voices were considered the human norm; women were inhibited from being authentic because few people were interested in hearing a woman's voice. Her protagonist in *A Woman of Genius* asserts: "From the earliest I have been rendered highly suspicious of the social estimate of women, by the general social conspiracy against telling the truth about herself."[10] *A Woman of Genius* and *The Arrow-Maker* thoroughly explore this dilemma.

Austin eventually resolved the dilemma when she developed a theory about the differences between men and women that gives women privileged access to creativity. In this theory, liminality allows a cultural reworking of the artist's status and relocates the sources of creativity. Arguing that creativity originates in the connections between mind and body, Austin finds that women are more capable of the liminal movement between mind and body necessary for true creative genius. With her self-construction in *Earth Horizon,* Austin puts this theory to work and succeeds in conceiving the artist as a woman, complete with a female body and capable, at times, of "telling the truth about herself." This persona is a powerful construction, but Austin's own life was too complex to accommodate her own theory, and her dilemma remains imprinted in her final work.

Like other women writing at the turn of the century, Austin often found herself between worlds in terms of narrative authority. Elizabeth Ammons observes that "the earlier generation of [women] fiction writers tried to conceive of authorship as an occupation compatible with the pervasive middle-class feminine ideal of domesticity. They therefore thought of themselves as writers, not artists."[11] They wrote as women, often reproducing their social role as nurturers in the construction of their narrative voice. Writing as an art, and the subjective freedom that implies, was the privilege of men. At the turn of the century, many women writers, including Austin, attempted to cross that gendered boundary and write not as women but as artists, appropriating the power of what had been male narrative authority. Austin's liminal strategies make such border crossings possible.

A Woman of Genius documents the struggle of the gifted woman who attempts to leave the Victorian world of her mother and enter modernity as an artist. Austin's narrative of Olivia's struggle to become an actress exemplifies these tensions, replicating what Marianne Hirsch calls the "female family romance" of the nineteenth century and bringing that plot into the modernist moment with its focus on the life of an artist. Hirsch argues that "the fantasy that controls the female family romance is the desire for the heroine's singularity based on a disidentification from the fate of other women, especially mothers. In modernist plots, this wish is supplemented by the heroine's artistic ambitions and the desire for distinction."[12] Austin calls on that nineteenth-century tradition (found, for example, in Jo in Louisa May Alcott's *Little Women*) and taps into modernist concerns about the development of the woman artist (exemplified by Lily Briscoe in Woolf's *To the Lighthouse*) who wants to be recognized as an artist, not stigmatized as "different."

A Woman of Genius presents the story of a woman struggling between dual identities, caught in a moment of cultural transition. Olivia tells us of the development of her genius and her successful stage career, as well as her conflicts with her mother, her painful marriage, and her love affairs. While Olivia wants to be an artist and to live differently from women like her mother, she does not necessarily want to reject all the familiar social structures and values that her mother's generation embraced. Unlike many of Austin's contemporaries (Mabel Dodge Luhan, for example), Olivia is not quite ready for the revolutionary future envisioned by the Bolsheviks, free-lovers, and other radicals of the 1910s, yet she is not satisfied with women's options of the past. In her view, the only place for a woman artist is on the stage; the world outside it provides her with little space to be herself. Olivia's life reflects Austin's own experience of estrangement, of leaving the traditional woman's life behind and entering a dimly lit realm of progressive politics, sexual freedom, and women's artistic development.

Olivia's struggles as an actress are a thinly disguised version of Austin's perception of her struggles as a writer. Ammons explains that "turn-of-the-century women writers found themselves, often in deep, subtle ways, emotionally stranded between worlds. They floated between a past they wished to leave . . . and a future that they had not yet gained. They were full members neither of their mothers' world, at the one extreme, nor of that of the privileged white male artist, at the other."[13] Olivia lacks both the traditional protections of womanhood and access to the privileges (and authority) of men who are artists. She succeeds when she refuses to act like a woman and acts like an artist instead. Her nonconformity separates her from middle-class culture and the domestic world of women. Her struggles—with her genius, her mother, her lovers—occur when she cannot leave her woman's body and experiences behind her, when she is forced to be woman and artist simultaneously.

Like Austin herself, Olivia believes that what separates her from other women—what distinguishes her as an artist—is her genius, which comes from maintaining the mystical vision of childhood, "the fairy wonder of the world." She explains: "I was not, I think, different in kind from the other children, except as being more consistently immersed in it and never quite dispossessed. . . . [T]his whole business of the biography has no other point . . . than to show you how far my human behaviour has been timed to keep what I believe most people part with no more distressfully than their milk teeth."[14] All children are granted similar abilities, but Olivia (and Austin) is exceptional in her recognition of the value of this childhood vision and her unwillingness to part with it. While Austin relies on the romantic tradition of the artist as child in her notion of the origins of artistic vision, she also moves the artist in the direction of liminality: this child is a presexual being, unencumbered with social expectations of masculinity or femininity, a free and androgynous spirit of genius. Austin views all artists, regardless of their sex, as sharing this visionary capability and being different from other people.

This distinction from ordinary life creates a conflict between the artist and the community. Early in the text, Olivia explains that the story she is relating describes her discovery of her genius and her realization of the conflicts that possessing genius can create for a woman:

I mean to put as plainly as possible how I felt it fumbling at my earlier life like the sea at the foot of a tidal wall, and by what rifts in the structure of living its inundation rose in me; by what practices and passions I was enlarged to it, and by what well meaning of my friends I was cramped and hardened. . . . This is the story of the struggle between a Genius for Tragic acting and the daughter of a County Clerk, with the social ideal of Taylorville, Ohianna, for the villain.[15]

While Olivia labors to understand her own genius, she also must face the disapproval and isolation that come with being a woman artist.

After the deaths of her child and, later, her husband, when Olivia's life takes a different route from her mother's, she realizes that her mother and women like her have access to something that she as an actress does not: the social protections of that single standard and the guidance of normative values. She recalls: "[I]t grew upon me during the days of my mother's illness that there was a kind of intrinsic worth in her which I, with all my powers, must forever and inalienably miss. With it there came a kind of exasperation, never quite to leave me, of the certainty of not choosing my own values, but of being driven with them aside and apart."[16] As a social outcast, Olivia finds herself among a group of people who appear to have no values; the only norms of behavior they share she finds deviant and sinful. By losing the securities of maternity and marriage, Olivia has unintentionally rejected the social values that continue to shape her worldview. She is morally isolated and suffers the loss of the social approval that supported her mother's life.

Olivia's isolation is exacerbated by her feeling that something is missing from her life, in spite of her success as an artist. After considerable professional struggle, she can say: "I was a successful actress, . . . I was well paid and well friended. . . . I was integrally a part of that half-careless, hardworking, well-living crowd so envied of the street. . . . And all the time I wanted something."[17] That "something" is a satisfying relationship. What would help her most, she feels, is the traditional woman's act of giving love. She explains: "For a man, to be loved is of the greatest importance, but with women it is loving that is the fructifying act."[18] Loving would round out her life, complete her genius; but love outside the conventional boundaries has a high price, and love within its confines stifles genius. Her passionate affair with Helmeth Garrett ends when he asks her to choose her art or him. When a fellow artist offers her a companionable marriage without passion at the novel's conclusion, Olivia is ambivalent. Although such a relationship promises security, it does not offer her a true opportunity to give love, the "fructifying act" that would act as a catalyst to her genius. The alternative, being alone, holds freedom but also a terminal loneliness, a life without the caregiving and attention that could have nurtured her art. Olivia's successful exploration of her creativity comes at a high cost.

With Olivia, Austin brings to her readers' attention the difficult situation of women artists: while their lives as artists place them outside the safety of social convention, they continue to be judged by the standards for women established by convention. Austin believed that the pragmatic concerns of artistic life weigh more heavily on women, who need money to avoid scandal more than men do. Austin's resentment of the bourgeois expectation that artists live on passion, not food, is expressed in Olivia's encounters with her comfortable upper-middle-class friends who fail to understand her need for money, a condition aggravated by her gender. On the one hand, women are paid less for doing the same work as men. Years later, Austin wrote of her frustration with this inequity: "I thought women should be free to make their contribution to society by any talent with which they found themselves endowed, and be paid for it at rates equal to the pay of men."[19] On the other hand, women without the protection of marriage need money to make themselves invulnerable to male predators. Out of money, approached by men willing to support her in exchange for sexual favors, Olivia tells her friends that she "fled to them to be saved from what . . . fretted all [her] finer instincts; to be ricocheted by them again on to that reef of moral squalour upon which the artist and woman in [her] were riven asunder."[20] In their bourgeois respectability, her friends fail to understand the impossible position of the woman artist who has neither the security of a husband nor success and wealth. Yet they, like Austin's readers, would be the first to castigate Olivia for failing to uphold Victorian mores.

Male artists, Austin believed, are judged not as men but as artists; they are expected to snub convention and live a life of passion, which qualifies them for membership in the Byronic tradition of artist as rebel. Examining the serial love affairs of her playwright friend, Jerry, Olivia rejects this way of life as unimportant to a woman artist, musing: "It came out for me in these moments that it is after all life that Art needs rather than feeling, and that, to a woman of my capacity, was to be supplied not by innocuous intrigues like Jerry's but by the normal procedure of living."[21] Austin's article "Greatness in Woman" states that "great women are often accused of being masculine in their time . . . and more often than not find it necessary to forego [sic] womanly rewards for the sake of maternal achievement."[22] For Austin, "womanly rewards" include the comforts of a home and family, a respected social position, and financial security—options rarely available to women artists. "Maternal achievement" involves directing one's genius toward social betterment, for the sake of others. Austin suggests here that women do not necessarily reject all aspects of their lives as women when they attempt to achieve something outside the domestic realm; many would like to be both women (as that category has been socially conceived) and artists.

In *A Woman of Genius,* Austin counters the cultural expectation that a woman who wants to achieve in the male realm will leave her body behind her. Society tells her that as an artist she must not be a wife or mother—a sexual being. And yet all the while she is forced to masquerade as a man in a man's world or she will be known as an oddity: a *woman* artist, actress, writer, and so on. In her women's guide to politics, *The Young Woman Citizen,* Austin writes that such women "must be understood as women, higher-powered, deeper-breathing, neither mimics nor angels. The Amazons were not born breastless."[23] Like many of Austin's chiseras, Olivia struggles to live her artist's life within her woman's body. She insists that her lover recognize both aspects of her being: "I'm those two things, a woman and a genius, and the woman was meant for you; don't think I don't know that and am not proud of it with every fibre of my brain and body."[24] While Olivia imagines her body finding a home in the arms of a man, she simultaneously asserts that it belongs onstage as well. In works from this period of Austin's formation as a writer, her depiction of liminality is mixed: androgyny is a fine state of being while performing, perhaps, but it's no way for a woman to live. For Austin, the artist, as a social identity, is still male.

Austin explores liminality more fully with her chisera figures than she does with Olivia, seeking alternatives to androgyny for women artists. But because they are often constructed as American Indian women, these chiseras exist in territory unfamiliar to Austin's readers. According to Melody Graulich, these "strong, prophetic women artists" can be "medicine women, influential women in their tribes; others are outcasts. Some live happily in their independent solitude; others long for human ties."[25] In her preface to *The Arrow-Maker,* Austin defines the Chisera as "simply the Genius, one of those singular and powerful characters whom we are still, with all our learning, unable to account for without falling back on the primitive conception of gift as arising from direct communication with the gods."[26] The Chisera of *The Arrow-Maker* is the most troubled of all Austin's chisera figures; she embodies a number of the tensions that we saw in *A Woman of Genius,* including the conflict an artist feels between communal expectations and individual needs. Like Olivia, her gender only complicates her position.

The Arrow-Maker, Austin's first commercially produced play, came out in 1911 as part of the New York New Theatre's attempt to bring indigenous American drama to the stage. It is based on material Austin collected during her years in rural California. In spite of its title, the play focuses less on Simwa, the arrow-maker, than on his lover, the Chisera. As Karen Langlois observes, the play "shows the close relationship between Mary Austin's personal life and literary work. Her 'authentic' folk play of Indian life was somewhat infused with the dynamics of her own emotions."[27] Austin is less concerned here with giving theatergoers a vision of American Indian life than she is with exploring the problems and possibilities of a gifted woman's relationship to her community and the cost of forcing women to leave their bodies behind when they enter the realm of genius.

The play centers on the Chisera's illicit love for Simwa. As the tribe's prophetess, the Chisera lives apart from the village and is not permitted to marry or have children because, as the elders and tradition have it, such personally satisfying experiences would interfere with her visionary abilities and role as moral guide of tribal affairs. In the first act, the Chisera complains of her isolation to Bright Water, the chief's daughter: "Oh, I am weary of the friendship of the gods! If I have walked in the midnight and heard what the great ones have said, is that any reason I should not know what a man says to a maid in the dusk—or do a kindness to my own kind—or love, and be beloved?"[28] The Chisera is a young woman who feels the stirrings of heterosexual desires, yet because of her enforced liminal status as an androgynous being, she is denied their satisfaction.

Simwa, the arrow-maker, cultivates a relationship with the Chisera, playing on her woman's desires to persuade her to intervene with the gods on his behalf so that he can become skilled in making arrows. As a male artist, he depends on a woman for inspiration and is free to explore his male sexuality—but not with the Chisera. Because he is politically ambitious, he decides to marry the chief's daughter, outraging the Chisera, who appears at their wedding only to cast a curse on their marriage. Simwa denies his former relationship to her and turns the Chisera's accusations against her. Instead of receiving some recompense from Simwa, she is thrust even further outside the community, and for insisting on the desires of her woman's body, she is labeled crazy. Simwa tells the confused tribal elders: "No doubt the woman is both mad and shameless."[29] Because Simwa refuses to acknowledge their former relationship, the Chisera withdraws her protection from the tribe, and their enemies are able to defeat them.

In the final act, the tribal elders confront the Chisera and attempt to force her to resume her position as the tribe's protector. But she refuses any status that insists on the neutrality of her gender, a role neither she nor the women of the tribe understand; she will not be forced into a position intended for men, insisting that she wants "the dole of women. Love and sorrow and housekeeping; a husband to give me children, even though he beat me."[30] Austin seems to be pointing out the Chisera's naïveté in this rather extreme desire: the Chisera equates being a woman with the socially enforced codes for women's behavior, including accepting a beating. At the same time, Austin is indicating that the tribe is wrong for denying the Chisera access to her womanhood, however it is defined.

In the end, the blame for the ruin of the tribe rests on the heads of the elders, who have enforced a code of conduct unsuitable for a woman. The Chisera argues that her powers would have been strengthened had she been allowed to have what ordinary women have: "Did ever a woman serve them [the gods] less because she had dealt with a man? Nay, all the power of a woman comes from loving and being loved, and now the bitterest of all my loss is to know that I have never had it."[31] Like Olivia (and Austin herself) the Chisera claims that women's creativity comes from their capacity to nurture, from "loving and being loved." The play ends with the Chisera's death; she dies because she had the audacity to claim both the desires of her woman's body and her gifts as a seer.

Although audiences of the 1910s may have enjoyed Austin's projection of the romanticized Indian, Austin used her Indians as props for her overtly feminist theme, and the play was a commercial failure. Austin explains its reception in *Earth Horizon*: "It was twenty years in advance of its time."[32] Perhaps she was right; an audience in 1911 probably was not ready to accept the woman artist as a specifically gendered being, as a woman and an artist. But Austin's feminism in *The Arrow-Maker* might raise some questions for contemporary readers. Austin validates the gifted woman as a whole woman, complete with a female body and sexuality, while making the "dole" of woman central to her power and creativity and its denial the source of tremendous pain and anguish. Like Olivia of *A Woman of Genius*, the Chisera seems limited by her body and its desires, bound by the parameters of womanhood. This representation may reflect Austin's own unhappy romantic experiences in New York, where she appears to have lived a sexually liberated but emotionally frustrating life.

Not all of Austin's chisera figures suffer for their desires. Especially in her earlier depictions, such as those in *The Basket Woman* and *The Land of Little Rain,* these figures seem more self-sufficient and less in need of a man, more stoic in their freedom from sexual desire, and more at ease with their liminality. The characteristics of these chiseras might reflect Austin's life during the time she created them; in the early 1900s, she was often separated from her husband and managed to care for her daughter and home by herself. She worked at her writing in the relative isolation of rural California, influenced by Native American spiritual practices and inspired by her own success in publishing her early efforts.

In "The Coyote Spirit and the Weaving Woman," included in *The Basket Woman* (1904), Austin's chisera figure, like that in *The Arrow-Maker*, is isolated from her village because of her extraordinary gifts. She is alone, the narrator explains, "because it was whispered among the wickiups that she was different from other people. It was reported that she had an infirmity of the eyes which caused her to see everything with rainbow fringes, bigger and brighter and better than it was."[33] As Austin makes clear to her readers, however, that "infirmity" is a gift, not an impairment. The woman's difference enables her creative abilities: "There were some who even said it was a pity, since she was so clever at the craft, that the weaver was not more like other people, and no one thought to suggest that in that case her weaving would be no better than theirs."[34] Unlike the Chisera of *The Arrow-Maker*, the Weaving Woman seems to be empowered by her liminal status, and her creativity is nourished by her uniqueness. Because she is not like the rest of the village, she need not fear the dangerous changeling, the Coyote Spirit: "Because she was not afraid of anything, she went farther and farther into the silent places until in the course of time she met the Coyote Spirit."[35] Her separation from the human community is interpreted not as a loss but as the source of her courage and her "fruitful" creativity. Although the Coyote Spirit is a highly charged sexual being (Austin is drawing on the Native American oral tradition of the coyote as a lust-filled trickster), the Weaving Woman is not threatened, because she is not controlled by sexual desire.

A similar figure appears in *The Land of Little Rain*. Seyavi, the Basket Maker, learned to live without men during a time of hardship for the tribe in which she lost her husband and had to care for their child alone. "That was the time Seyavi learned the sufficiency of mother wit, and how much more easily one can do without a man than might at first be supposed."[36] But Seyavi's strength comes from the fact that she is not androgynous; she draws on the experiences of a woman's body (sexuality, motherhood) yet has also prospered in her art, basket making. These American Indian women figures are creative, brave, and resourceful; they are unhampered by the needs and desires of their women's bodies, and they respond to their circumstances out of their "mother wit." Their liminality does not limit them to an existence between borders (as does that of Olivia or the Chisera) but permits them to cross borders, from woman to artist and back to woman. Their position strengthens rather than torments them.

This border-crossing form of liminality reaches its most powerful form in one of Austin's later chiseras, Dulcie Adelaide of *Cactus Thorn,* a novella written in the late 1920s but never published in Austin's lifetime.[37] Like Austin's other chisera figures, Dulcie is a liminal creature, a woman who lives a wanderer's life in the desert. Early on in the novella, when she encounters the man who will become her lover, she is depicted as existing somewhere between the human and the desert. "She might, like the horned lizard starting from under his foot, have assembled herself away from the tawny earth and the hot sand, or at a word resolve herself into the local element."[38] Dulcie's liminality allows her to exist outside the strictures of society, and she lives by her own moral code, which, as she explains to her lover, dictates "a different kind of rightness for different kinds of people."[39] Graulich notes that Dulcie's "philosophy of living sincerely is based on her spiritual integration with the land, and she tests her beliefs against her observations of nature around her."[40] Dulcie's morality, then, is not constructed but natural, in Austin's view, for it is based not on human notions of correctness, but on the natural justice of the desert.

Like the Chisera of *The Arrow-Maker,* Dulcie is spurned by a lover who chooses marriage with a conventional woman over his unlicensed relationship with her. Also like the Chisera, Dulcie confronts her former lover and demands justice for her hurt and rejection. However, Dulcie's personal vision frees her from becoming a victim; rather than being killed for her transgression, she kills the man who betrayed her trust and gets away with it, returning to merge with the desert at the novella's conclusion. Her liminality gives her freedom from the moral code that refuses her justice on her own terms and provides her with a sure sense of her own rightness and the firmness to act on it. In this later version of the chisera story, society is less powerful than the liminal figure; if it is unable to accommodate her, it is also unable to contain her. These last three chiseras have in common their ability to create (baskets or morality) according to their experience, to trust their knowledge as women. They are connected to something that Austin believes is more powerful than society's expectations for women, a matrix in which Austin blends women's bodies and nature.

Significantly, Austin's chiseras are frequently American Indian women who, by virtue of their race, were already on the margins of Austin's society and were, according to Austin, less fettered by the demands of that society's construction of femaleness. Austin's Indian women characters were shaped by her contact with Paiute and Shoshone cultures and her observations of women's lives within those tribes. Graulich observes: "Because they were able to merge the domestic life with the self-expressive life of the artist, because they lived so close to nature, which informed their art, because they seemed to unite culture and nature, these women—she called them 'chiseras'—had a powerful influence on Austin."[41] In *Earth Horizon,* Austin recalls learning the meaning of creative work from her early California experiences of visiting the local campody and following the Indian women around as they performed their domestic tasks. "It was in this fashion that she [Austin] began to learn that to get at the meaning of work you must make all its motions, both of body and mind. It was one of the activities which has had continuing force throughout her life."[42] This crucial connection between mind and body as an empowering creative force hints at why Austin repeatedly chose a "primitive" female figure as her emblematic artist. She viewed mind and body as connected best in a natural or "primitive" state, where social inhibitions cannot repress the flow of creativity.

Austin believed that her search—and that of other women artists—for the unity of mind and body caused a tremendous struggle. She could ignore the "social inhibitions" that repressed her creativity only by stepping outside the culture that created them, by adopting the ambiguities of a liminal identity. In her article "Woman Alone" she reminisces: "Being plain and a little 'queer,' it was hoped rather than expected that I would marry. My queerness consisted, at that time, . . . in stoutly maintaining against all contrary opinion that I would some day write."[43] By embracing her "queerness," or liminality, Austin gave herself a choice in her professional identity. She could choose to participate in a masquerade, leaving her woman's body to cross genders at times: "When I was a girl the great desire of every mother was that her daughter should turn out to be a perfect lady. Well, after twenty-five or thirty years of successful professional work, I find it hasn't always been possible to be all that, in my mother's day, being a perfect lady implied. But I have always found it possible to be a gentleman."[44] The male code provided a norm of behavior that allowed her to function as a professional writer, the male domain in which she found herself after successfully pursuing her gifts. Although liminality permitted her some flexibility in her self-construction as an artist, it complicated the process of finding her voice as a woman, of unifying mind and body.

But Austin never relinquished her desire to merge her identities as woman and artist, to write from a union of mind and body. In much of her nonfiction writing she theorizes about the difference between males and females, reevaluating what has been considered female and finding these very qualities conducive to creativity.

> There was a human norm, and it was the average man. Whatever in woman differed from this norm was a female weakness, of intelligence, of character, of physique. If the difference was in a direction pleasing to men, in charm, in humble-mindedness, in complaisance and provocation, it was counted to her credit. . . . Every sort of temperamental and intellectual divergence was judged a more or less successful attempt at provocation; and every variation from the male rhythm was a sickness.[45]

Women's differences were treated as monstrosities or abnormalities unless they conformed to the (male) construction of femininity. But, Austin insists, there exists for every woman, underneath this construction, a distant memory of a primal power that connects women to the spirit of the earth: "Among millions of modern women the cosmos still works, the wokonda [spirit] of the earth is a felt activity. But among other millions these influences have been cut off by the intervention of the falsely flattering persuasion of their ladyhood."[46] If only women would reject their status as ladies, Austin believed, they could gain access to "primitive" women's power, a power based on the union of mind and body that the chisera, as an artistic ideal, represents.

Austin attempted to circumvent the obstacles that inhibit this union by redefining the creative mind as female. Using herself as a model, Austin set up women's intuitive abilities in opposition to a certain rationality she ascribed to men. In *Experiences Facing Death,* she asserts that "logic" and "scientific patter" are "little more than ritualizations of the male approach."[47] Scientists, she says, cannot recognize the validity of intuition and mystical insight as a source of knowledge because, for them, data count only when the experiment or experience is repeatable. As the male language of rationality, science cannot accommodate what Austin would like to express: "[T]he felt experience of life must, in any conclusion of mine, always take precedence of the orthodoxies of science. . . . The Creative Factor in the universe does not work like a scientist who knows nothing and has it all to prove and find out, but like a novelist who knows it all, and strives only to arrange what he knows in patterns that will best display its attributes, its inwardness, its truth."[48] "The Creative Factor," Austin's term for a spiritual wellspring of creativity (and, perhaps, another of Austin's many terms for God) works like a novelist, from subjective knowledge. Austin elevates intuitiveness over rationality, subjectivity over objectivity; by moving creativity out of the male domain, she comes close to claiming it as naturally female.

Austin opposes the "male approach" with a female approach that is distinctively subjective and intuitive, able to comprehend the larger matters of existence. She explains: "But I am still far from admitting that the experienceable issues of life can be dealt with only, or properly at all, by the male ritual. . . . [W]e might understand both the pattern of evolution and the pattern of the good life better if we . . . studied the ritual of life processes. . . . Deep within the womb of life there may be activities going on. . . . I am at least aware of processes going on within myself."[49] The wisdom of women comes from the experience of "the ritual of life processes," and women's cyclic experience of their biology brings them closer to an understanding of human existence that relies not on measurable data but on an intuitive understanding of the female self. This biological body in its reproductive capacity—"the womb of life"—is naturally creative. In theory, Austin resolves the dilemma of women's creativity by inverting the value placed on their bodies, the same bodies that had undermined their authority in patriarchal culture.

Austin's pronouncements on women's creative capacities should be read as an oppositional strategy, a means of subverting male narrative authority. Her views of gender difference are far more complex, however. In her philosophical novel *Love and the Soul Maker,* she does not essentialize gender difference. There is no such person as the "wholly masculine" man or the "essentially feminine" woman.[50] There is really no clear formula for being a woman, she says; the only sure thing is that women are potentially as gifted as men. She goes on to say: "In this mutual crowding of the sexes into utterly untenable attitudes women have suffered the most. It is natural that from women as a class should come the most spirited rebellion. It is purely incidental that the struggle has shaped about the contest for political equality. Under all forms, the right women are fighting for is the right to be themselves."[51] Austin's views were very much in keeping with the "phenomenon of female avant-garde self assertion" of the 1910s.[52] By making intellectual creativity a female quality, Austin hoped that women writers could put aside the masquerade and "be themselves."

With her theory of women's privileged access to the creative matrix of mind and body, Austin appears to resolve the dilemma of the woman artist;

but theories are not always a sufficient response to the complexities of living. As certain as Austin was that her femaleness gave her the authority to create, she was equally certain that a woman's body was a liability for an artist in her culture. Her final attempt to reconcile the tensions between woman and artist can be found in her autobiography, *Earth Horizon*. This text is partially narrated by I-Mary, a powerfully liminal female persona. Like Austin's stronger chiseras, I-Mary is not androgynous; she bases her authority in her female body, yet easily crosses into the domain of the artist. I-Mary tells the story of Austin's development and success as a writer.

Earth Horizon also includes the story of Mary-by-herself, a persona that can be read as the aspects of femaleness that Austin wanted to reject, the version of femininity institutionalized in Victorian culture—the woman constrained by weakness, doubt, failure, and emotional needs. This voice appears also in the texts of her unpublished poetry and letters, and, in spite of Austin's attempts to filter it out, in glimpses and snatches in *Earth Horizon*. Graulich observes in her afterword that Mary-by-herself is "partially the poignant offspring of Austin's conflicted relationship with her mother, partially the outcast from social constructions of femininity that left her feeling as if she had failed as a woman."[53] While Austin names Mary-by-herself, she does not grant her much narrative space—except to recognize that persona as part of her past—and pushes her voice to the periphery of *Earth Horizon*.

I-Mary first comes on the scene before Austin can even read: "Mother was kneading the bread and Jim was studiously reciting his ABCs. At the other corner of the bread board, Mary was busy with a bit of pinched off dough and looking over his shoulder. 'A,' said Jim and 'O.' 'O,' said Mary, making her mouth the shape of the mark. Presently Jim pointed out 'I.' 'Eye?' said Mary, plumping one floury finger on her own. 'No,' said Mother, 'I, myself, I want a drink, I-Mary.'"[54] Austin establishes I-Mary as a reasoning, verbal persona connected to words and writing, equated with Austin's emerging identity as a writer.

Austin found her "true" voice while writing a description of the Hunter family's journey to the Tejon Valley in California when she was about twenty. She tells us that "Mary wrote an account of that journey, a few weeks afterward, for her college journal, in which all the derived and imitative influence of academic training fell away, and she wrote for the first time directly, in her own character, very much as she did in 'The Land of Little Rain.'"[55] After years of slow formation in the desert, this voice was put to work by Austin, who had recently married and was pregnant for the first time. She describes writing her first two short stories: "At any rate, it was as I-Mary walking a log over the creek, that Mary-by-herself couldn't have managed, that I wrote two slender little sketches."[56] Here we discover that it is I-Mary who has the confidence to transgress the male realm of the western sketch and write her own stories of the land. Austin's liminal identity as an artist (which she labels I-Mary) is bisexual, not wholly derived from male academic traditions, not burdened by the femininity of Mary-by-herself, but as certain of her female subjectivity as she is of her authority to write.

Critical to her development as a writer were Austin's experiences in the desert and mountains of southeastern California. As in the Old Testament tradition, Austin posits herself as a spiritual seeker in the desert, and her wise men are the medicine men and women with whom she talks. She reveals how a midwestern Victorian woman was able to turn away from her origins to construct herself anew. She insists that "nothing that happened to her in the ten years of Methodism prevented her from making use of salvation where she found it. . . . Mary did, as the major business of this story is to show, finally shed all the moralities that interfered with her soul."[57] Conventional religion and Victorian morals bound her creativity; Indian spirituality releases it. Contact with Indian culture helps Austin discover how "the cosmos" still works in her body, moving her further from her identity as Mary-by-herself, closer to her liminal identity as an artist, as I-Mary.

Creativity for I-Mary (as well as for other women artists) originates in her abilities as a mystic and seer; she tells us, "I kept it up, the foreknowledge, the clairvoyant seeing, for a long time."[58] Like Olivia, Austin posits the origins of her powers as a visionary in her childhood when she experienced God as a feeling of wonder and unity under the walnut tree in the meadow behind her house. Although this feeling evaded her during her young womanhood, she recaptures it in the desert: "On a morning Mary was walking down one of these [trails], leading her horse, and suddenly she was aware of poppies coming up singly through the tawny, crystal-sanded soil, thin, piercing orange-colored flames. And then the warm pervasive sweetness of ultimate reality, the reality first encountered so long ago under the walnut tree."[59] This is what gives her the powers of observation, the stamina for writing, the intuitive sense that allows her to discern the true meaning of all she sees. I-Mary's abilities as a mystic permit her, she believes, to discern the truth.

I-Mary's vision reveals the shape of Austin's own life and the shape of the world in which she lived—the society she both resisted and longed to be part of: "Up to this point the writer has done her work badly if you are not prepared to accept the major premise that Mary was more susceptible to ideas fermenting in the social atmosphere than to purely personal intimations of destiny."[60] She must transcribe her experience of mystically acquired knowledge textually: "She would be looking at something that all the world could see, had seen, without being stirred by it, and suddenly, from deep down, there would come a fountain jet of recognition ... often it would be new in the thought of her time."[61] Always in advance of her time, I-Mary insists she was misunderstood and misinterpreted, appreciated only later. Both what she sees and her means of expressing herself run counter to society's expectations. Mystical insight gives her "a more direct intuitional attack" and permits her to stand apart from the "male ritual of rationalization" of her society. I-Mary uses her female body—its experiences and insights—as a creative resource rather than suffering this body as a liability. She is similar to the powerful chiseras Austin created earlier in her career, finding in liminality the ability to cross boundaries of time and culture rather than being caught between them.

If we read for the story of Mary-by-herself, we find Austin's self-perception more troubled. The confidence of I-Mary is countered by fears of failure and a need for outside support. An early letter to her editor at Houghton Mifflin concerning her work on *The Flock* (1906) betrays this anxiety:

> You may put it down to the account of my isolated situation, or to pure femininity if you like, but, frankly, I cannot write without some point of attachment to the outside world of Art. I do well enough in touch with it, but as soon as the connection is broken I begin to faint. I would not be surprised if I still have to write to you about it occasionally until it is off my hands. It is so important to me to have some one looking over my shoulder.[62]

Austin needs to be part of a community of artists because she is a woman and cannot create alone. Her work, she decides in a letter to her friend Mabel Dodge Luhan, is an excuse to avoid the unhappiness of her personal life: "I get no light anymore. All my strength goes into trying to keep my work going. You see for years I have been hollow—emptied of all the things that make the personal life of woman, writhing into work and more work to keep from knowing how unhappy I was."[63] The voice of Mary-by-herself reveals that rather than providing personal fulfillment, Austin's writing was driven by the desire to silence the demons of a painful private existence.

Austin's identity as a writer was not simply the voice of the prophet on paper; it was a necessity, her only way of making a living. Written work was cash, a point driven home in Helen MacKnight Doyle's description of a visit to Austin in Santa Fe: "She took me into her writing room, a large, bare den with a businesslike desk and typewriter. Off this room was a vault where notes and manuscripts were neatly filed, tier on tier. 'This is my bank account,' she announced. 'This will see me through.'"[64] Although Austin felt plenty of economic pressure while she was married because of her husband's lack of business sense, she felt even more as a single woman after her separation and divorce. Her husband provided no financial assistance, and she was forced to support herself, which she did by writing. But using her creativity for economic support was a kind of catch-22 for Austin. A letter to Luhan expresses her need for economic security in order to be creative: "All the things I want could be secured by money. What I want is a permanent home, a resting place for my affections. If my heart was at rest I know that I could do better creative work."[65] But Austin had to create in order to build the home in which creativity could be fostered.

Austin did eventually succeed in building that home for herself in Santa Fe. She may even have found a "resting place" for her affections among her many friends and her niece, who was often with her during her last years. Yet, in *Earth Horizon,* Mary-by-herself hints at Austin's loneliness and reveals her rejection from her family as well as the lack of love and recognition she needed from her emotionally distant mother. If we read carefully, we can hear Mary-by-herself tell us that she was an unwanted child. Taking her mother's point of view, she explains: "It was plain to the wife of the half-invalided and not yet-established attorney, with one seriously ailing child on her hands, that another was not desired, was not, in fact, wanted."[66] Austin was haunted by the presence of Mary-by-herself until the end of her career. Shadowed by doubts and uncertainty, she longed for love and acceptance.

Mary Austin spent most of her professional life struggling to make peace between the woman she was expected to be and the artist she knew she was. She found life in the liminal territory that she carved out for herself both painfully isolating and liberating. Even though Austin's conception fluctuated from a position of being between worlds to the more powerful notion of liminality as the ability to cross boundaries, she never fully ex-

perienced the freedom that position implies. As much as Austin believed
that women are creatively empowered by the experiences of their bodies,
she continued to feel the weight of that body's cultural oppression, her maternal inheritance. These tensions continue to pull at feminist debates
about women's identity and resistance to social constructions. And if
women *could* leave their sense of dividedness behind in their struggles to
create, they might lose the distinctiveness of their voices, for their creations
are marked by these tensions. The power of the voice of I-Mary depends
on the existence of Mary-by-herself.

NOTES

1. Mary Austin, *The Arrow-Maker* (New York: Duffield, 1911), xi.

2. Esther Lanigan, in her biography of Austin, sees this sense of marginality as central to
Austin's self-definition. See Lanigan, *Mary Austin: Song of a Maverick* (New Haven: Yale University Press, 1989).

3. Austin, *Everyman's Genius* (Indianapolis: Bobbs-Merrill, 1925), 132.

4. Lanigan is the first to make note of Austin's use of liminality, observing: "The liminal
status she [Austin] consciously chose, which kept her aloof even from those closest to her,
was the vantage point of truth" (*Mary Austin*, 20).

5. Victor Turner, *The Ritual Process* (Ithaca: Cornell University Press, 1969), 95.

6. Virginia Woolf, *A Room of One's Own* (1929; reprint, New York: Harcourt Brace Jovanovich, 1981), 104.

7. Mary Austin, "Christ in Italy" (ca. 1910), MS, Mary Hunter Austin Collection, Huntington Library, San Marino, California (cited hereafter as Austin Collection), 52.

8. Susan Sniader Lanser, *Fictions of Authority: Women Writers and Narrative Voice* (Ithaca:
Cornell University Press, 1992), 6. Lanser's analysis of narrative authority is particularly
helpful in reading through Austin's occasional combativeness and giving shape to her usually invisible opponent.

9. Austin to Daniel Trembly MacDougal, 22 January 1922, Mary Hunter Austin Papers,
Center for Southwest Research, University of New Mexico, Albuquerque (cited hereafter
as Austin Papers).

10. Mary Austin, *A Woman of Genius* (New York: Doubleday, Page, 1912), 4.

11. Elizabeth Ammons, *Conflicting Stories: American Women Writers at the Turn into the
Twentieth Century* (New York: Oxford University Press, 1991), 10. This book is particularly
useful to Austin scholars because it sheds light on the distinctions between male and female
versions of literary modernism and draws on recent research in women's literary traditions
in the nineteenth century.

12. Marianne Hirsch, *The Mother-Daughter Plot: Narrative, Psychoanalysis, Feminism*
(Bloomington: Indiana University Press, 1989), 10.

13. Ammons, *Conflicting Stories*, 10.

14. Austin, *Woman of Genius*, 13.

15. Ibid., 4-5.

16. Ibid., 202.

17. Ibid., 376.

18. Ibid., 495.

19. Mary Austin, "Woman Alone," *Nation* 124 (2 March 1927): 83.

20. Austin, *Woman of Genius,* 202.

21. Ibid., 324.

22. Mary Austin, "Greatness in Women," *North American Review* 217 (January-June 1923): 200.

23. Austin, *The Young Woman Citizen* (New York: Woman's Press, 1918), 42.

24. Austin, *Woman of Genius,* 467.

25. Melody Graulich, introduction to *Western Trails: A Collection of Short Stories by Mary Austin* (Reno: University of Nevada Press, 1987), 25.

26. Austin, preface to *The Arrow-Maker,* x-xi.

27. Karen Langlois, "Mary Austin and the New Theatre: The 1911 Production of *The Arrow-Maker,*" *Theatre History Studies* 2 (1988): 81.

28. Austin, *Arrow-Maker,* 32.

29. Ibid., 109.

30. Ibid., 148.

31. Ibid., 153.

32. Mary Austin, *Earth Horizon: An Autobiography* (1932; reprint, Albuquerque: University of New Mexico Press, 1991), 315.

33. Mary Austin, *The Basket Woman* (Boston: Houghton Mifflin, 1904), 46.

34. Ibid., 47.

35. Ibid., 48.

36. Mary Austin, *The Land of Little Rain* (1903; reprint, Albuquerque: University of New Mexico Press, 1974), 103.

37. See Melody Graulich, preface to *Cactus Thorn,* by Mary Austin (Reno: University of Nevada Press, 1988).

38. Mary Austin, *Cactus Thorn* (Reno: University of Nevada Press, 1988), 39.

39. Ibid., 56.

40. Melody Graulich, afterword to *Cactus Thorn,* 108.

41. Melody Graulich, afterword to *Earth Horizon,* 387.

42. Austin, *Earth Horizon,* 274.

43. Austin, "Woman Alone," 82.

44. Mary Austin, "If I Had a Gifted Daughter" (ca. 1925), MS, Austin Collection, 13.

45. Austin, *Earth Horizon,* 156.

46. Mary Austin, "If Women Did" (ca. 1918), MS, Austin Collection, 7.

47. Austin, *Experiences Facing Death* (Indianapolis: Bobbs-Merrill, 1931), 57.

48. Ibid., 273.

49. Ibid., 58-59.

50. Mary Austin, *Love and the Soul Maker* (New York: Appleton, 1914), 249.

51. Ibid., 251.

52. Nancy Cott, *The Grounding of Modern Feminism* (New Haven: Yale University Press, 1987), 49.

53. Graulich, afterword to *Earth Horizon,* 379.

54. Austin, *Earth Horizon,* 46.

55. Ibid., 189.

56. Ibid., 231.

57. Ibid., 119.

58. Ibid., 346.

59. Ibid., 198.

60. Ibid., 114.

61. Ibid., 216-17.

62. Austin to W. S. Booth, 1 December 1904, Austin Papers.

63. Austin to Mabel Dodge Luhan, 22 May 1921, Mabel Dodge Luhan Collection, Beineke Library, Yale University (cited hereafter as Luhan Collection).

64. Helen MacKnight Doyle, *Mary Austin: Woman of Genius* (New York: Gotham House, 1939), 269.

65. Austin to Mabel Dodge Luhan, 10 May 1924, Luhan Collection.

66. Austin, *Earth Horizon*, 32.

CHAPTER SEVEN
A Taste for Center Stage
Consumption and Feminism in *A Woman of Genius*

ELIZABETH KLIMASMITH

As a cultural critic influenced by such thinkers as Thorstein Veblen and Charlotte Perkins Gilman, Austin consistently embedded a class analysis in her work. While Kathryn DeZur's postcolonial Marxist perspective helps her to identify property and ownership as central to Lost Borders, *Elizabeth Klimasmith looks through the lens of contemporary and Gilded Age theories of consumption, which often aligned consumer culture with female desire, to show how Austin and her semiauto-biographical heroine, Olivia Lattimore, "dismantle bourgeois social codes."*

In "A Taste for Center Stage," Klimasmith turns from lost borders to Austin's interiors, and discovers yet another liminal space. For Olivia, Klimasmith argues, the stage functions as a space in which a variety of roles can be enacted; A Woman of Genius *itself becomes a parable of a woman who uses consumption and feminism to define modern womanhood and redefine respectability and success. Showing just how perceptive Austin was about the class markers that separated middle-class and nonconformist women, Klimasmith reads the codes of taste, domestic interiors, and fashion in* A Woman of Genius *to reveal that Austin constructed the book as a history of the ways consumerism and feminism intersected in the much-maligned figure of the actress. "A Taste for Center Stage" is one of several essays in this volume that explore tropes of "performance" in Austin's work and life. Self-conscious about the parts women and men were asked to play in turn-of-the-century America, Austin sought more liberating roles. She reclaimed not only the theater, but also the city and the political arena as appropriate stages on which women could play (with) a range of roles as the curtain rose on the new century.*

In late nineteenth-century literature, the figure of the actress allegorizes capitalism's dangers. As her audience consumes her performance, the actress consumes her viewers sexually and economically. Mobile, capable of artifice, needing management, and coded as prostitute, the actress stands for all that simultaneously buttresses and threatens bourgeois society. There is no better example of an insatiable actress than the title character of Emile Zola's novel *Nana* (1880). Nana is more prostitute than actress; her best "acting" consists of appearing on stage gloriously nude. Following her increasingly sordid affairs with numerous other characters, Nana's putrefying body comes to stand in for the rotting French state under the Second Empire. Nana is not merely dangerous as an individual; her actions engender and implicate bourgeois society and its decay.

Although no such graphic depiction of an actress as a consuming force appears in American literature, literary actresses who negotiate and project the economic and sexual dangers of uncontrolled female consumption reflect similar currents of fear and desire. As industrialized cities came to dominate the American landscape, consumer culture, often imaginatively aligned with female desire, began to define the newly economically mobile middle class. Meanwhile, a new ideology called feminism was undermining the bourgeois standards of economic dependence and moral respectability central to nineteenth-century womanhood. Together, feminism and consumerism dramatically challenged the gender and economic status quo of the nineteenth century. As historian Albert Auster points out, actresses had "economic opportunities, as well as a social and sexual independence, enjoyed by few other women in the society. . . . Their position on the stage also gave actresses a great opportunity to aid in the struggle for women's rights and women's emancipation in the period from 1890-1920."[1] The figure of the actress, a woman who could profit from both consumer culture and feminism by rejecting Victorian mores, came to embody the cultural anxiety rooted in the economic and moral transition to modernity. Enter Olivia Lattimore and Carrie Meeber as Woman of Genius and Woman of Desire.

Olivia and Carrie, the central characters, respectively, in Mary Austin's 1912 novel *A Woman of Genius* and Theodore Dreiser's *Sister Carrie* (first published in 1900 but not widely available until 1912), helped to build the archetypal portrait of the actress in turn-of-the-century American literature. Carrie Meeber travels from her small midwestern town to Chicago and then New York, purveying her "naturally imitative" talents into a successful acting career.[2] Along the way, she has affairs with several men, one of whom descends to a naturalistic suicide by the gas jet in his Bowery lodging house as Carrie rises to a success spelled out in Broadway's new electric lights. Olivia, like Carrie, becomes involved with several men as she travels from rural Taylorville, Ohianna, to Chicago and finally New York, where she achieves success as a leading stage tragedienne. But the similarities end there.

The Gilded Age's most powerful cultural forces collide in the figures of these two actresses. For Carrie, who sheds any pretense to "respectability" when she moves into Charles Drouet's hotel room, the desire that consumer culture inspires becomes all encompassing. At the end of the novel, surrounded by marks of material wealth, Carrie only wants more. In contrast, Olivia steers by the star of respectable womanhood until she sees brighter lights on the horizon. As an actress, Olivia transforms herself from middle-class matron to working woman and in the process develops new standards for respectability. Through her "natural" good taste and talent for tragedy (itself a tasteful choice), Olivia plays a series of roles that allow her to tap into the growing power of 1910s feminism and write a script that recuperates her desires according to her paradigm of modern womanhood. Olivia is a woman who enters the worlds of art and consumption, consciously commodifies herself, and emerges dusty but intact, with her own voice, to tell her own story.

We can read *A Woman of Genius* both as a novel and as a history of the ways consumerism and feminism have played out through the figure of the actress. Olivia is clearly a product of her time; her desire to use acting for self-expression and profit closely adheres to the mores of consumer culture, while her political leanings reveal her to be a budding feminist by the novel's end. Thus, the theater becomes a stage on which Austin constructs a female character who becomes entangled with and then emerges from this swirl of competing ideologies. Historian Faye E. Dudden writes that "the theatrical enterprise thus contains two divergent possibilities for women: transformation and objectification. Theatre may enable women to rehearse the most radical projects of self-creation or it may reduce them to bodies and present them as objects."[3] Transformation and objectification are certainly present in *Sister Carrie* and *A Woman of Genius,* but Dudden's bifurcated view ignores the possibility that Austin presents—that the theater can allow women multiple options. In a world of changing economic and social pressures, acting becomes a mode of expression through which women may enact a range of roles between Dudden's polar possibilities. Olivia plays in the theater where consumerism and feminism meet.

As they leave their small midwestern towns, Olivia and Carrie reject the nineteenth-century village for the twentieth-century city, where the consumer-oriented society's standards of taste and idealized objects replace such domestic virtues as purity and piety. Historian T. J. Jackson Lears argues that "a fundamental cultural transformation" was shaping American "capitalist" society at this time.[4] In the nineteenth century, "the bourgeois ethos had enjoined perpetual work, compulsive saving, civic responsibility, and a rigid morality of self-denial. By the early twentieth century that outlook had begun to give way to a set of values sanctioning periodic leisure, compulsive spending, apolitical passivity and an apparently permissive (but subtly coercive) morality of individual fulfillment."[5]

Lears blames this shift on the infamous cultural elite, but other theorists argue that the transition he describes came from the bottom up as well.[6] Although both Olivia and Carrie become actresses, don costumes, and efface themselves to assume buyable personae on the stage, their motivations and negotiations differ. Olivia, for whom acting requires both talent and effort, balances the "individual fulfillment" with her "civic responsibility" and comes out in the black by, in essence, incorporating herself—investing in herself without losing her unique and salable gift. In contrast, Carrie enters the world of consumption, self-consciously makes herself consumable, and stumbles into an acting career that brings fame and economic success. Carrie, an accidental actress, is motivated by pure desire.

Certainly, Carrie and Olivia were far from alone in responding to the promise of the theater. The number of actresses in the United States rose from 780 in 1870 to 15,436 in 1910 and to 19,905 by 1920. Auster links this phenomenal jump to the growth of industrialism, urbanization, and consumption, explaining, "the rapid industrialization of the American economy, the increasing amounts of leisure time, and the weakening of clerical influence produced tremendous growth in the entertainment industry, and, by 1900, there were an estimated three thousand theaters throughout the United States." Despite the profession's rapid growth, a career as an actress remained a risky proposition for working-class women like Carrie and middle-class women like Olivia as well. According to social historian Tracy Davis, "Compared to teaching, the civil service, seamstressing, idleness, marriage, or obscurity, the theatre was a powerful lure for thousands of women (including those without capital, experience or artistic talent) who entered the profession at all levels." Along with risking her reputation, a woman took a financial risk when she attempted to enter the theatrical profession—far more actresses failed or eked out meager incomes than became stars. Olivia's and Carrie's achievements, while fictional, would have been historically exceptional.[7]

Carrie achieves fame and wealth as an actress because she commodifies herself completely. From the very beginning of the novel, Carrie embodies desire. When she is onstage, her expression is "a thing the world likes to see, because it's an expression of its longing." In the edition of *Sister Carrie* that was available in 1912, Carrie's first acting experience, in which she takes on the role of a sentimental heroine, is framed quite differently from her subsequent appearances onstage. As Laura in "Under the Gaslight," Carrie taps "the old melancholy of desire" to convey to her audience "the radiating waves of feeling and sincerity. . . . The magic of passion, which will yet dissolve the world, [is] here at work." Carrie's success moves her audience because she reflects the power of their shared desire. After this success, however, Carrie's acting career is limited to her role as Hurstwood's "wife." When that role is no longer profitable, Carrie turns to acting jobs that can pay the bills and purchase beautiful things. Her desire changes from a transforming force that enables artistic expression to a desire for things that makes acting necessary.[8]

Many critics have called attention to the power of objects and consumption in *Sister Carrie,* and Dreiser clearly emphasizes Carrie's objectness when she is onstage. For example, when she played the pouting pilgrim, "[t]he portly gentlemen in the front row began to feel that she was a delicious little morsel. It was the kind of frown they would have loved to force away with kisses. All the gentlemen yearned toward her. She was capital." This passage is at the nexus of several discourses of consumption. Carrie is objectified as a consumable morsel of food who appeals to her audience's salacious taste. Onstage she seems powerless, unable to resist the kisses they fantasize about forcing on her in their drive to possess her. As Dreiser says, Carrie embodies capital and as such remains eternally desirable and elusive. But as an objectified, objectifying being, Carrie is ultimately alone. She can invest her own capital to buy things, but she is happiest when she can desire more.[9]

Although Carrie succeeds as an actress, she is never portrayed as an artist; by the end of the novel her acting career seems to have devolved into mere display. *A Woman of Genius* offers a more concrete model of a successful woman artist, for Olivia balances the demands of production and consumption, avoiding Carrie's sacrifice of self while developing her creative talents. Olivia's greater accomplishment, however, is learning to express herself off the stage as well as on it. Like her creator, Olivia does this through the discourses of consumerism and feminism. In *Conflicting Stories,* Elizabeth Ammons situates Mary Austin as a member of a generation of female authors for whom creating literature *as art* was a priority: "[T]hese writers present a picture of a group of women breaking with the past; and the major break, I will maintain, consisted in their avowed ambition to be artists."[10] Austin's semiautobiographical depiction of Olivia's artistic success makes for a plot rarely seen in the genre of female *kunstleromanen,* of which *A Woman of Genius* may be considered a part. Unlike Avis in Elizabeth Stuart Phelps's *The Story of Avis,* Jo in *Little Women,* or Madeline in Mary Hallock Foote's short story "The Fate of a Voice," Olivia is not forced to choose between art and marriage. Only in Thea Kronborg's trajectory toward artistic triumph in Willa Cather's *The Song of the Lark* (1915), another all-too-rare story of an independent woman's artistic and economic success, do we see Olivia's rise reflected.

Olivia Lattimore's story echoes Mary Austin's life in important ways. Both women rejected the models of nineteenth-century womanhood their mothers and communities offered in favor of publicly visible careers as artists. Both had unhappy first marriages, and both had children who died. Both became involved in feminist movements and passionate love affairs; both tried to redefine spirituality. Indeed, some passages from *A Woman of Genius* appear in Austin's autobiography, *Earth Horizon,* with only slight modifications. Nancy Porter calls attention to several of these revisions, noting that Austin wrote the support she enjoyed from well-placed friends out of her novel in order to "heighten the rugged lines of [Olivia's] development as an artist." But in rewriting her story as Olivia's, Austin actually smoothed over more of her own personal and artistic conflicts than she roughened. For example, Austin wrote changes into Olivia's life that liberated Olivia to pursue her art in ways that Austin never could. Austin's own sister died in 1878 (when Austin was ten), but Austin gave Olivia Effie, the idealized sister in *A Woman of Genius* who offers Olivia money to support her career on the stage, never tattles, and ultimately provides a feminist perspective that allows Olivia to see her acting career as a positive force in a larger community of activist women.[11]

With its feminist ending, *A Woman of Genius* both cautions against and confirms the values of an urban economy based on consumption. As Olivia struggles to succeed as an actress, she must adopt the tenets of consumerism, even if it means sacrificing some of the pleasures of traditional womanhood. In delineating Olivia's struggle, Austin undermines the old standards of femininity, demonstrating the need for women to attain status in the "new commodity culture that challenged at its core the moral heritage of the nineteenth century." The moral heritage that Olivia rejects is best exemplified by her mother. Austin describes her own mother's generation pointedly in *Earth Horizon*: "The status of Wife and Mother, always spoken of in capitals, was sentimentally precious, a status of being treasured and apart. There was on all hands a general social conspiracy to keep the married woman's sense of her preciousness intact." In her classic essay "The Cult of True Womanhood," Barbara Welter claims that a dominant nineteenth-century model for white middle-class womanhood was based on "four cardinal virtues—piety, purity, submissiveness and domesticity." According to this model, in which production is figured as reproduction, women must submit to men economically as well as psychologically, entering the economy only as consumers. Olivia, like Austin, wants to assert her "womanhood," but she has no models to show her how to escape from an isolating "ladyhood." Thus, Olivia is largely alone as she makes the transition to an economy in which she can produce as well as consume.[12]

Olivia's alignment with the consumerism of her day is evident from the novel's earliest pages, when she casts her book and herself as entertainment for the reading public. Both she and her book play for and serve a target audience. Olivia challenges her audience's complacency, daring them to "escape the banality of believing that my having lived for a week in Chicago on 85 cents was in any way important to my artistic development and go so far as to apprehend it as it actually was, a foolish and unnecessary interference with my *business* of serving you anew with entertainment" (emphasis mine).[13] To express her inner artistic self, Olivia must necessarily "go public." In this early passage, Olivia's strong sense of her role in a consumer culture underlines her struggle to reconcile commingled but conflicting pressures to have children, create art, and earn money.

For Olivia, artistic success requires a certain level of material comfort. "[I]t matters not a little to Genius to be so cramped and retarded. I have arrived at seeing the uncritical acceptance of poverty and heartbreak as essential accompaniments of Gift, very much of a piece with the proneness of Christians to regard the early martyrdoms as concomitants of faith, when every thinking person knows they arose in the cruelty and stupidity of the bystanders" (5). Olivia rejects the commonly held view that geniuses must suffer by comparing it to what she sees as a common Christian fallacy, setting the stage for her rejection of Taylorville's repressive religious values in favor of the (a)moral universe of the economy. In order to succeed as an artist, Olivia participates in a consumer society, redefining purity, piety, and domesticity in order to fulfill her desires as a producer and consumer.

In addition to her dramatic flair, Olivia's "natural" good taste becomes one of the earliest indicators of her economic and artistic promise. A decade earlier, Thorstein Veblen argued in *The Theory of the Leisure Class* (1899) that cost, not intrinsic beauty, determines an object's appeal:

> By further habituation to an appreciative perception of the marks of expensiveness in goods, and by habitually identifying beauty with reputability, it comes about that a beautiful article which is not expensive is accounted not beautiful. In this way it has happened, for instance, that some flowers pass conventionally for offensive weeds . . . other flowers, of no greater intrinsic beauty than these are cultivated at great cost and call out much admiration from flower-lovers whose tastes have been matured under the critical guidance of a polite environment.[14]

Olivia will earn the money to purchase the things our "pecuniary canons of taste" deem valuable. But in a consumer economy, money isn't everything. "Matured under the critical guidance of a polite environment," taste helps to determine the difference between classes that the presence of an upwardly mobile, newly successful manufacturing class obscures. Taste, both inherited and learned, becomes a class marker. According to theorist Pierre Bourdieu, "To the socially recognized hierarchy of the arts . . . corresponds a social hierarchy of the consumers. This predisposes tastes to function as markers of 'class.'" In order to succeed in the twentieth century, Olivia must acquire the money to purchase goods *and* demonstrate that she can make discriminating choices. To demonstrate good taste, one must be able to read the codes that differentiate the flowers from the weeds. As Bourdieu states, "Consumption is . . . a stage in a process of communication, that is, an act of deciphering, decoding, which presupposes practical or explicit mastery of a cipher or code."[15]

Always a precocious reader, Olivia possesses the good taste that distinguishes her from her family while it helps mark her for eventual success.

> I was aware of a sort of gracelessness in their [her relatives'] vital processes, in much the same way I knew that the striped and flowered carpet in my mother's best room did not harmonize with the wall paper, and that the curtains went badly with them both. I have to go back to this, and to the fact that my clothes were chosen for wearing qualities rather than becomingness, to account for a behavior that . . . my mother complained of [as] . . . not taking an interest.
>
> How else was I to protect myself from the thousand inharmonies that chafed against the budding instinct of beauty: the plum-colored ribbons I was expected to wear with my brown dress, the mottled Japanese pattern upon the gilt ground of the wall paper. (28)

We can imagine Austin's intended audience letting out a collective groan at the thought of pairing plum and brown; this is a code she expects her middle-class readers to grasp readily. Importantly, the appreciation of beauty is noted as an instinct, and her possession of it marks Olivia as superior to her family and destined for greater things. Austin reinforces Olivia's sensitivity to aesthetics as she introduces codes of fashion and domestic interiors that Olivia and other members of her "true" class (if not her family) can read.

Olivia's ability to comprehend the cultural codes of middle-class taste separates her from old standards of womanhood and draws her toward the city, where she can cash in on and redefine domestic respectability. For example, when Olivia visits her Ohianna friend Pauline in Chicago, she laps up the luxurious atmosphere, coveting Pauline's possessions and yearning to trade Pauline's "hardwood furniture and afternoon teakettles" for "all the traditional sanctity and enthronement of women, for which I had paid with my body, with maternal anxieties and wifely submission" (84). Although she labels it absurd, Olivia's desire to cast off the mantle of reproduction and submission in favor of beautiful material objects marks an important step in her transition into a world of interpersonal connections made possible by things. In this world, purity, piety, and domesticity are devalued as cultural currency when compared with the luxury, convenience, and beauty that money can buy.

Olivia's experience of this jump to a new value system is linked with her first trip to the theater, which fills her with "intense, articulate excitement" and enables her to grasp the meaning of Pauline's possessions and surroundings (86). Pauline does have good taste, and we can see the class implications of her luxurious choices. Her teakettle becomes a symbol of consumption's power; Olivia's description of the "rows of them shining in the ticketed inaccessibility of seven dollars and ninety-eight cents" gives a clue to the power that goods beautifully displayed exert over her own sensibilities: "Pauline's wall papers were soft, unpatterned, with wide borders; her windows were hung with plain scrim and the furniture coverings were in tone with the carpets. When ladies called in the afternoon, Pauline gave them tea which she made in a brass kettle over a spirit lamp"(83). The atmosphere these visual tones create both soothes and enrages Olivia, for it reflects Pauline's easy access to the luxuries of beauty and taste that Olivia covets.

At the turn of the century, domestic interiors functioned both as class markers and as codes for their owners' psychological states. Karen Halttunen's essay "From Parlor to Living Room" traces the evolution of domestic space as a simultaneous projection and echo of personality and class status. According to *The House in Good Taste* (1913), written by social maven and interior decorator Elsie de Wolfe: "We are sure to judge a woman in whose house we find ourselves for the first time by her surroundings. We judge her temperament, her habits, her inclinations, by the interior of her home." So, while Olivia's response to her "background" (both her surroundings and her hereditary inheritance) may make her seem snobbish, Austin is in fact articulating through her character a well-accepted theory of personality as determined by (and shown in) purchases. Halttunen explains that "the commodified home became something more than a likeness or even an expression of the selves placed within it: it became something interchangeable with those selves, something out of which those selves were at once improvised and imprisoned, constructed and confined."[16]

Olivia's knack for reading codes of taste, especially in domestic interiors, also links her to other astute readers, such as Lily Bart in Edith Wharton's *The House of Mirth*. Lily's sensitivity to her surroundings is evident throughout the novel in her overwhelming fear of "dinginess." In Aunt Peniston's house, "[a]s was always the case with her, this moral repulsion found a physical outlet in a quickened distaste for her surroundings. She revolted from the complacent ugliness of Mrs. Peniston's black walnut, from the slippery gloss of the vestibule tiles, and the mingled odor of sapolio and furniture polish that met her at the door." Carrie Meeber, too, is repulsed by "ugly" interiors. At her sister's house, Carrie feels "the drag of a lean and narrow life. The walls of the rooms were discordantly papered. The floors were covered with matting and the hall laid with a thin rag carpet. One could see that the furniture was of that poor, hurriedly patched together quality sold by the installment houses." In *The Song of the Lark,* Thea Kronborg taps her artistic ability only after she has moved into an attic room that she has decorated with flowered wallpaper of her own selection. In turn-of-the-century literature, domestic interiors have the power to speak to and about creative women in a common language.[17]

For these characters, as for Austin, creativity can flourish only in a tastefully decorated space. In *Earth Horizon,* Austin constructs a theory connecting wallpaper, old-fashioned femininity, and writing: "Wall-paper had but recently made its way from the genteel East.... It was the way of people, when they wished to pay a modish compliment, to tell you your clothes fit 'like the paper on the wall'; pasted flat over an artificially firmed outline. It was about this time that 'glove-fitting' corsets came into vogue. What Mary meant by a wall-paper book was one you couldn't walk around in."[18] Here, wallpaper becomes a sign of eastern gentility gone awry. Outlines become artificial, corsets become even more constraining, literature becomes oppressive. Austin goes on to say that at that age she wanted to write "books you could walk around in." If she can't walk around in the wallpaper, Austin implies, she has no freedom to create. Similarly, in *A Woman of Genius,* patterned wallpaper is no longer au courant; indeed, it represents her husband Tommy's anachronistic helplessness. Unable to accumulate capital successfully, Tommy is impotent either to produce or to consume in a twentieth-century economy. Pauline's smooth brown walls, in contrast, are both tasteful and blank, respectable and unrestricted. And in Pauline's apartment, Olivia reconnects with her creative side.

The codes of taste in domestic space portrayed in *A Woman of Genius* simultaneously speak about Olivia and reveal the state of her relationships with her husband and with other women. For instance, while Olivia is away, Tommy decides to wallpaper the house to spare Olivia any sad associations with the death of their son. But his good intentions reveal a chink in their marriage:

Tommy had hit upon the idea of papering the room himself in the evenings after closing hours, and by way of keeping it a surprise, had chosen the paper to his own taste. Any one who kept house in the

early 80's will recall a type of paper then in vogue, of large unintelligent arabesques of a liverish bronzy hue, parting at regular intervals
upon Neapolitan landscapes of pronounced pinks and blues.
Tommy's landscapes achieved the added atrocity of having Japanese
ladies walking about in them, and though the room wanted lighting,
the paper was very dark. (86–87)

Current readers may not precisely recall this garish look, but Austin's language ("unintelligent," "liverish," "atrocity") calls for the same reaction
people today might have to appliances in shades of avocado and harvest
gold. Importantly, Austin distinguishes between the vogue that Tommy
obediently follows and Olivia's classic style. Although Tommy understands
the power of the domestic interior, he and Olivia speak different languages
of taste.

As Tommy fails to consume according to Olivia's standards, the wallpaper sets off reverberations that begin to widen the fracture in their marriage. Olivia states: "[I]t occurred to me that for the enlarged standard of
living I had brought home with me [from Chicago, city of goods], a man
of Tommy's taste was likely to prove an unsuitable tool" (87). Wallpaper,
furniture, and knickknacks play a game of show-and-tell—they show
Olivia just how far apart she and Tommy are in speech more eloquent than
either of them can express openly. The "astonishing fact that Tommy liked
plush furniture, and liked it red for choice" (71), marks the difference between Tommy and Olivia in a visible, readable way. By placing the blame
on Tommy's taste, Olivia exonerates herself from any accountability for
their marriage's collapse. If Olivia's refined taste excuses her somewhat
harsh treatment of Tommy, it also helps to elevate her in her audience's eyes
in terms of respectability, even as she turns to a career as an actress.

As I have pointed out, actresses threatened to overturn middle-class sensibilities in the early 1900s, especially the true-womanly virtue of purity. If
Carrie Meeber's career was scandalous, the same could be said of Olivia's
choice. Olivia disrupts the social order in several ways; for example, she
takes her maiden name as a stage name and leaves her husband in order to
pursue her own career. Although the importance of the bottom line in the
theater business disappoints her, she soothes herself by buying into consumerism, using her wages to indulge in purchases that both show her economic success and gratify the taste that marks her class standing. On her
way home from her first tour as an actress, she buys herself the much-de-

sired spirit lamp and brass teakettle just like Pauline's. But in small-town Higgleston's moral sphere, these symbols of urban domestic gentility backfire. In a scene that prefigures Carol Kennicot's entertainment efforts in Sinclair Lewis's *Main Street,* the women of Higgleston snub Olivia at her own tea party. Worse, once Olivia has revealed her plan to pursue a career in acting, the women's social neglect is accompanied by sexual advances from men who clearly link acting to prostitution. After she rebuffs him, the sleazy Mr. Montagu replies, "If you can't meet me like a woman of the world—you're a nice actress, you are" (129). Her occupation as actress quickly undermines Olivia's status as a respectable member of the small-town community.

In an earlier era (or the "earlier" space of Higgleston), Olivia's "transgressions" might have been fatal to her reputation. According to Victorian mores, women risked their reputations when they went on the stage. Actresses were pariahs because of their "mobility and professional equality," and "the easy and constant accessibility of actress to actor," both of which challenged bourgeois notions of separate spheres.[19] Davis notes that "[w]omen performers defied ideas of passive middle class femininity and personified active self sufficiency. Their visibility and notoriety in the public realm led to persistent and unfounded prejudices and very real sexual dangers in the workplaces. All of this contradicted public relations attempts to depict actresses as home-centered, modest, self-respecting females redolent of Victorian middle-class virtues. Their public existence seemed to preclude private respectability." Actresses' public visibility magnified these bad impressions and offenses to sensibility. In Britain, "daughters who 'fell' from virtue or trod the boards alike found themselves penniless, disinherited, and unprotected by respectable families; though patronized by men, they were condemned by women and their natural circles."[20] Historian Martha Banta suggests that similar concerns held true in the United States. Banta points to an article in the January 1912 issue of *Good Housekeeping* titled "Domesticity and the Theater" that features actresses enjoying lovely, scandal-free domestic lives in their kitchens with their husbands: "*Good Housekeeping* did its best to make stage actresses exciting but safe for middle-class consumption."[21] In *A Woman of Genius,* Olivia, too, recasts this cultural threat.

According to Higgleston's moral code, acting skirts the boundary between respectability and shame. Olivia conflates the two, emphasizing that the shame she experiences only drives her more deeply into acting. "People wonder why sensitive, self-respecting women are not driven away from the stage by the offences that hedge it; they are driven deeper and farther into its enfoldment. There is nothing to whiten the burning of its shames but the high whiteness of its ultimate perfection" (130). Carrie Meeber experiences even greater disapprobation. At the novel's end, the narrator admonishes her, "In your rocking-chair, by your window dreaming, shall you long, alone. In your rocking-chair, by your window, shall you dream such happiness as you may never feel." The narrator's castigation echoes contemporaneous anxieties about actresses' respectability.[22]

Actresses' reputation for sexual license both connects and divides Olivia and Carrie—the "fallen" Carrie acts to avoid prostitution, while for respectable Olivia, acting brings with it the danger of violation. Unlike Carrie, Olivia has experienced motherhood, which gives her a bourgeois respectability that the childless Carrie never has. Yet even motherhood is desentimentalized in *A Woman of Genius.* "And if you ask me why I didn't take the chance life offers to women to justify themselves to the race," Olivia says, "I will say that though the hope of a child presents itself sentimentally as opportunity, it figures primarily in the calculation of the majority, as a question of expense" (125). Economic reality pervades domesticity, making Olivia less eager, if not unwilling, to have another child. And rhetorically, Austin implicates most of the bourgeoisie in her assessment of motherhood, trading sentimentality for calculation and implicitly substituting creative production for maternal reproduction.

In rejecting motherhood, Olivia transforms another virtue of true womanhood, piety, to suit consumer culture. When she meets Mark Eversley, the great actor of the day, Olivia glimpses a world in which her powers can come to fruition and discovers a new way to worship. When Eversley in his sumptuous hotel suite tells her that she is a "woman of genius," Olivia becomes a supplicant to her talent for acting: "To be a genius is no such vanity as you imagine. It is to know great desires and to have no will of your own toward fulfillment; it is to feed others, yourself unfed; it is to be broken and plied as the Powers determine; it is to serve and serve, and to get nothing out of it beyond the joy of serving" (135). Here, the first-person narration serves as a way into Olivia's thoughts and allows her to become more than an onstage display like Carrie Meeber. Unlike Carrie, Olivia analyzes her artistic struggle (if a little pompously), voicing her views with a clarity utterly absent from *Sister Carrie.* In worshiping her gift, Olivia takes another step in transforming her value system by substituting acting for religion and transforming piety into self-fulfillment. Like Thea Kronborg in *The Song of the Lark,* or, later, Jake Rabinowitz in *The Jazz Singer,* Olivia must submit to and serve "the powers" that enable her to create, just as her religious mother worshipped another deity. But even if associating acting with religion makes her feel right, Olivia eventually rejects the restrictions of the domestic sphere for good. And after Tommy's death, Olivia must learn to read the public language of the marketplace on her own.

Launching her acting career in Chicago forces Olivia to face publicly many of the economic issues she has negotiated so adeptly within her own domestic space. In essence, her private domesticity goes public in the city, but not without complications. While she can read the economic language of spirit lamps and fire screens, she resists calculating her own market value. "To do what seemed necessary for the development of my gift . . . required money; and though there in Chicago was money for every sort of adventure that stirred the imagination of man, there was none for the particular sort of investment I represented. At least not at the price I was prepared to pay" (152). Olivia realizes that to invest in herself, she may need to sell off some of her respectability. As an actress, she is a commodity; at the same time she knows that in order to produce, she must consume. She tells Pauline, "I'm needing something new [to wear] myself . . . and I'm divided between the certainty that if I don't get an engagement I can't afford it, and if I don't afford it I probably won't get an engagement" (154). Olivia's quandary is historically grounded; Tracy Davis emphasizes that being fashionable was a job requirement for actresses. She quotes a 1916 source stating that actresses "must present an appearance of physical well-being and must wear 'smart' striking clothes."[23] Thus the actress confounds the "separate spheres" of production and consumption.

As it conflates the public sphere with the private, acting melds religion and art with consumption. To mark her transition to a consumer economy, Olivia experiences a billboard-induced epiphany in which advertising becomes her saving totem. As she rides the streetcar to audition for a part in a musical called "Flim-Flam" (which might have starred Carrie Madenda), she says, "I was dimly aware of moving, sitting upright, of paying my fare, and of great staring red posters that flashed upon me from the billboards. . . . Something was trying to get through to me" (203). As she tries to decode the mysterious message, Olivia attempts to return to the spiritual framework of her childhood, but her attempts to pray fail. "Now it occurred to me . . . that if the God of the church had cast me off, there must still be something which artists everywhere prayed to, a Distributor of Gifts who might be concerned about the conduct of His worshippers. I reached out for Him—and I did not know His name" (204). After realizing that the name on the billboards is literally that of her old mentor, Mark Eversley, Olivia wanders the streets calling out his name "as if it had been a charm" (205). Olivia reveres economic success as her mother worshipped God. The billboard speaks in a language (consumerism) she can read; fittingly, Olivia's artistic career is resurrected by the Distributor of Gifts, deity of the consumer economy.

To succeed in the public sphere, Olivia must become a product. More important, to effectively market herself she must relinquish control over her own product-ivity and turn the reins over to a professional—Morris Polatkin, "a speculator; he speculates in ability" (207). Immediately after learning that Polatkin will "put [her] gift on a paying basis," Olivia sees her talents return (207). But creativity has a price tag. In her first meeting with Polatkin, Olivia becomes uncomfortably aware that if she commodifies herself for Polatkin, she will completely become his product. He shapes her body, "follow[ing] out the outline of [her] figure with his thumb, flourishing out the alterations that made it more to his mind. 'Jalowaski would fix you so you wouldn't believe it was you,'" he tells her (210). Here, a man controls a woman's body, and a corset controls the shape she presents to the public. Polatkin pulls the strings.

With Polatkin, economics completely overshadows sentiment—he tells Olivia to stop wearing her mourning clothes and insists that they "have a contract from the start" (210). Even if their agreement will give Olivia the chance to act, Olivia's contract is strictly business. As business partners, Olivia and Polatkin function well. But there are personal conflicts, at least on Olivia's side, that prejudice her against Polatkin.

Perhaps the most troubling aspect of Olivia's first meeting with Mr. Polatkin is her attitude. She greets him with a noticeable sneer because he is Jewish, calling him, among other things, "the stodgy little Jew" (209). Her anxiety that a Jewish immigrant will be shaping her, investing in her, and in essence taking over her career echoes something other American women of that time may have felt when faced with the fact that, as Abraham Cahan points out in *The Rise of David Levinsky,* Jewish immigrants "had Americanized the system of providing clothes for the American woman of moderate or humble means. . . . had done away with the prohibitive prices and greatly improved the popular taste. The average American woman is the best-dressed average woman in the world, and the Russian Jew has had a good deal to do with making her one."[24] Although the idea of being dressed by immigrant hands may have made middle-class American women anxious, it allowed them to consume fashion in a new way. Similarly, Olivia must exchange control over her career for Polatkin's advice if she wants to succeed in the economy of the stage. Polatkin's influence, like the ghostly presence of her dead child and husband, saves Olivia from appearing too dangerous. His management paves the way for Olivia's success, both as a commodity and as an artist. As an added bonus, Olivia can finally live in a flat whose "lines and colors [are] in tune with [her] temperament" (218). Unlike Carrie, who is threatening because she is mobile and unmanaged, Olivia is well managed, and her mobility from this point on is upward.

Like many a good heroine, Olivia desires passionate love to round out her life, but even love speaks through economics. Olivia heads for London to rejuvenate herself, and there encounters Helmeth Garrett, in a beautiful house "stuffed full of the treasures of four hundred years of the selective instinct," including paintings by Velázquez, Holbein, and Titian (226). Thus, the onset of her affair with Helmeth is enmeshed in the web of conspicuous consumption that her success permits her, and she can experience her love for him only within the luxurious confines of wealth. Her consuming affair with Helmeth pays off by allowing Olivia to tap deep reserves of feeling unavailable to her before. Helmeth in essence becomes a means by which she can achieve more success on the stage.

Paradoxically, to act at the turn of the century was both to reject old standards of femininity and to gain a kind of power to which very few women had access. I quote Davis again: "The actress alone enjoyed an element of excitement and an unequaled degree of personal and sexual freedom in the practice of her trade. As Simone de Beauvoir observed, . . . by 'making their own living and finding the meaning of their lives in work, they escape the yoke of men . . . [and] in their self-realization, their validation of themselves as human beings, they find self-fulfillment as women.'"[25] Davis's evocation of de Beauvoir emphasizes connections between acting and twentieth-century feminism. But we can trace this connection back to feminism's earliest days, as Auster points out. Many actresses, including Mary Shaw and Lillian Russell, were active in feminist causes, especially the suffrage movement.[26]

Feminism not only validated women's decisions to pursue careers and achieve fame, it also challenged gender relations at all levels, politicizing the personal. For feminists, Nancy Cott writes, "[s]ex outside of marriage was . . . a personal form of direct action as risky, as thrilling, as full of a paradoxical sense of play and of deadly responsibility as throwing a bomb."[27] But for Olivia, sex remains a moral, not a political, act, and marriage and art remain irreconcilable. Olivia chooses the theater over Helmeth. After Helmeth has gone, Olivia tries to analyze why their affair failed and concludes that it is because she has no model for a two-career marriage. "Somewhere there must have been men and women working out our situation and working it out successfully, but the only example of life afforded us was not of the acceptable pattern" (266). Perhaps too late for Olivia and Helmeth, feminism began to render that pattern more acceptable.

Few signposts mark Olivia's path from a paradigm of womanhood marked by purity, piety, submissiveness, and domesticity to one identified as feminism. Consumption, sexuality, and art as religion offer her ways to redefine respectability as she bridges the gap to modernity. As an actress, Olivia takes on a role that allows her to be a product and a consumer, and she is in turn partially consumed by it. One of the ways Olivia avoids being completely used up is by beginning to channel her energies into a movement that seems to operate outside the world of goods. Her younger sister, Effie, points out that even though Olivia is one of only a few women to make the transition from an economy of morals to an economy of money, she can clear the way for others to follow: "Oh you! You're a forward movement yourself. All I am doing is herding the others to keep step with you. You know, Olivia, I've wondered if you didn't feel lonely at times, so far ahead that you don't find anybody to line up with. Every time I see a woman step out of the ranks in some achievement of her own, I think, 'Now Olivia will have some company'" (260). In Effie's view, feminism allows Olivia to redefine the economic terms of her career, see her acting as a service to others, and perform a public good that is outside of economic exchange.

Although acting is her business, politics is Olivia's service. "Last year I walked in a suffrage parade because Effie wrote me it was my duty, and the swing of it, the banners flying, the proud music, set gates wide for me on fields of new, inspiring experience . . . all the paths that lead to the Shining Destiny . . . why shouldn't women walk in them? I should think some of them might lead less frequently to bramble and morass" (290). In evoking the specters of Duty, Shining Destiny, and Patriotism, Olivia is playing on old forms. But she also plays with them. By reforming ideals of True Womanhood in favor of a feminist model, Olivia can join with and become a model for other women.

Olivia successfully manipulates the discourses of consumption and feminism in order to maintain her respectability as she dismantles bourgeois social codes. For her, both consumption and feminism are ultimately empowering. Nancy Cott points out, however, that by the 1930s, feminism's force had been diluted by the discourse of marketing. Corporations appropriated feminist discourse, subsuming a desire for equality with a desire to buy. "The culture of modernity and urbanity absorbed the messages of Feminism and re-presented them. Feminist intents and rhetorics were not ignored but appropriated" to sell products from toothpaste to cars.[28] Austin's feminism, however nascent in Olivia's story, remained powerfully linked to economics—as her final novella, *Cactus Thorn,* makes clear.

A Woman of Genius did not navigate the public economy as well as her heroine did. The novel was never commercially successful. Ironically, Austin's own autobiography, *Earth Horizon,* achieved the economic success that her fantasy rendering did not. Yet, in rewriting her own public and private trajectory as *A Woman of Genius,* Mary Austin provided a model for new womanhood that outstripped other fictional lives of the time and gave voice to a woman who succeeded in the paradigms of consumerism, feminism, and art.

NOTES

1. Albert Auster, *Actresses and Suffragists: Women in the American Theater, 1890-1920* (New York: Praeger, 1984), 6.

2. Theodore Dreiser, *Sister Carrie* (1907; reprint, New York: Bantam Books, 1992), 84.

3. Faye E. Dudden, *Women in the American Theater: Actresses and Audiences, 1790-1870* (New Haven: Yale University Press, 1994), 2.

4. T. J. Jackson Lears, "From Starvation to Self-Realization: Advertising and the Therapeutic Roots of the Consumer Culture, 1880-1930," in *The Culture of Consumption,* ed. Richard Wightman Fox and T. J. Jackson Lears (New York: Pantheon Books, 1983), 3. Novels helped to provide signposts for this transition. *A Woman of Genius* and *Sister Carrie* echo the texts Simon Bronner refers to: "Swept up by the tide of goods, turn-of-the-century Americans attentively read new texts geared to the consumer culture to understand what had happened to them and what could happen in the future. . . . In text and symbol, characters basked in the glory of attainment and lost something in the process" (Simon J. Bronner, "Reading Consumer Culture," in *Consuming Visions,* ed. Bronner [New York: Norton, 1989], 50-51).

5. Lears, "From Starvation to Self-Realization," 3.

6. Anthropologist Grant McCracken sees the culture of consumption as a web in which "consumption is thoroughly cultural in character ... [and] culture is profoundly connected to and dependent upon consumption" (McCracken, *Culture and Consumption* [Bloomington: Indiana University Press, 1988], xi).

7. Auster, *Actresses and Suffragists,* 31, 4; Tracy C. Davis, *Actresses as Working Women: Their Social Identity in Victorian Culture* (London: Routledge, 1991), 16. Davis is describing the rise of the acting profession in Victorian England, but the parallels between the rise of the theater in Britain and its rise in the United States are striking.

8. Dreiser, *Sister Carrie,* 385, 145. The University of Pennsylvania edition of *Sister Carrie* sheds even more light on Carrie as an actress, but in this essay I am concentrating on the version of the novel that was widely available in the early 1900s.

9. Ibid., 353. For consumption-oriented articles on *Sister Carrie,* see Alan Tractenberg, "Who Narrates? Dreiser's Presence in Sister Carrie," in *New Essays on Sister Carrie,* ed. Donald Pizer (Cambridge: Cambridge University Press, 1991); and Blanche Gelfant, "What More Can Carrie Want? Naturalistic Ways of Consuming Women," *Prospects: An Annual of American Cultural Studies* 19 (1994): 389-405.

10. Elizabeth Ammons, *Conflicting Stories: American Women Writers at the Turn into the Twentieth Century* (New York: Oxford University Press, 1992), 4. Ammons contrasts Austin with "middle-class white women at the middle of the nineteenth century ... who conceived of themselves as professional writers rather than as artists ... makers of new, challenging, and typically idiosyncratic forms" (5).

11. Mary Austin, *A Woman of Genius* (1912; reprint, Old Westbury, N.Y.: Feminist Press, 1985), 302. For example, Austin recasts this passage from *A Woman of Genius:* "[M]y mouth was dry with fever. I recall my mother standing over me and my being taken dreadfully with the need of that sustaining bosom, and her stooping to my stretched arms divinely ... and then ... I asked her to put me down again. I have had drops and sinkings, but nothing to compare with this, for there was nothing there you understand ... the release, the comforting ... it wasn't there ... *it was never there at all!*" (13). The passage appears, barely altered, in Austin's *Earth Horizon* (1932; reprint, Albuquerque: University of New Mexico Press, 1991): "When you lay in the crib forlorn with that dreadful feeling which went by the name of 'fevernague,' and you thought you would feel better if only Mama would take you up, as she did, and nothing happened!" (47). In smoothing out the obstacles she faced in her own life, Austin offered Olivia a convenient and socially acceptable way out of the dilemma of raising a child while pursuing her artistic career. Austin's own daughter, Ruth, was severely retarded, and Austin was unable to both write and care for her. By 1912, when Austin was living in New York and writing *A Woman of Genius,* she had institutionalized Ruth, a situation Austin found painful and that also drew censure from the community (*Earth Horizon,* 295). When Ruth died in 1918, Austin expressed her relief that Ruth would no longer have to suffer. See Mary Austin, *Literary America, 1903-1934: The Mary Austin Letters,* ed. T. M. Pearce (Westport, Conn.: Greenwood Press, 1979), 25-26. In *A Woman of Genius,* Olivia's son, Tommy, dies, and while the death is very painful for Olivia, it frees her to pursue a career as an actress without suffering the painful guilt Austin felt at "abandoning" her daughter. Austin also gave Olivia the beauty she claimed never to have had, a dashing, passionate lover (Helmeth Garrett), and a male friend to eventually marry.

12. Lears, "From Starvation to Self-Realization," 132; Austin, *Earth Horizon,* 24; Barbara

Welter, *Dimity Convictions* (Athens: Ohio University Press, 1976), 21.

13. Austin, *A Woman of Genius,* 5. All subsequent parenthetical references are to this edition.

14. Thorstein Veblen, *The Theory of the Leisure Class* (1899; reprint, New York: Penguin Books, 1994), 132.

15. Pierre Bourdieu, *Distinction: A Social Critique of the Judgement of Taste* (Cambridge: Harvard University Press, 1984), 2. As Werner Sollors asserts in *Beyond Ethnicity,* this conflict between what we inherit (what Sollors terms "descent") and what we learn ("consent") is a central conflict in American culture. See Sollors, *Beyond Ethnicity: Consent and Descent in American Culture* (New York: Oxford University Press, 1986).

16. Karen Halttunen, "From Parlor to Living Room: Domestic Taste, Interior Decoration and the Culture of Personality," in *Consuming Visions,* 177; Jean-Christophe Agnew, "A House of Fiction," in *Consuming Visions,* 136. Certainly "The Yellow Wallpaper" (1892), by Austin's friend Charlotte Perkins Gilman, clearly shows the power of domestic interiors to simultaneously shape and reflect a woman's personality.

17. Edith Wharton, *The House of Mirth* (1905; reprint, New York: Norton, 1990), 78; Dreiser, *Sister Carrie,* 10. Other examples of women whose rooms of their own are powerful sites of self are Sara Smolinsky in Anzia Yezierska's *Bread Givers* and Clarissa Dalloway in Virginia Woolf's *Mrs. Dalloway.*

18. Austin, *Earth Horizon,* 73.

19. Auster, *Actresses and Suffragists,* 57

20. Davis, *Actresses as Working Women,* xiv, 97.

21. Martha Banta, *Imaging American Women* (New York: Columbia University Press, 1987), 619-20.

22. Dreiser, *Sister Carrie,* 400. These lines were not a part of Dreiser's original ending. Literary historians speculate that Dreiser's wife, Sara, added them. So perhaps *Sister Carrie* is, at least partially, a woman's writing.

23. Davis, *Actresses as Working Women,* 32.

24. Abraham Cahan, *The Rise of David Levinsky* (New York: Harper and Row, 1960), 443-44.

25. Davis, *Actresses as Working Women,* 18-19.

26. Auster, *Actresses and Suffragists,* 6.

27. Nancy Cott, *The Grounding of Modern Feminism* (New Haven: Yale University Press, 1987), 42. Cott claims that the word *feminism* entered common usage in the United States around 1913 (13).

28. Ibid., 174; see Elizabeth Klimasmith, "Storytellers, Story-Sellers: Artists, Muses and Exploitation in the Work of Mary Austin," *Southwestern American Literature* 20.2 (1995): 21-34.

CHAPTER EIGHT

Can the Subalter Ego Speak?

Experiences Representing Mary Austin
on the Chautauqua Circuit

JUDY NOLTE TEMPLE

When Judy Nolte Temple accepted an invitation to "be" Mary Austin on the Chautauqua circuit, she was motivated, she says, by a feminist challenge to make sure women were well represented and by a desire "to do something playfully different." Temple's "Can the Subalter Ego Speak?" is something playfully different in our collection. It is an often humorous exploration of her costumes and conflicts as she "becomes" Austin in a series of lectures on environmental issues with a group of male academics representing John Wesley Powell, John Muir, and William Mulholland. (Austin's relationships with Powell and Muir are explored in essays by Mark Schlenz and Barney Nelson later in this volume.) Appropriately, though obliquely, Temple's essay celebrates the wit and humor often overlooked by Austin's critics but enjoyed by her "common" readers. Temple herself struggled to discover Austin's comic side beneath what she initially saw as her egotism and "uncompromising intensity," qualities sometimes stressed by earlier critics.

Although she questions whether her performances are merely "lite" literature, Temple's essay has a more serious side as she explores how playing Austin has given her insight into the politics of representation and appropriation, performance and education, and the assumptions behind her audiences' responses and questions. If we accept Hoyer's and Metcalfe's readings of Austin's self-conscious efforts to reinterpret unfamiliar Native American materials for her audiences, we can see that Temple follows in Austin's trail as she struggles to figure out how to re-present Austin to contemporary audiences. Always intrigued by performance, storytelling, and the oral tradition, and always concerned with speaking out for other women, Austin would surely appreciate Temple's way of "talking back" to history about feminism, environmentalism, and the West as she brings Austin's persona and Austin scholarship to an audience outside the academy.

The fact that I, a tenured middle-aged professor, wear an uncomfortable costume and pretend that I am Mary Austin in public may seem ludicrous, but how could anyone resist the following feminist *Mission Impossible* challenge? I was sitting in my phone-booth-size office doing routine academic tasks when I received the call. It was Dan Shilling, the director of the Arizona Humanities Council, with whom I have cordially worked numerous times on speakers' bureau activities and projects. He explained that the National Endowment for the Humanities (NEH) had given Arizona funds to develop a project that would bring environmental debates "to life" through chautauqua-style characterizations of western thinkers and doers such as John Muir, Gifford Pinchot, John Wesley Powell, and William Mulholland. Then he cut to the chase. "We also want to [my feminist instinct suspects he actually meant *ought to*] include a woman. Someone, I can't reveal who, suggested that you would make a good Mary Austin." My first instinct was to consider appearances—mine and Austin's. "Who thinks I look like Austin?" I demanded. But then I returned to my better self and remembered fondly that Mary Austin's autobiography, *Earth Horizon,* had been one of my dissertation possibilities when I was an American Studies doctoral candidate at the University of Iowa in the 1970s. My adviser had discouraged me from pursuing Austin because he considered her minor and regional. And, to be honest, Austin's autobiography also disheartened me with its lengthy opening genealogy and that daunting "I-Mary" stuff. I was about to turn down the invitation to enact Austin when Dan used The Plea that has lured me and other feminists into service on countless tenure, graduate, and award committees: "You will be the *only* woman in the project, and it's vital that women are represented well." I wish I could report that I astutely countered, "I'll do it *if* you also include another woman character such as Cather or O'Keeffe." Instead, seeing opportunities to renew my acquaintance with Austin and dig into the exciting new research on her, introduce others to this intriguing woman's work, and do something playfully different from the staid academic routine, I just said yes.

Embedded in my apparently simple decision to play (with) Austin were many of the issues facing postmodernist scholars and the writers of feminist biography today: Should anyone represent or speak for the other, especially an egoist like Austin, even if she is safely, silently dead? What political messages do we transmit consciously and unconsciously via any representation? When a single character carries the weight of representing Womankind in any endeavor, should the unpleasant complexities of her life be elided in the cause of uplifting women's history? As a teacher-scholar I wondered if the brief performance of an author's work was yet another sorry substitute for the written word in an era in which our students prefer CD-ROM hypertexts and growing audiences love recorded abridged "hypotext" books. On the other hand, if literature were made more accessible and appealing, would we better fulfill our roles as public educators? Could I attract attention to the relatively obscure Austin by becoming interestingly "Austin-tatious?"

My ambivalence about chautauqua reflected Austin's own experiences. While she was a child in Ohio, she voraciously read the informative chautauqua materials her mother received, but as an adult Austin joined other intellectuals who opposed the establishment of a summer chautauqua near Santa Fe, her home. She wrote, "I do not mean to say Chautauquas do not do fine work; my mother helped to establish one, and it was of great service to many people of the kind who seek culture en masse, rather than through individual initiative."[1] Would my performance as Mary Austin contribute to the dumbing down of audiences by feeding them "lite" literature?

Just how far afield of traditional, comfortable lecturing I had unwittingly ventured soon became clear as I and the other project participants watched a training video featuring the country's foremost chautauquan, Clay Jenkinson, giving a polished portrayal of Thomas Jefferson. Clay's Jefferson is witty, informative, wise, and a superb speaker of eighteenth-century English, a formidable model for us all. The video demonstrated how a chautauquan works with a large pool of ideas that are drawn on differently for each presentation, in contrast to an actor, who recites a set script. This modern-day format combines the original educational lecture circuit idea so popular in the late 1800s with a nonelectronic virtual reality game in which scholars "become" characters who speak from the past. Chautauqua tries literally to animate public interest in history by bringing its actors back to life, and to lure audiences into learning from scholars in costume. My tasks were to create a twenty-minute monologue of Austin's ideas, to prepare for a following question-and-answer session in which I would respond as Austin might, and then to close with a brief presentation of my own insights on Austin that would include contemporary scholarship.

Conceiving the opening monologue entailed a challenge similar to preparing an abstract, for scholars who make their living generating words hate to mince them. How could I distill Austin's ideas, which fill more than thirty-five books, into a twenty-minute monologue? How could I honor Austin without simplifying her complex life? This is a problem Jacquelyn Dowd Hall discusses in her essay about those second thoughts of the biographer.[2] The NEH project's focus on environmental writing made some textual choices easy: *The Land of Little Rain, Lost Borders,* and *The Land of Journey's Ending* could form a core. But chautauquans should not recite long passages from memory; rather, they paraphrase, sample, juxtapose, and "think aloud" in order to enliven ideas via the spontaneous spoken word. Having been trained as a writer to locate the apt literary epigraph to precede my own ideas, and taught as a reader that use of the perfect word is what distinguishes Art from mere utterance, I was appalled at having to select only a few of Austin's carefully crafted words. At first I relied on Austin quotation cards stuck between the pages of a prop book that I carried, for I was a print addict still tied to those index cards I had deployed in my high school debate days when debaters were warned not to insert our "distracting" personal voices into serious objective work by experts.

As I developed my monologue-as-Austin, my dramatic sense told me that I could not simply present her ideas as disembodied sound bites. I would need to include some context from Austin's life experiences to ground her ideas about the natural world: her discovery of I-Mary in the orchard, her wanderings with her notebook on the El Tejon ranch, her talks with the Paiute women. I went first to *Earth Horizon* to find her own assessment of what was significant.[3] Compared with more openly confessional autobiographies, Austin's circumlocution was disappointing and frustrating. Austin's distancing from her own life, signified by the then-common use of third-person narration, reminded me of Henry Adams and his manikin. But Austin was advisedly protecting herself—as did her pioneering contemporaries Charlotte Perkins Gilman, Edith Wharton, and Eleanor Roosevelt—from the moral criticism that Isadora Duncan's frank *My Life* had met in the late 1920s.[4] Only after I had read Austin's story in her own words, however vague, did I turn to the two most recent biographies by Augusta Fink and Esther Stineman.[5]

When we Arizona proto-chautauquans met again after two months of individual preparation, I was struck by one of those "women's ways of knowing" insights that I resist as a nonessentialist feminist. Of all the characters, only "Austin" talked about her personal life, her upbringing, her family, and their effect on her becoming a writer. At first I dismissed this difference as a result of there being fewer autobiographical sources available on the men and my assumption that my male colleagues were at this early point in our training less comfortable with the integration of the private and public personas. When I reviewed the Thomas Jefferson tape, however, I realized that "Jefferson" had not mentioned personal issues such as his alleged relationship with the slave Sally Hemming, although Clay Jenkinson said this issue often arose during the question-and-answer period. Why, then, had I chosen to personalize—and therefore expose—Austin? After a few harrowing experiences fielding questions from audience members critical of Austin's obvious pride in her accomplishments and her choices to leave behind her marriage and her daughter in order to write, I realized that I had rightfully assumed that as a woman, Austin would have had to defend herself, to explain why she should be able to roam beyond the domestic circle and into the wilderness, something assumed to be "natural" for the male historical characters. No one queried "John Muir" about the fate of the wife and children he left behind while he climbed trees in the Sierras, or asked the quintessential administrator "William Mulholland" how he ended up in a nasty custody battle with his estranged daughter. As Nancy Miller has observed, "To justify an unorthodox life by writing [or in my case, speaking] about it is to reinscribe the original violation, to reviolate masculine turf."[6] So, like Eleanor Roosevelt in the past and Hillary Clinton in the present, "Mary Austin" sometimes finds it necessary to fall back on domestic references to her famous pies in order to defuse an audience. In my first performance aside three male characters, I was glad that I had introduced Austin's biography for another reason, when the youngest person in the audience, an intrigued girl of perhaps twelve, eagerly asked "Mary" what her major had been in college. I am hoping that this integration of the private and public can be a model of what Charlotte McClure calls "ways to reinvent the pattern of womanhood, to learn of the existence of women who express in their own voices the natural capacity of women for public work and private love, for independence and connectedness."[7]

But what about the aspects of Austin's life that show disconnection and challenge contemporary definitions of love? When I initially included in my opening monologue an elaborate explanation of Austin's controversial decision to institutionalize her eleven-year-old daughter, Ruth, I could see people in the audience stiffen. I then decided to maintain that proud sense of personal inviolability that characterized women of my grandmother's generation and made it unthinkable to ask them about any personal mat-

ter such as birth control. I switched to using Austin's own strategy of public explanation, that Ruth had been "lost to her."The presence of this enigmatic comment in the monologue usually guarantees that someone familiar with Ed Abbey's atrocious introduction to the 1988 edition of *The Land
of Little Rain,* in which he calls Ruth a "mental retard" whom Austin
"dumped," will aggressively question me.[8] But by that middle part of the
program, I have usually succeeded in "becoming" Austin for my listeners,
who seem more empathetic when I am put on the defensive about this
difficult choice. Then, at the end of my program, in my role as feminist
scholar, I bring in the similar experience and public criticism of Charlotte
Perkins Gilman, talk about my students who give up child custody in order
to return to school, or bring in some historical context by recounting the
Joseph Kennedy family's decision to institutionalize their daughter Rose-
mary despite the support of live-in help and personal wealth. I often end
the monologue with one of Austin's poems, such as "Going West," or read
that sensuous passage from *Lost Borders*:

> If the desert were a woman, I know well what she would be: deep-
> breasted, broad in the hips, tawny, with tawny hair, great masses of it
> lying smooth across her perfect curves, full-lipped like a sphinx, but
> not heavy-lidded like one, eyes sane and steady as the polished jewel
> of her skies, such a countenance as should make men serve without
> desiring her, such a largeness to her mind as should make their sins
> of no account, passionate, but not necessitous, patient—and you
> could not move her, no not if you had all the earth to give, so much
> as one tawny hair's-breadth beyond her own desires.[9]

Thus reverting to the attributor at the end, I make my peace with Austin's
corpus by giving her the last word.

Since I anticipated sharing the stage with men costumed as if they had
just come from a boat on the Colorado River or a dam construction site
in California, I decided that I would dress "Mary Austin" as well in outdoor clothes. A vintage clothing expert and I perused magazines for pho-
tos of women in the outdoors circa 1900 and decided on a walking skirt
and a late-Victorian blouse modified to accommodate my late twentieth-
century broad shoulders. When I hurried to one engagement in a brisk
wind, however, I quickly discovered that my "walking" skirt functioned as
a sail unless I took smaller strides. But I adapted to the costume—to hours

of ironing the cotton clothes in hotel rooms, to the ankle-length hem that obscures my feet when I climb onto stages, to the staunch collar that supports my cameo pin and the large hat that chautauquans wear to signify that we are in character; the hat is removed when we return to portraying ourselves. At moments I ponder veracity, wondering as I struggle with twenty-five buttons at the back of my blouse if Mary Austin wore a bra toward the end of her life. But costume is the least problematic aspect of representing Austin, perhaps because she so enjoyed variously costuming herself, sometimes "going native" in velvets, donning a mantilla for a lecture, or appearing draped in white on a horse as she encouraged her Carmel neighbors in their fight against a fire.

Preparing to dress and speak as Austin in the opening monologue was much simpler than attempting to *think* like Austin for the question-and-answer sessions. This is the wild card of representation, in which Austin's cast of mind, as well as her voluminous public and personal writings, are on call. The first challenge was to maintain a semblance of early twentieth-century conversational English while hurriedly thinking with my own brain, which is overfilled with colloquialisms such as "cool." Dropping the hedging term "like," which I abhor in my children, was, like, more difficult than I care to admit. I used as my model the crisp, formal enunciation of Eleanor Roosevelt, a far cry from my own dropped g's. Even after several years of working with Austin's lexicon, I must warm up my brain for about thirty minutes before I feel able to talk without an offputting stiffness. How much I have yet to learn was revealed when I engaged in a heated debate about the accuracy of *Death Comes for the Archbishop* with "Willa Cather" as portrayed by professional chautauquan Betty Jean Steinhauser, who has been performing Cather for more than a decade. Her ease with Cather's everyday language as gleaned from the author's personal correspondence allowed Betty to chat, while I, in contrast, recited meticulously like a programmed robot in Disneyland's Hall of Presidents. Steinhauser also demonstrated that good scholarship can also be good theater, a valuable insight that freed me to portray more emotionally the woman who in *Earth Horizon* celebrated her *feeling* for experience and for the mystical.

This second part of the chautauqua performance, the question period with its give-and-take interaction, has both a troubling potential for misleading audiences and a great promise for addressing their current concerns within a historical context. I am still uncomfortable when I engage in a debate-style dialogue with another chautauquan, suspecting that we are merely multiplying our misrepresentations in the name of lively conversation. Generally, however, the audience's questions provide an opportunity to give a fuller, more balanced view of a complex person. Despite each moderator's request that the audience confine their questions to issues contemporaneous with Austin's life in order to maintain the suspension of disbelief, some presentism slips in. For example, "Austin" must appear surprised to learn from questioners that *Cactus Thorn* is their favorite fictional work, for she could not get the novella published during her lifetime.[10] In another case, a chautauqua debate sponsored by a local environmental group pitted "Austin" against "William Mulholland," director of the Los Angles Water District at the turn of the century as portrayed by Chris Smith, a professor of U.S. history at Arizona State University. An audience member praised "Austin" for her defense of the Owens River during the infamous dispute with Los Angeles over its waters and asked what her preservation goals had been. Much to the questioner's disappointment, "Austin" countered that she had not wanted to save the water, but rather to employ it to irrigate the fields near Lone Pine. I then continued to flesh out Austin's philosophy by summarizing the chapter "Other Water Borders" from *The Land of Little Rain,* in which Austin describes the wildlife living along the irrigation ditch. Although she calls the ditch the "proper destiny" of western streams, Austin opens the door of ambiguity by continuing, "It is difficult to come into intimate relations with appropriated waters; like very busy people they have no time to reveal themselves."[11]

It is humbling to field questions from informed audiences, for we scholars abhor admitting that we do not know something, and this comforting expert role is hard to shake in character. Just as I was being introduced for my very first solo performance, a woman sitting next to me in the audience whispered that she planned to ask "Austin" why she wasn't buried at El Morro. While I remembered that Austin's ashes had been placed on Mount Picacho near Santa Fe, I couldn't recall a thing about El Morro, so I sweetly turned to my potential questioner and asked, "Just why *am* I not buried there?" Luckily for me, she whispered the answer like a proud schoolgirl just before I ascended the stage. I am often asked about other public figures contemporaneous with Austin, since she knew such famous people as Jack London, Herbert Hoover, and Mabel Dodge Luhan. I was stymied early on when someone asked if Mary Austin was a close friend of Harold Ickes, once secretary of the interior, during her Santa Fe years. Austin's interests and locales were so broad that I can never remember all of her acquaintances, although I have found T. M. Pearce's collection of her correspondence with numerous colleagues a great help.[12] I now answer such who-do-you-know questions, the kind I abhor at cocktail parties, with a bluff by falling back on biographers' and friends' accounts of Austin's ego: "I don't recall that gentleman's name per se, but if he lived in Santa Fe when I did, he surely knew, as did *everyone,* who *I* was."

Another common type of question concerns a specific line in one of Austin's works. Although chautauqua may be a confection on the humanities circuit for those who have never read a word of Austin's, it provides committed readers a chance to brush up on their favorite work in order to ask "Austin" to expand "in person." While the most discomforting type of question asks me to complete an exact quotation started by the questioner (flashback to poetry recitation days in grade school and those excruciating mental blanks), I am passably good on her most famous works and can usually elaborate on an idea from a lesser-known piece that I hope the questioner will explore. I recognize that my aged brain and Austin's dense, lyrical prose preclude my memorizing vast passages of her work; the curious must *read* Austin. When "Austin" is asked about the more intimate details of her life, I sometimes find it frustrating because she protectively left so many questions about her sexuality and loves unanswered, and the chautauqua format does not allow me to metamorphose into the scholar who could set forth conflicting speculations by Austin's biographers for the audience to pursue.

I have been pursued by fans who enter the "cult of personality," asking me long after my presentation, when I am in street clothes, to answer more questions as if I were still Austin, writing to me as Austin, or requesting me to autograph-as-Austin one of her books. I draw the line at inscribing either Austin's "auto" or "graph," responding that I will sign my own name as a performer of "Mary Austin," which seems to disappoint the believers. Particularly deflating are the initial phone answering machine messages from event planners who request a return call from "Professor uh . . . Professor uh . . . oh please just have Mary Austin give us a call." But even perpetual I-Maryism has its satisfying surprises, as when I returned to my hotel room in Independence, California, still in costume after a performance, but obviously myself—exhausted, hat off, looking for my room key. The young Native American girl at the desk who handed me the key said, "I heard you in the park today and I'm memorizing one of your poems." Despite I-Judy's fatigue, "Austin" perked up and replied, "May I listen to you?" So while I read along, she recited "The Eagle," a difficult work written by Austin "in the Indian manner."

The most satisfying part of portraying Austin in the question mode is that I can "talk back" to the History that so marginalized this woman who was ahead of her time, and to individuals cowed by her old-fashioned look, her formal demeanor, and traditional gender etiquette. It gives me the power to combine my wit with Austin's in order to refute her critics. My finest moment occurred when an art history professor gave a slide presentation titled "Personification in Nature Painting" that was actually a stroking of his light pen over what he claimed were women's breasts and thighs in landscapes. As I listened and fumed, I considered possible responses. I knew what I wanted to say, but could "Austin" say it? I scoured my brain and remembered that Austin was indeed familiar with Freud's writings and critical of them. When "Austin" was asked for an impromptu commentary after the slide show, I mentioned Doctor Freud and his phallic theory and said that throughout the lecture I had, in contrast to the good professor, noted the artists' obsession with tall, erect pines. The female audience roared, and the professor, no doubt subdued by the presence of a beloved lady in Victorian collar as his nemesis, countered weakly that a painting of a mountain range he had termed "a recumbent pregnant maiden" had been seen similarly by many experts. "Austin" sweetly demurred: "But do you not also note, sir, in the foreground before the pregnant woman a bent-over *spent pine*?" (Audience members insist that while speaking I raised my forefinger stiffly upward and then collapsed it downward. I protest that this mild-mannered academic, who would never joke in public at the expense of a colleague, was momentarily possessed by the spirit of the feisty real-life Austin, who was renowned for her acerbic wit.) On another occasion at the University of California in Davis, "Austin" debated water-use ethics with a persistent but polite gentleman, blissfully unaware that he was one of the state's foremost water attorneys and adept at dismantling his opponents, but in this make-believe setting deferential to "Mrs. Austin." This cult of niceness sometimes compels me, the paid humanities speaker, to muzzle the cutting Austin wit in order to protect audience feelings, another legacy of my traditional training that says defensiveness can get in the way of knowledge. But chautauqua personalizes history and raises the emotional pitch, as I discovered when "Austin" chided a high school girl for her brash question about young Ruth and then recounted her pain at Ruth's institutionalization. I could see tears in my questioner's eyes, which made me feel un-nice, guilty, . . . and very powerful.

The final part of the chautauqua performance, in which I speak as the scholar, allows me to exercise my professorial prowess by providing Perspective, Relevance, and Humor. I feel my own spontaneous humor usually suppressed when in character. In interchanges with "William Mulholland," it exasperates me to play the outraged, defensive Austin to his jovial, victorious Irish engineer. In the scholarly venue, I can use my own communication skills to build connections between issues germane in Austin's time and in ours. The fate of the Colorado River waters still divides the West. Women of achievement are still suspect and are still ambivalent about being identified as feminists. We discuss the insights of identity politics and standpoint epistemology, which argue that no one can speak accurately for others, after hearing "Austin" speaking for Indians, the Land, and God. The anti-Semitism so evident in Austin's correspondence is a reminder that the overt bigotry acceptable in her time may still be a submerged part of the American grain. I also address the ambiguities of Austin as a prototype NIMBY, for she was a recent Anglo immigrant to the West who quickly deigned to write on behalf of preserving what *she* valued, as do many of today's New West residents.

The greatest benefit to my intellectual life of re-reading Mary Austin in order to re-present her has come in my graduate teaching. Two of my students are devoting substantial time to studies of Austin, and her works are included in many other students' examination reading lists. In an English Department seminar course, "Women's Narratives of the West," I gave three weeks to works by Austin that provide a case study of topics that provoke us today: the influence of the writer's gender on depictions of landscape (e.g., *Cactus Thorn*), subversion of the notion of a singular American western experience (*Land of Journey's Ending*), experiments with crossing genres, and the relationship between advocacy and co-option (Austin's claim that she "lapped up Indians" in *The American Rhythm*). Just how interrelated the intellectual and the emotional are became clear during a first-week discussion of Austin. When some students made Austin's "unnatural mothering" of Ruth the foreground for comments or belittled some of her problematic prose, I found myself responding viscerally, as if they were criticizing me. I had early in the seminar mentioned my Austin performances, glossing over them as theater versus our more serious classroom, but I now saw that my investment in Austin had generated an im-

pulse to protect her, which I resisted in the name of student-centered ped-
agogy. And indeed, others rose to her defense, and a fine seminar discussion was under way. Of all the writers covered in class, Austin provoked the
strongest responses among my students, who sometimes contradicted
themselves after reading yet more Austin. I did not offer to do a chautauqua presentation for the seminar, perhaps out of insecurity, or perhaps
in response to comments by some of my university colleagues who implied I could be doing something more "serious" in lieu of Austin characterizations. However, the ritualized make-believe of chautauqua seems to
me to be on the same continuum that texts request of readers. Just as Austin
"pretends" to guide us along western trails, we engage in a make-believe
contract in following her, similar to the one between performer and audience. Later, one of my students did sit in on an "Austin" performance at
the public library, and one of my junior colleagues applied to "be" Harriet
Beecher Stowe for a summer project in California. Both were attracted to
the concept of playfulness-for-pay, but I have mixed feelings about chautauqua for the untenured, for I fear that like most other deviations from
academia, such as Jane Tompkin's acknowledgment of having a bladder or
Nancy Miller's musings about her father's penis, only those who have serious status can play at being unserious.

My "Mulholland" colleague, Chris Smith, has had excellent experiences
in his history seminars by assigning his students the task of conceptualizing their own chautauqua characterizations as famous historians. Someone
always chooses Frederick Jackson Turner, of course, but thus far Smith's favorite is a male student's monologue "as" Patricia Limerick. Just as the notion of a male-identified Limerick contains some morsel of truth, so I am
sure that those who know me well find my cohabitation with Mary
Austin's ego no mere accident.

As I circumnavigate this land of little rain, collecting my honoraria and
charming audiences, I still ruminate on whether it is living or "lite" scholarship that I propound. I have found that chautauqua audiences are not
passive: they question, react, love, or hate. This is a precarious arrangement,
as I discovered when Ann Zwinger cajoled me into performing a "surprise" chautauqua before her unsuspecting Colorado College students. She
observed that they gawked and hesitated for a few minutes before they
gave themselves up to the fantasy of conversing with Mary Austin.

There is a slippery slope between performance grounded in a text and
engaging characterizations. I recall an event I witnessed after I had done

several Austin performances and was becoming aware of the effectiveness of this medium. I was at a reception in Tucson honoring the Margaret Sanger Papers project. We in the audience were first addressed by the head of Planned Parenthood of Southern Arizona, who gave a general overview of Sanger's years in Tucson from the 1930s until her death in 1966. I sat next to a ninety-something woman who had worked with Sanger and was correcting the speaker's dates under her breath, actively arguing with "history." Next to speak was historian Esther Katz, co-director of the Sanger Papers project, who has written on "the editor as public authority." She gave a brief, informative, and complex academic talk on Sanger, looking over her reading glasses in the classic scholarly way as she slowly lost her audience; the nonagenarian sighed politely . . . and then dozed. The last presentation was by an actress who had been portraying Sanger for almost a decade and who worked from a script written by someone else. Her presentation was based on Sanger's autobiography, which contains inaccuracies and powerful semifictional anecdotes characteristic of the genre. Katz stood in the doorway, studying our enthusiasm for this one-sided view of Sanger done by a costumed actress. My muttering neighbor no longer argued or slept. Like the rest of us, she sat up in her seat and empathized with "Sanger's" moving account of her work. Although "Sanger" said she would entertain questions at the end, she did not wait for the audience's initial shyness to subside so that questions could start. Rather, she bowed and exited to a round of applause quite unlike the tepid golf claps awarded the administrator and the academic. When I cornered "Sanger" and asked her my question, she responded that she was only an actress and that my query was beyond the scope of her knowledge; nor did she know where I could look up the answer. Thus "living history" in this case was actually the masterful performance of a "lite" and limited script. To the few of us with some knowledge of the multiple sides of the biography, it was mere—or misleading—entertainment, but perhaps to others it was a stimulus to read up on Sanger. Was a little bit of "Sanger" better than no Sanger at all?

In Austin's case, a little bit is probably enough. The strong advocacy that permeates her authorial voice, criticized as unseemly in a woman by many of her contemporaries, still raises resistance. I recall an experience at a reception held before my chautauqua performance. Not yet in costume, I had nonetheless mentally begun the transformation into Austin and was therefore taken aback when I was greeted at the door by a man who had clearly been liberally tasting the punch: "Aha. It's our Mary Austin. Everyone said she was a bitch." If versions of this question come up when I portray Austin, I rely on her own wonderful retorts about talent in women and the lesser men who pursued her. When I am the scholar, I mention today's personalities, female *and* male, who possess that disagreeable egotism so common in public figures. I also think of biographer Lois Rudnick's observations about Mabel Dodge Luhan, who like Austin seems doomed to be forever considered "not nice." During Luhan's lifetime, her conservative contemporaries criticized her for loving Indians, and today some feminists retrospectively criticize her for loving Indians in a patronizing way.[13]

As I grow more comfortable with the imperfect art of chautauqua, I am struck by the many ways it mirrors Austin's life. Popular in her time as a speaker, Austin never gained a wide audience for her written work, in part due to its uncompromising intensity. She, too, appropriated the voice of the Other, changing her demeanor when reciting "in the Indian manner" the poems she composed, and claiming in *The American Rhythm* that, on occasion, she had "become Indian." (She once literally appropriated an embarrassed Tony Luhan to sing Taos Indian songs for an audience without his prior consent, much to Mabel's chagrin.) Austin herself experimented with performance in the dramas—such as *The Arrow-Maker* and *Fire*—that she wrote, continued to revise, and could never bring to her complete satisfaction. Her writing pushed the boundaries of genres, just as today's performance art moves beyond the museum wall and the printed page. One poet explains that the artist must "[u]se [the] page as the start of an event that keeps going, off the page."[14] Austin herself used the trope of the journey and might applaud this one that embodies her books.

The tripartite chautauqua format ultimately allows me to have it all ways: I am first the auto/biographer, then the lively respondent to questions in living theater, and last the critical scholar, able to reinsert myself, enshrouded in the softer lens of "perspective." I have also come to admire the I-Mary strategy that Austin used as a forerunner to deconstruct the notion of a singular self. Thus the line that divides sky and land, the ring that Austin called by the Zia term "earth horizon," grows more permeable between myself and Austin as I recount and relive her experiences in performance. What started out a few years ago as intellectual curiosity turned quickly to sympathy when I paid a "site visit" to Santa Fe to find out if her beloved final home, Casa Querida, still stood. I was saddened when a tour bus driver I flagged down asked me if this Austin lady was alive or dead, and the tourist bureau employee placed Austin in the wrong century. (At least the people at the Gerald Peters Galleries knew who Austin was and that they occupy her former home.) My knowledge of Austin's indomitable spirit, so evident in her writing, has turned the sympathy to an ongoing empathy. When I contemplate a historical event, a song, a book, I wonder what Austin thought of it. I am still reluctant to guess, however, for I cannot become Mary Austin. But for my audiences, Austin has become me.

The multiple roles that feminist biographers inhabit in relation to their subjects all find a place in capacious chautauqua: daughter, voyeuse, mother, mirror, storyteller, performer, detective. Most recently, I have been trying to detect the sense of humor that Melody Graulich insists is present in Austin, but which I have missed in my zeal to "seriously" portray her while in unserious costume. I have found cutting wit, irony, and sarcasm, but not humor. It was only on Austin's home ground that her humor finally struck me: I was visiting Independence, California, and had completed a performance outside Austin's house where she had written *The Land of Little Rain*. The kind present-day owner of the home permitted me and others to visit her restoration-in-progress. Still in costume, I toured comfortably and felt no mystical Austin "presence." But the moment I stepped outside, a mighty wind snatched the signifier-hat off of my head, revealing me as the imposter. I shrieked with surprise, "Very, *very* funny, Mary," as I chased the hat, which "the wind" had blown completely off Austin's property. In the poem "Going West," which Austin wrote as her own eulogy, she proclaims, "When . . . the dust cones dance, Something in me that is of them will stir." Had Austin demonstrated that although she was clearly master of her estate, she had observed—with perfectly timed humor and stirring wind—the dress-up play of her *sub*alter ego? Perhaps Austin can be funny, once one gets to know her.

NOTES

Through this essay title I pay playful homage to my first academic role model, Gayatri Spivak, who introduced me to the adventure of literary criticism long ago at the University of Iowa.

1. Augusta Fink, *I-Mary: A Biography of Mary Austin* (Tucson: University of Arizona Press, 1983), 229.

2. Jacquelyn Dowd Hall, "Second Thoughts on Jessie Daniel Ames," in *The Challenge of Feminist Biography,* ed. Sara Alpern (Urbana: University of Illinois Press, 1992), 145.

3. Mary Austin, *Earth Horizon* (1932; reprint, Albuquerque: University of New Mexico Press, 1991).

4. Linda Wagner-Martin, *Telling Women's Lives: The New Biography* (New Brunswick: Rutgers University Press, 1994), 76–77.

5. Fink, *I-Mary*; Esther Lanigan Stineman, *Mary Austin: Song of a Maverick* (New Haven: Yale University Press, 1989).

6. Quoted in Carolyn G. Heilbrun, *Writing a Woman's Life* (New York: Ballantine Books, 1988), 11.

7. Charlotte M. McClure, "From Impersonators to Persons: Breaking Patterns, Finding Voices," in *Private Voices, Public Lives,* ed. Nancy Owen Nelson (Denton: University of North Texas Press, 1995), 226.

8. Abbey's masculinist introduction to *The Land of Little Rain* appears in the 1988 Penguin edition of the book and replaces Austin's own preface. My favorite edition of Austin's book is the University of New Mexico edition of 1974, which also contains the original illustrations and continues in print. A book that contains both *The Land of Little Rain* and Austin's later *Lost Borders* is *Stories from the Country of Lost Borders,* ed. Marjorie Pryse (New Brunswick: Rutgers University Press, 1987).

9. Austin, *Stories from the Country of Lost Borders,* 160.

10. Austin, *Cactus Thorn* (Reno: University of Nevada Press, 1988).

11. Austin, *The Land of Little Rain* (Albuquerque: University of New Mexico Press, 1986), 139.

12. Thomas Matthews Pearce, *Literary America 1903-1934: The Mary Austin Letters* (Westport, Conn.: Greenwood Press, 1979).

13. Lois Rudnick, "The Male-Identified Woman and Other Anxieties: The Life of Mabel Dodge Luhan," in Alpern et al., eds., *The Challenge of Feminist Biography,* 116–38.

14. Poet Vito Acconi, quoted in Gregory Battcock and Robert Nickas, eds., *The Art of Performance: A Critical Anthology* (New York: Dutton, 1984), xii.

CHAPTER NINE

Mary Austin, I-Mary, and Mary-by-Herself
Collaboration in *Earth Horizon*

LINDA K. KARELL

Like Judy Temple's essay, Linda Karell's "Mary Austin, I-Mary, and Mary-by-Herself" takes up the politics of representation, this time in Austin's autobiography, which has fascinated, confounded, and sometimes aggravated readers. As Austin's friend Charlotte Perkins Gilman insightfully recognizes in her 1912 review of A Woman of Genius, *women who write about their own talent and achievement risk criticism. Gilman writes of the novel's heroine: "Olivia is not a loveable person—as is often the case with geniuses. In the pursuit of her work, or perhaps we should say, in her work's pursuit of her, she is forced to sacrifice not only much that was dear to her, but the dearest wishes of others. This also is frequently the case with geniuses. We are quite used to its expression in men" (280).[1] Like Carew-Miller, Karell sees Austin as struggling with the dilemma of female genius and how to claim and represent it. Karell argues that Austin solved the dilemma by using "provocative and subversive" ways to challenge autobiography's focus on singular subjectivity and individual authorship.*

As we have seen in other essays in this collection, Austin repeatedly stretched generic boundaries, and Earth Horizon *is no exception. Karell sees the presence of* Earth Horizon's *multiple narrators and Austin's elaboration of various generative sources of her creativity as demanding an unconventional approach to the text. She approaches* Earth Horizon *as a collaborative work, using recent theories of collaboration in the writing process and revisionist readings of the genre. In constructing an autobiography that eludes the conventions of the unitary self, Karell argues, Austin claims a diffuse subjectivity that relies on connection—between her many component selves and between herself and others—in a remarkable act of self-creation.*

Early in her 1932 autobiography, *Earth Horizon,* Mary Austin relates a "prophetic" event in the life of her maternal grandmother, Hannah Graham. Hannah's husband, a tailor, made his wife a custom-fitted dress from fine broadcloth, "an act so unprecedented that it narrowly escaped being scandalous."[2] Because she offended the conservative tastes of the community, Hannah was promptly disciplined by the Methodist church and publicly called forward while a sermon on vanity was preached: "One must suppose that the church was well filled on that occasion, and that it was at the properly dramatic moment—I am sure that Hannah would have seen to that—the young matron walked down the aisle with her limping and totally unperturbed Scotchman beside her, *wearing that particular dress!* It was so exactly the thing Mary would have done!" (19-20). Rather than wearing a daring dress as her mode of resistance, however, Austin writes about her grandmother's "scandalous story," affirming her affinity with her grandmother in order to claim Hannah as a collaborative source in her refusal to capitulate to cultural expectations that violate her own vision of female creativity.

Austin's "particular dress" is *Earth Horizon.* In it she challenges the basic tenets of the genre of formal autobiography, including its insistence on veracity, linear narrative, singular subjectivity, and individual authorship. She investigates female subjectivity and its relation to creativity by positing an influential matrilineal heritage to form a collaborative history of resistance; she establishes a collaborative, multivocal subjectivity in place of the traditional singular subject of autobiographical writing; and she points to Native American literature, in its traditional oral and collaborative forms, as a prior text underlying her success as a writer.[3] Looking at Austin's text through the lens of collaborative writing provided by recent theorists in textual production and composition theory allows us to see the challenges she poses both to the genre of autobiography and to conceptions of female subjectivity.

In her introduction, Austin states one of her clearest goals for her autobiography: to credit "the stamp of ancestral influences." She feels herself fortunate "to have been brought up intimately in touch with ancestral history, and so aware as few people are, of the factual realities of transmitted experiences." She insists that her sense of "ancestral rootage" has been both her "greatest pleasure" and "the major importance" for writing the autobiography (viii). In the first section of *Earth Horizon,* a tribute to Austin's great-grandmother entitled "The Saga of Polly McAdams," Austin transforms oral stories into an alternate written history and claims Polly as a temperamental and emotional mentor: "except for Polly, you might suppose that Mary was hatched from a cuckoo's egg" (14). By crediting her female ancestors for their "influences," Austin creates a prior text from their lives, a text that she can claim collaborated in the creation of her identity: "Whatever in Mary makes her worth so much writing about has its roots in the saga of Polly and Hannah and Susanna Savilla, in the nurture of which she grew up" (14). Austin's search for origins denies the illusion of the "self-made" identity in autobiographical writing, while her insistence on the centrality of female ancestry as a collaborative component of identity privileges an earlier cultural understanding of collaboration as intertextuality.[4]

Yet, Austin's efforts to claim a usable, coherent text in her female ancestry are blocked by her mother, Susanna Savilla Hunter, whose responses to crucial events in Austin's life undercut the image of collaborative female resistance and posit opposition and the collective force of cultural condemnation of female ambition instead of support. *Earth Horizon* chronicles Austin's sense of abandonment in her relationship with her mother. When Austin's first story is published in the *Overland,* for example, her mother's response is lukewarm. "Susie read it aloud to her, but she could never be got to express an interest in it. 'I think you could have made more of it,' Mary finally dragged out of her. Where was now the triumph and encouragement that should go to one's first professional adventure!" (240). After Austin's daughter, Ruth, is born with severe mental disabilities, Austin receives a letter from her mother: "I don't know what you've done, daughter, to have such a judgment upon you" (257). Her mother's blame creates in Austin a "grief too long borne in secret for surface recovery" (257). By quoting her mother's words, Austin creates a competing text documenting women's distance from one another, a text that erupts only to be silenced in secret grief where "no one ever does speak to me about it" (257).

Austin addresses this narrative and emotional disjunction by positioning her mother as a strong activist in the public arena. Involved in the Woman's Christian Temperance Union, Susanna took her daughter with her to meetings. The prohibition movement and her mother's commitment to it stand out for Austin as a bridge between mother and daughter, between abandonment and love: "I remember the first woman who was allowed to speak in our church on the right of women to refuse to bear children to habitual drunkards, and my mother putting her arm across my knees and taking my hand in one of the few natural gestures of a community of woman interest she ever made toward me" (142). Although Austin is unable to invest her mother with the same prefeminist subversive tactics she sees in her grand-mother, she is careful to strike a balance between Susanna as a model she can claim fully and one she must repudiate utterly. Instead, Susanna be-comes the narrative embodiment of a blurred boundary on which the sub-versive aspects of the autobiography rely. Neither wholly this nor com-pletely that, Susanna is an example of the cultural obstacles to female creativity that Austin both internalizes and struggles to reject.

Austin clarifies these competing aspects of collaborative female inheri-tance when she discusses Susanna's death. At the hour of her mother's death, Austin has a vision of her: young, happy, telling her daughter that "there was no need for Mary to take the train now, since everything was well with her" (273). Austin learns later, in a telegram from her brother, that Susanna's last words were "take care of Mary." Her vision of her mother culminates in an unassailable union never experienced in life, which, coupled with the uncharacteristic tenderness of her mother's final words, offers Austin some consolation for a lifetime of distance.

But the very grief Austin feels at her mother's death reasserts the simul-taneous union and division that marked their relationship: "There is an el-ement of incalculable ravening in the loss of your mother; deep under the shock of broken habit and the ache of present grief, there is the psychic wound, the severed root of being; such loss as makes itself felt as the com-panion of immortality. For how should the branch suffer, torn from the dead tree? It is only when the tree is green that the cut bough bleeds" (273). Although Austin must go back to her grandmother and great-grandmother to assert a prior text that she can claim collaborated in creating her identity, it is the conflicted text Austin makes of her mother's life and death, the image of a "severed root of being" in a matriarchal family tree, that most consistently informs her vision of female subjectivity as multiple, collabo-rating together but replete with fissures; linked but not identical.

Austin develops her complex understanding of female subjectivity in her self-construction throughout *Earth Horizon*. Her subjectivity is cleaved—not simply in half, but into various personas. Some of these per-sonas are subtly differentiated, marked by inconsistent changes in voicing, grammar, or syntax, while others are announced in the text. The most ob-vious persona is Mary Austin the author, whose achievements justify the autobiography and who is reconstructed by the text. Closely related is

Mary Austin the narrator, striving for omniscience but, as she often interrupts her narrative to tell us, frequently baffled at the complexity she encounters in relating her life story. In addition, there are the yoked personas of Mary, Mary-by-herself, and I-Mary, a representation of multiple subjectivity central to the collaborative aspects of the autobiography because Austin associates each persona, directly and indirectly, with her early development as a writer.

As she writes, Austin alternates between the first and third persons, frequently referring to herself as "Mary" or using the subjective or objective case to refer to herself as "she" or "her." Although it is an awkward narrative approach, the alternation repeatedly challenges the assumed stance of unitary selfhood privileged by traditional forms of male autobiographical writing by announcing these differences within herself rather than suppressing them. Despite its claims to unmediated truth telling, the "I" of autobiography is specifically gendered. Sidonie Smith writes, "Single letter, single sound, the 'I' appears unitary, bold, indivisible. In its very calligraphy and enunciation (in English at least) it defies destabilization, dissemination, diffusion. But that 'I' is gendered and it is male."[5] In *Earth Horizon*, Austin grapples with the obstacles encountered by female authors writing autobiographically in a literary genre conventionally dedicated to telling the life stories of great men. She must claim the narrative authority of the autobiographical "I" in a genre that excludes her as Other, while at the same time subverting the constraints of the unitary subjectivity that justifies her writing. Austin does both in *Earth Horizon* by refashioning the traditional subject of the autobiography, the bold "I," to present herself as multiple selves who never coalesce into a unitary subject. The linked personas Austin calls Mary, Mary-by-herself, and I-Mary, in combination with the other divisions of selfhood represented in the text, complicate even this critique. Austin inevitably introduces competing desires and conflicts among the personas. Each persona, in its fluid interconnection, forms a part of the collaboration that is *Earth Horizon,* and through them Austin contextualizes the autobiographical "I," revising and revealing it as a collaborative construction when she attributes agency for her writing to a variety of personalities, events, and influences.

On one level, Austin's use of a collaborative mode of narration is pragmatic, a recognition of the multiple selves, multiple voices, and multiple influences she felt defined her writing. On another level, it is an extremely effective writing strategy, anticipating recent work in the collaborative nature of textual production.[6] Multiple authorship, whether defined as process or as result, has been difficult to theorize adequately, in part because the concept of individual authorship has been made to seem inevitable in the humanities. Collaborative textual production challenges that inevitability. With it depart claims to autonomy, to the individual as the site of originality, and to the privileged status of the author in the production of a text—all concepts that help consolidate the idea of the self as unitary, organic, and self-knowing; and also literature, in this case autobiography, as a transcendent medium through which experience can be directly represented. In "On the Author Effect: Recovering Collectivity," Martha Woodmansee points out that "from the Middle Ages right down through the Renaissance new writing derived its value and authority from its affiliation with the texts that preceded it, its derivation rather than its deviation from prior texts."[7] The idea of derivation from prior texts is key to Austin's collaborative endeavor in *Earth Horizon*. The prior texts she chooses to identify and claim, however, are not masterpieces of male autobiography; rather, they are the oral stories of women's history and Native American storytelling, traditions that repeatedly deny the single authority of a named author—traditions that, in other words, refuse the coherent gendered identity of the authorizing "I."

Yet Austin does not fully forgo the authority of the autobiographical "I." Indeed, she cannot, because that "I" signifies an authority Austin wishes to claim, one that gives her entry into the realm of autobiographical representation and helps to limit criticism for transgressing the bounds of gendered expectations of female creativity. Austin herself apparently has the traditional male-gendered template for autobiographical writing in mind when she writes in the introduction, "When first it was proposed to me that I write my autobiography, I anticipated great pleasure in the undertaking, for I thought it meant the re-living of my important occasions, the setting of them in their significant order, and so bringing the events of my life into a pattern consistent with my acutest understanding of them" (vii). Austin understands that ordering events, creating the normative linear narrative, is a part of the pleasure of autobiographical writing, and yet she often assumes the pose of striving to meet, rather than to challenge, the formal expectations of autobiography. We are justified for refusing to take Austin at her word, or at least at her first word, because her forthcoming hint, "I anticipated . . . ," immediately alerts us that this traditional strategy failed. When she continues by writing, "But I found that there was more to an autobiography" than her expectations first suggested, including "the choice of incidents," she launches her critique of the tenets of autobiography and the notion of the organic and unified self it seeks to reveal (viii). Austin's critique is linked to the collaborative aspects of *Earth Horizon* when the "I" of the introduction becomes suspect within the text—when the different representations of "Mary" appear.

The process of subverting the tenets of formal autobiography continues throughout the introduction, which is signed simply "M.A.," a designation apparently meant to signal the reader that it corresponds to Mary Austin, the author of the upcoming autobiography; yet this correspondence is quickly rendered fluid. Austin asserts, "It has always been a profound realization of my life that there was a pattern under it" (vii). Her statement lays claim to a spiritual essence, a prior text from Native American culture that provides the "earth horizon" of her title, which precedes and guides the life story, further undercutting the notion of the self-made subject free of the culture that formal autobiography rests on and re-creates. Austin insists on the pattern rather than the more traditional autobiographical frame. By deflecting attention from herself to the spiritual symbol of another culture, Austin resists the claims to singular genius that autobiography implies. What is more, her cross-cultural appropriation, while debatably a colonizing maneuver that I will discuss in more detail later, emphasizes the differences between cultures rather than insisting on universality. Of course, the "pattern" Austin claims is in itself a multiple construct, affected by her cultural positioning as a heterosexual, white, midwestern woman struggling for financial and emotional security at a particular historical moment. These elements of the pattern are sometimes in conflict with one another, and Austin must balance her occasional desire for an essential, unchanging identity with her awareness of identity as shifting and contingent. The difficulty of maintaining that balance is evident in the apparent contradictions of the text, in the ways Austin's representations of her "selves," her attitudes, and her actions sometimes conflict with each other.

One of these points of conflict appears in the first-person address throughout the introduction, which seems to claim a coherent subjectivity. However, while the "I" of the introduction is aligned with the initials M.A., much of the introduction's purpose is to emphasize and explain the difficulties of maintaining that coherent self in the process of writing autobiographically. Austin elaborates on the difficulty of knowing which events are important, and in so doing links the status of authorship with the presence of the pattern: "It is not enough to say that, since one has arrived at the point at which an autobiography is demanded, the pattern has not been wholly defeated" (viii). This passage, along with the entire introduction, alerts readers to the tension that exists throughout *Earth Horizon:* Austin's affinity for abstract rhetoric, the passive voice, and multiple negative constructions undermines authority while linear assertion gives way to qualifications, digressions, and abstraction. A second tension is evident in Austin's attempt to claim a unified self in the face of a heightened awareness of the fractures in that unity, fractures that are compounded by her acknowledgment of multiple sources of agency. It is an astutely doubled strategy because, by asserting the inspiration of the preexisting pattern, Austin lays claim to a higher authority, yet the intimacy of the first-person address works to coalesce the persona of Mary Austin, author and subject of the ensuing life story.

As Austin interweaves those collaborative forces into her autobiographical narrative, she creates a textual form that is itself a challenge to established forms of autobiographical writing. Once the autobiography proper begins, Austin chooses an unconventional narrative mode to relate it, assuming a more removed narrative stance by referring to herself in the third person. Rather than apologizing for the shifts between first- and third-person address, she insists on their validity as true to her experience. She is aware that she risks criticism: "I must write these things the way they happened to Mary, swiftly flashing, in a flame spurt. . . . Often [the idea, the event] would be new in the thought of her time. And nothing Mary does has so irritated the critics against her as her habit of writing these things in all the shining sharpness of her first perception of them" (216-17). Challenging the expected division between fact and fiction, or between past and present, could make Austin a publishing risk, but she nonetheless vents her annoyance with the strictures of autobiographical expectations: "[A]ll this Mary business is a nuisance; having to stop and tell why she did things and what she thought about them" (204). Well into the second half of *Earth Horizon,* Austin interrupts her third-person narrative with a lengthy first-person description of the difficulty and responsibility in writing an autobiography:

Here I come upon the unfeasible task, the true presentation of a life-story uninformed by the contributory solutions snatched in passing from lives unable to profit by their own instruction. . . . I suppose every life that attains any degree of expressiveness is largely lessoned by these things. . . . I recognize no right of mine to minute particularity in the lives that did not actually press constructively on mine, and at the same time admit my indebtedness to the truth those lives revealed. I am aware that any autobiography written with due regard to such acknowledgments must seem to present the chief figure in it as moving through the ample space of admitted importance. (245-46)

Unhesitatingly revealing that she knows that the constraints placed on autobiography do not coincide with the actualities of a life, Austin consistently shifts her notion of autobiography to include the effects of others on both her writing process and her identity. Austin's characteristic abstractness in this address further undermines her authority as a "chief figure" by requiring the participation and substantial interpretative abilities of her readers.

The literary persona of Mary Austin is at once troubling and necessary. Austin works to create this persona, but at the same time she also feels separate from it, and separated from others by it. Her discomfort is evident when she returns to her college years later as a published author: "I was shocked even to find figures warmly remembered out of that so happy intimacy, putting me apart across the years as Mrs. Austin" (175). The distance in this sentence between the "I" who was shocked and the public figure, "Mrs. Austin," can be measured in more than years or accomplishments: the palpable difference between the two identities precludes a return of "happy intimacy." The "I," signifier of identity and indivisibility, cannot traverse the distance to include "Mrs. Austin." The self is divided by the gaze of others, resulting in a loss that Austin does not attempt to suppress or recover. When Austin shifts between first person and third person elsewhere in the text, the echo of division is recalled, but so is Austin's insistence on the illusionary intimacy of the autobiographical "I."

The most baffling and intriguing aspect of Austin's autobiography is her representation of Mary, Mary-by-herself, and I-Mary. Austin describes Mary-by-herself as a shy, uncertain child who of the three most fully feels the absence of her mother's love; I-Mary is the more confident, capable persona Austin associates with books and, significantly, with her eventual authorship. Mary and Mary-by-herself become conflated identities after the arrival of I-Mary when Austin is four years old and learning to read a primer with her older brother, Jim. Contrary to autobiography's assump-

tion that "I""defies destabilization, dissemination, diffusion,"[8] Mary, trying
to understand the letter *I,* mistakes it for "eye," and her mother must correct her: "I, myself . . . I-Mary" (46). The ensuing experience transforms
Austin: "Something turned over inside her; the picture happened. . . . And
inside her, I-Mary, looking on. I-Mary, I-Mary, *I-Mary!*" (46). This scene of
literal "self" awareness comes to Austin as a surprise, suggesting that
women's subjectivity is not a foregone conclusion, an inevitable event. This
inaugural moment of subjectivity functions as a key to Austin's association
of I-Mary with the ability to write and with her conception of collaboration: Austin bestows selfhood onto I-Mary; only I-Mary can withstand
criticism and remain unaffected by it. I-Mary does not replace the other
persona, Mary-by-herself; she assists her.

Austin consistently writes of I-Mary as a distinctly separate entity, although she is clearly aware that, to others, I-Mary is indistinguishable from
Mary or Mary-by-herself: "She came so suddenly and always so inevitably
that I doubt if anybody ever knew about her, or could have been made to
understand" (46). Austin insists on I-Mary's reality: "Certainly she would
not have described the I-Mary experience as a feeling. It was a reality, as
real as when in dreams you pick up your feet and go floating in the desired
direction. . . . I-Mary was as real as that" (74). Austin steadily upholds this
sense of an alternate reality as a valuable component of her creative ability
and spiritual insight: "When you were I-Mary, you could see Mary-by-
herself as part of the picture, and make her do things that, when you were
she, could not be done at all; such as walking a log high over the creek,
which gave Mary-by-herself cold prickles even to think about" (74).

Austin's association of I-Mary with writing explains her importance.
"Always until she was quite grown up, I-Mary was associated with the
pages of books. The mere sight of the printed page would often summon
her, and since her coming was comfortably felt . . . it was sought in the contemplation of print" (46). Because it was in the process of learning to read
that Austin had her first experience of "self" awareness, the link between
I-Mary and printed text was tightly forged. I-Mary, quite understandably,
would become a collaborative partner later in Austin's life when she began
the difficult and demanding process of writing, offering her not only comfort but also a singularly trustworthy experience of ability and confidence
unmatched elsewhere.

The dangers of a life as a woman writer are emphasized later in *Earth
Horizon* when the metaphor of I-Mary traversing the log reappears, linked
with authorship:

There was that stream of knowingness which ever since adolescence I had felt going on in me, supplying deficiencies, affording criterions of judgment, creating certainties for which no warrant was to be found in my ordinary performance, setting up in me the conviction, which as experience I have named I-Mary, that all I know has always been known by me and used as known. At any rate, it was as I-Mary walking a log over the creek, that Mary-by-herself couldn't have managed, that I wrote two slender little sketches. (230-31)

The "two slender sketches" signify a beginning that I-Mary literally enables because she brings to Austin the experience of a competent self and binds that experience with the realm of books and writing.

Austin's understanding of I-Mary fluctuates throughout her autobiography. What is first claimed as a separate entity whose appearance can be coaxed becomes the name for an experience of self-knowledge that Austin takes as evidence of the pattern she claims underlies her life. Although Austin's conception of I-Mary shifts, I-Mary remains in a collaborative relationship with Austin, upholding her as a writer, giving her confidence and self-assurance. As a separate entity, I-Mary is a co-creator of Austin's "slender little sketches." I-Mary also implicitly collaborates in *Earth Horizon* when she is transformed into Austin's experience of "the pressure of knowledge, all the knowledge in the world" (154).

Just as Austin must find a way to include female ancestry as a prior text that collaborated in the construction of her identity, she also searches for a way to claim her religious inheritance; in this case, however, it is a text she radically revises by incorporating Native American beliefs. Austin was uncomfortable with the Methodist beliefs of her family and community as a child, feeling that "Heaven sounded more boring than church," and she eventually linked a long period of spiritual unhappiness and alienation to her participation in organized religion (53). As a young child, Austin had an experience she describes as "earth and sky and tree and wind-blown grass and the child in the midst of them came alive together with a pulsing light of consciousness. . . . I remember the child looking everywhere for the source of this happy wonder, and at last she questioned—'God?'— because it was the only awesome word she knew" (371, n. 13). Here Austin seems to fulfill the traditional obligations of autobiography by linking herself to an experience of universality, and the search to recover this experience is central to Austin's eventual conception of herself as a writer. But Austin's apparently traditional approach also functions as an acknowledgment of her difference from those around her, steadfast Methodists with whom she was at odds even as a child. Austin's description of God is not a claim to wholeness; it is evidence of her incompleteness, the partiality of subjectivity, a point she emphasizes when the feeling leaves her for much of her childhood. It is also one of many narrative episodes in which Austin's struggle to find usable prior texts illuminates the role of collaboration in her development as a writer; she regularly describes her achievements, both personal and professional, as the culmination of external sentient forces acting in relationship with her, forces she reorganizes and revises for inclusion in her autobiography.

Even after it is revised to incorporate God experientially and I-Mary's function as granting transcendent knowledge, Austin's Methodist religious training cannot sustain her in crisis. During her adolescence, following the deaths of both her beloved sister and father, I-Mary disappears, along with the experience of unity and unique individual vision Austin associates with her: "No longer were things experienced vizualized [sic] as things seen. . . . God was not found under the wide elms and cloudy maples with which the way to school was lined. There was no sort of emergency in which I-Mary came, nor answered to if called" (94). Apart from suggesting adolescence as the cause, Austin offers no concise explanation for I-Mary's disappearance, but we can find a hint when she writes, "Against the trauma of grief children are doubly helpless" (91). Austin's helplessness ceases only after her college graduation, when she moves to California with her family. There she directs her mind to learning about the desert landscape, its indigenous peoples, and the animals there and is "released from the long spiritual drought that was coincident with her commitment to organized religion" (198). This "release" enabled Austin to incorporate collaborative aspects of Native American oral literature into her spiritual perceptions and writing, a point I will return to shortly.

Feminist theories of autobiography show us the risks Austin takes with her representations of multiple selfhood traced across prior texts. Austin's metaphor of the log high over the creek, which she uses twice in nearly identical phrasing, emphasizes the risks women take when they write and the fear they face of being unable to maintain a necessary delicate balance between success and failure, praise and blame. The stakes of writing for women here are high, and terrifying. Austin's initial surprise at the concept of subjectivity, the "I" of "I-Mary," and her subsequent experience of her as separate—as arriving to protect her, comfort her, or achieve for her—

reveal another dilemma of female authorship: not granted subjectivity, women must create it and wrestle for it. While it is possible to read Austin's experience as a form of multiple personality brought on by the trauma of her mother's physical and emotional distance and later integrated into a single persona, the autobiography does not bear out this reading. Although I-Mary is mentioned less frequently as the narrative focuses on Austin's adulthood, continuing shifts between first- and third-person narration reveal that Austin never achieves a single, unified subjectivity, just as her autobiographical narrative never becomes smoothly or consistently linear.

Late in her autobiography (and in her life) Austin emphasizes her ability to re-create herself. Austin was noted, perhaps even notorious, for acts of self-creation and calculated self-promotion during her lifetime, but as she matured, some of her most notable feats of self-creation concerned her commitment to Native American issues and artistic expression. Without formal training in literature, ethnography, or anthropology, Austin wrote numerous short stories with Native Americans as her theme, "re-expressions" of what she called "Amerindian verse," and sometimes took on the behaviors, associations, and beliefs of Native Americans in her personal life, often at the cost of pointed ridicule. Why would a woman who experienced the status of outsider so bitterly throughout her life consistently re-create herself as a target for criticism? The answer may be related to Austin's experience of subjectivity through the appearance of I-Mary, her association of I-Mary with writing, and her experience of Native American beliefs as usable prior texts for her formulation of collaborative identity. In *Earth Horizon,* Austin writes of an encounter with the Paiutes: "She entered into their lives, the life of the campody, the strange secret life of the tribe, the struggle of Whiteness with Darkness, the struggle of the individual soul with the Friend-of-the-Soul-of-Man. She learned what it meant; how to prevail; how to measure her strength against it. Learning that, she learned to write" (289).

Austin's dichotomous and elusive view of Indian spirituality is troubling, but her attribution is clear: she learned her craft from Indians. The personal struggle, the collaborative relationship formed out of that struggle, and the experience of eventual literary success echo Austin's earliest experiences of texts: reading, and then writing, with I-Mary to guide her. For Austin, autobiography is a form in which she can credit the forces of her life, and the distinct personas of her self, for their collaborative relationship in her writing. Austin acknowledges this relationship when she writes that this form of prayer "is described here because it proved, though in the beginning I had no notion that this would be the case, the answer to the problem of creative activity" (277). Although here Austin attributes her ability to write to the Paiutes, the experiences do not so much suggest that Austin found a substitute for I-Mary and the pleasures of selfhood that I-Mary conveyed as that she found another manifestation of that experience, one that integrated her unconventional spiritual beliefs with her experience of subjectivity residing in texts.

Near the end of her life, Austin published *The American Rhythm: Studies and Reexpressions of Amerindian Songs* (1930), perhaps her most extensive claim to expertise in Indian literary forms. Criticized for being inadequately researched and documented, and presented in Austin's own rather mystical vocabulary, *American Rhythm* nonetheless utilizes the collaborative strategies she valued elsewhere in her writing, and it did help to solidify her reputation as an expert on Native American literature. In *Earth Horizon,* Austin even claims to have a "far-off and slightly mythical Indian ancestor of whose reality I am more convinced by what happened to me among Indians than by any objective evidence" (267), an assertion that one critic appropriately questions as "problematic if Austin made such a claim to enhance her status as an Indian expert."[9] Biological Indian ancestry is doubtful; more likely Austin was appealing to a sense of spiritual compatibility, but there is no way to be sure. At worst, Austin was self-infatuated and appropriated Native American literature and culture in response to her own need to establish herself publicly as an expert on Native American concerns. At best, she was searching for a way to record her cross-cultural experience in a genre not meant to accommodate divergence from its established boundaries.

Austin's behavior here is debatably a colonizing maneuver; she claims expertise without an intimate understanding of the tribes she studies or their languages, and her "reexpressions" tell us considerably more about Austin and her growing confidence than they do of legitimate Indian literature. While intention, to the degree that we can recover it, does not justify appropriation, it can render that behavior understandable. Although Austin describes her use of Native American themes as an active collaborative relationship, it is unknown to what degree, if any, the Native Americans she knew agreed to that collaboration or even saw it in those terms.[10] On the other hand, contemporary scholars of Native American literature have shown repeatedly that "authority" and the signature of the author do not function in Native American literary forms as they do in European tradition. Arnold Krupat writes, "American Indian literature, until very recently, has been notoriously lacking in its possession of named authors."[11] The absence of an author's signature and the oral, performative basis of Native American literature make it traditionally a collaborative literature. Although Austin found a compatible understanding of the collaborative nature of literature and rediscovered her childhood feeling of unity through her encounters with Native American cultures, she never fully entered a tribal identity. Nor, I would argue, does she claim to, at least in *Earth Horizon*. Austin is careful to position herself in her autobiography as the enthusiastic and grateful student, a positioning that emphasizes a collaborative relationship but also keeps her marginal, a white woman outside. Late in her life, Austin kept to the lessons of that life by not abandoning the insight provided by her marginal position and by trusting in a collaborative process despite its cost in criticism and rebuke.

Earth Horizon is a provocative life story, detailing the conflicting desires of a child to be loved, a woman to be accepted, and an author to be esteemed. In it, Austin negotiates between the unitary subjectivity that is a generic component of autobiographical writing and her own deeply felt understanding of herself as multiple personalities whose ancestry and involvement with others collaborated in her writing and in the creation of her identity as an author. By refashioning the subject of her autobiography to incorporate multiple personas, the role of female ancestors in collaborative identity, and the importance of cross-cultural relationships in her writing, Austin revises the very form of autobiographical writing and insists on the need, particularly for women writers, to acknowledge the role of multiplicity and difference in their writing. Yet even more poignantly, *Earth Horizon* reminds its readers that to follow where her vision of creativity leads, a woman must create herself, going against a web of social conventions, often without support and in the face of ridicule and humiliation. The bold "I" of the autobiographic adventure remains bold in *Earth Horizon,* but it is no longer indivisible after Austin uncovers the hidden costs and struggles required to maintain it.

NOTES

1. Quoted in Melody Graulich, "'I Thought at First She Was Talking about Herself': Mary Austin on Charlotte Perkins Gilman," *Jack London Journal* 1.1 (1994):148–58.

2. Austin, *Earth Horizon* (Cambridge, Mass.: Riverside Press, 1932), 19. Page numbers

follow subsequent quotations in the text.

3. In grateful recognition of the collaborative relationship that exists between a writer and her editor, I thank Melody Graulich for her suggestion that I think about Austin's uses of prior texts in her autobiography.

4. See Martha Woodmansee, "On the Author Effect: Recovering Collectivity," *Cardozo Arts and Entertainment Law Journal* 10 (1992): 279-92.

5. Sidonie Smith, "Resisting the Gaze of Embodiment: Women's Autobiography in the Nineteenth Century," in *American Women's Autobiography: Fea(s)ts of Memory,* ed. Margo Culley (Madison: University of Wisconsin Press, 1992), 79.

6. Several recent book-length studies have begun to set forth the range and implications of collaborative writing. See Lisa Ede and Andrea Lunsford's *Singular Texts/Plural Authors: Perspectives on Collaborative Writing* (Carbondale: Southern Illinois University Press, 1990); Jack Stillinger's *Multiple Authorship and the Myth of Solitary Genius* (New York: Oxford University Press, 1991); Wayne Koestenbaum's *Double Talk: The Erotics of Male Literary Collaboration* (New York: Routledge, 1989); and *Significant Others: Creativity and Intimate Partnership,* ed. Whitney Chadwick and Isabelle de Courtivron (London: Thames and Hudson, 1993). Individual articles and special journal issues also explore the fertile area of collaboration and its challenges to established conventions in literary studies. See *Tulsa Studies in Women's Literature,* ed. Holly Laird, 13.2 (Fall 1994) and 14.1 (Spring 1995); Lisa Ede and Andrea Lunsford, "Why Write . . . Together?" *Rhetoric Review* 1 (January 1983): 57-68; Ede and Lunsford, "Why Write . . . Together: A Research Update," *Rhetoric Review* 5 (Fall 1986): 71-84; Ede and Lunsford, "Rhetoric in a New Key: Women and Collaboration," *Rhetoric Review* 8.2 (1990): 234-41; Carey Kaplan and Ellen Cronan Rose, "Strange Bedfellows: Feminist Collaboration," *Signs* 18.3 (1993): 547-61; Brenda Carr, "Collaboration in the Feminine: Daphne Marlatt/Betsy Warland's 'Re-Versed Writing' in *Double Negative,*" *Tessera* 9 (1990): 111-22; and Phyllis F. Mannocchi, "Vernon Lee and Kit Anstruther-Thompson: A Study of Love and Collaboration between Romantic Friends," *Women's Studies* 12 (1986): 129-48.

7. Woodmansee, "On the Author Effect," 281.

8. Smith, "Resisting the Gaze," 79.

9. See Karen S. Langlois, "Marketing the American Indian: Mary Austin and the Business of Writing," in *A Living of Words: American Women in Print Culture,* ed. Susan Albertine (Knoxville: University of Tennessee Press, 1995), 165.

10. See Betsy Klimasmith, "Storytellers, Story-Sellers: Artists, Muses, and Exploitation in the Work of Mary Austin," *Southwest American Literature* 20.2 (1993): 21-23.

11. Arnold Krupat, "An Approach to Native American Texts," in *Critical Essays on Native American Literature,* ed. Andrew Wiget (Boston: G. K. Hall, 1985), 120.

CHAPTER TEN

Waters of Paradise

Utopia and Hydrology in *The Land of Little Rain*

MARK SCHLENZ

In her performances of "Mary Austin," Judy Temple tries to "bring environmental debates to life." The next four essays explore how Austin's own work brings to life environmental debates, in her own time and in ours. In "Waters of Paradise," Mark Schlenz connects Austin's ideas about social organization with her understanding of water use by the native people and the Spanish settlers of the Southwest, and with the "hydrographic vision" of John Wesley Powell. In Schlenz's reading, both Powell and Austin offered utopian visions of communal organization in the West, developed from their close study of the region's landscapes and peoples; placed in historical context, their prophetic visions of a "paradise regained" reveal the ironies in the lost paradise of the contemporary West. The "tragic key" in which Austin writes, Schlenz argues, reveals a tension between idyllic visions of community based on bioregional theory and historical reality. Contemporary ecological theorists, he suggests, are often themselves caught in a similar struggle between imagining what might be and offering a realistic vision of life in the West.

Schlenz's discussion of Austin's exploration of western water use positions her between Powell and his most recent biographer, Wallace Stegner, who are generally viewed as major figures in the history of western settlement. Schlenz implicitly argues for Austin's importance as a central figure in western studies as well. Like DeZur, Hoyer, and others, he reveals how Austin saw the West as offering a regenerative vision often at odds with her realistic observation of western life, a vision she nevertheless saw as a "native alternative to imported European communism."

Mary Austin's meditations on the meaning of landscape for American cultural history, developed through both her fiction and nonfiction, resulted in her articulation of a distinct, environmentally grounded, utopian concept of social formation that might be termed "bioregional" in today's ecological language. Her lifelong interest and involvement with natural and political histories of water in the West as they influenced settlement patterns in arid lands led Austin to argue "for the settling of the Colorado Basin according to the village pattern of small-scale communalism, local integrity, self-sufficiency, and 'aesthetics as a mode of life behavior,'" a pattern she termed "village socialism."[1]

Austin details her concept of village socialism in an article focused on water-rights conflicts in the West entitled "The Indivisible Utility," in which she explains that the organizing principle of village socialism in the American Southwest, evidenced throughout the ancient histories of Pueblo peoples, is the *acequia madre* (mother ditch), "which symbolizes the cooperation made possible when the land necessitates sharing precious water resources."[2] Later, in *The Land of Journeys' Ending,* Austin would write,

> When a crop can flourish handsomely on the run-off of natural watersheds, a family may subsist satisfactorily by itself for everything except its social occasions. But when a river is to be diverted in its course to irrigate the fields, then, by the same tie that they bind the river to the service of the corn, men bind themselves by the tie of the indivisible utility. Rain falls on radical and conservative alike, but the mother ditch makes communists of them all. That is, it makes for cooperative effort with psychological implications, to which the term "communism" is a clumsy, crab-like approach.[3]

Austin's argument for "village socialism"—for human settlement patterns that would reflect hydrological realities of arid lands—echoes John Wesley Powell's 1890 report before Congress on the Irrigation Surveys and his proposal for organizing municipalities in the new western states around the natural boundaries of hydrographic basins rather than by the orthogonal grid of the Jeffersonian land survey system. Powell was eventually removed as head of the U.S. Geological Survey for his unpopular expression of what we might regard today as a precursor of bioregional concepts of social formation. To late nineteenth-century free-market capitalists, Powell's plan for social cooperation, demanded by the coordinated use of an essential natural resource, seemed to threaten a socialist attack on the principle of primitive accumulation.

In the decades following Powell's proposals, associations with socialism became even more problematic for American social thinkers, and as her statement above indicates, Austin was at some pains to dissociate her ideas from Marxist theory and political discourse. As Lois Rudnick notes, Austin consciously developed her concept of village socialism as a native alternative to imported European communism through the argument that "the natural factors of land and climate in the Southwest have created communities with the kind of environmental awareness, broad social vision, and economic equality that 'would fill the self-constituted prophets of all Utopias with unmixed satisfaction.'"[4] While in "The Indivisible Utility" Austin acknowledges and laments deplorable health and social conditions in contemporary Pueblo communities, she explicitly grounds her social prophecy for post–World War I America in the evolutionary experiences of native communities and concludes her article with the statement that "[h]ere, not in the cafes of Prague or the cellars of Leningrad, is the still turning wheel on which the fair new shape of society is molded."[5]

Like Powell, Austin first arrived at her utopian social conceptions through personal observations of the natural and human histories of the American Southwest rather than through academic study of political economy. Also like Powell, she juxtaposed the English—or riparian—tradition of water law, which grants first privilege to owners of land adjoining a stream, with the Spanish tradition of "beneficent use" or "appropriative rights," in which precedent use guarantees continued privilege to a stream's waters and protects users from subsequent diversions by upstream property owners. Austin's first major work, *The Land of Little Rain,* presents a vision of Utopia possible only if the realities of aridity and fair use of hydrologic resources directly affect social formation. Against the contentious historic backdrop of evolving water law and reclamation policy in the American West, however, Austin's utopian vision, like Powell's proposal for settlement patterns based on community-based water allocations, succeeded entirely in its evocation of a desired pastoral democracy while it failed utterly to accurately predict or determine the future.

As a result of this dissonance, Austin's utopian representation of Spanish traditions of water use in the American West generates an ambivalence between the nostalgic and the prophetic—a textual tension between the sense of a paradise lost and the promise of a paradise regained—that gives the text its irony. The way of life promised throughout *The Land of Little Rain* is mourned as Austin's fictive form transforms the social optimism of popular local color and the lyricism of natural-history essay traditions into a story of the tragedy of modern civilization's alienation from its environment and its failure to fulfill its own identity.[6]

As a story of a lost utopia, *The Land of Little Rain* beckons readers to an imagined community of regional wholeness even as it signals the failure of the hydrographic vision in the American West first articulated by Powell and later developed by Austin. As a fictional prototype for the concept of village socialism she would articulate in the 1920s during the debates surrounding the Boulder Dam federal reclamation project, then, "The Little Town of the Grape Vines," the book's conclusion, raises questions regarding the relations of literary production and the intersections of environmental and social history—questions that demand serious attention of "green" cultural studies and emerging ecological criticism.[7]

Social Formation and the Hydrographic Vision of John Wesley Powell

As early as 1878, Powell caused considerable congressional consternation with his *Report on the Arid Region of the United States,* which included two proposed bills designed to reorganize fraudulent and disastrous land-use policies facilitated by the Pre-emption Act (1830), the Swamp Lands Act (1851), the Homestead Act (1862), the Timber and Stone Act (1873), and the Desert Lands Act (1877). Based in part on his observations of successful communal irrigation by Native Americans, Hispanics, and Mormon settlers, Powell's report recognized that, practically speaking, land beyond the one hundredth meridian was useless for farming and ranching without irrigation systems that were beyond the means of most individuals, and, further, that federal provision to form cooperative water districts for homesteading citizens was necessary to thwart the rapid monopolization of water rights by large capitalist interests.

The first fight over Powell's proposals led to his being passed over as founding director of the newly consolidated United States Geological Survey in favor of Clarence King. When Powell eventually came to the post in 1881, he continued developing his program for land law reform in the West through his Irrigation Surveys. In testimony before the House Committee on Irrigation in 1890, Powell again attacked the orthogonal grid system of the U.S. Land Survey and argued once more for reformed land laws that would recognize idiographic, hydrological realities in settlement patterns and develop appropriate political systems for the West. By then Powell envisioned hydrographic basins as geographic keys for social formation in the arid region—a notion far beyond the parameters of his initial private-water-district proposals of 1878. Powell presented his up-scaled program to the general public in a series of three articles for *Century.* "Institutions for the Arid Lands" explicitly outlines a prescient biore-gional theory for the harmonious natural and cultural integration of western timber lands, pasturage, irrigable lands, and human communities.

Powell's outline of the respective roles of local, state, and federal institu-tions in the administration of hydrographic districts relegated to local communities the adjudication of "questions of water rights, timber rights, pasturage rights, and power rights" as well as the rights to generate capital through self-taxation and financing.[8] State courts would settle litigation between people of different districts, and state inspectors would maintain public safety regulations. Through its geographic surveys, land allotment policies, and general statutes for the proposed incorporation of settlers within individual hydrographic basins, the federal government would pro-vide a unifying framework for decentralized administration of the hydro-graphic district system.

By 1890, Powell apparently had lost hope of achieving appropriate set-tlement patterns through the type of private cooperatives described in his report of 1878. He now believed, radically, that only the federal govern-ment could slow the incredible waste of natural resources he had witnessed in the West. Although Powell's plan was attacked by his enemies as "social-ist"—and although Powell is sometimes today regarded as "one of the ma-sons who troweled mortar on the cornerstone of an American welfare state"—biographer John Upton Terrell claims that Powell "vigorously dis-avowed any political theory that would prohibit the possession of private property" and argues that "Powell could not be justifiably called a social-ist, for he was not advocating government ownership of production or government control of the distribution of all manufactured and agricul-tural products."[9]

Although much twentieth-century federal reclamation policy claims Powell's work as its blueprint, Wallace Stegner, Powell's most recent and popular biographer, describes his plan as a too-radical—and ultimately un-acceptable—challenge to laissez-faire practices of western settlement dur-ing his time. Powell's plan "had been his vision of the way in which, by the help of science, justice and happiness could be guaranteed for the people and the region to which he was most attached . . . that the waste could be stopped, the random ill-advised mob of settlers directed by scientific knowledge and planning and steered into becoming colonists and communities." But, as Stegner explains, "[t]he myths surrounding free land were among the most durable the nation ever developed." Although his utopian plan proceeded from a scientist's faith in the ability of reason—in this case through scientific planning—to provide for the improvement of human conditions, Powell naively underestimated the force of what Stegner calls "the cussedness of the human race."[10]

Ironically, as American cultural critic Alan Trachtenberg notes, it was the threat of government regulation rather than government financing of natural resource development that ultimately defeated Powell's plan in the Congress: "Powell and others . . . proposed plans for orderly land use of remaining public resources, especially water supplies for desert regions. But public planning was anathema to Congress and private entrepreneurs, who did not shrink from public subsidy of business. So the unimaginable wealth of nature's gift was funneled by the people's representatives into private hands."[11]

With the passage of the Reclamation Act of 1902, after private and state efforts to set a workable irrigation policy had failed, western senators and congressmen—who had believed through the 1890s that suggestions that reclamation should be the federal government's task were an insult to their constituents—miraculously changed their attitudes toward federal reclamation projects, and, in Marc Reisner's words, "the American West quietly became the first and most durable example of the modern welfare state."[12] Reisner considers the passage of the Reclamation Act

such a sharp left turn in the course of American politics that historians still gather and argue over why it was passed. To some, it was America's first flirtation with socialism, an outgrowth of the Populist and Progressive movements of the time. To others, it was a disguised reactionary measure, an effort to relieve the mobbed and riotous conditions of the eastern industrial cities—an act to save heartless capitalism from itself. To some, its roots were in Manifest Destiny, whose incantations still held people in their sway; to others, it was a military ploy to protect and populate America's western flank against the ascendant Orient.[13]

Whatever the motives behind it, the act signaled the end of practical hopes for the environmentally guided social formations envisioned in Powell's plans of 1878 and 1890. Efforts of late nineteenth-century westerners to direct their regional destinies through private, local, or state-governed water development were essentially drowned by the Reclamation Act of 1902 and the twentieth-century flood of federal reclamation legislation that followed.

In 1903, Mary Austin published *The Land of Little Rain,* a collection of literary sketches that synthesizes nonfiction traditions of American nature writing with local color traditions of short fiction to trace the intricacies of life in arid western lands. *The Land of Little Rain* incorporates Austin's detailed observations of natural and human histories in the West, her personal experience of reclamation history as a homesteader and as the wife of a would-be private water developer in the interior desert valleys of southeastern California, and her passionate life search for meaningful natural and social patterns through aesthetic experience. The book reports Austin's own hydrologic surveys and her personal quest for utopic social formations in arid regions, drawing on—and drawing up—the "pioneer" life she lived in the southwestern extremes of the "post-Turnerian" frontier during many of the years when Powell was making his controversial public reports and proposals.

By the time Austin published *The Land of Little Rain,* the Reclamation Act had already put into motion a future entirely unimagined in the development dreams of her husband, Wallace, and the men of Inyo County. Initially the people of the Owens Valley believed that their wildest irrigation fantasies would at last be realized, and they welcomed the Reclamation Bureau into their valley. But larger political realities soon evaporated their dreams. The city of Los Angeles, more than two hundred miles away, began to manipulate provisions of the Reclamation Act to divert the Owens River from the service of inland agricultural and ranching communities to the profit of rapid metropolitan growth in coastal southern California. During the struggle between the people of Owens Valley and the city of Los Angeles over rights to the vast watershed of the eastern Sierra Nevada, Austin decided to leave her husband. As Los Angeles prepared to drain the Owens Valley's precious waters, she left Inyo County and the house she had recently built in Independence. She never returned to her beloved land of little rain.

Austin's decision to leave the Owens Valley, I suggest, marks a necessary point of departure for present-day readers journeying through *The Land of Little Rain* in search of Las Uvas and critical comprehension of Austin's concept of village socialism. Contemporary "green" critics should cer-

tainly consider the utopic vision of Austin's environmentally grounded social prophecies against the subsequent geographic history of hydrologic
exploitation in the Owens Valley and greater eastern Sierra regions. Today
the noxious clouds of alkali dust that rise and blow from the long-dry bottom of Owens Lake obscure the vision and pit the windshields of endless
streams of skiers and vacationers from the greater Los Angeles Basin. Just
north of Lone Pine, Austin's template for the little village of the
grapevines,[14] the newly widened highway passes close by remains of the
entrance gate to Manzanar, now a national historic site, one of several
desert camps where thousands of Japanese American citizens were de-
tained during World War II.[15] In extending its "water privileges" further
north through basins east of the Sierra Nevada, Los Angeles has jeopar-
dized the survival of an entire ecosystem at Mono Lake.

As an unrealized utopia, the promise of *The Land of Little Rain* presents
a particularly problematic version of the pastoral. Austin complicates the
pastoral by dramatizing tensions inherent in its literary tradition between
the pastoral as a forever lost Golden Age and the pastoral as the "timeless
idea of the tranquillity of life in the country."[16] On one hand, Austin presents Las Uvas as an organic society that, in contrast with intervening complexities of modern life, evokes nostalgic longing for the loss of simpler
ways. On the other hand, she holds out the village as an ever-present "rural
retreat" for the fulfillment of desires frustrated by contemporary life. She
accomplishes this by depicting an idealized village that never actually existed in the Owens Valley, but which she claims may still be found despite
her refusal to reveal its location.

Manipulation of desire, then, rather than its fulfillment, accounts for the
continued appeal of *The Land of Little Rain*. Similarly, Austin's later articulation of village socialism, while perhaps efficacious in promoting a critique of present and emerging social formations, ultimately failed to provide models for progressive reformation. When considered within the
context of the region's actual environmental history of hydrologic exploitation, Austin's conflations of nostalgic and utopic pastoral tensions
problematize her work for contemporary ecological critics.

In the Land of Little Rain

At the metaphoric center of Austin's map of the land of little rain lie the
conditions of aridity—climatic, emotional, intellectual, and spiritual.
Springing from the desert's dryness, the ways of water provide productive

paths for life, society, art, and philosophy. Nature and culture, individuals and communities are defined and interconnected in the book by their relations to water. The sketches move from ostensibly objective surveys of the ephemeral boundaries of a topographic region—defined primarily by its aridity in the opening title sketch—and chart a route to a utopic community, "The Little Town of the Grapes," where the scarcity of water nourishes exemplary social cohesion. *The Land of Little Rain* begins as an observant traveler's description of a desolate landscape and ends by presenting a map of imagined intersections of geography and social formation that represents a regional ideal, a utopian integration of people and place, a harmonious community of humans and nature joined by the paths of water.

Austin invites readers into an unbounded land beyond the pale of human administration, a "Country of Lost Borders" where "[n]ot the law, but the land sets the limit."[17] As a representation of an unlocatable country perfectly governed by natural laws—in this case laws governing the precious distribution of life-sustaining water—*The Land of Little Rain* announces its utopian commitments in the first sentences of the text. In the tradition of the pastoral, nature provides for human need without the necessity of human toil; in the pastoral utopia of Austin's desert, nature provides political government for those who recognize its bounty on its own rather than on human terms.

Austin follows her description of the aridity of "The Land of Little Rain" with the argument that the desert's apparent desolation owes more to agrarian anthropocentrism—to humans' evaluation of all land in terms of its agricultural potential—than to actual conditions there: "Desert is a loose term to indicate land that supports no man; whether the land can be bitted and broken to that purpose is not proven. Void of life it never is, however dry the air and villainous the soil" (3). Throughout the sketch, Austin recounts the remarkable adaptation of diverse and profuse plant communities to the scant, but nonetheless adequate, precipitation of the region. But with her wonder at the impressive population of such apparent loneliness, Austin shifts from detailed observations of topography and biology to speculation that further establishes the imaginative character of her landscape and the utopian longings of her journey:

If one were inclined to wonder at first how so many dwellers came to be in the loneliest land that ever came out of God's hands, what they do there and why stay, one does not wonder so much after having lived there. None other than this long brown land lays such a hold on the affections. The rainbow hills, the tender bluish mists, the luminous radiance of the spring, have the lotus charm. They trick the sense of time, so that once inhabiting there you always mean to go away without quite realizing that you have not done it. (11)

Like Homer's land of the lotus-eaters, Austin's pastoral desert frees travelers from toil and desire and removes them from the world of labor and longing through liberation of the imagination. Described thusly, the land of little rain becomes a utopian never-never land where "[t]he palpable sense of mystery in the desert air breeds fables" (12).

As she quests after the realities of water, Austin herself tells the stories and fables of the land that bring to life the natural facts of her desert. Yet, she insists, her stories, bred of the desert air, are redolent of the soil—more the heritage of the storyteller's direct regional experience than the inheritance of literary convention. "[I]s it not perhaps to satisfy expectation that one falls into the tragic key in writing of desertness?" she asks (12). In Austin's desert, however, "it is possible to live with great zest, to have red blood and delicate joys." But such rewards are reserved for true seekers (such as herself), for whom natural facts—especially the fact of water in the desert—open always into greater significance: "At any rate, it was not people who went into the desert merely to write it up who invented the fabled Hassaympa, of whose waters, if any drink, they can no more see fact as naked fact, but all radiant with the color of romance. I, who must have drunk of it in my twice seven years' wanderings, am assured that it is worth while" (13).

As seen through the eyes of the initiated, the limits set on plant, animal, and human life by the desert inspire a vital, stubborn adaptability—what Austin later calls "the courage to sheer off what is not worth while" (78). In Austin's desert, "to live deliberately, to front only the essential facts of life," is more than Thoreauvian luxury;[18] these are absolute conditions of survival. Through geographically enforced economy, plants, animals, and humans conform to a life that, although exacting, rewards observation of natural limits with spiritual expansion: "For all the toll the desert takes of a man it gives compensations, deep breaths, deep sleep, and the communion of the stars" (13).

In "Water Trails of the Ceriso," Austin shows how this human spirit is determined by—and discovered through the ability to follow—natural paths of water. It is through detailed observation of constraining and liberating conditions of particular geographies, Austin asserts, that human imagination can be most free. The fullest physical and spiritual existence is achieved through this geographically inspired imagination, through pragmatic adaptation to shifting patterns of life revealed through physical landscapes rather than by rigid adherence to human abstractions of rational order. Water trails inscribed by animals on the terrain provide a surer guide to sustenance than the surveyor's rule: "Venture to look for some seldom-touched water-hole, and so long as the trails run with your general direction make sure you are right, but if they begin to cross yours at never so slight an angle, to converge toward a point left or right of your objective, no matter what the maps say, or your memory, trust them; they *know*" (18-19). As for Thoreau, Austin's insistence on pragmatic attention to physical experience, the knowledge of natural things, opens into metaphysical insight.

Austin's water trails wander from ostensibly objective observations of the landscape through progressively subjective reflections on increasingly complex organizations and interrelations of life. In "The Streets of the Mountains," "Water Borders," "Other Water Borders," and "Nurslings of the Sky," she traces water trails from headwaters high in glacier-sculpted mountains, down through steep water-carved river canyons, to valley streams, to irrigation ditches, and, finally, to their return to the skies in eternal cycles of evaporation and precipitation. As she moves from her hydrographic description of her region's topography to speculations on the psychic effects of desert landscapes, she points out that all mountain streets in the Sierra of her description are water trails for travelers seeking fulfillment. The hydrology of mountain canyons then becomes the organizing structure for Austin's detailed observations of the habitats, flora, and fauna of the eastern Sierra Nevada. In "Water Borders" Austin meditates in even further descriptive detail on "the fashion in which a mountain stream gets down from the perennial pastures of the snow to its proper level and identity as an irrigating ditch" (131). But in "Other Water Borders" Austin's focus shifts dramatically to the effects of hydrology on human history as her water trails lead her at last to the violent struggles over water use that began with American occupation of the region.

"It is the proper destiny of every considerable stream in the west to become an irrigating ditch," states Austin at the opening of this sketch; but it is clear from the tales she tells that she also believes the destiny of an irrigating ditch is to nourish neighboring fields and not—via the L.A. aqueduct—a distant, burgeoning metropolis. Austin's purely fictional tale of "old Amos Judson's" battles at the water gate draws on incidents described in her autobiography from her days on the Tejon and Mountain View Dairy ranches. Describing the battle between Henry Miller and other ranchers in the San Joaquin Valley in *Earth Horizon,* Austin writes,

> Farmers aligned themselves, as they thought their interests best served, under the reigning Duke, and guarded their ditches with shot guns. Armed employees of the great companies went about cutting dykes and tearing out water gates: all of which, as it reacted into the homes of company employees and small farmers alike, Mary was made aware through the talk of the women. One morning she would see white water-birds against the warm colored dykes, performing their wingspread dances, and the next, grim figures sitting with their guns across their knees. When active warfare was about to break out, the courts intervened.[19]

In "Other Water Borders," herons stalk "the little glinting weirs across the field" while old Amos Judson sits "asquat on the headgate with his gun, guarding his water-right toward the end of a dry summer" (139). Amos owned half of Tule Creek while "the other half pertained to the neighboring Greenfields ranch," but

> [y]ears of a "short water crop," that is, when too little snow fell on the high pine ridges, or, falling, melted too early, Amos held that it took all the water that came down to make his half, and maintained it with a Winchester and a deadly aim. Jesus Montaña, first proprietor of Greenfields,—you can see at once that Judson had the racial advantage,—contesting the right with him, walked into five of Judson's bullets and his eternal possessions on the same occasion. (139-40)

"That," Austin writes, "was the Homeric age of settlement and passed into tradition" (140). With the passing of Jesus Montaña—and the exoneration of his Anglo murderer—Austin symbolically acknowledges the passing of Spanish water-use traditions in the American West.

As Austin explained decades later, in a passage from *Earth Horizon* obviously informed by Powell's nineteenth-century hydrographic arguments,

> the Spanish colonists had employed, for the allocation of waters, a usage by which control of water was made contingent upon "beneficent use" rather than by ownership of the land through which it

flowed. Such control was acquired by "appropriation"; that is to say, by declaration of the intention to use, made at the point of diversion from the natural channel, and promptly followed by practical provision for use. . . . In California, the hasty Act of Legislature, before the State was admitted, established arbitrarily the English riparian rule. But early in the homesteader's westward movement, it began to be seen that much food-bearing land was, by the riparian rule, deprived of the necessary irrigation, while vast quantities of water wasted in the control of riparian holders.[20]

In the years following the killing of Jesus Montaña the violence and bloodshed continue. Austin finally resolves the conflict, and perhaps the tension she had felt in the homes of San Joaquin farmers, by twisting it into a sort of domestic comedy that ends through voluntary, mutual cooperation—and the introduction of new technology—between former combatants:

> Every subsequent owner of Greenfields bought it with Amos in full view. The last of these was Diedrick. Along in August of that year came a week of low water. Judson's ditch failed and he went out with his rifle to learn why. There on the headgate sat Diedrick's frau with a long-handled shovel across her lap and all the water turned into Diedrick's ditch; there she sat knitting through the long sun, and the children brought out her dinner. It was all up with Amos; he was too much of a gentleman to fight a lady—that was the way he expressed it. She was a very large lady, and a long-handled shovel is no mean weapon. The next year Judson and Diedrick put in a modern water gauge and took the summer ebb in equal inches. (140-41)

What had required governmental and court intervention to resolve and enforce in the San Joaquin Valley, Austin settles in *The Land of Little Rain* with humor, community spirit, and scientific progress. But while the tale amuses with a surface calm, troubled waters still run deep through the actual history of federal reclamation policy in the West—and, I would argue, throughout Austin's text. After tracing Sierra streams to the irrigation ditches of the Owens Valley, Austin follows her water trails past the village weirs and out into the tulares. Beyond here, however, she will not follow: "The tulares are full of mystery and malaria. That is why we have meant to explore them and have never done so" (148). Instead, by way of foreshadowing her only reference to the location of Las Uvas, she concludes her wanderings in this sketch leaving her readers to wonder at "the secret of the tulares" (148).[21]

Before her metaphoric return to the tulares in the tale of Las Uvas, Austin inserts the last of this sequence of sketches, "Nurslings of the Sky." In it, she wanders yet a bit further along her water trails into descriptions of global hydrological cycles and speculations about the almost religious significance of weather. Just as Thoreau realized, through much contemplation, that the water of the Ganges flowed in Walden Pond, so Austin concludes this sketch by acknowledging the spiritual significance of the natural facts she has pursued throughout *The Land of Little Rain:* all life is interconnected by a cosmic network of water trails.

Lost Utopias: The Failure of the Hydrographic Vision

At the conclusion to her wanderings through *The Land of Little Rain,* Austin returns at last to her ultimate concern with interconnecting structures of environmental and social experience. Following the natural paths of water, Austin's text finally discovers an idealized course of the human spirit as she and her readers arrive ultimately at Las Uvas. As Marjorie Pryse explains, "Austin 'defines the path' of human emotional and spiritual experience by focusing on geological, biological, and botanical details of the desert in . . . *The Land of Little Rain.* [S]he discovers patterns that animals and human beings make in their search for water, and ends with examples of the highest forms the discovery of water can take—in 'The Little Town of the Grape Vines.'"[22] At Las Uvas, where Sierra streams reach village weirs and strips of tillage, the stresses of desert aridity give way completely to an imagined community of ease and modest plenty where the inhabitants "keep up all the good customs brought out of Old Mexico or bred in a lotus-eating land" (164). The inhabitants of Las Uvas sing through the night and sleep through midday, and "the mere proximity of a guitar is sufficient occasion" for a dance (164). At Las Uvas, marriage is a blessing easily come by, and fathers are known to quit their jobs in neighboring mines to live with their families in poverty. At Las Uvas, an Irish priest baptizes "little Elijias, Lolas, Manuelitas, Josés, and Felipés," and each year following the celebration of the Sixteenth of September when the flag of Old Mexico is again replaced by the Stars and Stripes, the national anthems of Mexico, America, France, Cuba, Chile—of all the lands represented by the people of the village and region—are sung in a unified community chorus. In the final paragraph of *The Land of Little Rain,* Austin beckons her readers to an idyllic natural community where even the architecture is geomorphic; where animals and people work and live together; where folks are bound by their relationships and are free from want, crime, and guilt; and where the alienation and cares of modern life give way to the kindly, earthy "ease of El Pueblo de Las Uvas": "Come away, you who are obsessed with your own importance in the scheme of things, and have got nothing you did not sweat for, come away by the brown valleys and full-bosomed hills to the even-breathing days, to the kindliness, earthiness, ease of El Pueblo de Las Uvas" (171).

Yet, Austin demurs from "discovering" the actual geographic location of Las Uvas except as a literary *nowhere* hidden like "the heron's nest in the tulares" (163). As the sketch of a pure utopia, a true nowhere, "The Little Town of the Grape Vines" locates itself within a long literary tradition in which elements of nonfictional discourses of geography, natural history, and political economy are deliberately joined in fictional representations of ideal and attractive, but ultimately unlocatable, locations.

El Pueblo de Las Uvas is a multicultural paradise where an isolated, interracial human community is harmonized through integration with its natural environment. It is a vision of cosmopolitan spirit joined with bioregional sensibility to give shape to a truly sustainable concept of social formation. As Marjorie Pryse has noted, Las Uvas "serves as a resting place" for the peripatetic philosophizing of Austin's wanderings through *The Land of Little Rain;* but Austin has no intention of giving the lie to her "pastoral haven" by supplying concrete directions to the contented village (xxvii). In a phrase that evokes Sarah Orne Jewett's "A White Heron," "Austin suggests that Las Uvas exists, but leaves it to the reader to find" (xxvii). "Where it lies, how to come at it, you will not get from me," Austin writes, "rather would I show you the heron's nest in the tulares" (163).

Ultimately Austin's imaginary utopia remains lost in figurative waters. Furthermore, as the histories outlined here illustrate, her hydrographic vision, like Powell's, remains obscured by the actual course of federal reclamation policy and its determining influence on social formations in the post-Turnerian West. Austin herself wrestles with the eclipse of her prophetic vision by historical reality in *The Ford,* written fifteen years later. *The Ford* is an attempt at a more realistic mode of fiction, but, as Anne Raine explains elsewhere in this volume, here again Austin's analysis fails to satisfactorily sort out complexities of environment, water law, and actual potentials for progressive social formations.

In a later reflection on her time in Inyo and the writing of *The Land of*

Little Rain, Austin writes, "though I was there in the midst of it, I began to write of the land of little rain as of something very much loved, now removed."[23] The pervasive touch of the reminiscent mood to *The Land of Little Rain* adds perhaps its strongest literary affect. A sense of tragic loss pervades Austin's oeuvre, and in *The Land of Little Rain* it is perhaps the sense of the irrecoverable loss of a beloved space and time—and an ideally imagined *genre de vie*—that moves readers. This emphasis on an emotional affect—which is, of course, the rhetorical aim of fictive discourse—far outweighs the informational effects of the work's ostensibly nonfictional elements of natural history and science. Ironically, when writing of her desert utopia as a paradise lost, despite her optimistically promised "communion with the stars," Austin does, in fact, fall into the tragic key. For her, however, the tragedy is not so much the destruction of human spirit by desert desolation as it is the desolating human destruction of the spirit she finds in the desert.

Contemporary "green" literary and cultural critics must develop readings of literary landscapes that foreground the ecological fates of the actual geographies they represent. The regional fate of the Owens Valley has been to water the phenomenal population and growth of what postmodern geographers designate the quintessential post-Fordist cosmopolis,[24] while desert has reclaimed the village weirs and gardens of Austin's utopia. Consideration of Austin's concept of village socialism against the backgrounds of Powell's unsuccessful proposals for regional organization of hydrographic districts, the reclamation history of the Owens Valley, and Austin's ultimate failure to influence the Boulder Dam issue is relevant to critical assessments of contemporary utopic concepts of environmentally grounded social formations. Consideration of Las Uvas as the fictional prototype for Austin's village socialism raises larger questions about the definitions and functions of American nature writing, and for emerging ecological literary criticism.

Austin's literary representation of an idyllic western community presumably organized around the Spanish tradition of beneficent use of scarce water resources came out a full quarter century after Powell's *Arid Region*: at the historic moment at which the hydrographic regional development Powell envisioned was irretrievably lost in the wake of policies launched by the Federal Reclamation Act of 1902. Critical readers of the utopian vision promised by *The Land of Little Rain* must ask what accounts for Austin's romanticization of already rejected concepts of coordinated resource use and social formation. Further, students of Austin's career must consider how to account for her resurrection of Powell's concept of the hydrographic district a full two decades after she had personally witnessed the Chinatown appropriation of Owens Valley water by the city of Los Angeles that was enabled by Reclamation Act policies.

More generally, and importantly, contemporary "green" cultural critics must consider not only how environmentally grounded concepts of social formation in current ecological discourse such as Kirkpatrick Sale's bioregionalism, Gary Snyder's watershed consciousness, and even the biogeographic island theories of conservation biology undergirding Dave Foreman's Wildlands Project bear positive family resemblances to the failed hydrographic visions of Powell and Austin, but also how they may be vexed with similar dispositions toward failure. To what extent do these concepts of coordinated resource use and social formation, like Powell's and Austin's pastoral utopias, depend on manipulation of nostalgic longing for imagined, organic regional wholeness bound by "natural law" to motivate progressive social reform? Plainly put, we must consider to what extents rhetorics of region, as utopic visions haunted by lost Edens, offer prophecies of impossible futures approached from pasts that never were.

NOTES

1. Shelly Armitage, "Mary Austin: Writing Nature," introduction to *Wind's Trail: The Early Life of Mary Austin,* by Peggy Pond Church (Albuquerque: Museum of New Mexico Press, 1990), 24.

2. Quoted in Lois Rudnick, "Re-Naming the Land: Anglo Expatriate Women in the Southwest," in *The Desert Is No Lady: Southwestern Landscapes in Women's Writing and Art,* ed. Vera Norwood and Janice Monk (New Haven: Yale University Press, 1987), 21.

3. Mary Austin, *The Land of Journeys' Ending* (reprint; Tucson: University of Arizona Press, 1983), 89.

4. Rudnick, "Re-Naming the Land," 243.

5. Mary Austin, "The Indivisible Utility," *Survey Graphic* (December 1925): 301-6, 327.

6. Sean O'Grady writes in *Pilgrims to the Wild: Everett Ruess, Henry David Thoreau, John Muir, Clarence King, Mary Austin* (Salt Lake City: University of Utah Press, 1993) that "[d]esire in Austin's work is always predicated upon loss—lost borders, lost loves, lost lives" (129).

7. See Mary Austin, "The Colorado River Project and the Culture of the Southwest," *Southwest Review* 13 (1922): 110-15.

8. John Wesley Powell, "Institutions for the Arid Lands" (1890), in *Selected Prose,* ed. George Crossette (Boston: David Godine, 1970), 41-52.

9. John Upton Terrell, *The Man Who Rediscovered America: A Biography of John Wesley Powell* (New York: Weybright and Talley, 1969), 229.

10. Wallace Stegner, *Beyond the Hundredth Meridian: John Wesley Powell and the Second Opening of the West* (New York: Penguin Books, 1953), 338, 316, 309.

11. Alan Trachtenberg, *The Incorporation of America: Culture and Society in the Gilded Age* (New York: Hill and Wang, 1982), 23.

12. Marc Reisner, *Cadillac Desert: The American West and Its Disappearing Water* (New York: Penguin Books, 1987), 114-15.

13. Ibid.

14. In *Earth Horizon* (1924; reprint, Albuquerque: University of New Mexico Press, 1991), Austin writes:

> About half the population of Lone Pine were true "Mexicans"; not early Californians (Spanish), but descendants from one of the refugee groups of the last disturbance before Porfirio Diaz, still so immensely patriotic that they always made more of the Sixteenth of September than the Fourth of July. They had settled in Inyo about the time of Cerro Gordo. There was the remnant of gentility among them—manners, old silver, and drawn work. I do not know from what States they hailed, but they seemed to be largely akin, and the Indian blood most noticeable among them was Yaqui.

Although this description fits more or less neatly with the history and details she attributes to Las Uvas in *The Land of Little Rain,* Austin's Lone Pine apparently did not share anything like the degree of ethnic harmony depicted in "The Little Town of the Grape Vines," as her further autobiographical comments reveal: "It was not good form at Lone Pine to make social equals of the Spanish-speaking families . . . ; but Mary collected folklore, Spanish idioms, and cooking recipes among them with great gusto" (251-52).

15. This is a particularly ironic historical twist since at least one explanation for Teddy Roosevelt's refusal to respond to the petitions of the people of the Owens Valley in their struggle with Los Angeles claims that he believed metropolitan development of coastal California to be critical to the nation's defense against the growing strength and interests of Japan.

16. Raymond Williams, *The Country and the City* (New York: Oxford University Press, 1973), 19.

17. Mary Austin, *The Land of Little Rain* (1903; reprint, Albuquerque: University of New Mexico Press, 1991), 3. Subsequent page numbers cited parenthetically refer to this edition.

18. Henry David Thoreau, *Walden,* in *The Portable Thoreau,* ed. Carl Bode (New York: Penguin Books, 1975), 343.

19. Austin, *Earth Horizon,* 211.

20. Ibid., 206.

21. Geographer Robert A. Sauder writes in *The Lost Frontier: Water Diversion in the Growth and Destruction of Owens Valley Agriculture* (Tucson: University of Arizona Press, 1994) that he considers the Owens Valley the ideal historical case study for assessment of Powell's hydrographic theories, and documents the geographic extent and rich habitat values of long-vanished tule wetlands in the center of the valley that were among the first ecological casualties of the Los Angeles aqueduct.

22. Marjorie Pryse, introduction to *Stories from the Country of Lost Borders* (New Brunswick: Rutgers University Press, 1987), xx. Subsequent page numbers cited parenthet-

ically refer to this edition.

23. Austin, "How I Learned to Read and Write," reprinted in *My First Publication,* ed. James D. Hart (San Francisco: Book Club of California, 1961), 64.

24. See, in particular, Edward Soja's geographic history of Los Angeles in *Postmodern Geographies: The Reassertion of Space in Critical Social Theory* (London: Verso, 1989).

CHAPTER ELEVEN

Mary Austin's
The Land of Little Rain
Remembering the Coyote

MICHELLE CAMPBELL TOOHEY

While Mark Schlenz's discussion of John Wesley Powell's "hydrographic" vision shows how Austin could profitably borrow ideas from male thinkers, in "Remembering the Coyote" Michelle Campbell Toohey argues that Austin, in contrast to her male contemporaries, positioned her nature writer as part of the ecosystem she described, creating a rhetorical and political strategy that challenged both the androcentric perspective and the attendant ecological exploitation some male nature writers implicitly endorsed. By writing from a "heterarchic" rather than a "hierarchic" position, Toohey suggests, Austin revised the genre of nature writing at the turn of the century. Like DeZur and Melody Graulich, Toohey sees Austin as resisting "the colonization of nature," using, for instance, an active rather than passive, acted-on sentence structure to give nature agency.

Like many Austin critics today, Toohey places Austin's work in historical context, in this case comparing The Land of Little Rain *with early-twentieth-century articles and essays on nature writing, the desert, and Native Americans that appeared in the same periodicals in which Austin published. She also uses the poststructuralist critical insights of Barthes, Foucault, and particularly Bakhtin, whose principle of "dialogic" writing provides her with her central approach to Austin. Toohey argues that Austin's nature writing takes the shape of an "ecological dialogue" between the writer, the land, its human and nonhuman inhabitants, and the reader. Like other critics in this volume, she sees Austin as challenging and crossing borders, both thematically between self and "other," and formally as she "ruptures the boundaries of nature writing."*

Once at Red Rock, in a year of green pasture, we saw two
buzzards, five ravens, and a coyote feeding on the same carrion,
and only the coyote seemed ashamed of the company.[1]

At the turn of the century Mary Austin challenged the predominantly male sphere of nature writing in the United States, a genre oscillating between the rationality of Enlightenment absolutes and the romanticism of anthropomorphic tropes. Although the approaches to nature in this genre might have differed, the prescribed role of nature writer required a cultural position that could justify the colonization of nature, a political necessity for a nation intent on expanding its physical boundaries at any cost. As a single mother struggling to support herself by writing "around the edges of her life," as did so many other nineteenth-century women, Austin's goal to author texts about nature must have seemed almost laughable to her male counterparts. How could a woman, already intimately identified with an objectified, penetrated, and romanticized nature, create a speaking position from which to feed "on the same carrion" without ordering her own death in the process? Patrick Murphy describes her solution: "[I]n order to have a woman's nature writing, there must be a breaking of genre conventions established by men, and accepted by women, working within patriarchal structures."[2] As the coyote nature writer embarrassed by the methods of her contemporaries, Austin broke prescribed genres, interrogated ideological codes from within, and redefined not only her own speaking position but also the speaking positions of other marginalized participants in the ecosystem.

In 1903, Houghton Mifflin published Mary Austin's *The Land of Little Rain*. That same year, *Atlantic Monthly* and the *North American Review* printed an earnest debate between John Burroughs and William J. Long surrounding what Long called the "Modern School of Nature-Study." Both men perceived the discourses of science and nature as dichotomous but puzzled over how the genre of nature writing should treat this polarity. In his *North American Review* article Long theorizes: "First, the study of Nature is a vastly different thing from the study of Science."[3] Similarly, Burroughs's opening sentence states: "The literary treatment of natural history themes is, of course, quite different from the scientific treatment, and should be so."[4] Although these two popular writers agree that scientific and literary treatments of nature use disparate methods, the first requiring exact and objective observation and the second depending on suggestive and evocative images, they strongly and strangely debate how the humanizing factor fits into this particular genre. Unlike Austin, who engendered an ecological dialogue that heterarchically values human and nonhuman voices alike, both Long and Burroughs unquestioningly accepted the Enlightenment prescription that nature is properly defined as an object of observation, collection, and categorization.

In "The Literary Treatment of Nature," published in *Atlantic Monthly* in 1904, Burroughs argues that, although the writer must awaken human sentiment by contemplating nature, he should restrict himself to describing nonhuman action that is "not the kind that involves reason."[5] But Burroughs's anti-rational animal stance is somewhat problematic in its indignation toward rendering nature anthropomorphically: "I do not want the animals humanized in any other sense. They all have human traits and ways; let those be brought out,—their mirth, their joy, their curiosity, their cunning, their thrift, their relations, their wars, their loves."[6] In other words, the writer can attribute all human traits but reason to animals. Ironically, Burroughs excludes war, mirth, curiosity, love, and the other emotions as rational properties. Does his argument also denigrate such attributes, intimating that they are somehow secondary and associated with a marginalized nonhuman world? Burroughs's argument might seem to the contemporary reader confusing at best, dissembling at worst; but contextually the debate between Long and Burroughs was a serious attempt to derive prescriptive formulas for the proper relationship between the scientific and literary discourses in nature writing at the turn of the century.

A review of Long's remarks makes it easier to appreciate Burroughs's point of view as arguably progressive. While Burroughs says that the discourses of science and nature writing are equally "true" and need no poetic interpretation,[7] Long postulates a Neoplatonic romanticism: "This upper world of appreciation and suggestion, of individuality interpreted by individuality, is the world of Nature, the Nature of the poets and prophets and thinkers. Though less exact, it is not less but rather more true and real than Science, as emotions are more real than facts, and love is more true than Economics."[8] Disagreeing emphatically with Burroughs, Long suggests that a rarefied, artistic improvement of nature is possible through the intervention of "poets, prophets, and thinkers" and the valorization of emotion over reason. He describes the naturalist as a kind of romantic guide seeking animal individuality, insisting again that it is only through personal style in nature books that "we are to interpret the facts truthfully."[9] He even goes so far as to claim that without an intense human sympathy "the living creatures are little better than stuffed specimens."[10]

From this kind of pervasive androcentric egotism, privileged white men developed the national policy of ecological exploitation, inclusive of

human and nonhuman nature, still present in American ideology. Is Burroughs's approach any better? Despite his attempts to desentimentalize nature, his discourse of reason supports a colonizing violence no less detrimental than the narcissism of Long. Both postulate an alienated human
control as given: man separate from nature is in control of defining nature.
It is ironic to find Mary Austin's story about "Mahala Joe" directly following the Burroughs article in *Atlantic Monthly* because neither Burroughs
nor Long includes Austin, who had just published *The Land of Little Rain,*
as a credible nature writer in his list of male contributors. But then, Austin's
dialogic style precludes any inclusion in such monologic discussions.

Austin's style of discourse suggests that she cared very little about a debate centered on abstract prescriptions that tried to define from an androcentric perspective. Furthermore, she seems to identify the nature writer
not as a human who has the power to stand outside and name with humanizing superiority in the ways that Burroughs and Long suggest but as
"the lean coyote that stands off in the scrub from you and howls and
howls" (17). This coyote/nature writer is an integral part of the ecosystem
as she takes on speaking positions at once distanced from and participating
in her surroundings. Her role is to activate a dialogic process in which all
inhabitants of the ecosystem find space to foreground both their needs and
their desires.

Unlike Long's and Burroughs's attempts to lift the veil of an objectified
nature, Mary Austin's discourse does precisely what Roland Barthes suggests in his "Theory of the Text": "The current theory of text turns away
from the text as veil and tries to perceive the fabric in its texture, in the interlacing codes, formulae and signifiers, in the midst of which the subject
places himself and is undone, like a spider that comes to dissolve itself into
its own web."[11] In *The Land of Little Rain* Austin places herself within a
dominant ideological fabric of interlacing codes that colonize the land,
Native Americans, and women while she tries to deconstruct formulas and
signifiers of that ideology. Her discourse struggles within the dualistic
Western discourse, resisting the assumptions that humans are exterior to
and custodial of nature, that Eurocentric Americans have the right to ob-
jectify and commodify any resource they want to consume, and that marginalized groups (human and nonhuman alike) are passive receptors content with such exploitation. She says of the intermittently successful
pocket hunter, a white male entrepreneur who tries to find gold in the
desert in order to gain access to the wealthy English middle class: "the land

tolerated him as it might a gopher or a badger. Of all its inhabitants it has the least concern for man" (45).

Like the spider of Barthes's text, Austin's subjects shift, ontologically dissolving in their own webs. Because the material subject of her discourse in *The Land of Little Rain* is the dialogic relationship of all members of the ecosystem in the country of lost borders, her writing is extra-abundant, at times "above all compassing of words" (3). Such discourse blurs the chronic borders of hierarchical power positions, deliberately chooses a model of interanimating webs over great-chain-of-being justifications, and is deeply and mystically political in its praxis. She posits the practical adaptation of inhabitants found in the "Streets of the Mountains" as an alternative to androcentric "house habits": "No doubt the labor of being comfortable gives you an exaggerated opinion of yourself, an exaggerated pain to be set aside. Whether the wild things understand it or not they adapt themselves to its processes with greater ease" (109). She describes the process that goes on in the streets of the mountains as "world-formative"; the inhabitants "left borders and breathing-space" to continue an open-ended interchange of possibilities, valuing the multiplicity of difference as the basis of survival.

Austin's "dissolving" of the dominant ideological discourse occurs in the preface as she chronicles the dialogic relationship between the writer as subject and the reader as subject. She begins by discussing the proper ways of naming, the traditional task of the author inscribing a subject into the symbolic order. In the dominant ideology, naming originates "in the poor human desire for perpetuity" (3), but the Indian fashion of naming is associational and recognizes a multiplicity of namers who base their name giving on specific, relational circumstances. Such naming ruptures static, prescriptive categories and opens the symbolic order of language to speaking positions outside the voice of the dominant ideology. According to Austin, the Eurocentric desire for a central author independently controlling the text is not appropriate to the process she is about to incubate. From the first sentence her readers experience the "question of caesurae which break up the instant and disperse the subject into a plurality of possible positions and functions."[12]

Rather than locate Austin within the institutional canon prescriptively as a certain type of writer producing a certain type of text, we, as readers, must live with her work in the same way she advocates living in the desert: "One must summer and winter in the land and wait its occasions" (4). First, she suggests that we are responsible to the text in ways that she is not:

"You see in me a mere recorder, for I know what is best for you; you shall blow out this bubble from your own breath" (68). Arguably, she is more than a mere recorder in this satiric comment on other authors, but her encouragement to readers to respond to her text from their "own breath" supports her commitment to a mutually constitutive discursive style. Second, as we live with and respond to her text we must adapt to a discourse that crosses genres, constantly naming through poetic, narrative, scientific, political, and mystical occasions: "There are many areas in the desert where drinkable water lies within a few feet of the surface, indicated by the mesquite and the bunch grass (*Sporobolus airoides*). It is this nearness of unimagined help that makes the tragedy of desert deaths" (11). Austin writes a country of lost borders not easily found in the canonized versions of map naming, suggesting to readers that questions of longitude and latitude are irrelevant in a place where "not the law but the land sets the limits" (9). The individual author no longer autonomously chooses how to write the text, whether to humanize or not to humanize, because the landscape also participates fully in shaping the discourse it needs.

The land also interpellates Austin's readers. Austin's use of direct address positions her readers as participating subjects, positing that they too have a unique relation to the land: "The earth is no wanton to give up all her best to every comer, but keeps a sweet, separate intimacy for each" (3). Again the earth acts as agent in naming the properties of intimacy for individual participants. Furthermore, the readers' relationships to this text are recognized as ontologically open-ended; epistemological truth does not exist, "only a sort of pretense allowed in matters of the heart" (3), a pivotal position negating any kind of transcendental romanticism. In her preface Austin positions her readers as Mikhail Bakhtin's listeners-as-respondents, encouraged to interact as speakers voicing their own situational knowledge rather than reacting as passive nonparticipants.[13] The readers of *The Land of Little Rain* are invited into intimacy with both the land and Austin's discourse, invited "to have such news of the land, of its trails and what is astir in them as one lover of it can give to another" (4). The sensuousness of Austin's discourse throughout the text sustains the intimate connection of writer, reader, and the land that she promises.

Stylistically, Austin chooses her discourse carefully to promote an inclusive political agenda operating as a hostile agent within the colonizing discourse of expansionism. Her main concerns in *The Land of Little Rain* circle around issues of the land, Native Americans, and women. Again she promotes a heterarchical model of all participants in the ecosystem inter-acting in dialogue rather than one of Western man androcentrically con-trolling the universe. She refuses to privilege a discourse that colonizes and consumes an objectified nature; rather, she uses a style that ruptures and turns back on the dominant discourse to counteridentify, and eventually to disidentify, while still maintaining credibility in particular discursive styles. A comparative analysis of articles about the American desert con-temporary with *The Land of Little Rain* published in *National Geographic* and *Harper's Bazaar* clarifies Austin's uniquely dialogic approach.

Although Austin and her contemporaries use the same scientific facts to discuss nature, the different cultural positions of these speakers significantly affect their translation of their observations. "The American Deserts," an anonymous article published in *National Geographic* in 1904, mirrors much of the scientific content of *The Land of Little Rain*: it discusses the resiliency of the desert plants, corrects the definition of the desert as "without vege-tation," and notes the ability of Native Americans to adapt their lifestyle to the desert.[14] In "Plant Life in the Desert," published in *Harper's Monthly* in 1905, Ernest Ingersoll specifically agrees with Austin's discussions of indi-vidual plant characteristics: the rolling weeds, the root structure of the mesquite, the creosote bush.[15] Finally, Robert H. Chapman's article, "The Deserts of Nevada and the Death Valley: U.S. Geological Survey," published in *National Geographic* in 1906, two years after *The Land of Little Rain* came out, describes mining towns in a desert topography that includes "moun-tain ranges, high plateaus, mesas, and buttes, exclusive valleys."[16]

The facts and observations put forth in these articles and Austin's text derive from the same scientific discourse that catalogues species, topogra-phy, and adaptability to environment, but the boundaries constructed by their identification with the dominant ideology are entirely different. For the male writers, the boundaries are maps and tables based on economic concerns. For example: "A complete solution of the mysterious strength of the desert plants will prove of great economic value to the United States aside from the important information it will give regarding the funda-mental processes of protoplasm."[17] Even the anecdotal asides in these dis-courses reproduce a language of economic priority. Chapman reserves his enthusiasm and approbation for the "real development in Death Valley . . . by the parties interested in borax" and "a modern hotel with a wonderful variety of refreshment, solid and fluid, served to a nicety, including ham-mered-brass finger bowls by men in conventional black evening clothes."[18] This economic discourse either objectifies the desert into a somewhat challenging product to be conquered and exploited or romanticizes it as an existentially threatening power, as in an *Outing* magazine article published in 1904: "A curse seems to have struck the very vegetation which is weird and fantastic, befitting the surroundings."[19] But Austin denies both concepts of nature. "[T]he desert breeds its own kind," she says; "each in its particular habitat" (12); "the storms of hill countries have other business" to interact with watercourses and manure pines (133); and the desert stars "make the poor worldfret of no account" (17). For Austin, scientific discourse should interrogate the processes of the ecosystem as they interrelate between participants, human and nonhuman alike, rather than considering solely how they affect human economic potential.

Austin revises the "poor worldfret" by distancing herself from the androcentric discourse of colonization. William Scheick has suggested that Austin's position as a "mere recorder" indicates an artistic frustration that disfigures the landscape in her "unfulfilled search for divine assimilation."[20] But Scheick's conclusions assume a desire in Austin for Emersonian transcendence frustrated by the limits of an androcentric mind unable to eradicate her own death. He also ignores the satiric context of Austin's remark that she is "a mere recorder" of a woman's death, which male authors might exploit to meet the genre requirements of medieval romance or western tales. But Austin's desires as a writer have little to do with transcendence based on man's privileged relationship with God or the colonization of nature that results from such an ideological construct. When she relates the horrific death of a pregnant Native American woman abused and abandoned by a man (significantly) from New England, she offers no metaphysical justification. With a directed sense of irony, she remarks that the town named a gulch after this "squaw" because the man who found her consequently discovered gold that day. Is it Austin or a culture exploitative of women and its own environment that cannot eradicate a fear of death?

Scheick further portrays Austin biographically as an unfulfilled, "physically unattractive woman," again reducing the speech act of a constructed narrator into the physical details of a woman writer he finds personally unappealing. While Scheick may conclude that Austin's temporal identity is "a barrier to the divine," Austin herself is much more inclined to refigure a narrator who listens to alternate speaking positions rather than silence them with the stare of Emerson's "transparent eyeball." Scheick's attempts to discredit Austin along transcendental lines prescribed by male norms for nature writing (and, we might suspect, feminine beauty) misread an author of proven political involvement whose gaze is decidedly fixed on the marginalized status of women, minorities, and the environment.[21]

Rather than use the limits set by the land as a metaphor for her own artistic inadequacies, as Scheick suggests, Austin positions the land as another speaking subject in an interactive ecosystem. The land, not humans, determines the adaptability of life in the desert. Unlike the scientific discourse of her contemporaries, which discusses the desert with passive sentence structure, Austin uses an active construction that places the land as agent with an intention very different from Long's suggestion that only human individuality can interpret nature: "There are hints to be had of the way in which a land forces new habits on its dwellers" (15). As Austin observes the land, the personal voice of the author in the preface is replaced by a generic "one" who witnesses the ways of the land but does not have the power to affect them in any way. Austin now positions herself as the observant coyote who is "of no account" in comparison to the magnitude of the ecological process.

Although Austin personifies the land and its nonhuman inhabitants, she does not humanize them hierarchically with either the romantic sentimentality or the existential determinacy apparent in the popular nature discourse discussed above. The power in Austin's personification exists in the heterarchical, adaptive relationship of the desert inhabitants to their ecosystem: "The desert floras shame us with their cheerful adaptations to the seasonal limitations" (11). Human beings are not the privileged masters of the desert. They are simply another species that sometimes adapts effectively, as the community of Las Uvas does; or the pocket hunter, who survives, unaware of "how much he depended for the necessary sense of home" found in the desert (47); or the one who "wastes so many seasons' effort, so many suns and rain to make a pound of wool!" (90). Austin shows ecological concern for the exploitative efforts of human beings, but that concern never becomes unbalanced paranoia, because "[c]uriously, all this human occupancy of greed and mischief left no mark on the field, but the Indians did, and the unthinking sheep" (76). In her efforts to convince readers that they too must learn to adapt for their own physical and spiritual survival, Austin shifts from the position that the reader must somehow save the land out of altruistic notions to the reality that the land will always survive; it is the human occupancy of that land that is at risk.

Austin suggests that her readers can learn much from Native Americans and their relationship to the land to minimize such risk: "The Shoshones live like their trees, with great spaces between" (57). Throughout her text she stresses that the Indians leave a mark that is relationally appropriate for human habitation in the ecosystem, and that other humans new to this land need to observe and apply the knowledge the Indians can teach them. We are aware from the first sentences of *The Land of Little Rain* that Austin's discourse departs from contemporary views of the official, stereotyped Indian. In the *Handbook of American Indians North of Mexico*, published by the Smithsonian Institution in 1907, Frederick Webb Hodge provides an ethnographic study of the Indians, "in preparation for a number of years," which begins, interestingly enough, with a discussion of the "curious errors" that have resulted in naming the Native Americans.[22] The purpose of the handbook is to catalogue and correct those errors: "It has been the aim to give a brief description of every linguistic stock, confederacy, tribe, subtribe, or tribal division, and settlement known to history or even to tradition, as well as the origin and derivation of every name treated, whenever such is known, and to record under every form of the name and every other appellation that could be learned."[23]

In light of Austin's discussion of how the Native Americans name referentially from a particular moment in a relationship, an official document that attempts to definitively record Indian names seems suspect. For the authors of this handbook, naming reverts to the scientific discourse of static classification antithetical to the relational adaptation of Native American practice. In the ethnographic report on the Shoshone and Paiute, whom Austin also mentions, the same scientific discourse colonizes and universalizes the Shoshone in the past tense: "In general character they were fierce and warlike."[24] The past tense predominates in this report, indicating that either all Native Americans are dead at this point in history or that the living tribes, sometimes mentioned in the present tense, retain none of the characteristics imposed by this Anglo-American construction. The report goes on to discuss the Shoshones' counterparts in the desert, the Paiutes, to whom "the opprobrious name of 'Diggers' was applied." This tribe is categorized relatively: "Representing as a class, as they undeniably do, a culturally low type of Indian, they were by no means as low as many writers of repute have asserted."[25] The desire here to scientifically catalogue the Paiute as hierarchically better than contemporary sentiment might allow reproduces the detached dimension of a colonizing discourse that masks itself in altruism.

Such a mask of colonizing altruism becomes insidious when considered in relation to the discourse in Francis Amasu Walker's article "The Indian Question." Walker begins by saying: "Equally obdurate must one be to the seductions of Indian ethnology" and the temptation "to dwell upon the history of Indian tribes" because such eastern romanticism will divert the reader from the true task at hand: "The Indian question naturally divides itself into two: What shall be done with the Indian as an obstacle to national progress: What shall be done with him when, and so far as he ceases to oppose or obstruct the extension of railways and settlements."[26] Again the readers of such turn-of-the-century texts find only two options available to them as far as the "Indian question" is concerned: they can either develop a false altruism that still objectifies other human beings as empathetically passive, or they can concur with the American political solution of genocide for the Native American populations, whom the Naturalization Act of 1790 described as "domestic foreigners." These two viewpoints formulate the primary genres from which Austin constructs her secondary text arising "in more complex and comparatively highly developed and organized cultural communication."[27]

Austin approaches the secondary text of the "Indian question" again in dialogic style: she introduces individual Native Americans of the narrator's acquaintance to her readers. Storytelling about Shoshone land, she tells the reader that, prior to going there, she "had seen it through the eyes of Winnenap in a rosy mist of reminiscence, and must always see it with a sense of intimacy in the light that never was" (55). The narrator moves from a personal observation to a retelling of what Winnenap, the Shoshone medicine man who is neither a romanticized noble savage nor a fierce obstacle to national progress, has told her. Winnenap assumes flesh and bone as the hostage Shoshone who despises his captors, the Paiutes, but who nevertheless becomes a contributing member of the tribe "to save his honor and the word of his vanished kin" (55). As medicine man, he even accepts his death as a tribal necessity after patients die under his care, but he also has the potential to construct his own heaven with "the free air and free spaces of Shoshone Land" (61). Winnenap never becomes a colonized object, as Austin verifies by referring the entire chapter on Shoshone land to his authority.

In the chapter "Shoshone Land" the reader hears through Winnenap's discourse a Native American who is tribally resistant but still committed to the community; a man whose "savageness" interacts with the necessities of his environment; a shaman who protects a complex social system by self-sacrifice. Readers must react to the complexity of Winnenap's social position and reject the monologic, prescriptive constructions of Native American men posited by dominant American ideology. Donna Haraway's re-visioning of scientific knowledge in *Simians, Cyborgs, and Women: The Reinvention of Nature* summarizes Austin's discursive relationship to Winnenap's story and to subsequent accounts of the inhabitants of the land of little rain. Haraway suggests that "[t]he alternative to relativism is partial, locatable, critical knowledges sustaining the possibility of webs of connections called solidarity in politics and shared conversations in epistemology."[28] Instead of presenting romanticized vignettes of universalized characters alienated from the readers' space and time, Austin creates locatable speaking subjects whose particular knowledge offers pragmatic conversation to readers who want to understand the land she is describing from alternate worldviews.

Metaphorically, Austin's own situated knowledge at times reproduces the dominant ideological theme that Indians are somehow closer to the natural order than whites: "Young Shoshones are like young quail, knowing without teaching about feeding and hiding, and learning what civilized children never learn, to be still and to keep on being still, at the first hint of danger or strangeness" (58). But she turns this reproduction just enough so that the reader sees the relational shift. It is not so much that the Shoshone children are somehow better adapted biologically to nature than the white children; rather, these children have remained united to a natural order. They instinctively know how to survive without an artificial, Eurocentric education that favors alienation rather than connection. Knowledge for "primitive people," Austin believes, is a "sort of instinct atrophied by disuse in a complexer civilization" (144). Again we experience the Eurocentric duality of the dominant discourse, primitive against civilized, but Austin has consistently questioned the definition of those terms as necessarily dichotomous throughout the text.

Her chapters on Jimville and Los Uvas expand the theme of civilization and how it relates to the ecosystem that she develops in *The Land of Little Rain*. The casual reader might conclude that Austin represents Jimville as the satiric trope of western individualism versus the primitive/peasant utopia in Los Uvas, but such an assumption overlooks Austin's complexity in relocating humans within the ecosystem. These two towns, located very near each other, form the locus of adaptation to the land. The residents of Jimville cultivate an honor code that holds as "moral distinction" "as much ground as you can shoot over, in as many pretentions as you can make good" (69), while the inhabitants of Los Uvas live by an honor code based on relational responsibility and artistic imagination. The crux of Jimville's inability to thrive ("You could not think of Jimville as anything more than survival" [65]) is not that civilization is inherently evil; rather, Jimville's problems stem from a worldview that sees "behavior as history . . . untroubled by invention and the dramatic sense" (70). The result is a male-dominated society that Austin represents in the following way: "Along with killing and drunkenness, coveting of women, charity, simplicity, there is a certain indifference, blankness, emptiness if you will of all vaporings, no bubbling of the pot" (71). Austin finds no "mean-spiritedness" here or even egotism, just a lack of "any new thing to gape and wonder at" (72). Once they have depleted the economic potential of the land, the inhabitants of Jimville are unable to connect to the surrounding environment, resulting in the lethargic isolation of outmoded stagecoaches barely held together by wire. The exploitation of women, minorities, and the environment creates the myth of the individual who can only anesthetize himself with drink and count on hunches for survival.

In contrast to Jimville, Las Uvas might easily be seen as an exotic primitive utopia, but again Austin uses a prescribed genre to disrupt the dominant discourse. Interestingly, Las Uvas is unlocatable in the Greek sense of the lotus-eaters' land to which she refers. And although she describes the methods and means to get to Jimville, she refuses to say where Las Uvas "lies, how to come at it" (143). With much description of natural lushness connected to social celebrations of dance, music, and song, Austin initially creates a stereotypical image of pastoral abundance based on imagination that could be easily contrasted genre-wise to the satire of Jimville's occupants. But just as the people of Jimville reveal qualities beyond the western romances written by such authors as Bret Harte, the inhabitants of Las Uvas surpass mere tropes for romantic idealization. The imagination they need to survive is hardly a narcissistic recollection in tranquillity.

With the first sentence of "The Little Town of the Grape Vines" Austin introduces serious political concerns into this genre of the pastoral, telling her readers that the people of Las Uvas "make more of the Sixteenth of September than they do of the Fourth of July" (143). The most significant story of this chapter is not about the happy primitive; rather, it centers on the Mexican people's colonization of California, another result of the Anglo-American "eastern enterprise" (144). The people of Las Uvas are a community struggling to preserve their own collective identity through the celebration of a holiday that marks independence in their native land, now colonized by American aggression. Are they unrealistic romantics who refuse to accept the reality of the present? Not at all. Austin says: "You are not to suppose that they do not keep the Fourth, Washington's Birthday, and Thanksgiving . . . but the Sixteenth is the holiday of the heart" (148). While the people of Las Uvas accept the real political situation—the American flag dominating their days—their imagination creatively sustains their cultural integrity in the image of the flag of Old Mexico gracing their celebrations.

Textually, in Las Uvas Austin represents a community resistant to the annexation of Mexican land and culture by American enterprise that entices men like José Romero away from his family with good wages. But Las Uvas, now lacking the economic success that mining once brought it, not only survives but thrives because its imaginative adaptation is based on communal needs rather than individual enterprise. "Honor" in Las Uvas considers the needs of the family above individual greed. It makes marriage "easily come by" (146) and regenerates a society in which "every house is made of earth" (148) and there is no "incentive to thieving or killing" because the town's "little wealth" is "to be had for the borrowing" (149). Austin suggests that "ease" for the human species must come from a mutual interplay of human need in the ecological community in the same way that other species survive. In reality, the people of Las Uvas will thrive because, as a community, they are able to lower one flag and raise another in a ritualistic celebration of change and adaptation without losing their identity and traditions. Austin suggests that this ability to operate from relational adaptation is also the basis of human survival in the ecosystem.

In the earlier chapter about Seyavi, "The Basket Maker," Austin creates the dialogue that shows her readers the possibilities of working, as Patrick Murphy discusses, "from a concept of relational difference and anotherness rather than Otherness."[29] She does this primarily through her recurrent feminist agenda of heterarchically respecting the speaking positions of those groups negatively identified with nature and the land.

Just as she respects the situational knowledge of Winnenap, Austin refuses the stereotypical image of Native American women in her Basket Maker. "Seyavi made baskets for love and sold them for money, in a generation that preferred iron pots for utility" (95). Significantly, Austin does not abstract the Indian woman artist, as Agnes Laut does in "The Indian's

Idea of Fine Arts" (*Outing*, 1904). Laut describes a romantic Indian heroine: "She is ageless, this creature, with the color of berry stain in her
bronzed cheeks, and muscles like a gladiator."[30] Austin's Seyavi lives
through the "crude time" when women "became in turn the game of con-
querors" (94), finding a way to survive from her artistic, sensual desire.
Laut's Indian woman artist, Fighting Mistah, is "stabbed to death in her
tepee by the other women of the tribe, who could no longer bear her
dominant will."[31] In these two authors we again see oppositional approaches to the patriarchal discourse. Even though she is trying to render
Fighting Mistah in heroic terms as "bigger than life," Laut succeeds only in
reproducing the viewpoint that independent, gifted women have to die, if
not by men's hands then by the design of other women who cannot sustain such strength. Furthermore, Laut's sentimental approach to the Indian
woman as a westernized version of the independent female artist rein-
scribes the artificial strictures of the nineteenth-century cult of domesticity that denied such women a legitimate place in society. Austin gives readers a very different sense of the woman she chooses to carry her artistic
discourse.

Uniting every form of exploited Otherness characteristic of nineteenth-century America, Seyavi is female, Native American, poor, and a
single working mother who lives from the spirituality of the land rather
than the dogma of the religious institution. According to Western standards, she has few redeeming qualities, but Austin makes it clear that Seyavi
is her model because she defies alienated otherness and lives relationally:
"Every Indian woman is an artist,—sees, feels, creates, but does not phi-
losophize about her processes" (95). We are brought back again to the difference between the perspectives of Mary Austin, who is not engaged in
transcendental closure, and Burroughs and Long. While Burroughs and
Long use academic debate to carve out prescriptive theory, Austin creates
Seyavi to explore where her writing can lead her in the practical process
of discovering her own art.

In Seyavi, Austin places the desire and "mother wit" of feminine discourse, the sensuality of the columbine, and the dancing and dressing of
hair that take place in ritualized art. Unlike many contemporary Cartesian
knowers who find truth through abstract reasoning, Austin gives to Seyavi
the revolutionary potential of all women, particularly herself. In *Desire in
Language: A Semiotic Approach to Literature and Art*, Julia Kristeva describes
the artist's process: "Theoretical discourse is not the discourse of a repudi-

ated subject, but of one searching for the laws of its desires, operating as a hinge between immersion in the signifier and repudiation (it is neither one nor the other), its status unknown."[32] In just such a discursive process, Austin covets Seyavi's baskets and has a "keen hunger . . . for bits of lore and the 'fool talk' of her people" (96) because she sees her own position of authorship as incomplete, "its status unknown." She also realizes that Seyavi's spirituality is so strong that "having borne herself courageously to this end she will not be born a coyote" (99). Austin, however, who has not yet achieved such spiritual grounding, must still struggle as the coyote scavenging through available discursive options while trying to fulfill her artistic desires.

The discourse of the coyote, with whom Austin finds such an affinity throughout *The Land of Little Rain,* may define where she sees herself as writer and activist, the "I-for-another" space interpreting her own praxis. Austin says she is still looking for Seyavi's columbine, but while she looks she will continue to howl in the distance as the scavenger coyote within the dominant discourse. Her style of cross-genre nature writing in *The Land of Little Rain* calls into question the necessity of prescriptive boundaries. Through satiric storytelling she instructs us with scientific clarity about the particular interpellations of our ecosystem while she simultaneously makes us laugh at the cultural idiosyncracies of our own constructed Jimvilles. Ultimately, her poetic discourse, interpenetrating with other genre styles, will intensify the sensual desire that leads to the mystical in Austin's writing.

In a popular short story written in 1901 and published in *Harper's Monthly,* George Bird Grinnell tells the story of a coyote that saved a little Indian girl by acting as her guide through hostile territory. Although the coyote could not remain with the little girl after she returned to her people, it was not forgotten.[33] Significantly, Austin's work has recently been "not forgotten" because it provides an antecedent for another of Haraway's observations: "Politics rests on the possibility of a shared world. . . . You've got to contest for the discourse from within, building connections to other constituencies."[34] By critically appreciating Austin's ability to interrogate nature writing from within the limits of a prescribed genre and, ultimately, to rupture those boundaries with her own artistic expression, we can begin to connect her historical contribution to the energies we need to transform our future. As contemporary folk wisdom suggests, "If you don't know where you've been, you can't know where you're going."

NOTES

1. See Mary Austin, *The Land of Little Rain*, in *Stories from the Country of Lost Borders*, ed. Marjorie Pryse (New Brunswick: Rutgers University Press, 1987), 36. Subsequent quotations are cited parenthetically in the text.

2. Patrick Murphy, *Literature, Nature, and Other: Ecofeminist Critiques* (Albany: State University of New York Press, 1995), 340.

3. William J. Long, "The Modern School of Nature-Study and Its Critics," *North American Review* 179 (1903): 43.

4. John Burroughs, "The Literary Treatment of Nature," *Atlantic Monthly* 94 (1904): 38.

5. Ibid., 39.

6. Ibid.

7. Ibid., 42.

8. Long, "The Modern School," 688.

9. Ibid., 692.

10. Ibid., 693.

11. Roland Barthes, "Theory of the Text," in *Untying the Text*, ed. Robert Young (New York: Routledge, 1990), 39.

12. Michel Foucault, "The Order of Discourse," in Young, ed., *Untying the Text*, 69. Foucault theorizes the discontinuity of discourse that disrupts traditional categories of time as succession and subject as unified, positing the violence that universalizing presuppositions do to textual analysis.

13. Mikhail Bakhtin, *Speech Genres and Other Late Essays*, ed. Caryl Emerson and Michael Holquist, trans. Vern W. McGee (Austin: University of Texas Press, 1986), 68.

14. "The American Deserts," *National Geographic* 15 (1904): 152–63.

15. Ernest Ingersoll, "Plant Life in the Desert," *Harper's Monthly* 110 (1905): 576–91.

16. Robert H. Chapman, "The Deserts of Nevada and the Death Valley: U.S. Geological Survey," *National Geographic* 17 (1906): 482–97.

17. "American Deserts," 151.

18. Chapman, "Deserts," 494, 491.

19. Charles Holder, "The Heart of Darkness," *Outing* 45 (1904): 419.

20. William J. Scheick, "Mary Austin's Disfigurement of the Southwest in *The Land of Little Rain*," *Western American Literature* 27.1 (1992): 44.

21. For an in-depth discussion of women nature writers, including Mary Austin, and how their approaches differ from prescribed genre expectations, see Patrick Murphy's essay "Voicing Another Nature," in *A Dialogue of Voices: Feminist Literary Theory and Bakhtin*, ed. Karen Hohne and Helen Wussow (Minneapolis: University of Minnesota Press, 1994), 59–82.

22. Frederick Webb Hodge, *Handbook of American Indians North of Mexico*, Bureau of American Ethnology Bulletin 30 (Washington, D.C.: GPO, 1907), i.

23. Ibid., viii.

24. Ibid., 555.

25. Ibid.

26. Francis Amasu Walker, "The Indian Question," *Outlander* 75 (1874): 17.

27. Bakhtin, *Speech Genres*, 62.

28. Donna Haraway, *Simians, Cyborgs, and Women: The Reinvention of Nature* (New York: Routledge, 1991), 191.

29. Murphy, "Voicing Another Nature," 63.

30. Agnes Laut, "The Indian's Idea of Fine Arts," *Outing* 46 (1905): 354.

31. Ibid., 363.

32. Julia Kristeva, *Desire in Language: A Semiotic Approach to Literature and Art* (New York: Columbia University Press, 1980), 120.

33. George Bird Grinnel, "Little Friend Coyote," *Harper's Monthly* 102 (1902): 5.

34. Donna Haraway, "The Actors Are Cyborg, Nature Is Coyote, and the Geography Elsewhere: Postscript to 'Cyborgs at Large,'" in *Technoculture*, ed. Constance Penley and Andre Ross (Minneapolis: University of Minnesota Press, 1991), 4.

CHAPTER TWELVE

The Flock

An Ecocritical Look at Mary Austin's Sheep
and John Muir's Hoofed Locusts

BARNEY NELSON

In her discussion of Isidro, *Nicole Tonkovich points to Mary Austin's allegorical use of sheep and lambs. In* "The Flock: *An Ecocritical Look at Mary Austin's Sheep and John Muir's Hoofed Locusts," Barney Nelson offers a new reading of* The Flock, *which is generally viewed as a dated pastoral of uncertain genre. Using the insights of recent critics, especially Richard White's essay "'Are You an Environmentalist or Do You Work for a Living?': Work and Nature," Nelson reads* The Flock *as a multivoiced political allegory in which Austin defends the lifestyles of working-class and rural people and questions the assumptions of the emerging conservation movement.*

Like Michelle Campbell Toohey, Nelson claims that Austin's antihierarchical relationship to the rural western landscape challenged the dominant perspectives of her nature-writing peers—here encapsulated in John Muir's and Austin's writings on sheep. In Nelson's reading, the authors' differing portrayals of sheep and shepherds reflect their differences on controversial issues in the turn-of-the-century West: the domestic and the "wild"; business and tourism; anarchy, democracy, and capitalism; land use, grazing rights, and national parks. Like Tonkovich, Nelson concludes by demonstrating the contemporary political relevance of a work critics generally overlook.

Around the turn of the century, just before she wrote *The Flock* (1906), Mary Austin watched Los Angeles steal the water from her Owens Valley neighbors.[1] She watched John Muir lead a push to expand Yosemite Valley's boundaries, taking extensive private lands away from rural people in order to "preserve" and "protect" those lands inside the new national park boundary. She watched as some of those newly "protected" lands quietly became railroad right-of-way, laying the foundation for the development of the most lucrative big business the West ever produced: tourism.[2] Finally, she watched as the new national park closed thousands of acres of high Sierra meadows to summer sheep grazing, putting even more of her Owens Valley neighbors out of business. Austin had probably also just read Frank Norris's *The Octopus* (1901), a novel suggesting that California and the nation were at the mercy of a huge, ruthless, manipulative railroad monopoly.

As *The Octopus* opens, a band of sheep has accidentally wandered onto a railroad right-of-way into the path of a fast-moving train. What ensues is "a slaughter, a massacre of innocents. The iron monster had charged full into the midst, merciless, inexorable. To the right and left, all the width of the right of way, the little bodies had been flung; backs were snapped against the fence posts; brains knocked out. Caught in the barbs of the wire, wedged in, the bodies hung suspended. Underfoot . . . the black blood, winking in the starlight, seeped down into the clinkers."[3] As Norris's description of these innocent victims of the thundering machines of big business suggests, much of the rhetoric and symbolism regarding private and public land, rural and urban conflict, water rights and railroads, socialism, capitalism, and democracy centered on sheep. During the high-stakes land battles between businesses promoting tourism, cities seeking water rights, and local rural residents trying to preserve their communities and livelihoods, two authors in particular concentrated their politics into literary allegories using sheep: Mary Austin and John Muir.

According to William F. Kimes's excellent annotated summary of Muir's early published work, Muir began cursing sheep publicly in 1872 through numerous articles in the *San Francisco Examiner*, the *Oakland Daily Evening Tribune, Century* magazine, the *San Francisco Daily Evening Bulletin, Scribner's Monthly*, and the *Overland Monthly*.[4] Muir's most famous antisheep essays, "Wild Sheep of California" and "Wild Wool," first appeared in 1874 and 1875, respectively.[5] Books Muir published in 1894 (*The Mountains of California*) and 1901 (*Our National Parks*) also condemned sheep. These texts were instrumental in rallying popular support to ban sheep grazing within Yosemite National Park's boundaries. Austin was obviously aware of Muir's writing. She briefly mentions him in her first book, *The Land of Little Rain* (1903), as a "devout man," and they evidently met in 1904.[6] I read Austin's 1906 book, *The Flock*, as a series of direct challenges to Muir's published denigration of sheep.

In 1982 Vera Norwood noted that *The Flock* was "written at a time when John Muir was referring to sheep as 'hoofed locusts.'"[7] Although Norwood would later argue that Austin was "inspired in part by John Muir's call to preserve natural landscapes," a close reading comparing Austin's and Muir's views reveals strongly opposed ecological perspectives. Muir favored preserving "pristine wilderness" as a place for leisure and study, not work, and he revered those parts of the West that most resembled Europe—its mountains, waterfalls, and lush woodlands—as inspirational to writers and artists. Austin, on the other hand, believed land should be valued as a place to live and work and argued that ranking land into hierarchies and preserving the most beautiful encouraged abuse of the unbeautiful. On both literal and symbolic levels, Muir and Austin wanted to protect natural resources from ravaging hordes, but their perceptions regarding the identity of those hordes differed considerably. Muir feared the common rural masses and their domestic animals; Austin feared the unquenchable urban thirst for water and recreation. Muir wanted to preserve beautiful places for escape and enjoyment; Austin wanted to preserve sustainable rural communities.

Using a complex collected essay pattern that Carl Bredahl calls "divided narrative," Austin constructed *The Flock* as a boundary-blurring collection of sketches about sheepherding in the Sierra, merging nonfiction and myth into a multivoiced, dialogic narrative.[8] This communal narrative genre, later of much interest to class and postcolonial theorists such as Mikhail Bakhtin and Trinh T. Minh-ha,[9] enabled Austin to work within the nonhierarchial oral tradition and disclaim an authoritative voice. The very structure of the book supports her attempt to give democratic authority to the common working class. Carefully crediting her sources in the first chapter, Austin cites historic California sheepherders, from Hispanic landowners to the "Basco" shepherds. "I suppose of all the people who are concerned with the making of a true book, the one who puts it to the pen has the least to do with it," she says. "This is the book of Jimmy Rosemeyre and José Jesus Lopez, of Little Pete, . . . of Noriega, of Sanger and the Manxman and Narcisse Duplin, and many others."[10] With this introduction, Austin creates a humble, journalistic persona in order to characterize the shepherds as authority figures and give them voices in the book.

A detailed history of the sheep industry in California is followed by lyrical allegoric vignettes about sheep management, shearing, shepherd ways, grazing the Sierra, weather sense, flock mentality and habits, sheep dogs, wars with cattlemen, predators, the Tejon Ranch, and the coming of a national park. Through what she calls the "pale luminosity" of sheep dust rising along the Long Trail, Austin conjures "the social order struggling into shape" (57) and follows the ancient storyteller's tradition of using sheep to represent the human masses. Carefully presenting the wild habits of domestic sheep, Austin's allegory ranges from biblical authors who wrote that the meek would inherit the earth—and who were quite familiar with docile flocks that could quickly explode into an uncontrollable sea of running anarchists—to Thoreau.

In the sketch entitled "The Sheep and the Reserves," Austin blatantly argues against Muir's call to ban grazing within Yosemite National Park, declaring that even the rangers often sympathized with law-breaking shepherds and looked the other way while they sneaked back into their old summer haunts. The rangers, she claims, "despised . . . the work of warding sheep off the grass in order that silly tourists might wonder at the meadows full of bloom" (93). Austin obviously wrote *The Flock* as a response to both political activism promoting tourism and national parks, and the underlying economic and cultural class divisions such activism encouraged. Her final chapter, "The Shade of the Arrows," uses a Paiute saying that "no man should go far in the desert who cannot sleep in the shade of his arrows" to warn against visiting a "wild" place when one does not truly understand how to survive there. This saying seems to encapsulate the theme of *The Flock:* working shepherds belong in the Sierra; tourists do not. Austin privileges local working people rather than sightseeing visitors and supports the needs of rural communities.[11]

Although the story line of *The Flock* is obviously based on a political controversy raging in California at the turn into the twentieth century, the conflicts it describes are ancient ones. A glowing 1906 review in *Nation* compares Austin to Virgil, saying, "Baldly stated, [*The Flock*] is no more than a study of the sheep industry in California, with a slender thread of historic narrative, a picture of sheep herding, a word for irrigation. This summary of *The Flock,* however, bears about as much relation to the actual achievement as a statement that the first book of the Georgics is a treatise on agriculture."[12] The struggle Austin illuminates in *The Flock* is a modern one as well. "Are You an Environmentalist or Do You Work for a Living?" asks Richard White in the title of a provocative essay published in William Cronon's controversial collection, *Uncommon Ground: Rethinking the Human Place in Nature* (1995). *Uncommon Ground* explores wilderness as an Edenic construct of the imagination, a pristine place where no one works.

White posits that modern environmentalists, while "celebrating the virtues of play and recreation in nature," often "take one of two equally problematic positions toward work." They either "equate productive work in nature with destruction" or they "ignore the ways that work itself is a means of knowing nature."[13] Almost one hundred years earlier, Mary Austin allegorically attempted a similar literary argument in *The Flock*. She saw a grave political danger in imagining sheep, so often symbolic of common people, as ravaging hordes.

Muir scholars have traditionally interpreted Muir's sheep allegories as ecocentric rather than anthropocentric. Thomas Lyon, for instance, observes that "Muir's conversion of the lamb . . . into a devilish, 'hoofed locust,' is a fine example of his imaginative inversion of cultural values."[14] I argue, however, that as an allegory, Muir's hierarchical reversal, which places a higher value on wild sheep than on domestic ones, is xenophobic, riddled with allusions to class divisions, and takes on a chilling elitist aspect. Austin challenged Muir's tendency to privilege what Thorstein Veblen had just labeled "the leisure class" over work-based local communities and his desire to appropriate rural places in order to provide playgrounds. As indigenous peoples of various races were pushed aside for the "greater public good," which almost always turned out to be oppressive, urban, and in some way promoting big business, Austin rose to defend her friends and neighbors. I argue that *The Flock* blends natural history, politics, and allegory into a genre-blurring narrative championing local shepherds in their losing battle against the quickly developing tourist business.

Realizing how powerfully Austin had structured her literary argument supporting working shepherds, Muir may have felt that both Yosemite National Park and tourism itself were threatened. Muir's book *My First Summer in the Sierra* (1911) may well have been written in reaction to *The Flock*. Although today we read *My First Summer* as a published journal, in fact, more than forty years passed between the actual experiences and the writing and publication of the book. Muir supposedly spent the summer of 1869 working for Pat Delaney as a sheepherder in the Sierra. *My First Summer,* however, was written in 1910 and published in 1911. According to the editors of Muir's papers, the original journal from which Muir supposedly composed the book is missing. The collected papers do, however, contain another unpublished journal entitled "Twenty Hill Hollow," which Muir began on 1 January 1869 and kept while working in the fenced pastures of the San Joaquin Valley for John Connel. The papers also contain Muir's working draft of *My First Summer.* Both documents reveal extensive contradictions and changes between Muir's private observations, his publication drafts, and his early and later published work.[15] If indeed Muir worked from an early journal when he wrote *My First Summer,* that journal was probably heavily rewritten. In an interesting analysis comparing the "young" Muir as sheepherder and journal keeper with the "old" Muir as author, Michael Cohen says that *My First Summer* is "deceptively straightforward," and although "an honest and truthful book, it is also narrated with all the skill that a novelist might muster."[16]

By the time Muir published *My First Summer,* Yosemite was embroiled in the bitter struggle between those who lived and worked in the Sierra and those who wanted to preserve it. Muir had also married into a very wealthy California family, and his circle of friends now included the nation's educated, wealthy political elite. Understandably, although wanting to claim sheepherding expertise through personal experience, he also wanted to avoid the stigma attached to that occupation. His glacier theories had once been dismissed as the simple ideas of a sheepherder.[17] So Muir tries to make it clear to the reader of *My First Summer* that he had agreed to go along only as a respectable scholar, eager for the opportunity to study the geology and biology of the high mountain meadows, and was merely making sure the real sheepherder did his job.[18] Through this stance, Muir emphasizes the class division between himself and the common shepherd. Leo Marx describes this as creating a "distinction between the countryman who actually does the work and the gentleman (or poet) who enjoys rural ease."[19] Yi-Fu Tuan calls it a "special kind of play," common in both Eastern and Western cultures, in which "the high-born pretend to be simple farmers, thus imitating children who in their games pretend to be engaged in serious work."[20] Nor is this worldwide need to pretend to work confined to a single time period. White argues that environmentalists today have edited out the labor of the body and "have replaced it with a story of first white men at strenuous play or in respectful observation." The reason, he says, "[e]nvironmentalists so often seem self-righteous, privileged, and arrogant" is because they identify nature with play and make it "a place where leisured humans come only to visit and not to work, stay, or live."[21] In truth, when John Muir first arrived in California in 1868, he was a penniless thirty-year-old drifter in desperate need of a job, not a gentleman scholar on holiday.

On the subjects of sheep, shepherds, and sheepherding, Muir contradicts

Austin's descriptions in *The Flock* almost line for line. Austin's sheepherder seldom carries a six-shooter; Muir's usually does.[22] Austin rhapsodizes over the wonderful meals she has eaten at a shepherd's fire; Muir says the sheepherder's food is "far from delicate" (*Flock*, 82–83; *First Summer*, 81). Austin argues that "[t]he smell of sheep is to the herder as the smack and savor of any man's work"; Muir makes fun of the sheepherder's desire to sleep next to the sheep "as if determined to take ammoniacal snuff all night" (*Flock*, 93; *First Summer*, 129). Austin calls ridicule of shepherds simple prejudice and argues that the fact "[t]hat most sheepherders are foreigners accounts largely for the abomination in which they are held and the prejudice that attaches to the term" (*Flock*, 55–56). Muir claims the sheepherder wears "everlasting clothing" consisting of pants waterproofed by drips of "clear fat and gravy juices" that have clustered into stalactites and become imbedded with bits of nature. These greasy clothes do make the sheepherder a collector of specimens, jokes Muir derisively, again keeping the class divisions clear, but he is "far from being a naturalist" (*First Summer*, 130).

Austin persistently questions cultural, educational, political, and language hierarchies; Muir just as persistently characterizes himself as superior to shepherds because they are, in his view, dirty, uneducated, and racially other. Austin suggests that because shepherds often speak an(other) language, outsiders come to the "unfounded assumption" that most sheepherders are "a little insane." She suggests further that their outdoor life "nourish[es] imagination and they have in full what we oftenest barely brush wings with" (*Flock*, 61–63). Although Muir claims that mountain hardships produce strength and wisdom in himself and fellow mountaineers, he believes this same solitary outdoor life adversely affects the shepherd: "seeing nobody for weeks or months, he finally becomes semi-insane or wholly so" (*First Summer*, 24). Austin states emphatically, "With all my seeking into desert places there are three things . . . I have not seen, —a man who has rediscovered a lost mine, the heirs of one who died of the sidewinder and a shepherd who is insane" (*Flock*, 65). Muir just as emphatically states, "The California shepherd, as far as I've seen or heard, is never quite sane for any considerable time" (*First Summer*, 24). Commenting on today's version of this argument, White asserts that modern environmentalists, "[h]aving demonized those whose very lives recognize the tangled complexity of a planet on which we kill, destroy and alter as a condition of living and working, . . . can claim an innocence that in the end is merely irresponsibility."[23] The attitudes of Austin and Muir toward the working shepherd expose many of the stereotypes about the poor and racially other that the environmental justice movement has recently begun to scrutinize. Modern versions of this debate often use much the same rhetoric, and domestic animals still allegorically represent the clashing cultures and class values.

Austin challenged the stereotype of rural people as ignorant and illiterate wherever she found it. In her work she recognizes art in humble places, granting sophistication to basket makers and pocket hunters, and remembering that she never found a better companion with whom to discuss French literature than a dark shepherd she calls "Little Pete." She respects and recognizes shepherds' creativity: they are poets, wood carvers, musicians, philosophers.[24] Austin believed that the perception of ignorance often stemmed from language barriers, and she writes defiantly in *The Flock* that "these Bascos are a little proud of the foolish gaspings and gutterings by which they prevent an understanding" (60, 63). Austin's defense of sheepherders reflects her pattern of respectful representation of indigenous, regional cultures. She often preferred the company of Shoshone, Paiute, and settlers from Old Mexico to that of her white neighbors, whose creeds, she points out, "are chiefly restrictions against other people's way of life."[25]

On the surface, it would seem that John Muir, having actually worked as a shepherd, had more personal knowledge of sheep than did Austin and therefore would be the more reliable authority. However, "Twenty Hill Hollow," the journal he actually wrote at the time he worked with sheep, reveals his inexperience with herding. In the journal, Muir describes losing one hundred lambs and two hundred "old sheep" in one night, after which the boss called to ask if Muir had ever lambed a band of ewes. Muir writes, "I answered that I had not, & that I had not the slightest idea of the duties." The boss quickly relieved Muir of the ewe band and sent what would have been considered an easier-to-care-for band of wethers, castrated male sheep. Muir, however, found the wethers wild and totally uncontrollable. He describes spending the first day trying to "train" them to behave, running them with the dogs. This training proves to be another error in judgment. The next day he writes, "a good many of my sheep are dying." All along, he blames his losses not on his own lack of shepherding skill but on the weather—San Joaquin Valley weather, mind you, not Mount Whitney's.[26] Muir may have been born in Scotland, a country where sheep have grazed steep green hills for thousands of years, but he was no shepherd.

In contrast to Muir, Austin claims no personal experience herding sheep. Instead, she presents herself as a simple reporter, asking questions, listening to shepherd stories around campfires, and retelling them in a multivoiced narrative that respectfully gives the shepherds themselves the voice of authority. At her best, Austin practices the humble techniques of journalism and storytelling, meticulously gathering facts and stories from many different points of view rather than trusting to her own knowledge. In fact, however, Austin probably possessed a deeper personal understanding of the rural culture than Muir. She grew up "in a farming country, of farming kin"[27] and spent two years homesteading on the borders of California's old Tejon Ranch and fifteen in the Owens Valley, living for almost two decades among shepherds and beside the "Long Trail" that wound through the Sierra (*Flock*, 12). She also wrote her book as events happened, not forty-two years later. She knew and respected the shepherds she wrote about and tried to represent the culture from the inside.

A close reading and comparison of Muir's private papers and published work reveals many inaccuracies and contradictions. Perhaps partly motivated by his own embarrassing inability to handle what he considered a simple, unskilled job, Muir publicly cursed sheep for their "reckless ravages" and called them "ruthless denuders" and "hoofed locusts." However, his early private journal observations and descriptions of the San Joaquin Valley contradict these published statements. By the time Muir first saw the valley, sheep had been grazing it for more than one hundred years; there were more than 300,000 of them in the valley in 1833 (*Flock*, 7). Yet, in 1868, Muir described the heavily grazed valley as "the floweriest piece of world I ever walked."[28]

Austin points out that California shepherds came from countries where sheep, flowers, steep pastures, and crystal streams had coexisted, and probably coevolved, for thousands of years (*Flock*, 32, 52). And while she admits that "[y]ou will find proof . . . in the government reports" that sheep grazing can cause damage if shepherds are not given their own "fixed" pastures, she makes clear that the damage should not be blamed on the shepherds, who are just following orders, or on the sheep, who like all creatures "use the face of the earth to better it" (*Flock,* 172, 206-10). "No doubt," she argues, "meadow grasses, all plants that renew from the root, were meant for forage" (*Flock,* 100). Shepherds and sheep alike merely follow the same labor techniques practiced by good gardeners when they pinch back, prune, fertilize, and burn in order to produce more blooms and healthier plants.[29] She explains that what may appear to be destruction may actually be cultivation. By grazing through pastures in early spring as growth begins, and again in the fall after seeds have dropped, sheep make ideal gardeners for flowering plants. Defending even the sheep themselves as laborers, Austin observes that their pruning and droppings fertilize and strengthen the beautiful flowered meadows and asks, "Is it not the custom [everywhere] to put sheep on worn-out lands to renew them?" (*Flock*, 170, 208–9). Muir wanted to protect the Sierra as "pristine wilderness" to be used only for recreation and to develop the sensibilities of privileged middle-class "mountaineers." Austin valued the Sierra as a vital part of an ecological web necessary for sustaining life.

Austin also realized that to imagine the Sierra a pristine wilderness or a Garden of Eden was to ignore centuries of Native American land management. The open, sunlit, parklike quality of the "pristine" Sierra so attractive to tourists had been maintained by fire, first by native people, then by shepherds.[30] In *Savage Dreams* (1994), Rebecca Solnit describes the removal of the Mariposa tribes from Yosemite Valley and argues that "the gap between our view of landscape and of history is full of lost stories, ravaged cultures, obliterated names."[31] As White says, although "academic historians have produced a respectable body of work . . . that concentrates on how Indian peoples shaped the natural world they lived in . . . by and large, this literature has been dismissed. . . . Working people of mixed race can't carry the story line" that environmentalist writers favor, of a "first white man" and an "untouched paradise," or of "the wonder of a world before work."[32] Ironically, Muir wanted to protect the Sierra "wilderness" from the very people and animals who had been maintaining it.

Austin, however, does not simply present a rhetorical argument about sheep grazing. Her characterization of working people, her use of both symbolism and fact, her focus on storytelling and its democratic implications, and her creation of a journalistic persona all work together to achieve *The Flock*'s unity as an argument supporting the democratic principles of equality and government by consent of the governed. She uses her powerful allegory to illuminate human relationships: the struggles between shepherds are similar to animal or tribal wars over hunting territories or struggles between modern economic ideologies. When the land belongs to no one and its welfare is no one's responsibility, then every year, she argues, the "best contriver" will possess the best pastures. In "The Strife of the Herdsmen," Austin explains how shepherds, under orders from their employers and with their own traditional sense of responsibility toward the welfare of their sheep, were forced to match wits against each other and the forces of God, beast, weather, and park rangers to feed their flocks. Desperate shepherds infringed on the national park and, she says, "came out boasting, as elated, as self-congratulatory as if they had merged railroads or performed any of those larger thieveries that constitute a Captain of Industry" (*Flock,* 197).

Although this comment sounds like social Darwinism, Austin's political views were neither socialistic nor hierarchical. Lawrence Clark Powell calls her a "Fabian Socialist": that is, someone supporting gradual social progress while avoiding direct confrontation with the state.[33] However, in Austin's mind the allegoric "flock" was not a cohesive, socialistic, cooperating group, but a seething stew composed of highly independent individuals. A sentence from *The Flock* seems to summarize her politics: "The flock-mind is less than the sum of the intelligences of individual sheep" (109). Austin's rural people were not helpless innocents in need of protection from powerful, more intelligent capitalists. Indeed, she stresses that the "sheepmen had always the advantage in superior knowledge of the country, of meadows defended by secret trails and false monuments, of feeding grounds inaccessible to mounted men, remote, and undiscovered by any but the sheep" (*Flock,* 198). Some shepherds, like Narcisse the Red, who appears as a red-tinged Mephistopheles character, enjoyed the game immensely (*Flock,* 158). Austin believed in the struggle and was not asking to have rural people "protected" from the captains of industry. She never waivered in her faith that "common" people could and should take care of themselves. In direct contrast to social Darwinists, she did not believe that the "best people" always rose to the top. Her shepherds were in constant flux from the estate of owner to hireling, and such cyclic flux, she says, makes all shepherds philosophers (*Flock,* 61).

Sheep, shepherds, and sheepherding, as described by Muir and Austin, provide an excellent allegorical lens through which to expose tensions between the leisure class and the often mixed-race working class. Such tensions have existed throughout history, and White outlines the same threat to the modern West: "[I]f we do not come to terms with work, if we fail to pursue the implications of our labor and our bodies in the natural world, then we will return to patrolling the borders. We will turn public lands into a public playground; we will equate wild lands with rugged play; we will imagine nature as an escape, a place where we are born again. It will be a paradise where we leave work behind."[34] Almost one hundred years ago, Austin made a similar argument that societies that overlook the contributions of rural working people risk decline.[35]

Muir and Austin were both well aware that sheep have traditionally symbolized the humble human masses. Comparing their respective descriptions of the "lambs of God" at the allegoric, political level reveals ominous differences and deeply opposed philosophies. Even Muir's earliest writing shows no affection or sympathy to the masses and their children. "The mongrel manufactured misarranged mass of mutton and wool called a sheep band which I have tended lo these six weeks with a shepherd's care are now rapidly increasing in number by little thick legged wrinkled duplicates, unhappy lambs born to wretchedness and unmitigated degradation."[36] He never wavers from this position.

In contrast, Austin, with affection, humor, and respect, describes lambs as they struggle to adapt to the unique regional challenges of the Long Trail. "Young lambs are principally legs, the connecting body being merely a contrivance for converting milk into more leg, so you understand how it is that they will follow in two days and are able to take the trail in a fortnight, traveling four and five miles a day, falling asleep on their feet, and tottering forward (*Flock*, 25). Allegorically, Muir's young "lambs of God" are a burden on society, increase the strain on natural resources, and face a life of permanent and increasing poverty. In Muir's allegory, someone will have the unpleasant burden of taking care of the helpless female masses, who are rapidly breeding more and more ragged children. Austin, in contrast, allegorically characterizes young lambs as the hope of the future. Quickly able to stand on their own feet, they totter forward, even when physically exhausted. She feels a fierce pride for the nation's youth.

Muir's numerous allegories, published both before and after *The Flock,* equate common sheep with the working class and wild sheep with the leisure class. In contrast to the dirty, helpless, and out-of-shape common domestic sheep, wild sheep are able to go "wading in snow, roaming through bushes, and leaping among jagged storm-beaten cliffs" while remaining clean and self-confident, wearing "a dress so exquisitely adapted to its mountain life that is it always found as unruffled and stainless as a bird."[37] Muir's common sheep are "poor, dusty, raggedy, famishing creatures," whose brains "must surely be poor stuff."[38] Although "Twenty Hill Hollow" often describes a wildness in domestic sheep that Muir found uncontrollable, his political rhetoric and published writing present them as plodding dullards.[39] Wild sheep, which climb the highest peaks, are obviously superior in Muir's mind: "The wild sheep ranks highest among the animal mountaineers of the Sierra."[40] He argues that "the domestic sheep is expressionless . . . the wild is elegant . . . the tame is timid; the wild is bold. The tame is always more or less ruffled and dirty; while the wild is as smooth and clean as the flowers of his mountain pasture." He even credits wild sheep with the ability to appreciate beauty.[41]

Muir's various allegorical attempts to create a hierarchy supporting leisure land-use politics drifts into pathetic fallacy when he claims that wild animals are "as free from disease as a sunbeam," never weary or sick, and that "nothing truly wild [is] unclean."[42] Nature never allows her wild animals "to go dirty or ragged."[43] No famine occurs in the wild, "no stagnation, no death," not "one drop of blood"; and he is sure wild animals never experience "a headache or any other ache amongst them."[44] With a view that seems to presage White's observation that modern environmentalists have a tendency to imagine their activities as benign because they "do not have to face" what they alter, Muir's "happy" wild animals nibble mountain plants so daintily that they never crush a flower or mar a leaf.[45] According to J. Moussaieff Masson and Susan McCarthy, the sentimentalized view that the natural world is "a place without war, murder, rape, and addiction," where "animals never lie, cheat, or steal," is "embarrassed by reality."[46]

Austin's is the more clear-eyed vision. Her animals, both wild and domestic, realistically live in the valley of the slant-winged shadow of death. One reviewer observes that although Austin "stops for queer speculations on the development of the animal mind," she "does not sentimentalize about them: she makes the limits of instinct quite as clear as its scope."[47] While Muir's wild animals leave no scar on the landscape, Austin's wear mazes of white trails that eventually converge at water. Her bighorns starve in their tracks, trapped in deep snow; predators lurk at water holes; hawks patrol every trail and flyway. Austin uses accurate and detailed natural history of real sheep to express her respect for the intelligence of both common animals and common people. She finds the natural laws that operate within flocks and between shepherds, dogs, predators, and sheep quite similar to the natural laws that operate within society and between races. In *The Flock* she carefully explains the complexity of sheep social structure as a culture: sheep intelligence, range of emotion, cravings, watch keeping, selection of leaders, and communication patterns. She describes their recognition, exclusion, and finally acceptance of strangers. Reviewing *The Flock* in 1930, Henry Chester Tracy said that the chapter entitled "The Sun in Aries," about "lambing and the ways of lambs and ewes," contains "more pure authentic science of behavior in it than you will find in many passages of heavier reading."[48]

In addition, Austin describes sheep adoption, kidnapping, and the intri-

cacies and idiosyncracies of the flock mind, which, she says, is neither natural nor permanent, but artificial and temporary. She notes that once a
sheep is separated from the flock, the shepherd must go and find it because
it will not return on its own: "[I]t is as if for them the flock had never
been." Also, she supposes, sheep may very well understand the arm signals
and will of the shepherd, but they only grudgingly obey, feeling "a little re-
sentful of the importunity of the dogs" (*Flock*, 110, 119, 117, 127). Real
sheep, Austin suggests, when studied deeply, the way shepherds study them,
can help humans understand our own political problems. Real sheep are
not stupid, easily controlled, or of one mind, although they do have a few
idiosyncracies. Ecologically, in order to sustain the complicated web we
call life, the plants, soils, insects, water, and animals, whether wild, domestic, or human, all depend on one another—even locusts.

As Kevin Starr describes in *Americans and the California Dream, 1850-
1919*, at the time Muir and Austin were writing, Californians were frustrated with corrupt government and ruthless monopolies engaged in a
brutal, "greedy[,] and unregulated" struggle.[49] Socialism was becoming a
popular alternative among disillusioned urban workers. Read allegorically,
these lines Muir deleted from the early draft of *My First Summer* show
both a dislike and a fear of the common human masses:"The sheep are behaving worse than ever because hungrier than ever. . . . They broke away
suddenly as if a plan had been formed during the night like the plan of a
mutinous crew on shipboard. I fancy too that they would have knocked us
in the head ere they had left us if only they had been able for they seem to
be as wicked & ungovernable as they possibly have the power to be."[50] In
the published version, however, Muir or his editors chose to delete Muir's
mention of this fear. The final published version admits to no emotion
other than pity. Muir appears as a kindly monarch, fearlessly in charge, the
sheep helpless and afraid without him:"Having escaped restraint, they were
like some people we know of, afraid of their freedom, did not know what
to do with it, and seemed glad to get back into the old familiar bondage."[51]

Privately, in his journal, Muir found flock politics unfathomable and
verging constantly on complete anarchy, but by the time he published
"The Wild Sheep" in 1874, he was ready to claim that a domestic sheep "is
only a fraction of an animal, a whole flock being required to form an individual."[52] Austin, carefully explaining complex social structures, argues
that sheep can think for themselves but simply find life less complicated
when they select and follow leaders. She claims that the "earliest impor-

tant achievement of ovine intelligence is to know whether its own notion or another's is most worth while, and if the other's, which one" (*Flock,* 109-10). Muir fears the genuine wildness he sees both in sheep and in the common masses, while Austin, like Thoreau, believes that this real wildness will save the world. Like Thoreau, she finds it lurking just below the thin veneer of domesticity and breaking out when oppressed people or animals reach a point of desperation. At the end of *The Flock,* she calls this natural wildness one of the "arrows" that inhabitants of the wild must learn to sleep in the shade of in order to survive.

The predator-prey relationship as portrayed by Austin and Muir also takes on an ominous tone when allegorically juxtaposed with the ruthless California politics of the day. In Muir's idealistic descriptions of wild predators, he again uses hierarchical metaphors: "Perhaps no wild animal in the world is without enemies, but highlanders, *as a class* have fewer than lowlanders."[53] As Thomas Lyon has suggested, because Sierra peaks substitute as heaven, and the devil's tracks are seldom found above timberline, Muir's mountaineers are seldom bothered by the devilish predator.[54] Muir's "devil" refers to common humans, common sheep, dogs, predators—perhaps all animals except celestial mountaineers. While Muir's predators remain sinful thieves, they prey mostly on domestic sheep, which Muir finds acceptable.

Austin's complicated view of the predator-prey relationship is again more heterarchical and less judgmental. She does not consider predators thieves or devils but simply animals who are following their own natural behavior patterns. She sprinkles her writing with constant reminders that under the right circumstances we are all animals and thieves: "Times when there is moonlight, watery and cold, a long thin howl detaches itself from any throat and welters on the wind" (*Flock,* 93). She argues that problems with predators are caused by close herding and relates an incident that occurred at El Tejon during the drought of 1876, when fifty-eight thousand head of starving sheep were turned loose in December to die. The staggering flocks slowly disappeared into the bear-, cougar-, and wolf-infested mountains. The next fall, when rains finally replenished lowland meadows, fifty-three thousand head of healthy sheep trailed themselves back down for the winter (*Flock,* 235).

Sheep and predators have shared the same pastures since time began, and Austin never sees sheep as huddled, helpless masses too stupid to take care of themselves. Shepherds have no quarrel with predators, she says. "It is only against man contrivances, such as a wool tariff or a new ruling of the Forestry Bureau, that the herder becomes loquacious. Wildcats, cougars, coyotes, and bears are merely incidents of the day's work, like putting on stiff boots of a cold morning, [or] running out of garlic" (*Flock*, 176). Bears, she muses, often stroll harmlessly over sleeping shepherds at night or burn their paws trying to rob frying pans. "Or so it was," she states pointedly, "in the days before the summer camper found the country" (*Flock*, 186). On an allegorical level, common people have always been able to survive and make a living in spite of predators, but perhaps the summer camper will prove too great a foe. "Tourists," Wallace Stegner once said, "can be as destructive as locusts."[55] History may prove campers even more destructive than hoofed locusts and more dangerous to rural areas than thieves.

If a duel over grazing Yosemite was indeed being fought between the two authors, Mary Austin lost the battle. Sheep bells no longer tinkle through high Sierra meadows. Muir's persona "worked" on the reader; Austin's did not. Although critics consistently list *The Flock* as one of Austin's best books and say her sheep have the "potency of symbol,"[56] the book has usually been read as a charmingly outdated pastoral that inspired the reader to want to "lie under the sky with dogs and flocks, lulled to sleep by the 'blether' of ewes and the bark of distant coyotes."[57] By 1930, Tracy was already calling *The Flock* one of Austin's "least known volumes"; modern critics dismiss it as "a study of the ways in which the insistent claims of motherhood can inhibit one's distinctive voice."[58] In contrast, *My First Summer* has consistently remained in print, perhaps because Muir's persona appeals to readers who want to imagine themselves as superior to the common masses. Muir's persona says, "Come along with me; only you and I truly appreciate this wilderness." Only Muir and the reader can name each plant. No one else, not even tourists, can appreciate the "glorious objects about them."[59] Readers vicariously identifying with Muir's superiority do not see themselves as common tourists; they are "true mountaineers" and naturalists.

In contrast, Austin's humble, democratic persona of naive reporter happily tags along behind shepherds and gives them credit for extensive knowledge gained through their daily work as they climb into the meadows with the flocks. She dismisses the idea of risk, saying city dwellers are often incredulous that a person can "go about" these mountains "unhurt and unoffended by the wild" (*Flock*, 265). The Sierra, she says, is a maze of sheep trails, footpaths, and shepherd camps. Tucked away at the edge of most large meadows are food, shelter, and firewood. Rural western hospitality traditionally welcomes anyone to these supplies (*Flock*, 265). Even the distinguished Joseph LeConte, leading a group of hungry hikers, once robbed a shepherd of his dinner right off the fire—with Muir's help and blessing.[60] The presence of shepherds in the Sierra took any true risk out of traveling light in Muir's day, a fact often overlooked by young hikers who succumb to exposure and exhaustion trying to follow in Muir's footsteps, some of which may have been made only by his persona.

Readers who prefer to think of themselves as inherently superior to the "average" citizen are put off by Austin's persona because it humbles them. She insinuates that, at least in the mountain pastures, working shepherds possess a certain kind of common sense and wisdom that highly educated visitors or housebound readers on vicarious adventures have never learned. White's modern version of the argument makes clear that "[w]ork once bore the burden of connecting us with nature," but today we attempt to make this connection through leisure, and "play cannot bear the weight."[61] Austin's persona seems to warn the reader to "[s]tay away and leave these mountain pastures to the people who have given their lives to them." And keeping people away was probably her intent. Even as a child, when Mary Austin was admonished by her mother not to "antagonize people" but instead to try to "draw people to you. Mary would reply stubbornly, 'And what would I do with the people after I have drawn them to me?'"[62]

Perhaps Muir never considered the cumulative effect of his own behavior: by drawing people to the mountains through his books, he might have been the "worst enemy the wilderness ever had."[63] Today, more than two million travelers stand in line to see Yosemite Falls. The "beautiful" well-kept gardens full of flowers, "grass up to a bear's hips," and "champagne water" that Muir encountered during that long-lost first summer with the sheep have been replaced by two hotels, four swimming pools, five grocery and general stores, five souvenir shops, two golf courses, six gas stations, a bank, a hospital, campsites for six thousand people, and a vast motel and parking lot complex.[64] The meadows are ribboned with deep backpacker trails, park police wear riot helmets, and campers must carry water purification kits. When society privileges leisure over work, as White points out, "[n]ature may turn out to look a lot like an organic Disneyland, except it will be harder to park."[65]

Ultimately, Muir won the political battle over Yosemite, but in my view Austin left him in the dust of the Long Trail (now, ironically, called the John Muir Trail). Arguing on one level against banning shepherds and sheep from Yosemite, at a deeper level she argues against dividing people, animals, or places into hierarchies and classes. She defends indigenous working people and recognizes the importance of ecological interdependence between a place and all its inhabitants. Through sheep, both real and allegorical, she champions equality and government based on consent of the governed. She believes cultures that remain in closest contact with natural rhythms and resources will prove sustainable.

How threatening *The Flock* may have been to California or national politics in 1906 is probably impossible to determine today, but Austin's later friend, President Theodore Roosevelt, who developed the national park system, appears to have been enough impressed by her arguments to send a forestry expert out to talk to her.[66] Permanent federal grazing leases, a method she recommends in *The Flock* to help stop grazing abuses on public land (171-72, 209), were implemented and are still in effect today. *The Flock* deserves rereading; it is much more than a simple pastoral. White argues that modern "[e]nvironmentalists must come to terms with work."[67] Austin and I argue that environmentalists must also come to terms with land, animal, and human hierarchies.

NOTES

1. For critical reviews linking Austin's novel *The Ford* with California water politics, see, for instance, Benay Blend, "Mary Austin and the Western Conservation Movement: 1900-1927," *Journal of the Southwest* 30 (1988): 12-34.

2. In *John Muir and the Sierra Club: The Battle for Yosemite* (San Francisco: Sierra Club, 1965), Holoway R. Jones posits, "The role of the Southern Pacific in the establishment of the California parks is one of the most provocative conservation questions yet to be exposed by the historian" (44). His book includes an intriguing summary, including maps, about the battle for Yosemite. Noel Perrin suggests, "It's a coincidence, but a nice coincidence, that the year in which [Muir] began to describe the Western mountains as wonderful places, sacred ground, God's outdoor temples, was the same year [1869] in which the transcontinental railroad was completed" (Noel Perrin, "Forever Virgin: The American View of America," in *On Nature: Nature, Landscape, and Natural History* [San Francisco: North Point Press, 1987], 20).

3. Frank Norris, *The Octopus* (1901; reprint, New York: Signet, 1964), 42.

4. William F. Kimes, *John Muir: A Reading Bibliography* (Palo Alto: W. P. Wreden, 1977).

5. John Muir, "Wild Sheep" (1874), 419-28; and "Wild Wool" (1875), 871-76, in *John Muir: The Eight Wilderness Discovery Books* (Seattle: The Mountaineers, 1992).

6. Mary Austin, *The Land of Little Rain* (1903; reprint, New York: Penguin Books, 1988),

94. Although Frank Stewart claims in *A Natural History of Nature Writing* (Washington, D.C.: Island Press, 1995) that Austin was "thirsty to meet" Muir and was "swept away" by his stories (134), Austin pointedly notes in her autobiography that Muir had a "habit of talking much, . . . the habit of soliloquizing" (Mary Austin, *Earth Horizon* [Boston: Houghton Mifflin, 1932], 298). The Huntington Library collection of Austin's papers contains a clipped article written by Muir entitled "The Hetch-Hetchy Valley: A National Question" and published in *American Forestry* 16 (1910), further evidence that Austin followed Muir's work.

7. Vera Norwood, "The Photographer and the Naturalist: Laura Gilpin and Mary Austin in the Southwest" (1982), in "Mary (Hunter) Austin 1868-1934," *Twentieth-Century Literary Criticism,* vol. 25 (Detroit: Gale, 1988), 39-40. In this article, Norwood argues that Austin was unsympathetic to the national parks and sympathetic to the shepherd. Eleven years later, however, Norwood changed her mind. That later ecofeminist review appears in *Made for This Earth: American Women and Nature* (Chapel Hill: University of North Carolina Press, 1993), 279.

8. A. Carl Bredahl Jr., *New Ground: Western American Narrative and the Literary Canon* (Chapel Hill: University of North Carolina Press, 1989), 49.

9. Trinh T. Minh-ha, *Woman, Native, Other: Writing Postcoloniality and Feminism* (Bloomington: Indiana University Press, 1989).

10. Mary Austin, *The Flock* (Boston: Houghton Mifflin, 1906), 114. All subsequent parenthetical notations, unless noted otherwise, are from this edition.

11. In May 1997 the Center of the American West at the University of Colorado at Boulder sponsored a conference called "Seeing and Being Seen: Tourism in the American West." The conference flyer advertised a discussion of ideas such as using folk societies (Indian, Hispanic, Mormon, ranching, mining, logging) as "attractive 'foreign' alternatives" and turning peoples' homes into "veritable theme parks." Provocative questions appeared on the flyer: "[D]oes tourism prove to be yet another form of extraction and colonialism?" "What are the relations of power in tourism?" "Does [tourism] devalue people by forcing them into subservient, seasonal, low-paying jobs?" In short, the conference organizers took exception to the idea that "outdoor recreation is typically benign."

12. "A Review of *The Flock*" (*Nation,* 1906), collected in "Mary (Hunter) Austin 1868-1934," 17.

13. Richard White, "'Are You an Environmentalist or Do You Work for a Living?': Work and Nature," in *Uncommon Ground: Rethinking the Human Place in Nature,* ed. William Cronon (New York: Norton, 1995), 171. White says that he "phrased this issue so harshly not because I oppose environmentalism (indeed, I consider myself an environmentalist)" but precisely because he thinks environmentalism must play a key role in addressing many political issues. I, too, have chosen to present my argument "harshly" and blatantly biased toward Austin's views. I believe the rural viewpoint has been stifled for so many years that an angry tone is justified. As Austin well knew, rural people have had no voice in either literature or politics. Their voice needs to be heard and respected by today's environmentalists.

14. Thomas J. Lyon, *John Muir* (Boise: Boise State College, 1972), 30.

15. Muir worked sheep at least four times. He sheared sheep during the late summer of 1868 for John Connel. That fall and winter, he herded for Connel in the fenced pastures he would later call the "bee-pastures" of the San Joaquin Valley. A year later he worked in the fenced pastures for Pat Delaney. In the summer of 1869, Muir went with a band of sheep

into the Sierra, working for Pat Delaney. In the fall of 1870, he again worked for Delaney, this time in the fenced pastures near LaGrange. From the John Muir Papers, 1858-1957, ed. Ronald H. Limbaugh and Kirsten E. Lewis (Microform), Alexandria, Va., Chadwyck-Healey, 1986, chronology; information about the missing journal appears in the introduction. "Twenty Hill Hollow" is in reel 23; the working draft of *My First Summer* (hereinafter "draft") is in reel 31.

16. Michael Cohen, *The Pathless Way: John Muir and the American Wilderness* (Madison: University of Wisconsin Press, 1984), 350-51.

17. Edwin Way Teale, *The Wilderness World of John Muir* (Boston: Houghton Mifflin, 1954), xix. In 1890 Muir had been forced to defend his reputation in a letter to the editor of the *Oakland Daily Evening Tribune* that ran under the lengthy title "John Muir in Yosemite. He Never Cut Down a Single Tree in the Valley. Twenty Years Ago He Was Employed by Mr. Hutchings to Saw Lumber from Fallen Timber." But this may not have been quite truthful. As an example of the many discrepancies between Muir's private and published work, in the early draft of *My First Summer,* Muir describes cutting down silver firs to build a sheep corral—but the passage was struck before publication (Muir, "draft," 51).

18. John Muir, *My First Summer in the Sierra* (1911; reprint, New York: Penguin Books, 1987), 5.

19. Leo Marx, *Machine in the Garden: Technology and the Pastoral Ideal in America* (New York: Oxford University Press, 1967), 99.

20. Yi-Fu Tuan, *Dominance and Affection: The Making of Pets* (New Haven: Yale University Press, 1984), 31.

21. White, "Are You an Environmentalist?" 177, 173.

22. Austin, *The Flock,* 83; Muir, *My First Summer,* 129. Subsequent quotations from these works are followed by parenthetical page numbers.

23. White, "Are You an Environmentalist?" 185.

24. Curiously, in 1878 Muir also published a kindly statement about shepherds: "Back among the hills, and in almost every town and hamlet, there are shepherds, tradesmen or laborers, who, while working hard for a bare livelihood, yet zealously pursue some branch of natural history . . . hungering and thirsting after knowledge for its own sake" (qtd. in Kimes, *John Muir,* 21). This statement may have appeared when Muir's glaciation theories, which he began to publish around 1872, were being attacked by Josiah Whitney as the simple ideas of a sheepherder.

25. Austin, *Land of Little Rain,* 106.

26. Muir, "Twenty Hill Hollow," 46-53.

27. Austin, *Earth Horizon,* 227.

28. Letter dated 19 July 1868, Muir Papers, reel 1.

29. Numerous scientists back up Austin's views. See Neil West, "Biodiversity of Rangelands," *Journal of Range Management* 46 (1993): 2-13; and Dan Daggett, *Beyond the Rangeland Conflict: Toward a West That Works* (Salt Lake City: Gibbs Smith, 1995).

30. See Thomas C. Blackburn and Kat Anderson, *Before the Wilderness: Environmental Management by Native Californians* (Menlo Park: Ballena Press, 1993); Gary Paul Nabhan, "Cultural Parallax in Viewing North American Habitats," in *Reinventing Nature? Responses to Postmodern Deconstruction,* ed. Michael E. Soulé and Gary Lease (Washington, D.C.: Island Press, 1995); and Gary Snyder, *The Practice of the Wild* (San Francisco: North Point Press, 1990), 92.

31. Rebecca Solnit, *Savage Dreams: A Journey into the Landscape Wars of the American West* (New York: Vintage Books, 1994), 222.

32. White, "Are You an Environmentalist?" 175-76.

33. Lawrence Clark Powell, "Mary Austin: *The Land of Little Rain,*" in *California Classics: The Creative Literature of the Golden State* (1971; reprint; Capra Press, 1982), 44-52.

34. White, "Are You an Environmentalist?" 185.

35. Among Austin's collected papers is a clipped article entitled "Agriculture and Moneyculture" that reminds the reader that historians have traced the fall of both Greece and Rome to the fall of their agricultures. The article is in the Mary (Hunter) Austin Collection, Huntington Library, San Marino, California, AU box 131, folder 1.

36. Muir, "Twenty Hill Hollow," 46-47.

37. Muir, "Wild Wool," 872.

38. Muir, *My First Summer,* 64, 114.

39. Muir, "Twenty Hill Hollow," 6-7.

40. Muir, "Wild Sheep," 419.

41. Ibid., 421-22.

42. Muir, *My First Summer,* 68, 226.

43. Muir, "Wild Wool," 872.

44. Muir, *My First Summer,* 73, 96.

45. White, "Are You an Environmentalist?" 185; Lisa Mighetto, ed., *Muir among the Animals: The Wildlife Writings of John Muir* (San Francisco: Sierra Club, 1986, xvii); "Bears," from *Our National Parks* (1901), in *Muir among the Animals,* 161.

46. J. Moussaieff Masson and Susan McCarthy, *When Elephants Weep: The Emotional Lives of Animals* (New York: Delacorte Press, 1995), 42.

47. "Review of *The Flock,*" 17.

48. Henry Chester Tracy, "Mary Austin" (1930), in "Mary (Hunter) Austin 1868-1934," 24-25.

49. Kevin Starr, *Americans and the California Dream, 1850-1915* (New York: Oxford University Press, 1973), viii.

50. Muir, "draft," 93.

51. Muir, *My First Summer,* 57.

52. Muir, "Wild Sheep," 425.

53. Ibid., 18; emphasis added.

54. Lyon, *John Muir,* 16.

55. Wallace Stegner, *Where the Bluebird Sings to the Lemonade Springs: Living and Writing in the West* (New York: Penguin Books, 1992), 55.

56. Editors of *Twentieth-Century Literary Criticism,* plus numerous critics quoted therein. The quote comes from the same collection: Vernon Young, "Mary Austin and the Earth Performance," 1950, 31.

57. "Review of *The Flock,*" 17-18.

58. Tracy, "Mary Austin," 24; David Wyatt, *The Fall into Eden: Landscape and Imagination in California* (New York: Cambridge University Press, 1986), 87.

59. Muir, *My First Summer,* 104.

60. Elizabeth Stone O'Neill, *Meadow in the Sky: A History of Yosemite's Tuolumne Meadows Region* (Fresno: Panorama West Books, 1983), 30.

61. White, "Are You an Environmentalist?" 174.

62. Augusta Fink, *I-Mary: A Biography of Mary Austin* (Tucson: University of Arizona Press, 1983), 33.

63. Galen Rowell, "Along the High, Wild Sierra: The John Muir Trail," *National Geographic* (April 1989): 466–93, 480; Ezra Bowen, *The High Sierra: The American Wilderness* (Washington, D.C.: Time-Life Books, 1972), 63.

64. Bowen, *High Sierra,* 166.

65. White, "Are You an Environmentalist?" 185.

66. Austin, *Earth Horizon,* 289.

67. White, "Are You an Environmentalist?" 174.

CHAPTER THIRTEEN

"The Man at the Sources"

Gender, Capital, and the Conservationist Landscape
in Mary Austin's *The Ford*

ANNE RAINE

*In "The Man at the Sources" Anne Raine explores how gender and capital shape
the western landscape in Austin's recently reissued novel* The Ford. *In Raine's
reading, Austin's "progressivist model" situates the artist "within social relations of
modern capitalism," blurring the lines dividing art from business, ecosystems from
economies, and nature from cultural production. For Austin, artistic production and
the land are always located in and defined by "particular material landscapes." Her
emphasis on the materiality and particularity of Austin's approach to art and the
land links Raine to other authors in this collection, especially Kathryn DeZur and
Tara Hart. But her reading of environment in* The Ford *as "simultaneously social, economic, and ecological" allows her to explore Austin's novel both as a literary
production pitted against the prevailing tide of naturalism and as an enactment of
then-current land-use debates.*

According to Raine, The Ford *critiques naturalism as a model for social
relations, for the novel argues that even modernity's landscape is manageable, and
further, that its wise management is a social responsibility. The novel's setting—a
western landscape enmeshed in a web of industry, art, government, and business
relations—comes to represent an alternative modern landscape. Although rural,
this landscape does not stand as a nostalgic or utopian counterpoint to the modern
world (see Schlenz for a contrasting view); rather, it is consistently involved and
implicated in the relations that govern modernity's more urban landscapes. Simultaneously with her reworking of the naturalist model of relations between people and
the land, Austin revises the familiar form of the bildungsroman, undermining male
protagonist Kenneth Brent and ironizing the form's potential for* The Ford's
*female protagonist, Kenneth's sister Anne. In Anne's view, the land is malleable
and salable; this belief, Raine argues, combined with Anne's concern for the*

community's future within its particular landscape, positions Anne Brent as the embodiment of Austin's modernist paradigm for relations between people and the environment.

In her 1922 essay "The American Form of the Novel," Mary Austin alludes rather ominously to the "scores of novels, eyeless and amorphic, kept moving on the submerged social levels by the thousands of readers who never come any nearer the surface of the present than perhaps to be occasionally chilled by it."[1] For Austin, the mass circulation of second-rate novels participates in but fails to reflect on the vast flow of social forces that constitutes modernity. In contrast to the naturalist view of modernity, the novel of "prophetic form" should reconstruct the present not simply as a flow of inscrutable subterranean forces, but as a lucidly reflecting surface whose shrewd revelations of "place, relationship and solidarity" may be chilling, but enable the recognition and cultivation of "the green bough of constructive change." For Austin, in other words, the modern novel's formal success depends on its progressive potential. Successful novels, she writes, "will eventually be found to lie along in the direction of the growing tip of collective consciousness" because they "deal with patterns that . . . have a constructive relation to the society in which we live." And to develop such a "constructive relation," the novelist cannot adopt the authorial pose of a "superior being standing about with his hands in his pockets, 'passing remarks,'" but instead must "be inside his novel," and "see himself as he is seen by the people with whom he does business" (85-87). By positioning herself within the social relations of modern capitalism, Austin's American novelist can render "the color, the intensity and solidarity of experience *while it is passing*" and at the same time "fix upon the prophetic trend of happenings" (86).

Austin proposes a modernist vision that is simultaneously aesthetic, pragmatic, and prophetic; like Emerson's "The Young American" and Frank Norris's portrait of the railroad magnate as the epic poet of industrial capitalism, her progressivist model of cultural production posits modern art and modern business as intertwined or coterminous rather than inevitably opposed.[2] Shifting between commercial and organic images of national community, she echoes Emerson's argument that literary form, like government, "has been a fossil; it should be a plant"; and that given the fact of modernity, "our part is plainly not to throw ourselves across the track, to block improvement and sit till we are stone, but to watch the uprise of successive mornings and to conspire with the new works of new days."[3] Like Emerson, Austin views the land and the commercial-industrial system as two crucial factors in American social and spiritual progress.[4] But while Emerson sees social evolution as inseparable from natural processes because both manifest the same spiritual laws, Austin argues more concretely that cultural practice is embedded in the ecological as well as the social environment: not in universal Nature, but in particular material landscapes.[5]

Despite her valorization of "the quality of experience called Folk, and the frame of behavior known as Mystical," Austin's work as a political and environmental activist argues that attentiveness to the land is as much scientific and practical as aesthetic and mystical, and in fact is essential to good business sense.[6] As Reuben J. Ellis observes, Austin's interest in environment and adaptation paralleled then-current theories of evolutionary biology, process psychology, and pragmatic philosophy, and her use of "close observation and inductive exposition" to describe and interpret western landscapes and indigenous peoples "speak[s] to the liberal faith in 'facts' and the scientific method as debunkers of superstition and agents of progress."[7] A 1925 letter opposing the proposed Boulder Dam affirms Austin's earlier "prophecy" that if urban developers "resist the deep-seated factors of cultural evolution" such as the land's aridity and the farmers' water needs, "presently the land itself [will] speak." She insists that intuiting socioecological consequences is "not poetry," or "even prophecy in the sense that it proceeds from any supernormal or hifalutin faculty," but "plain deduction from known facts and measured forces."[8] In place of Emerson's poet's eye that "can integrate all the parts" of the landscape, Austin posits a pragmatic and prophetic "structural capacity" that her modern novelist shares with the social psychologist, the ecologist, and those able "to pronounce the word capitalism without a hiss."[9] The range of her professional and political work suggests that the "green bough of constructive change" depends as much on these modern forms of knowledge as on any purely aesthetic or mystical vision.

Austin's view of cultural practice as "prophetic pragmatism" is central to her 1917 novel *The Ford*,[10] whose stark contrast to her better-known desert writings is important because it demonstrates the provocative complexity of Austin's "environmental imagination," to borrow a phrase from Lawrence Buell. In contrast to *The Land of Little Rain*'s lyrical evocations of sublime "desertness," where "not the law, but the land sets the limit," *The*

Ford constructs a conservationist fictional space in which it is no longer possible to perceive the nonurban landscape as a remote, resistant, and elusive "country of lost borders." Relations between human beings and the physical landscape are inextricable from social and economic structures: even the open range beyond the ranch fences is not wilderness, but "government land" fragmented by "invisibly divided squares" of private property (*Ford,* 55). The river delta is not a wild space teeming with nonhuman life, but a "glittering hieroglyphic" signifying the river's unfulfilled desire to "tur[n] mills or whirring dynamos," to "wate[r] fields and nurs[e] orchards"; the "watery waste," in other words, is a negative sign of the river's productive potential within the human regional economy (*Ford,* 34).[11] Several of the characters are lovingly attentive to the "intimate properties of the earth" and its plant and animal life (*Ford,* 414), but their relations with the local landscape take place within a systematically surveyed terrain traversed by flows of information and capital as well as of natural resources. The oil pipeline and the controversial aqueduct that would redistribute water from rural farms to city reservoirs are only part of the modern communication and distribution networks, which also include railroads, telegraph and telephone lines, and the U.S. Postal Service. In *The Ford,* both urban and rural spaces are structured not only by ecological relationships, but by systems of governmental, technological, and corporate power that also form part of the landscape with which, and within which, individuals must come to terms.

Admirers of Austin's desert writings are likely to be ill at ease in the systematized modern landscape of *The Ford,* and those who read Austin as an exemplary ecocentric writer may be disturbed by the novel's overt anthropocentrism. In *The Land of Little Rain,* Austin responds to the desert's sublime indifference to human agency and selfhood by decentering the individual human subject and imaginatively unsettling the boundaries between self and other, human and nonhuman, organism and environment, structure and process.[12] If that text represents Austin writing, as she asserts, "directly, in her own character,"[13] this "character" only "fleetingly gives [itself] a shape and a history," and more often registers its distinctive presence precisely through its permeability, both to "other people's stories" and to "diffuse perceptual centers" through which the speaker "imagine[s] the desert as it might look through the eyes of birds and animals."[14] In contrast, *The Ford* replaces this diffusion of narrative persona with a narrative form based on the bildungsroman, a genre centrally concerned with es-

tablishing the distinct "shape and history" of its male protagonist in relation to his social environment.[15] Austin's novel subverts the bildungsroman's anthropocentric and androcentric conventions not with experiments in ecocentric perception, but by redefining environment as
simultaneously social, economic, and ecological, and by ironically juxta-
posing Kenneth Brent's narrative of self-construction with his sister Anne's
less histrionic and more efficient progress toward individual agency.

Rather than examining the intrinsic value or affective power of desert
ecology, *The Ford* explores how different relations to landscape produce or
enable differing configurations of social and economic power. It considers
the relation between gender identity and socioecological practice, and
projects the possibility of ameliorating regional and individual economic
disparities by irrigating "desertness" into farmland. Precisely for this reason, the book's recent reissue by the University of California Press is
timely: Austin's feminist, conservationist novel anticipates the concerns of
many 1990s environmental activists, historians, and cultural critics for
whom the dialectical relation between nature and culture is inseparable
from the sociospatial relations of gender, race, and class.[16] Less convincing
but no less important than her better-known desert writings, *The Ford* is
Austin's provocative attempt to articulate a viable relationship between the
acute ecological sensitivity of *The Land of Little Rain* and her equally acute
awareness of the need for nonurban space to be recognized and reimag-
ined as part of the landscape of capitalist modernity.

The Ford is a fictionalized account of the 1905 controversy over water
rights in Owens Valley, California, where Austin and her husband were active in an unsuccessful struggle to prevent the Owens River water from
being diverted from local irrigation projects to the Los Angeles city water
supply.[17] The novel traces the coming of age of Anne and Kenneth Brent
and their childhood friends Frank, the son of local capitalist and land baron
T. Rickart, and Virginia, the daughter of Rickart's ranch manager. Anne
and Kenneth spend their childhood on their parents' ranch, but when
drought strikes the valley, their father sells Las Palomitas and tries to restore
his fortunes and satisfy his wife's social ambitions by investing in oil development with other local farmers. A born rancher who dreams of revital-
izing the valley through irrigation, Steven Brent is a poor businessman. The
farmers strike oil but are unable to store and transport it when Rickart un-
expectedly gains control of the oil pipeline, causing their financial ruin and
precipitating the death of Mrs. Brent, who dies after aborting an unwanted

pregnancy. After this tragedy, Anne refuses to marry; she becomes a successful real estate agent and eventually buys back the ranch for her father.
Meanwhile, Kenneth becomes an apprentice in Rickart's San Francisco
law office, flirts with the bohemian socialism to which Virginia introduces
him through her career as a labor agitator and would-be actress, and tries
to heal the psychic wounds of his father's failure and his mother's death by
defining his own vocation and the larger problems of gender and socioeconomic inequality. Kenneth eventually resolves his confusion by returning to the valley, reaffirming his affective and spiritual bond with the land,
and trying to rally the farmers against the water-diversion project engi-
neered by Elwood, a San Francisco booster, and against Rickart's bid for
control of the valley's water rights. While the novel endorses Kenneth's
utopian coming of age, its ironic treatment of his sexist assumptions and
his limitations as a businessman and political strategist casts considerable
doubt on his potential to revitalize the rural community. Austin describes
his agonized wrestling with the "angels" of capitalism, socialism, feminism,
and the land with alternating sympathy, amused tolerance, and exasperation, and proposes the practical and "long-sighted" feminist real estate developer Anne Brent as a far more promising protagonist for the modern
novel of "constructive change."[18]

The Ford frames the problem of incompatible water-use proposals as
part of a larger question about competing forms of foresight: the valley's
social, economic, and ecological future depends on competing readings of
the land and its potential, and the futures of individuals depend on their
ability to envision and establish a "constructive relation" to a social and
material landscape already incorporated into modern capitalist sociospatial
relations. Austin's complex view of the rural landscape in The Ford differs
dramatically from that of John Muir and other wilderness preservation advocates who launched an influential campaign to prevent the Hetch-
Hetchy Valley from becoming a reservoir for San Francisco. The Hetch-
Hetchy activists saw their campaign as a sacred mission to protect the
natural landscape's intrinsic aesthetic and spiritual value from contamina-
tion by urban and technological expansion and the hegemony of exchange
value.[19] In a famous statement, Muir called the proponents of the dam
project "temple destroyers, devotees of raging commercialism," who "have
a perfect contempt for Nature, and, instead of lifting their eyes to the God
of the mountains, lift them to the Almighty Dollar. Dam Hetch Hetchy!
As well dam for water-tanks the people's cathedrals and churches, for no
holier temple has ever been consecrated by the heart of man."[20]

In contrast, Austin foresaw the impending desolation of Owens Valley not as the destruction of sacred wilderness, but as "the *return* of a great acreage of orchard and alfalfa to desertness," which would support urban development while "wiping out . . . the best of the few remaining chances for people of limited means to obtain homes on Government land."[21] For Austin, the farmers and businesspeople living and working in Owens Valley complicated the preservationist binary between crassly commercial urban space and pristine, nonurban Nature. Like other conservationists, she recognized that the borders between human economies and natural ecosystems could not be so neatly drawn,[22] and she defined the issue at stake as "how far it is well to destroy the agricultural interests of the commonwealth to the advantage of the vast aggregations of cities."[23] Like other conservationists, Austin believed that the best alternative to urban expansion and its attendant social and ecological problems was not wilderness preservation but regional development.

Originally a doctrine of scientific management of surplus water and public pastureland, conservationism by 1910 had become a broad-ranging "moral crusade" concerned, among other things, with the revitalization of rural life.[24] As William Kahrl notes in his study of the Owens Valley Project, both the conservationist principle of efficient use of "waste waters" and the ideal of the family farm were integral to the irrigation movement in California, where the expansion of irrigated agriculture seemed "the driving wheel of social and spiritual progress" as well as of economic development.[25] Supported by legislation such as the 1902 Reclamation Act, irrigation was to "extend opportunities for settlement and self-reliance to the common people by creating a whole new class of lands which would be made habitable through irrigation." Class conflict over land use would be eliminated, not by "breaking up the holdings of western corporate interests and redistributing their properties among a new class of resident farmers," but by scientifically restructuring rural space to accommodate both corporate interests and a revitalized agrarian individualism.[26] This model of regional development addressed widespread concern about the fate of the individual farmers who remained, in Austin's phrase, "producers rather than players of the game" (*Ford,* 289) in the era of urbanization, big business, and expanding managerial and distributive networks. It appealed to popular images of an idealized rural past in its attempt to reconstruct, through modern scientific management, family farm–based modes of production and social life that were becoming obsolete in the "age of incorporation."[27] Yet it also posited the nonurban landscape as a legitimate and progressive site of modernity, distinct from but no less modern than the spaces of the city. Combining Progressive Era social interventionism with scientific knowledge disseminated through national agencies such as the Reclamation Service and the Association of Agricultural Colleges and Experiment Stations, the conservation and rural revitalization movements sought to modernize the rural landscape and to insist, as Austin does in *The Ford,* that the landscape of modernity does not end at the city limits.

If the national system of railroads gave nineteenth-century progressives an exhilarating image of the technological annihilation of space and time that would modernize and Americanize the landscape, water conservation offered an alternative metaphor for progressive regional and national integration as a system of rationalized distribution, not of citizens and commodities, but of natural resources. This utopian image resonated even in texts not directly concerned with the problem of food production in arid regions: Edward Bellamy's decidedly urban novel *Looking Backward,* for example, uses irrigation as a figure for centralized distribution of social wealth, imagining human labor as a "fertilizing stream which alone render[s] earth habitable" and must be "regulated by a system which expend[s] every drop to the best advantage" to prevent "some fields [from being] flooded while others [are] parched, and half the water [runs] wholly to waste."[28] As Austin observes, water companies rivaled the railroads in "play[ing] the part of Providence" in western settlement and economic development; while the railroad companies pioneered what would become standard managerial methods in modern business, irrigation projects were central to the development of twentieth-century resource management and regional planning.[29] But if the need for irrigation figured "the complete helplessness of the individual in the arid West" without "an available water supply, organizing capacity, and that commodity known as capital," the water companies made production possible, and so seemed more intrinsically benevolent than the monopoly-controlled railroad system described in *The Octopus* as "the ironhearted monster of steel and steam, implacable, insatiable, huge—its entrails gorged with the lifeblood that it sucked from an entire commonwealth."[30] Norris's naturalistic image of the railroad as a monstrous organism evokes anxiety about the "miscegenation of the natural and the cultural" in the landscape of modernity.[31] But like Frederick Jackson Turner's description of commercial expansion as "an ever richer tide" pouring through "the arteries made by geology . . . until at last the slender paths of aboriginal intercourse have been broadened and interwoven into the complex mazes of modern commercial lines," the conservationist image of irrigation made the expansion of capitalist industrial technology seem reassuringly, rather than threateningly, continuous with the networks and flows of natural forces.[32]

Biologist and agricultural educator Liberty Hyde Bailey was one influential rural revitalization advocate who used conservationist imagery to reinvent the American farmer as both gifted producer and successful manager.[33] Bailey's book *The State and the Farmer* (1908) critiques popular nostalgic distress over the spectacle of the "abandoned farm," arguing that empty farm buildings indicate not the decline of American agriculture, but rather its changing practices. Small farms, Bailey says, have become larger agricultural enterprises that complement tilled fields with pastures, fallow lands, and timber stands, and augment working knowledge of local ecology with technological innovation, rationalized production and distribution methods, and systematic knowledge of changing urban and global markets. While some fail, many farmers have proved that the "fittest" can indeed survive—and expand their power and property holdings—by combining hands-on experience with a "rational outlook" and "respect for ideas in print," and by adopting new, scientific approaches to the business of farming. Like *The Ford's* "long-sighted" capitalists, Bailey's modern farmer occupies a strategic position within a "ganglionic" network of canals, railroads, telegraph lines, mail order services, newspapers, agricultural periodicals, educational outreach programs, and banking systems.[34] Similarly, the farmer's vital importance to society lies in his unique position as "the man who stands at the sources": He is both the producer of nourishment and wealth, and the "natural conservator of the native resources of the earth," who manages flows of crops, soil, and water as shrewdly as he manages flows of information and capital.[35] By constructing agriculture as conservation, Bailey both naturalizes farming and rationalizes natural processes; his heroic vision of the farmer-as-conservationist conflates natural with economic flows, production with distribution, and the farmer-as-producer with the farmer-as-businessman, and so invests farming with the cultural capital of modern science and commerce, and agribusiness with the moral capital of traditional agrarian values.

Yet while attributing modern agricultural success to rural values and local knowledge, Bailey insists that rural life can be revitalized only through federal and state government agency. Echoing Emerson's assertion that "[g]overnment must educate the poor man" and that the very landscape "seems to crave government," Bailey argues that while the ganglionic networks are now primarily "concentrative or centripetal . . . piling up wealth in small cities and towns," progressive governments must expand their "distributive or centrifugal" capacity to transfer wealth from cities back to rural producers and disseminate vital medical, sociological, and agricultural knowledge into "the open country."[36] "It is not only important to farming," Bailey writes, "but absolutely essential to the nation that the man at the sources be reached": local agricultural societies must be "assembled, solidified, and educationalized" into a centralized hierarchy for national progress toward "definite social ends."[37] Bailey's obsession with systematizing rural space, like the California movement to restructure rural space through irrigation, suggests that behind his utopian rhetoric lay an anxiety about the ability of "the man at the sources" to survive in the modern capitalist landscape without being either consumed by "the organized interests of the business world" or subsumed into a rural mass movement that too closely resembled organizations of "the labor-union kind."[38]

In the modern landscape of both *The State and the Farmer* and *The Ford,* the individual farmer "born to wrestle with the earth" is a compelling yet deeply problematic figure (*Ford,* 228). Austin shared Bailey's concern for the farmers' economic prospects, and in opposing the Owens Valley Project she supported the "profounder moral right" of rural producers to conserve water for irrigation over the claims of an urban society she considered economically parasitic and culturally barren.[39] But in *The Ford,* she is highly skeptical of the farmers' ability to read the modern landscape in a viable way. In the landscape of modernity, the characters who succeed are those, like Bailey's farmer-conservator and Austin's American novelist, who have pragmatic and prophetic insight into how the landscape has changed. Unlike the homesteaders, Timothy Rickart and Anne Brent are able to see the landscape not as an object of manual labor and conjugal desire, but as a map of socioeconomic relationships and of real estate and resource claims to be measured, managed, and sold. Unlike John Muir, and contrary to the expectations of most late twentieth-century environmentalist and ecofeminist readers, Austin does not suggest that the managerial and entrepreneurial gaze is automatically a desecration of the land. In both *The Ford* and her autobiography, she presents it simply as the "structural capacity" that allows her enterprising capitalists to "arrive directly without noticeable fumbling at the structural features of any situation," to "maintain within the main structures an immense amount of detail which was inherent in the situation itself," and so to see farther ahead than those still deluded by an obsolete pastoral imaginary.[40] Kenneth and others are struck by the "likenesses of method" with which Anne and Rickart benefit from the "noticing disposition" that allows them to intuit connections between apparently "inconsiderable items" (*Ford,* 274); locating themselves strategically within the modern distributive and communicative networks, they access and manage the flows of information, capital, and resources to secure for themselves, and perhaps for their communities, "an especial privilege in futures" (*Ford,* 227).

Unlike Bailey, who conflates production and distribution to posit "the man at the sources" as the successful manager of both, Austin suggests that production and management are fundamentally incompatible: the farmers' inability to outmaneuver Rickart and Elwood is caused by "the very elements which made them good farmers, producers rather than players of the game" (*Ford,* 289). While the rural landscape offers developers like Elwood and even ineffectual visionaries like Steven Brent "a clear call to realization" that speaks of "canals, highways, towns" or of "water and power [and] farms," the homesteaders find the land's voice "compelling" but "inarticulate" and productive of a kind of "enslavement" (*Ford,* 273, 361). Bound to the land by affection and physical labor, they respond to both drought and capitalist expansion by continuing to "tu[g] at the dry breast of the valley" rather than by imagining in any practical way how to transform their environment with development projects that serve local needs rather than urban growth or corporate profits (*Ford,* 225). The inauspiciously named Homestead Development Company is defeated less by lack of capital or by Rickart's or Elwood's machinations than by its own narrowness of vision, by the "invincible rurality" that binds the farmers to their own plots of land and makes them fear any enterprise that might "grow beyond their individual capacity to deal with it" (*Ford,* 221). Faithful to "the partial gods of their own boundaries," they lack organizing or "structural capacity," and so remain "completely out of the game," immobile as the stone "figures in the group of the Laocoön ... serpent-wrapped, their mouths open and no cry to issue from it," trapped in the coils of the "octopus" of modern capital rather than assuming a strategic managerial position within its ganglionic system (*Ford,* 409, 368).

In her compelling description of the farmers' defeat, Austin draws on the imagery of American literary naturalism to conflate nature and capital, not as manageable systems and flows, but as vast, impersonal, and only

partly apprehended forces whose power manifests itself in the homesteaders' invincibly rural temperament. The farmers become iconic figures paradoxically dwarfed, defeated, subsumed, and ennobled by monumental
forces both within and external to themselves: the discrepancy between
their reading of the modern landscape and that of the successful capitalists
gives their inevitable defeat "the quality of ancient tragedy; the tragedy of
men defeated, not squalidly by other men, but by forces within themselves
which had the form and dignity of gods" (*Ford,* 290). Invoking what Mark
Seltzer calls "a miscegenation of the natural and the cultural: the erosion of
the boundaries that divide persons and things, labor and nature, what
counts as an agent and what doesn't,"[41] Austin's powerful language dis-
solves the preservationist binary between nature and commerce into a naturalist landscape of mysterious forces and flows beyond human comprehension or control.

But if *The Ford* constructs a naturalist "melodrama of uncertain agency"
in its compelling portrayal of the farmers' predicament, it also lucidly critiques the different forms of agency by representing them as complemen-
tary forms of partial blindness. The farmers labor in the "half-blind social
struggle" represented by the one-eyed socialist organizer who is the "temperamental Pioneer of social revolution" (*Ford,* 191-92); the capitalists,
meanwhile, engage in the half-blind pursuit of profit embodied in the un-
scrupulous prospector Jevens, whose one cast eye has "a separate intelligence of its own" (*Ford,* 8). With their eyes "far fixed upon the ultimate triumph," rural producers and bohemian socialists suffer "incredible
immediate defeat" because they misinterpret the relationship between
labor and capital "in the terms of personal conflict" (*Ford,* 191, 204). Meanwhile, the "half-gods whose divinity is conferred by dollars" succeed not
by scheming against them, but by "taking the shortest distance between
two points, ignoring the human element" altogether (*Ford,* 287, 385). For
Rickart, laws are "not human institutions at the making of which men
prayed and sweated, but so many hazards and hurdles of the game": "The
most that he knew of mortgages, overdue installments, foreclosures, were
their legal limitations; he did not know that men are warped by these
things and that women died of them. It was as if a huge bite had been taken
out of the round of his capacity, and left him forever and profitably unaware of the human remainder" (*Ford,* 176). Through this analysis of both
failures of foresight, *The Ford* critiques naturalism's limitations as a model
for constructive socioecological relations. While attributing both forms of

"half-blindness" to innate temperamental differences, Austin nonetheless insists that the landscape of modernity is not intrinsically unmanageable, and that human agents possess the capacity and the social responsibility to propagate the "green bough of constructive change."

When he returns to the valley after his apprenticeship as a corporate lawyer, Kenneth Brent disrupts the naturalist tableau of the "half-gods of capital" and the "temperamental, the incurable pioneer[s]." He rides into the breach between "the kind of a man T. Rickart had become and the sort that was fleeced by him" (*Ford,* 386, 87, 295). Like Bailey's "man who stands at the sources," Kenneth embodies the spirit of rural revitalization, combining business and legal expertise with traditional rural values and intimate working knowledge of soil and stream. While claiming to be "done with business" because he is now a producer, he aspires to "produce an irrigation canal and a farming district" as well as alfalfa and mutton, and eventually becomes both a farmer and the president of a new water conservation company (*Ford,* 406). Kenneth's dual capacities are prefigured in his childhood "double consciousness" of both "public, boyish interest in the activities of the oil fields" and "absorbed, contemplative pleasure in which the piercing of the sod by the first faint spears of the brodea marked an epoch, and the finding of the first meadow-lark's nest a momentous discovery" (*Ford,* 90–91). Wavering between filial respect for Rickart's inhuman but impressive "structural capacity" and desire for the "maternal breast" of the rural landscape, he sympathizes with the farmers' vulnerability to both capitalism and the land, and shares Steven Brent's "desire to cover their lack with his own larger outlook" (*Ford,* 294).

Despite his good intentions, however, Kenneth's return as "Brent of Palomitas" resolves neither the novel's plot nor its central problem of "constructive relation." The plot continues for sixty more pages of revelations, setbacks, resolutions, and deliberations, during which the female characters critique the way Kenneth's rural revitalization project is circumscribed by his relentless personal project of masculine identity formation. Kenneth's renewed association with "the grazing flocks, the ribbed hills, the steady fall of the valley seaward" inspires him to argue that "it wasn't any feeling for the System that had got him, it was a feeling for the land," and that "the biggest fact in [his] existence" is that he is "Brent of Palomitas." Virginia objects that "you can't stop with just getting after the individual" because "it all comes back to the Cap[italist System]" (*Ford,* 404), but the novel's own sensitivity to landscape and satirical treatment of Virginia's fashionable socialist phrases undermine the force of this otherwise quite plausible critique.[42] Anne, however, is no less impatient with the homesteaders and her brother for what she considers their lack of "structural capacity" and myopic preoccupation with their own individual relationships to the land, and her dual status as a skilled and respected businesswoman and the novel's real heroine lends considerable weight to her liberal feminist critique of Kenneth's romantic agrarianism.

Succeeding at real estate "the same way other people are musicians and writers," because she likes it, Anne bases her own relationship to land on managerial rather than manual labor, and on a theory of property in which the market and legal systems overrule labor in determining value and ownership (*Ford,* 199). Like another successful female capitalist, Alexandra Bergson in Willa Cather's *O Pioneers!,* Anne disregards her brother's agrarian conviction that "the earth was the right and property of those who worked it, and that its values should accrue to them if to anybody" (*Ford,* 436). Like Alexandra, who prospers by emulating "the shrewd ones" who buy up "other people's land [and] don't try to farm it,"[43] Anne possesses what Austin calls "the gift of detachment": she can "buy land without wanting to work it . . . with the distinct intention of unloading it on somebody else who believed himself elected to work it and was willing to pay handsomely for the privilege" (*Ford,* 178). Anne's and Alexandra's investment skills depend on detachment from their brothers' Lockean view of property, in which, as Howard Horwitz writes, "property is created by mixing with nature one's labor, an inalienable part of the self," and so figures as "an analogue to subjectivity . . . a structure of representation and reproduction in which self is experienced."[44] Although Alexandra is also a producer who sets her face toward the land "with love and yearning" and "expresses herself" in the soil, she ultimately "loves the land not for its service but for its resistance to human will." For her, longing and personhood are not "absolute, or absolutely individuated" but only "for a little while."[45] As Horwitz argues, Cather's narrative of sublimely impersonal love for the land challenges natural-rights assumptions about the inalienability of both property and selfhood by disentangling "love from yearning, from identificatory desire, from viewing possessions as monuments to the self."[46]

Austin furthers this critique of natural-rights theory by pointing out how men's impulse to produce both property and selfhood by "mixing with nature their labor" feminizes the land as object of conjugal desire. In *Earth Horizon,* she describes the "spell of the land over all the men who had in any degree given themselves to it, a spell of its lofty and intricate charm, which worked on men like the beauty of women" to "set up in men the desire to master and make it fruitful."[47] Looking at "the almost untouched valley as a man might look at his young wife, seeing her in his mind's eye in full matronly perfection with all her children about her," men like Steven Brent view the land's "potential fecundity" as both "invitation and the advertisement of man's inadequacy" (*Ford*, 35, 225), while women like his wife and daughter "look at one another with sharp—or weary— implications of exasperated resignation."[48] But unlike some later ecofem- inists, Austin objects not to the men's desire to own and develop the land, but to the lack of "organizing capacity" that prevents them from doing so effectively. In *The Ford,* the river itself wants to "tur[n] mills or whirring dynamos," to "wate[r] fields and nurs[e] orchards," but is "discouraged at last by the long neglect of man." The land "doesn't mean crops" to Anne as it does to Steven and Kenneth, but it does mean "people—people who want land and are fitted for land, and the land wants—how it wants them!" (*Ford,* 34, 199). While Rickart uses his entrepreneurial skills to accumulate capital for himself and his son, Anne uses hers to make real estate a prof- itable *and* progressive "liberal profession" and scientific managerial practice that she claims will ensure socioecological harmony: "Say a certain piece of land will grow prunes or potatoes; then you've got to have prune peo- ple or potato people. . . . I can make a Socialist out of a prune man . . . by keeping him six years on a piece of ground that was only meant to grow potatoes" (*Ford,* 234). Like Emerson's "true lords, *land-lords,* who under- stand the land and its uses and the applicabilities of men" and "mediat[e] between want and supply," Anne is "an agent for the land," using scientific analysis of "soil constituents and subsoil and drainage" to identify the land's intrinsic use values, and then selling it to the person best suited to realize its productive potential.[49] Alexandra Bergson ultimately argues, with John Muir, that the land "belongs" only to "the people who love it and under- stand it," suggesting the insignificance of both labor-based and legal prop- erty claims in the face of nature's transcendence.[50] Anne, however, argues that "you can absolutely find out what land is good for, and . . . it only be- longs to the people who can do those things." Like Bailey's, her practice affirms the natural-rights bond between property and persons as based on inalienable qualities inherent in both, yet denaturalizes this bond by point- ing out its dependence on and mediation by an expanding network of sci- entific, legal, and business institutions (*Ford,* 234).

Like his more enterprising daughter, Steven Brent recognizes that the arid western landscape undermines the masculine myth of "absolute and absolutely individuated" selfhood inherent in property, since "a man cannot simply appropriate individual holdings" of land and "make any quarter-section of it bear."[51] But like the other farmers, he lacks the capital and "organizing capacity" to sublimate his love for the land into a system of resource management that would nurture its potential fecundity. Enamored of "the promise of the land," the "residue of the romantic mining experience [and] allure of the desertness," men like Brent "spen[d] their lives going around and around in it," feeling themselves "enchanted by its longer eye-reach, its rainbow horizons; but in fact it [is] the *timeless space* that [holds] them."[52] Their form of foresight fails to be truly "prophetic" (that is, historically progressive) because it remains a contemplative, individualized desire for conjugal relation with the feminized landscape rather than a participatory attentiveness to socioecological structures and processes that is "true for the observer and successful in the outcome" because it is "related to the main structure as the twig is to the branch and the leaf to the twig."[53]

Anne, therefore, desires for her brother a *bildung* that will unsettle his devotion to the "partial gods of his own boundaries" (*Ford,* 409) and make him, as Alexandra Bergson hopes for her brother Emil, "fit to cope with the world" by developing in him "a personality apart from the soil."[54] Before Anne "wake[s] Kenneth to a sense of the future," he labors in "the snare of that strange, intimate delight, the mastery over his own body": the "satiny, smooth feeling of his skin and the taut muscles shor[e] him up against the sense of family defeat" and his father's subsequent "slackness of . . . surfaces" (*Ford,* 163, 161). Kenneth's "wholly pagan revelations of identity" focus on the boundaries of his own body rather than on the plots of land that ensnare the homesteaders. But the disciplining of his own body helps him to lift the traumatic question of the reasons for his father's failure and his mother's death "out of the obscure region of his feelings about them" to become "events merely, hard, reasonless features of the landscape in which he [is] to find his way about," though he does "not yet think of any way out and beyond them" (*Ford,* 162). This link between affirming the boundaries of individual selfhood and finding one's way in the socioecological environment also characterizes Kenneth's attitude in the struggle to revitalize the valley: "at the moment nothing mattered so much to young Brent as that he should take his own measure. Whatever he was up against,—laws, institutions, the passions and prejudices of other men,—he must know once and for all its nature and its name" (*Ford,* 398). And for him, the question of social agency in the landscape of modernity is insep-arable from his own identificatory desire for the land. Having proposed his plan to put all the farmers' land and water claims in escrow to keep Rickart from buying them up and selling them out, "Brent of Palomitas" becomes literally "the man who stands at the sources" as he camps out and works on his own water-rights claim; his contact with the maternal landscape supplies "the need he stood in of healing and reassurance," and he grows "brown and leaner and at ease with himself, a kind of ease … inexplicable to Anne almost to the point of irritation" (*Ford,* 414).

While she shares her father and brother's "feeling for the land," which binds "them to it through the nurture of common experience," Anne's vo-cation is social rather than ecological. Her attentiveness to the land is in-strumental rather than affective, focused on use values rather than aesthetic or ecological ones (*Ford,* 403, 361). Once she has "learned all that [is] nec-essary to the construction of the work in hand," she loses patience with Kenneth and Ellis's affectionate absorption in the details of local ecology (*Ford,* 414). And unlike Kenneth, Anne believes that "taking one's own measure" only counts if it is "successful in the outcome." While recogniz-ing its valuable masculinizing function for her brother, she views his soli-tary retreat into physical labor on his claim as "a sort of sublimated mud-pie making" that doesn't "settle anything," but merely allows him to ignore the reality that his Thoreauvian return to nature will only last "until she or Rickart or somebody of the same stripe [comes] along and [takes] it away from him" (*Ford,* 414, 431). By constructing his relation to the land as a matter of individual identity and labor rather than social or corporate power, Kenneth makes another shortsighted misreading of the landscape of modernity. Rather than establishing a "constructive relation," he merely "escape[s] the necessity of settling anything, of having to decide things that are important to be decided" (*Ford,* 430).

Anne's impatience with Virginia suggests her agreement with Emerson that "our young people have thought and written much on labor and re-form, and for all that they have written, neither the world nor themselves have got on a step"; and her impatience with Kenneth echoes Emerson's assertion that "[s]o many things are unsettled which it is of the first im-portance to settle,—and, pending their settlement, we will do as we do."[55] But if Austin agrees with Emerson that progressive socioecological evolu-tion emerges out of "muscular activity" rather than mere "intellectual tast-

ing of life," her conception of "settlement" unsettles the opposition between intellectual and material production. For her, "settlement" refers
both to the intellectual process of decision making *and* to the materially
productive human settlement of the landscape that her real estate practice
will bring about.[56] But through Anne's ironic critique of Kenneth's masculine quest for identity through working the land, Austin also insists that
"muscular activity" is no more progressive than the "eyeless and amorphic"
novels she deplores, as long as both are directed toward individual self-pro-
duction rather than toward "the structural features of any situation" and
the "growing tip of *collective* consciousness."[57]

Retelling the Owens Valley events in her autobiography, Austin writes,
"All this Mary business is a nuisance; having to stop and tell why she did
things and what she thought about them" in the face of "affairs of the ut-
most constructive importance to the commonwealth, to which her status
was that of a short person at a circus parade."[58] This wry remark suggests
why Kenneth remains the "hero" of *The Ford* when Anne is clearly its
working model of constructive practice. Virginia's dramatic but ineffectual
narrative of "finding herself" as the "Friend of Labor," "Spirit of the West,"
and "woman of genius" suggests that rewriting the male bildungsroman as
a female "Development of the Ego" has limited progressive potential. Instead, Austin ironizes both narratives of self-construction by contrasting
them with Ellis's and Anne's less introspective outlook (*Ford, 242, 307*). Ellis
surprises Kenneth by asking "a thousand questions of the land and the trail
and the new life that came crowding to her quick, excited notice" rather
than seeming "in the least interested" in him or in herself. And in contrast
to the meticulous narration of Kenneth's every thought and emotion,
Anne's development is more indirectly marked in the admiring but con-
descending comments of the men she outwits, and in Kenneth's belated
realization that his sister has "views" (*Ford, 296, 170*). Anne is blunt and
forceful in promoting her own practice of real estate as socioecological engineering, but her monumental stature as *The Ford*'s model of progressive
womanhood and conservationist practice is announced not by a self-de-
scription like Kenneth's "I'm Brent of Palomitas," but by Kenneth's revelation that while he had "accepted for his sister, as most men had for all
women, the necessity that one or the other thing in her should waste," "he
saw now that it wasn't necessary, but simply stupid. It wasn't in the least
that a woman couldn't be both as big as Anne was, and as womanly, but
that men weren't big enough to afford her both within the scope of their
lives" (*Ford, 372–73*).

Anne, who like Ellis is of a "noticing disposition," returns to Palomitas not to reconstruct her mother's house and garden in her own image, but to make it a center of operations from which one can see "full from the veranda the perspective of the valley" as far as "the line of the Caliente fence and the breach in the Coast Range, curving seaward"; or, if one chooses, take in "nothing at all but the banks of red geraniums, the new-planted beds, and the red rambler working close under the waves, with here and there a lifted, inquiring streamer" (*Ford,* 393). Through this "inconsiderable" image, Austin unobtrusively delineates the relational capacity that is central to Anne's success precisely by decentering her personal identity, by drawing attention away from herself and toward what she sees. In its graceful affiliation of intimacy and distance, Anne's perspective quietly overlooks the boundaries of property and identity in which Kenneth and the homesteaders are so intensely invested, and suggests a mode of vision that is neither "half-blind" nor torn, as in Kenneth's "double consciousness," between two conflicting views. Through the exquisite impersonality of this image, Austin suggests an affinity between Anne's disturbingly instrumental "structural capacity" and Ellis's more stereotypically feminine gift for intuiting and nurturing personal and ecological relations, which at first glance appears far more compatible with the perspectives of later twentieth-century ecofeminism. In the context of Anne's successful practice, the view from the veranda suggests a mode of vision that can operate simultaneously at multiple scales. Such a vision depends not only on "the estheticization of a particular place-bound relation to nature," which in the case of men like Kenneth ends up "fetishizing the human body [and] the Self," but on a more abstract structural understanding of "broader socioecological processes occurring at scales that cannot be directly experienced and which are therefore outside of phenomenological reach."[59] The subtlety of Austin's methods and "views" is perhaps easier to discern in *The Land of Little Rain,* in which her anti-androcentric deconstruction of individual narrative voice asserts itself more directly; but in *The Ford,* her critique registers its presence in, against, and around the edges of the narrative of self-construction, to be noticed by readers, like *Earth Horizon*'s Mary, who have "edged in," "scrooged and peeked between the elbows," and "judge[d] many times what was going on from what taller people said."[60]

Late twentieth-century readers whose environmental imaginations have been shaped more by John Muir's preservationism than by Liberty Hyde Bailey's conservationism will be disturbed by the extent to which

Anne's "gift of detachment" obstructs her "feeling for the land." From our perspective, her conservationist faith in modern progress, capitalist entrepreneurship, and privatized social engineering makes her an unlikely candidate for an ecofeminist heroine. Yet *The Ford*'s pragmatic and prophetic insistence that nonurban space is inescapably part of the landscape of modern capitalism lends considerable weight to Anne's mode of foresight, and provides an important complement to the individual affective relations with the nonhuman landscape that make *The Land of Little Rain* so luminous with attention and desire. If, as Tara Hart argues elsewhere in this volume, the textual strategies of Austin's less anthropocentric desert writings "keep possibility alive" by constructing a "conditional female occupation of a suspended space" and a relation to landscape that is perpetually unsettled, *The Ford*'s commitment to the human beings who make their living in the landscape insists on the centrality of "settlement" to the construction of a viable *working* relation between human and natural economies. In *The Organic Machine,* Richard White observes that "[e]nvironmentalists, for all their love of nature, tend to distance humans from it" by stressing "the eye over the hand, the contemplative over the active, the supposedly undisturbed over the connected," and argues for an understanding of natural and human economies as a single system of energy and labor.[61] Underlying Bailey's and Austin's vision of conservationist regional development is a similar argument that a pragmatic and prophetic relation to the landscape *in which we live* must accommodate a reading of human work on and in the natural environment as not always and automatically a desecration. There are naturalist moments in *The Ford* when the plight of the farmers and the ugliness of the oilfields stand as dystopian images of "that mysterious quality taken on by the works of man, power ungoverned by sensibility"; but the Brent family's collaborative rural revitalization project shows that both sensibility and power are necessary for effective resistance to male dominance and capitalist instrumentality (*Ford,* 145). For Austin, constructive socioecological practice requires both compassion and a more impersonal awareness that "the structural features of any situation" encompass self and other, culture and nature, human and nonhuman landscapes. When the young Kenneth Brent imagines even the oil derricks as "tall, iron trees— for does not iron come up out of the earth even as oak and pine?" this unsettling novel leaves the question open (*Ford,* 92).

NOTES

1. Mary Austin, "The American Form of the Novel" (1922), in *Beyond Borders: The Selected Essays of Mary Austin,* ed. Reuben J. Ellis (Carbondale: Southern Illinois University Press, 1996), 84-88, 85.

2. See Clare Eby's lucid argument that Shelgrim the industrialist rather than Presley the writer is the epic poet of *The Octopus,* and that Norris's novel celebrates rather than opposes the epic project of capitalist expansion embodied in the railroad. Clare Virginia Eby, "*The Octopus*: Big Business as Art," *American Literary Realism* 26 (1994): 33-51.

3. Ralph Waldo Emerson, "The Young American" (1844), in *Collected Works,* vol. 2 (Boston: Houghton Mifflin, 1921), 379.

4. "I think we must regard the *land* as a commanding and increasing power on the citizen, the sanative and Americanizing influence, which promises to disclose new virtues for ages to come. . . . [T]he uprise and culmination of the new and anti-feudal power of Commerce is the political fact of most significance to the American at this hour" (ibid., 370).

5. In *The American Rhythm,* Austin argues that poetry originates in affective motor responses to the experience of "rhythmic forms" in the natural environment, and that adaptation to the American landscape produces an affinity between Native American and modernist poetry. While valorizing "folk" and "mystical" relations to landscape, she suggests that subjectivity and culture are rooted both in the land *and* in the commercial-industrial system whose "new attacks on the mastery of time and space" transform the landscape and the "whole new scale of motor impulses . . . built into the subconscious structure of the individual" (Mary Austin, *The American Rhythm: Studies and Reexpressions of Amerindian Songs* [1923; rev. ed., Boston: Houghton Mifflin, 1930], 9).

6. Mary Austin, *Earth Horizon* (1932; reprint, Albuquerque: University of New Mexico Press, 1991), vii.

7. Reuben J. Ellis, introduction to *Beyond Borders,* 18.

8. Austin, "The Future of the Southwest," *New Republic,* 8 April 1925, 186.

9. Austin, *Earth Horizon,* 205.

10. Austin's conception of the "prophetic" resonates with Cornell West's term for the intellectual tradition of American pragmatism, and her model of socioecological practice prefigures West's view of "prophetic pragmatism" as a form of "left romanticism" that "tempers its utopian impulse with a profound sense of the tragic character of life and history": "Prophetic pragmatism is a form of tragic thought in that it confronts candidly individual and collective experiences of evil in individuals and institutions—with little expectation of ridding the world of *all* evil. Yet it is a kind of romanticism in that it holds many experiences of evil to be neither inevitable nor necessary but rather the results of human agency, i.e., choices and actions" (Cornell West, "Prophetic Pragmatism," in *Pragmatism: A Reader,* ed. Louis Menand [New York: Vintage-Random House, 1997], 406). Mary Austin, *The Ford* (1917; reprint, Berkeley: University of California Press, 1997). All subsequent parenthetical notations refer to this edition.

11. Even in *The Land of Little Rain,* "[i]t is the proper destiny of every considerable stream in the west to become an irrigating ditch," and "it would seem that the streams are willing" (Mary Austin, *The Land of Little Rain* [1903; reprint, New York: Penguin Books,

1988], 85).

12. As Kathryn DeZur points out in her essay in this volume, these unsettled boundaries are racial and cultural as well.

13. Austin, *Earth Horizon,* 189.

14. Lawrence Buell, *The Environmental Imagination: Thoreau, Nature Writing, and the Formation of American Culture* (Cambridge: Harvard University Press, 1995), 176-77.

15. See Elizabeth Abel, Marianne Hirsch, and Elizabeth Langland, eds., *The Voyage In: Fictions of Female Development* (Hanover: University Press of New England, 1983).

16. I have in mind the social ecology and environmental justice movements and some forms of ecofeminism that complicate mainstream environmentalism's emphasis on nature preservation by pointing out how the category of "nature" is defined and used to support various forms of socioeconomic oppression or to override the claims of indigenous peoples or those who live and work "in nature"—subsistence farmers and loggers, for instance—to participate in decisions about land use. See the essays in *Ecology,* ed. Carolyn Merchant (Atlantic Highlands, N.J.: Humanities Press, 1994); and *Uncommon Ground: Rethinking the Human Place in Nature,* ed. William Cronon (New York: Norton, 1996). See also, for example, the work of Howard Horwitz in American studies, Donna Haraway in feminist science studies, William Cronon and Richard White in environmental history, and David Harvey in geography.

17. See William L. Kahrl, *Water and Power: The Conflict over Los Angeles' Water Supply in the Owens Valley* (Berkeley: University of California Press, 1982).

18. The biblical image of Jacob wrestling with the angel is central to *The Ford.* In *Earth Horizon,* Austin writes that while for John Muir "the spirits of the wild were angels, who bore him on their wings through perilous places," for her the spirit of the desert was an elusive and terribly beautiful woman whose "dreadful, never-to-be appeased desire" inspired her answering desire to come back, as Kenneth does in *The Ford,* "to wrestle with the Spirit of the Arroyos" (188).

19. The Hetch-Hetchy campaign failed as well, but its premises were much more influential on the mandates and conceptual boundaries of mainstream environmental groups such as the Sierra Club, which, ironically, have often been forced to follow Muir's lead in preserving nature by marketing "wilderness" as a profitable tourist attraction.

20. John Muir, *The Yosemite* (1912; reprint, Garden City, N.Y.: Anchor-Doubleday, 1962), 202.

21. Austin, "The Owens River Water Project," *San Francisco Chronicle,* 3 September 1905, 19; emphasis added.

22. William Cronon similarly critiques the boundary between Chicago's urban history and the natural history of its hinterland: "Nature's Metropolis and the Great West are in fact different labels for a single region and the relationships that defined it" (Cronon, *Nature's Metropolis: Chicago and the Great West* [New York: Norton, 1991], 19).

23. Austin, "Owens River Water Project."

24. See Samuel P. Hays, *Conservation and the Gospel of Efficiency: The Progressive Conservation Movement, 1890-1920* (Cambridge: Harvard University Press, 1959).

25. Kahrl, *Water and Power,* 30.

26. Ibid., 32.

27. See Alfred D. Chandler, *The Visible Hand: The Managerial Revolution in American Business* (Cambridge: Harvard University Press, 1977), on the "managerial revolution" in Amer-

ican business. Also see the influential discussions of Gilded Age economics in literary and cultural history in Walter Benn Michaels, *The Gold Standard and the Logic of Naturalism:American Literature at the Turn of the Century* (Berkeley: University of California Press, 1987); and in Alan Trachtenberg, *The Incorporation of America: Culture and Society in the Gilded Age* (New York: Hill and Wang, 1982).

28. Edward Bellamy, *Looking Backward* (1887; reprint, New York: Penguin Books, 1982), 228-29.

29. See Chandler, *The Visible Hand;* Hays, *Conservation.*

30. Austin, *Earth Horizon,* 199, 271; Frank Norris, *The Octopus* (1901; reprint, New York: Airmont, 1969), 224.

31. Mark Seltzer, *Bodies and Machines* (New York: Routledge, 1992), 21.

32. Frederick Jackson Turner, "The Significance of the Frontier in American History" (1893), in *The Turner Thesis: Concerning the Role of the Frontier in American History,* ed. George Rogers Taylor (Boston: D. C. Heath, 1949), 7.

33. For a useful discussion of the nineteenth-century roots of Bailey's position, see Alan I. Marcus, *Agricultural Science and the Quest for Legitimacy: Farmers, Agricultural Colleges, and Experiment Stations, 1870-1890* (Ames: Iowa State University Press, 1985). Marcus argues that the development, promotion, and institutionalization of agricultural science enforced a distinction between "agriculturists" and "scientific professionals" and so implied that "farmers properly belonged within the business community" (219).

34. Liberty Hyde Bailey, *The State and the Farmer* (New York: Macmillan, 1908), 14, 16.

35. Ibid., 56-57.

36. Emerson, "Young American," 384; Bailey, *The State and the Farmer,* 125.

37. Bailey, *The State and the Farmer,* 115-16.

38. Ibid., 120, 122. The nineteenth-century Populist movement clearly underlies this anxiety about rural mass politics, even though organized labor generally did not support the Populists because they addressed the interests of "*employing* farmers" rather than wage-earning farm workers (Trachtenberg, *Incorporation,* 176). As Marcus points out in *Agricultural Science and the Quest for Legitimacy,* Populist revolt was partly motivated by ambivalence toward the kind of institutionalized agricultural science that Bailey represented and promoted as president of the Association of American Agricultural Colleges and Experiment Stations.

39. Austin, "Future," 186.

40. Austin, *Earth Horizon,* 205. In this section of her autobiography, Austin is describing Henry Miller, a San Joaquin capitalist and land baron whom she admired and used as the model for Rickart in *The Ford.*

41. Seltzer, *Bodies and Machines,* 21.

42. Here, Kenneth and Virginia rehearse two "half-blind" perspectives that still obstruct dialogue between some forms of ecological and Marxist theory. See David Harvey, *Justice, Nature and the Geography of Difference* (Cambridge, Mass.: Blackwell, 1996); and Merchant, ed., *Ecology.*

43. Willa Cather, *O Pioneers!* (1913; reprint, New York: Penguin Books, 1989), 68.

44. Howard Horwitz, *By the Law of Nature: Form and Value in Nineteenth-Century America* (New York: Oxford University Press, 1991), 222-23.

45. Cather, *O Pioneers!,* 65, 84, 308; Horwitz, *By the Law of Nature,* 223, 235.

46. Horwitz, *By The Law of Nature,* 235.

47. Austin, *Earth Horizon,* 270.

48. Ibid., 271.

49. Emerson, "Young American," 384; Austin, *Ford,* 200.

50. Cather *O Pioneers,* 308.

51. Austin, *Earth Horizon,* 270-71.

52. Ibid., 284-85; emphasis added.

53. Ibid., 205.

54. Cather, *O Pioneers,* 213.

55. Emerson, "Experience" (1844), in *The Oxford Authors: Ralph Waldo Emerson,* ed. Richard Poirier (Oxford: Oxford University Press, 1990), 222, 225.

56. Ibid., 222.

57. Austin, *Earth Horizon,* 205; Austin, "American Form of the Novel," 85, 86 (emphasis added).

58. Austin, *Earth Horizon,* 205.

59. Harvey, *Geography of Difference,* 303-4.

60. Austin, *Earth Horizon,* 204.

61. Richard White, *The Organic Machine* (New York: Hill and Wang, 1995), x.

CHAPTER FOURTEEN

Walking Off an Illness?
Don't Go West, Young Man

The Construction of Masculinity in *Cactus Thorn*

MELODY GRAULICH

Austin's portrayal of strong and independent women has long attracted feminist critics, but more recently critics have begun to explore her efforts to rethink masculinity in such works as The Basket Woman, The Ford, *and* Starry Adventure. *In "Don't Go West, Young Man," Melody Graulich draws on recent work on the construction of American manhood by Anthony Rotundo and Gail Bederman to explore the "strenuous rest cure"—the curative trip west undertaken by men who had experienced some kind of breakdown. In her satiric treatment of the way Grant Arliss uses the West in his "recovery" of his potency and power in* Cactus Thorn, *Austin suggests the intersections between constructions of virile manhood, racism, and imperialist impulses during the Progressive Era.*

Graulich's essay, like most of the others in Exploring Lost Borders, *presents Austin's work as enmeshed with the politics of her time. Like Tonkovich in her reading of the apparently escapist* Isidro, *Graulich reads the apparently romantic* Cactus Thorn *as exploring connections between regional and national politics, between national and international concerns. Like DeZur, she turns to "A Case of Conscience" as a text that particularly reveals Austin's views on nationhood and imperialism, and she too sees Austin as raising crucial questions about property and ownership of land and people. Together with other contributors to this volume, she views Austin as a theorist of "the West," one whose theories grew from the landscapes she inhabited and from ongoing cultural explorations. Creating that theory in a variety of forms, from poetry and drama to nature writing and ecocriticism, from fiction and autobiography to cultural criticism and political allegory, Austin reminds us today of the West's historical diversity and complexity, of the rewards that still beckon in western exploration.*

As part of a tribute to her dead friend Mary Austin, Mabel Dodge Luhan shared the following anecdote:

> One day while staying with us at the Big House she emerged from her room at noon and paced up and down the portal looking all in.
> "What's the matter, Mary?" I asked her.
> "I killed a man this morning," she replied.
> It happened to be Lincoln Steffens, who had walked out on her some years previously. She had not minded losing him, what she couldn't take was that it was *he* who withdrew. . . . So of course she had to destroy him.[1]

When I wrote my afterword to the first publication of *Cactus Thorn,* I, like Luhan, read Austin's portrayal and eventual murder of the hypocritical Grant Arliss as a satisfying act of vengeance, although I recognized its larger political significance.[2] Austin felt personally betrayed by Steffens, but she also came to see him as representative of supposedly radical politicians who failed to rethink their relations to and attitudes about women and marriage, men whose "personal expression . . . contradicted and reversed the political expression."[3] Her motives mirrored her message: the personal *is* political.

But while *Cactus Thorn* presents a political critique, it also offers a cultural critique: Austin's satiric response to a recurring image of the West in our literary history as the refuge where easterners broken in body or mind come to regain their psychic health. (Anachronistically, I think of this place as the "Betty Ford West.") Like Progressive Era figures Theodore Roosevelt and Owen Wister, and such fictional characters as Harold Frederic's Theron Ware, Grant Arliss comes west because he has had some kind of "breakdown"; he feels "spiritual insufficiency" and, more suggestively, a kind of uncertainty and "impotence."[4] Unhinged by the competition to assume power and authority in the modern world, by what some historians have called a "masculinity crisis" among middle-class turn-of-the-century men, he seeks regeneration in the West.[5] Although the West has traditionally been an asylum for men, throughout her career Austin staked claim to that healing landscape for women, representing the West as a place where women like the Walking Woman, troubled by an "unsoundness of mind," can be "healed at last by the large soundness of nature." In *Earth Horizon* she suggests that she, like the Walking Woman, "had begun by walking off an illness." Thus the West provides space for a new construction of womanhood.[6] Yet especially in *Cactus Thorn* she raises questions about whether some male characters in search of a (re)new(ed) manhood are able to make sense of the land's lessons, able to walk "off all sense of [the] society-made values" she often associated with the East and with cities ("Walking Woman," 97). As is often the case with Austin's feminist analyses, she proves prescient in anticipating recent explorations of the cultural construction of "manliness" during the Progressive Era, explorations that suggest intersections between constructions of virile manhood, racism, and imperialist impulses.

Austin was well aware of the cultural politics of disease, particularly attitudes about the causes and treatment of nervous disorders. She suffered a "breakdown" after her first year at college that, she said, "was supposed to have been caused by overwork. . . . It had more to do with something Mary was unable to explain, least of all to a physician of those days . . . [with] the deep-seated conviction that all illnesses of women were 'female' in their origin, and could best be cured by severe doses of housework and child-bearing. 'The *only* work,' said Dr. Hankins, 'a female should do is beside her own fireside'" (*Earth Horizon,* 151–52). That midwestern small-town doctor was not so advanced as S. Weir Mitchell, who treated the woman who was to become Austin's friend, Charlotte Perkins Gilman, at about the same time. Or perhaps he was simply more pragmatic, for the lower-middle-class women he treated could hardly take to their beds for the extended periods Mitchell's "rest cure" prescribed. But both doctors shared similar assumptions about the causes of mental distress—too much mental activity—and the ultimate goal of treatment: return to the domestic roles women were meant to play.

Both Austin and Gilman, of course, came to see their breakdowns as representing their dis-ease with those very roles, and both wrote stories about the mad and frustrated women they would have become had they accepted their doctors' treatment. Both women ultimately saw the West as a place of personal liberation and healing, a place of refuge from constricting expectations, and it was in the West that both began to write seriously about women who hungered for more out of life, women who took charge of their own lives.[7] In her western wanderings, Austin found her own "remedy"; malnourished from eating only meat, she gorged on wild grapes in a scene she later rendered symbolic:

But there was more to the incident than that; there was the beginning of a notion in Mary's mind of a poor appetite of any sort being cured by its proper food; that there was something you could do about unsatisfactory conditions besides being heroic or a martyr to them, something more satisfactory than enduring or complaining, and that was getting out to hunt for the remedy. This, for young ladies in the eighteen-eighties, was a revolutionary discovery to have made. (*Earth Horizon,* 195)

And so Austin prescribed for herself what we might call the "walking cure," a regimen she kept up for the rest of her life.

The rediscovery of "The Yellow Wallpaper" in the 1970s and its rapid canonization made Weir Mitchell a notorious figure in an epidemic of feminist scholarship about women's health and the medical establishment, and about the rest cure and its role in the lives of such famous turn-of-the-century figures as Gilman, Edith Wharton, and Jane Addams.[8] Historians explored the misogynistic cultural implications in diagnoses of "hysteria" and "neurasthenia." But until recently, little attention has been paid to *male* neurasthenics and the cultural implications of their dis-ease with their gendered roles, although neurasthenia may have been "equally common among males and females."[9]

In 1885, the same year Dr. Hankins suggested to Austin that she do handwork by her fireside, Weir Mitchell treated Owen Wister, who had also suffered the kind of vague breakdown usually associated with neurasthenia. A talented musician, Wister had hoped to become a composer and had studied music in Europe, but his sharply critical father saw his accomplishments there as "stuffed with worthlessness, bad habits, and elements of failure" and insisted that he return to enter a brokerage firm, a job Wister detested. When he failed there, his father suggested law school.[10] Wister responded by completing a novel, *A Wise Man's Son,* not surprisingly "the story of a young man whose father forced him into business."[11] When he sent the book to W. D. Howells, his "mentor," Howells called it a "rebellious" work and recommended against Wister showing it to a publisher.[12] Wister accepted Howells's judgment, but his health collapsed, and he was sent to Mitchell. Mitchell prescribed "rest" to both male and female patients, but his definitions of what that constituted varied widely. He sent Wister west. His prescription: enjoy the stimulation of meeting new people, even "humble" ones, and live an active out-of-doors life; he specifically told Wister to take along riding clothes.[13] In 1886 he recommended the same trip to the artist Thomas Eakins after Eakins had been fired from the

Pennsylvania Academy of Fine Arts for pulling a loincloth off a male model in front of women students. Refining a famous phrase from Wister's Harvard classmate and longtime friend Theodore Roosevelt, who also went west following an undefined breakdown, we might term this advice "the strenuous rest cure."[14]

In many ways, Wister is a representative male neurasthenic. According to Anthony Rotundo, the disease afflicted "comfortably situated, middle-class men"; its most common symptoms were "insomnia, tension, depression, and (especially) fatigue accompanied by an utter lack of energy"; and it "was especially a disease of youth and early middle age." Neurasthenia was generally believed to be caused by overwork, and the usual recommendation was, logically enough, relaxation, or the "rest cure." In Rotundo's reading of the "cultural meaning" of the disease, "neurasthenia involved men's negative feelings about work."[15] In fact, breakdowns "often happened at times of vocational crisis" when men were trying to fulfill their fathers' or others' expectations about work. Rotundo continues:

> Looked at in terms of gender, male neurasthenia amounted to a flight from manhood. It not only meant a withdrawal from the central male activity of work, but it also involved a rejection of fundamental manly virtues—achievement, ambition, dominance, independence. A man who steered away from the middle-class work-world was avoiding a man's proper place. . . . A man who broke down was making a statement, however unconscious, of his negative feelings about middle-class work and the values and pressures surrounding it. In doing so, he made a gesture of serious opposition to manhood in his own time.[16]

As part of his "flight from manhood," the male neurasthenic "was also finding refuge in roles and behaviors marked 'female': vulnerability, dependence, passivity, invalidism. Even a man who traveled to recuperate was pursuing the life of cultivated leisure which was associated with women."[17]

Rotundo names William and Henry James, among others, as examples of men who traveled to recuperate, but his conclusion is based on European travel. Western travel offered men such as Wister a different resolution to their struggles with what was expected of them. Rather than offering a flight from manhood, it offered them what David Leverenz has called a "crucible for man-making."[18] If their breakdowns were caused by their uncertainty about how to go about achieving the "fundamental manly virtues" rather than by a rejection of them, the West provided new ways to attain them. In the West men could learn the self-assertion that would allow them to return to the civilized world and stake their claims. The West also provided new philosophies ("the strenuous life"); aphorisms or metaphors ("speak softly but carry a big stick"; "smile when you call me that"); and material (*The Virginian;* Francis Parkman's *The Oregon Trail* [1849]; Roosevelt's *Ranch Life and the Hunting-Trail* [1888]) men could use to achieve success. And if "lack of energy" was a covert expression for impotence, western travel was associated with vigor, with increased virility and power the traveler could carry home, like Roosevelt's famous "big stick," and put to use as he rejoined society.

Anxious men who could not afford a trip west could become armchair travelers, if we accept Jane Tompkins's analysis of the "cultural work" of the western, as developed around the turn of the century by Wister and Zane Grey, whose *Heritage of the Desert* (1910) is a particularly interesting companion piece to *Cactus Thorn*. Tompkins reads westerns as expressions of anxiety about the power of Victorian women's novels, which often present domesticated, demasculinized figures like the minister or the Christian male, and about "women's invasions of the public sphere between 1880 and 1920." Enacting "the destruction of female authority," the western "is about men's fear of losing their mastery, and hence their identity, both of which the western tirelessly reinvents."[19] Read in this context, *Cactus Thorn* is a satiric response to the western, showing the consequences of that reinvention.[20]

When we meet Austin's Grant Arliss, in "flight" from New York politics, he *has* lost his mastery, and he knows it (*Cactus Thorn,* 23). He has begun "to wonder [about] the mystery of his waning appetite for leadership, his reluctance to accept the opportunity held out to him" (12-13). A progressive reformer who has inspired his followers, Arliss lacks a "program"; although he has advocated "the elimination of private interest from public life," he has no "new system" to "justify" his protest (23, 18). But his immediate crisis is brought on by the necessity of forming a coalition with a powerful political patriarch, the "old war horse, Henry Russel Rittenhouse" (23). Arliss is not ready to play hardball with the big boys. "He had called upon himself to rise to the opportunity which he himself had created, and nothing came. In the face of the staring possibility that nothing would come from anywhere, Arliss broke into a sudden sweat of panic" (23). Austin's repeated sexual imagery, exaggerated to the point of satire, makes clear that she sees this anxiety attack as gendered. As if she hadn't made her point clear enough, Austin closes her paragraph by suggesting that the breakdown leads directly to feelings of "impotence" and "despair" (23).

As a reformer and a critic of American culture, Arliss has good reason to feel anxious about his masculinity. During the Progressive Era, the manhood of reformers was often challenged, either directly or through metaphors embedded in political language. Rotundo concludes that "the men who guarded the political arena," men like Henry Rittenhouse, "imagined that acting on reform impulses unsexed a person."[21] When Theodore Roosevelt was elected to the state assembly in 1882, newspaper writers referred to him as "Jane-Dandy" and "Punkin-Lily." If Gail Bederman is right that by "the last decades of the nineteenth century, middle-class power and authority were being challenged [by women, ethnic groups, and the working class] in a variety of ways which middle-class men interpreted—plausibly—as a challenge to their manhood," Arliss's political bedfellows raise questions about his virility.[22] Hence the pressure to earn the support of Henry Rittenhouse only reminds Arliss of his "unfruitful state," of the "nature of his present lack" (*Cactus Thorn,* 19, 21). No wonder he is anxious, unable to rise to what he sees as a challenge.

Despite the "years of European travel" that gave him the easy manner and knowledge on which he has built his political career, Arliss decides to "fle[e] westward" (*Cactus Thorn,* 17, 18). Austin connects Europe with the "spiritual lethargy" that would come to characterize modernism (17), and Arliss recognizes that he is in danger of becoming cowed and ineffectual, another Prufrock. As in the formula western of the period, the West offers a new world for another Adam, a place for a man to regenerate his "hope and faith," a setting for personal reinvention, for the liberation and satisfaction of desire (18). Seeking "the freedom he had come so far to find," Arliss sees the West as an agent in his renewal; he hopes to "find himself" and eagerly wonders "what the West might do to him" (7, 20).

Like many westerns, *Cactus Thorn* explores that very question. As we have seen, Austin believed in the West's healing powers, the opportunities it provided for challenging social convention. But she turns Arliss's question around: at what cost, at whose cost, his "recuperating powers" (61)? What might he "do" to the West, what "use" will he put it to? The West might indeed offer Arliss—and, through him, the United States—a regenerative social vision. In much of her own work Austin moved from personal to cultural healing and transformation, presenting the West and its regional cultures, its racial diversity, its landscape as offering a compelling alternative to what she saw as the sterile (perhaps even impotent) and empty despair of modernism, cut off from roots in real places.[23] Instead Arliss takes and uses the West, and its resources, to create a masculine image that will enable him to take power and make capital out of a symbolic mining of the West. Ironically, this reformer's achievement of a "healthy" manhood particularly rests on racial, gender, and class superiority.

Austin embodies the West in Dulcie Adelaid Vallodón, who seems to "have assembled herself from the tawny earth," a young woman capable of healing Arliss and guiding him to that redemptive social vision (4). In the most obvious sense, Arliss has a lay with the land, to paraphrase Annette Kolodny, and indeed he brings to the West the set of assumptions Kolodny explores, a yearning for a sexualized paradise available for his use.[24] Austin anticipates Kolodny's critique and allows the West to fight back. Devastating satire is Austin's sharpest weapon, her cactus thorn. Arliss, she suggests, uses Dulcie's body to achieve that "elusive quality of self-inflation called inspiration" (20). In many lines like this and in her image patterns, Austin deflates Arliss's "desire" to create a comic treatment of his "healing" as infatuation. Yet Arliss *does* return east with new vigor and authority as a result of his western experience. Austin is certainly satirizing the idea that sexual experience leads to male empowerment. But Arliss takes more than Dulcie's body. Because Austin makes so clear that Dulcie's "philosophy," her ways of seeing, her relationship to regional peoples, and her identity all represent her western experience and the land itself, Arliss's western "healing" comes at the expense of the West and represents an act of imperialism.

Dulcie has thought deeply on what the desert has to offer, on the sources of its "power," on how to "live sincerely," on how its lessons challenge "made up" social constructions of human behavior (75, 12). She is one of Austin's many far-seeing desert women, and as with the others, Austin connects her wisdom directly to her relationships with the land and with American Indians, in this case Paiutes. Significantly, Dulcie is not trying to become an Indian or to imitate or appropriate; she wants to learn. "When I'm out with the Indian women, . . . gathering roots and materials for basket making, it's not that I expect to make baskets or drink their medicine, it's the things you sort of soak up from the earth while you're with them, the things that make women wise. I don't know if I can explain—it's not as if they learned about willows and grasses in order to make baskets, but as if they learned to make baskets by knowing willows" (41). Dulcie learns that cultural production should follow from knowing and respecting the natural order of things. So, she believes, should social institutions: "You have to begin with what loving is, and cut your marriage accordingly" (12). She counters the "made-up ideas" of "society and religion and politics [and] the city" with an intense respect for and responsiveness to the desert, which exists in its own right, "goes on by itself, doing things that you don't see either the beginning of, or the end, except that it has very little to do with men" (46, 47). As Betsy Klimasmith has argued, Arliss "uses Dulcie's ideas to further his own career," recognizing "the appeal Dulcie's mysterious wisdom will have to other urbanites afflicted with ennui" (8–9).[25]

By attributing the source of Dulcie's ideas—"that mysterious wisdom which she shared with the Indian women," generated from knowledge of the processes of nature—Austin demonstrates that Arliss's successful new program appropriates others' lives and worldviews (54). (Austin might well be critiqued for romanticizing the "mysterious wisdom" of "others.") In fact, Arliss, who in his "unfruitful state" has been unable to "rise to the opportunity" presented by Henry Rittenhouse's daughter, Alida, repeatedly finds the "fruity brownness of [Dulcie's] skin" sexually exciting (14). Alida, it is apparent to Arliss, is "to be had and used only through marriage"; but he has quite different assumptions about Dulcie, whom Austin repeatedly connects to Indians and to Mexico, suggesting a mestizo heritage (22). Her indeterminate but certainly mixed racial background further embodies the multiracial, multicultural West that Austin so valued. Dulcie takes her last name from her mother, whom she describes as a "southerner," and in the context of this novel the south is Mexico. The prefix "Valla" suggests an opening between two natural elements, a junction, in Spanish. Her first name also underscores the connection. She is named Dulcie after her birthplace, Agua Dulce, or Sweetwater, a ranch with an artesian well. The weapon she will ultimately use against the invader, Arliss, was given to her mother by a Mexican admirer. On her guitar Dulcie plays Spanish melodies, perhaps "part of her mother's repertory" (55). She follows Mexican politics, noting with approval Arliss's assessment of the Mexican Revolution: "not that a bloody and violent revolution has occurred but that the political energy of a people has been set free for constructive activity"

(40).[26] Here as elsewhere, Dulcie is attracted to Arliss's apparently progressive politics because they seem to reflect her own beliefs, developed as a western outlier; her "program" would be based on cultural and racial intersections and blending. Like Gail Bederman, who points out that Roosevelt's phrase "the strenuous life," which became the mantra for progressive manhood, was actually the title to a speech he gave on imperialism, Austin explores the ways manhood, imperialist assumptions, and racism intersect.[27]

In a series of images that expose Arliss's hypocrisy about the use of the West's natural resources, Austin further suggests how his regeneration depends on exploitation. Inspired by Dulcie's ideas and body, Arliss, previously in a state of "dryness," finds that "the fountains of his mind [are] broken up" (19, 53). In further sexual satire, Austin shows how Arliss's mind flows from his body, symbolized by the previously clogged, "disused" fountain that Dulcie manages to "rehabilitate" (39). An artificial water source, the fountain was built at his absurd "Italian" villa by a local pocket miner, who, according to Dulcie, "just about tore the insides out of the hill, getting at the rich streaks" (39). Arliss's efforts to distance himself from this miner are telling. "Arliss found in her description his favorite indignation. That, he protested, was how men went about the earth, snatching and rending, and even as they tore at the hills for a handful of gain, they despoiled and exploited one another. Once he was launched on the social protest he slipped easily into the born politician's facility of denunciation, and quoted freely from himself" (39). Dulcie does not recognize Arliss's fundamental insincerity, although Austin's scathing narrative undermining tears away at his character; ultimately, of course, he will reveal himself as a version of the very men he critiques.

Austin makes these passages even more ironic by identifying Dulcie with the West's natural resources, particularly water and minerals, which lie deep within the earth, and the sun, associated with energy, passion, and desire. (A veritable ecosystem, Dulcie is also linked to plant and animal life.) As a westerner, Dulcie recognizes the inevitable scarcity of natural resources, and her beliefs are also based on a strong preservationist ethic that eventually causes her to question all forms of ownership. Repeated water imagery connects Dulcie to artesian wells, like that for which she was named. The Adelaid was a famous mine in Leadville that generated numerous battles over property rights, and Austin connects the mining of the desert to Dulcie's body in many passages: "From the mouth of the canyon they could see far up the range between the reddish flanks of the canon, the ruined scar of the mine" (39). (Austin met Georgia O'Keeffe at Luhan's house at about the time she was writing *Cactus Thorn*.) Indeed, Arliss is given directions to Dulcie by a "mining engineer" who explicitly connects sexual desire, manhood, and imperialistic urges: "'S a great country,' he said, letting his eyes wander from the high window to the round-bosomed hills and the cradling dip of the land seawards. 'And a man-size job to conquer her . . . make her bear . . . great civilizations'" (24). Feeling a "returning pulse of power" in response to the primitive, Arliss finds himself heating up in the presence of "this pale brown girl, as if she were, like the land, but the outward sheath of incredible hot forces" (20, 8). As he misreads the "flame-colored" cactus flower to which she is likened, Arliss misunderstands Dulcie's embodiment of the desert: she does open to the desert sun and heat, but her desire is not for self-inflation but for a receptivity to the life forces around her.

Arliss, whose politics have verged on socialism, returns to the East "in that mood of robust individualism which comes to a man satisfied in all his instincts" (59). Empowered by his man-size conquering, he has appropriated the desert's and Dulcie's sources of power and is now ready to inspire others. "Those of his followers who were privileged to hear Grant Arliss on his first platform appearance after his return from the West never forgot it. It was like hearing . . . him burst suddenly into full power. Younger men who had gathered around him chiefly out of their own desperate hope for *something,* some way out of their own political sterility, men who had felt that Arliss *could* produce the materials of fire, and had yet remained doubtful if he *would,* found themselves dazzled into confidence. Dazzled and yet warmed. There was a blaze" (79). Significantly, Arliss's "program" remains vague, lacks substance; it is his persona that has changed. "They found him greatly improved by his Western holiday. Filled out; bodily and, well, personally" (80). As Theodore Roosevelt did, Arliss uses the West to construct a new, virile self, even a new body.[28] With his fountain unplugged, he has learned how to negotiate with Henry Rittenhouse: he will seal their coalition by marrying Rittenhouse's daughter, who will become what he desires in a wife, a "fenced and valued possession" (54). He has learned the ways of capitalism. Alida is the medium of exchange that binds the two men together, and she will serve Arliss as she served her father: "Alida sat close to her father's elbow with that complete acceptance of [Arliss's] own as well as her father's importance and of herself as a suitable background for it" (81).

Her value depleted, her passion consumed, Dulcie is abandoned, "used—exploited," and she knows it (98). Arliss's power and authority have come at her expense. In the all-consuming, "faintly illuminated" city, where earth has turned to pavement and sun to "electric lamps," where the "piled-up plunder of the world . . . glittered from behind the plate glass windows," Dulcie appears to lose her power (84, 98, 97). Noting her "docility," Arliss pities her (96). But Austin's West is hardly docile, and Arliss can save his pity for himself, as is his practice: "The picture of himself as the source of suffering in others filled him with a sincere misery almost as acute as the thought of his own suffering at someone else's hands" (96). When Dulcie realizes the use to which Arliss has put the desert West's crucial lesson—the necessity "to live sincerely"—she enacts the threat that has been in evidence throughout the novella in the descriptions of natural forces (75). Austin manages to extend Arliss's hypocrisy into his grave. As he misreads the West, so does the eastern "public" misread the motives for his death: he is "remembered as martyr to the cause of justice and true democracy to which he had dedicated the life he lost" (98). The description of the murder weapon, a "dagger of foreign workmanship," tells two intertwined stories: it simultaneously reveals the racism of the authorities who associate all violence with "foreigners" and represents Austin's understanding of the very real rage of the colonized (99).

In the discrepancy between the public myth of Arliss's life and the covert truth, we can discover a clue to the cultural critique encoded in *Cactus Thorn,* a clue that takes us back to Tompkins's reading of the cultural work of the western. Throughout her career, in works as diverse as *The Basket Woman, The Ford,* and *Starry Adventure,* Austin attempted to deconstruct the social forces defining manhood and then reconstruct what it meant to be a man; many of her male characters develop a self-conscious sense of manhood by listening receptively to the lessons of the land and to ethnic voices. She naturally resisted the "tireless reinventions" of the violent, sexually dominant, and "masterful" masculinity in the western—and resisted even more the symbolic use of the West as embodied in land, women, and ethnic minorities. If male readers, suffering from the vague malaise about their manhood associated with neurasthenia, could go west with popular western heroes and experience a vicarious potency, the violence safely contained, then Austin would sharpen her cactus thorn, her tongue.[29] *Cactus Thorn* satirically undermines the dominance of the popular western's mythology, revealing its appropriations of the West and offering a threatening counternarrative of retaliation.

Of course, Austin too was putting the West to her own use, and she closes the novel with a characteristically romantic image of female escape. As a train carries Dulcie once more into the western landscape in "relief after great shock and pain," we return to the West as healing asylum (99). Austin's West is often a symbolic refuge for women outlaws on the run after expressing their rebellion and anger. Austin offers Dulcie sanctuary there as one who, unlike Arliss, can receive its riches without consuming them.

In a story she wrote some years before *Cactus Thorn,* Austin satirizes another hypocritical, "consumptive" man. I close my discussion with "A Case of Conscience" because in it Austin challenges even more directly the rights of outsiders to use and appropriate a racialized West. Saunders, the narrator tells us immediately, is "an average Englishman with a lung complaint" who comes west to be cured.[30] At Ubehebe, the same Maiden's Breast Arliss heads for to find Dulcie, Saunders meets Turwhasé, a Shoshone, and begins to live with her. They have a child. "Turwhasé," the narrator says, "was as much married as if Church and State had witnessed it; as for Saunders, society, life itself, had cast him off" (48). The narrator sarcastically suggests that Saunders's story hints at "the myth of the renewal of life in a virgin embrace" (48). After a visit to a doctor he suddenly finds himself cured, able to return home. There is no question of taking Turwhasé; Saunders knows he can make a "very good marriage at home" (48). But out of a sense of duty, he decides to take his half-breed child.

Saunders soon regrets his decision: the child pines; strangers look at his "brat" with scorn; he pays a woman to keep the child out of his sight. Then he is confronted by Turwhasé, who has tracked him for four days. "'My baby!' she said. 'Give it to me! . . . Mine!' she said, fiercely. 'Mine, not yours!'" (50). He hands her the baby and then takes out all his money and "pour[s] it in her bosom." Turwhasé laughs, scatters the coins on the ground, and walks away "with dignity" (50). Saunders, a "smug" Englishman, returns to his colonial empire. But Turwhasé keeps her baby—and the West holds onto its future.

NOTES

1. Mabel Dodge Luhan, "Mary Austin: A Woman," in *Mary Austin: A Memorial,* ed. Willard Hoagland (Santa Fe: Laboratory of Anthropology, 1944), 21.

2. Luhan goes on to assume that Austin committed her "destruction" of Steffens in *No. 26 Jayne Street* (1920), which is certainly true. And yet Austin claims in *Earth Horizon* that she wrote *Jayne Street* in New York, and while she savagely ridicules the politician based on Steffens, he is very much alive at the novel's end. It is much more likely she was "done in"

by writing the ending of *Cactus Thorn,* never published during her lifetime but written in New Mexico.

3. Mary Austin, *Earth Horizon* (1932; reprint, Albuquerque: University of New Mexico Press, 1991), 337. Subsequent parenthetical page numbers refer to this edition.

4. Mary Austin, *Cactus Thorn,* ed. Melody Graulich (Reno: University of Nevada Press, 1988), 22, 13, 23. Subsequent parenthetical page numbers refer to this edition.

5. Gail Bederman, *Manliness and Civilization: A Cultural History of Race and Gender in the United States, 1880-1917* (Chicago: University of Chicago Press, 1995), 11.

6. Mary Austin, "The Walking Woman," in *Western Trails: A Collection of Stories by Mary Austin,* ed. Melody Graulich (Reno: University of Nevada Press, 1987), 93. Subsequent parenthetical page numbers refer to this edition.

7. For a fuller treatment of their relationship and their mutual influence, see Melody Graulich, "'I Thought at First She Was Talking about Herself': Mary Austin on Charlotte Perkins Gilman," *Jack London Journal* 1.1 (1994): 148-58. I see the encounter between these two women who had so much in common and so much to share as significantly shaping Austin's fiction, particularly such stories as "The Walking Woman" and "Frustrate," in which two women come together in transformative moments. Austin definitely knew "The Yellow Wallpaper"; there was a copy in her library when she died, inscribed "To Mary Austin— with real admiration and interest. Charlotte Perkins Gilman 1910."

Cather's Thea Kronborg of *The Song of the Lark* (1915), a novel surely influenced by Austin's work, is another fictional heroine who recovers in the West and realizes her artistic potential there.

8. For a particularly balanced treatment of Mitchell, see Suzanne Poirier, "The Weir Mitchell Rest Cure: Doctor and Patients," *Women's Studies* 10 (1983): 15-40.

9. E. Anthony Rotundo, *American Manhood: Transformations in Masculinity from the Revolution to the Modern Era* (New York: Basic Books, 1993), 189.

10. Darwin Payne, *Owen Wister: Chronicler of the West, Gentleman of the East* (Dallas: Southern Methodist University Press, 1985), 66.

11. Jane Tompkins, *West of Everything: The Inner Life of Westerns* (New York: Oxford University Press, 1992), 136.

12. Payne, *Owen Wister,* 74.

13. Ibid., 76.

14. In fact, while some critics have focused on the extreme inactivity and isolation of Mitchell's rest cure as portrayed by Gilman, he prescribed widely various treatments. He often sent both men and women to Europe for "vacations," treatment he had recommended for both of Wister's parents.

15. Rotundo, *American Manhood,* 185-86, 190.

16. Ibid., 191-93.

17. Ibid., 191.

18. David Leverenz, "The Last Real Man in America: From Natty Bumppo to Batman," in *The American Literary History Reader,* ed. Gordon Hutner (New York: Oxford University Press, 1995), 273.

19. Tompkins, *West of Everything,* 9, 44-45.

20. For an excellent discussion of Austin's "The Walking Woman" as a revision of formula westerns in the context of Progressive Era politics, see Faith Jaycox's "Regeneration

through Liberation: Mary Austin's 'The Walking Woman' and Western Narrative Formula," *Legacy* 6.1 (1989): 5-12.

21. Rotundo, *American Manhood,* 272. Rotundo quotes a wonderful passage by Senator John Ingalls of Kansas (from 1886), who said that male reformers were "effeminate without being either masculine or feminine; unable to beget or bear; possessing neither fecundity nor virility; endowed with the contempt of men and the derision of women, and doomed to sterility, isolation and extinction" (272).

22. Bederman, *Manliness and Civilization,* 10, 170.

23. For a more extended discussion of how the "radical visionaries" who moved to New Mexico after World War I saw it as a "fertile ground on which to rebuild the world," in sharp contrast to European-based or urban modernism, see Lois Rudnick's *Utopian Vistas: The Mabel Dodge Luhan House and the American Counterculture* (Albuquerque: University of New Mexico Press, 1996), 33. Rudnick points out that "[t]he Anglo expatriates' hunger for spiritual and psychic renewal often blinded them to the more unpleasant social, political, and economic realities that surrounded them," particularly the exploitation of racial minorities, both economically and culturally (35). Throughout her career Austin was certainly susceptible to that critique; the portrayal of "Indian George" and Catameneda as servants in *Cactus Thorn* seems unexamined, though perhaps Arliss misunderstands their role in Dulcie's life. But in her portrayal of Arliss, Austin removes the blinders.

24. Annette Kolodny, *The Lay of the Land: Metaphor as Experience and History in American Life and Letters* (Chapel Hill: University of North Carolina Press, 1975).

25. Betsy Klimasmith, "Storytellers, Story-Sellers: Artists, Muses, and Exploitation in the Work of Mary Austin," *Southwestern American Literature* 20.2 (1995): 8-9. Austin is certainly open to charges of romanticizing and appropriating American Indian materials herself, an issue explored by other essays in this volume. In "Storytellers, Story-Sellers," Klimasmith presents a compelling reading of the differences between Austin's narrators and Arliss in their approach to their "subjects."

26. Throughout her life, but especially around the time she was writing *Cactus Thorn,* Austin was intrigued by the cultural influence of Mexico on the southwestern United States. She was much involved in the Spanish colonial arts movement and in supporting and developing programs for bilingual education for Spanish-speaking children. In 1930, she went to Mexico, a trip she found profoundly moving; she described herself as "overflow[ing] with tears" when viewing the murals of Diego Rivera, whom she also met, and as seeing many intersections between his work and hers (*Earth Horizon,* 365).

27. Bederman, *Manliness and Civilization,* 184.

28. In *Theodore Roosevelt: A Life* (New York: William Morrow, 1992), Nathan Miller discusses how Roosevelt used his western experience to construct a new image:

> Roosevelt had three major liabilities in politics: he was an aristocrat, he was an intellectual, and he was an easterner. Altogether, he spent only about three years in the Bad Lands, a period interrupted by sometimes lengthy stays in the East. Yet he so successfully identified himself with the West that for the remainder of his life, the public thought of him as a rough-riding cowboy rather than a New York dude. This western experience removed the stigma of effeminacy, ineffectuality, and intellectualism that clung to most reformers. (163-64)

In *Earth Horizon,* Austin comments that she and Roosevelt were "rather good friends" during the years she lived in New York (324).

29. Despite one recent U.S. president's personification of the western reader as male, there has been considerable debate about who actually reads westerns. In "Zane Grey's Western Eroticism," for instance, William Bloodworth suggests that Grey, who sometimes published in women's magazines, wrote for women readers (*South Dakota Review* 23.3 [1985]: 5-14). While I, like Tompkins, find Grey's westerns "thrilling," I think Austin would have seen the popular western as appealing primarily to male fantasies about the West.

30. Mary Austin, "A Case of Conscience," in *Western Trails,* 44. Page numbers follow subsequent quotations in the text.

Works Cited

Abel, Elizabeth, Marianne Hirsch, and Elizabeth Langland, eds. *The Voyage In: Fictions of Female Development*. Hanover: University Press of New England, 1983.

Adams, Ansel. "Notes on Mary Austin." In *Mary Hunter Austin: Author, Poet, Lecturer, Naturalist*, 7. Independence, Calif.: Mary Austin Home, 1968.

Agnew, Jean-Christophe. "A House of Fiction." In *Consuming Visions*, ed. Simon J. Bronner. New York: Norton, 1989.

Alcott, Louisa. *Little Women*. 1869. Reprint. New York: Random House, 1983.

Allen, Paula Gunn. "Meanings." In *Symposium of the Whole*, ed. Jerome Rothenberg, 173-87. Berkeley: University of California Press, 1983.

Almaguer, Tomás. *Racial Fault Lines: The Historical Origins of White Supremacy in California*. Berkeley: University of California Press, 1994.

"The American Deserts." *National Geographic* 15 (1904): 152-63.

Ammons, Elizabeth. *Conflicting Stories: American Women Writers at the Turn into the Twentieth Century*. New York: Oxford University Press, 1991.

Applegate, Richard B. *Atishwin*. Socorro, N.Mex.: Ballena Press, 1978.

Armitage, Shelley. "Mary Austin: Writing Nature." In *Wind's Trail: The Early Life of Mary Austin*, by Peggy Pond Church. Ed. Shelley Armitage. Santa Fe: Museum of New Mexico Press, 1990.

Armitage, Susan. "Through Women's Eyes: A New View of the West." In *The Women's West*, ed. Susan Armitage and Elizabeth Jameson, 9-18. Norman: University of Oklahoma Press, 1987.

Ashcroft, Bill, Gareth Griffiths, and Helen Tiffin. Introduction to *The Post-Colonial Studies Reader*, ed. Bill Ashcroft, Gareth Griffiths, and Helen Tiffin, 7-11. New York: Routledge, 1995.

Auster, Albert. *Actresses and Suffragists: Women in the American Theater, 1890-1920*. New York: Praeger, 1984.

Austin, Mary Hunter. "Aboriginal American Literature." Mary Austin Collection, Box 25. Huntington Library, San Marino, California.

——. "The American Form of the Novel." 1922. In *Beyond Borders: The Selected Essays of*

Mary Austin. Ed. Reuben J. Ellis, 84-88. Carbondale: Southern Illinois University Press, 1996.

——. *The American Rhythm.* New York: Harcourt, Brace, 1923.

——. *The American Rhythm: Studies and Reexpressions of Amerindian Songs.* Boston: Houghton Mifflin, 1930.

——. *The Arrow-Maker.* 1911. Rev. ed. Boston: Houghton Mifflin, 1915.

——. *The Basket Woman: A Book of Fanciful Tales for Children.* Boston: Houghton Mifflin, 1904.

——. *The Basket Woman: A Book of Indian Tales for Children.* Boston: Houghton, 1910.

——. *The Basket Woman: A Book of Indian Tales.* Reprint. Reno: University of Nevada Press, 1999.

——. *Beyond Borders: The Selected Essays of Mary Austin.* Ed. Reuben J. Ellis. Carbondale: Southern Illinois University, 1996.

——. *Cactus Thorn.* Reno: University of Nevada Press, 1988.

——. *California: Land of the Sun.* New York: Macmillan, 1914.

——. "Caller of Buffalo." *Poetry* (June 1928): 32.

——. "Campo Santo at San Juan." In *Mary Austin: Woman of Genius.* Ed. Helen M. Doyle, 228-29. New York: Gotham House, 1939.

——. "Can Prayer Be Answered?" Installments I and II. *Forum* 91 (1934): 269-72, 363-66.

——. *The Children Sing in the Far West.* Boston: Houghton Mifflin, 1928.

——. *Christ in Italy.* New York: Duffield, 1912.

——. "The Colorado River Controversy." *Nation,* 9 November 1927, 510-12.

——. "The Colorado River Project and the Culture of the Southwest." *Southwest Review* 13 (1922): 110-15.

——. "The Coyote Doctor." Unpublished play in the Mary Austin Collection. Huntington Library, San Marino, California.

——. "The Divorcing of Sina." *Sunset* 40 (January-June 1918): 26-30.

——. "Do We Need a New Religion?" *Century* 100 (September 1923): 756-64.

——. *Earth Horizon: Autobiography.* 1932. Reprint. Albuquerque: University of New Mexico Press, 1991.

——. *Everyman's Genius.* Indianapolis: Bobbs-Merrill, 1925.

——. *Experiences Facing Death.* Indianapolis: Bobbs-Merrill, 1931.

——. *Fire: A Drama in Three Acts.* Published serially in *Play-book* [of the Wisconsin Dramatic Society] 2 (October-December 1914): 3-25, 11-26, 18-30.

——. *The Flock.* Boston: Houghton, 1906. Reprint. Reno: University of Nevada Press, forthcoming.

——. "The Folk Story in America." *South Atlantic Quarterly* 33 (January 1934): 10-19.

——. *The Ford.* Boston: Houghton Mifflin, 1917. Reprint. Berkeley: University of California Press, 1997.

——. "Frustrate." In *Western Trails: A Collection of Stories by Mary Austin.* Ed. Melody Graulich, 228-35. Reno: University of Nevada Press, 1987.

——. "The Future of the Southwest." *New Republic,* 8 April 1925, 186.

——. "Greatness in Women." *North American Review* 217 (January-June 1923): 197-203.

——. *The Green Bough—Tale of the Resurrection.* Garden City, N.Y.: Doubleday, 1913.

——. "Home Thoughts in the City." *Folksay IV* (1932): 91.

———. "How I Learned to Read and Write." Reprinted in *My First Publication,* ed. James D. Hart. San Francisco: Book Club of California, 1961.

———. "How I Would Sell My Book, 'Rhythm.'" *Bookseller and Stationer,* 1 May 1923, 7.

———. "Imagism: Original and Aboriginal." *Dial,* 23 August 1919, 163.

———. "Indian Arts for Indians." *Survey* 60 (1 July 1928): 381-88.

———. "The Indivisible Utility." *Survey Graphic* 8 (1925): 301-6.

———. Introduction to *American Indian Poetry: An Anthology of Songs and Chants,* ed. George W. Cronyn. 1918. Reprint. New York: Ballantine Books, 1991.

———. Introduction to *The Path on the Rainbow,* ed. George W. Cronyn. 1918. Reprint. New York: Liveright, 1934.

———. *Isidro.* Boston: Houghton Mifflin, 1905.

———. *The Land of Journeys' Ending.* 1924. Reprint. Tucson: University of Arizona Press, 1983.

———. *The Land of Little Rain.* 1903. Reprint. Albuquerque: University of New Mexico Press, 1974; New York: Penguin Books, 1988.

———. *The Land of Little Rain.* 1903. In *Stories from the Country of Lost Borders.* Ed. Marjorie Pryse. New Brunswick: Rutgers University Press, 1987.

———. Letter to Carey McWilliams, 29 April 1932. Quoted in Benay Blend, "Mary Austin and the Western Conservation Movement." *Journal of the Southwest* 30.1 (1988): 12.

———. Letter to Ferris Greenslet, 11 November 1918. Reprinted in *I-Mary: A Biography of Mary Austin,* by Augusta Fink, 185. Tucson: University of Arizona Press, 1983.

———. Letter to Franklin K. Lane, 16 January 1919. Box 1, Mary Austin Collection, Huntington Library, San Marino, California.

———. *Literary America, 1903-1934: The Mary Austin Letters.* Ed. T. M. Pearce. Westport, Conn.: Greenwood Press, 1979.

———. *Lost Borders.* New York: Harper Brothers, 1909.

———. *Lost Borders.* In *Stories from the Country of Lost Borders.* Ed. Marjorie Pryse, 155-263. New Brunswick: Rutgers University Press, 1987.

———. *Love and the Soul Maker.* New York: Appleton, 1914.

———. "Mahala Joe." *Atlantic Monthly* 94 (1904): 44-53.

———. *The Man Jesus.* New York: Harper, 1915.

———. Mary Hunter Austin Collection. Henry F. Huntington Library, San Marino, California.

———. "Night Wind, Wake!" *Out West* (April 1904): 318.

———. "Not to You Only, O Pythian." *Nation,* 1 December 1926, 601.

———. *One-Smoke Stories.* Boston: Houghton, 1934.

———. "The Owens River Water Project." *San Francisco Chronicle,* 3 September 1905, 19.

———. "Poetry in the Education of Children." *Bookman* (November 1928): 270-73.

———. "Regionalism in American Fiction." In *Beyond Borders: The Selected Essays of Mary Austin.* Ed. Reuben J. Ellis, 130-40. Carbondale: Southern Illinois University Press, 1996.

———. "Religion in the United States." *Century* 104 (August 1922): 527-38.

———. "Rio Abajo." *Saturday Review of Literature,* 12 April 1930, 1.

———. "The Song-Makers." *North American Review* 194 (August 1911): 239-47.

———. *Stories from the Country of Lost Borders.* Ed. Marjorie Pryse. New Brunswick: Rutgers University Press, 1987.

———. *Western Trails: A Collection of Stories by Mary Austin.* Ed. Melody Graulich. Reno: University of Nevada Press, 1987.

——. "Woman Alone." *Nation* 124, 2 March 1927.

——. *A Woman of Genius.* New York: Doubleday, Page, 1912. Reprint. Old Westbury, N.Y.: Feminist Press, 1985.

——. *The Young Woman Citizen.* New York: Woman's Press, 1918.

Bailey, Liberty Hyde. *The State and the Farmer.* New York: Macmillan, 1908.

Bakhtin, M. M. *Speech Genres and Other Late Essays.* Ed. Caryl Emerson and Michael Holquist. Trans. Vern W. McGee. Austin: University of Texas Press, 1986.

Banta, Martha. *Imaging American Women.* New York: Columbia University Press, 1987.

Barthes, Roland. "Theory of the Text." In *Untying the Text: A Poststructuralist Reader,* ed. Robert Young, 31–45. New York: Routledge, 1990.

Bean, Lowell J. "The Artist and the Shamanic Tradition." In *Ethnology of the Alta California Indians II: Postcontact,* ed. Lowell J. Bean and Sylvia B. Vane, 963–70. New York: Garland, 1991.

Bean, Lowell J., Sylvia Brakke Vane, and Jackson Young. *The Cahuilla Landscape: The Santa Rosa and San Jacinto Mountains.* Menlo Park, Calif.: Ballena Press, 1991.

Bean, Walton, and James J. Rawls. *California: An Interpretive History.* 5th ed. New York: Mc-Graw-Hill, 1988.

Beck, Peggy V., Anna Lee Walters, and Nia Francisco. *The Sacred: Ways of Knowledge, Sources of Life.* Redesigned ed. Tsaile, Ariz.: Navajo CC Press, 1992.

Bederman, Gail. *Manliness and Civilization: A Cultural History of Race and Gender in the United States, 1880-1917.* Chicago: University of Chicago Press, 1995.

Bellamy, Edward. *Looking Backward.* 1887. Reprint. New York: Penguin Books, 1982.

Berkhofer, Robert F., Jr. *The White Man's Indian.* New York: Vintage Books, 1978.

Blackburn, Thomas C., ed. *Flowers of the Wind: Papers on Ritual, Myth, and Symbolism in California and the Southwest.* Socorro, N.Mex.: Ballena Press, 1977.

Blackburn, Thomas C., and Kat Anderson. *Before the Wilderness: Environmental Management by Native Californians.* Menlo Park, Calif.: Ballena Press, 1993.

Blend, Benay. "Mary Austin and the Western Conservation Movement." *Journal of the Southwest* 30.1 (1988): 12–34.

Bloodworth, William. "Zane Grey's Western Eroticism." *South Dakota Review* 23.3 (Autumn 1985): 5–14.

Blunt, Alison, and Gillian Rose, eds. *Writing Women and Space: Colonial and Postcolonial Geographies.* New York: Guilford Press, 1994.

Borah, Woodrow W. "The California Mission." In *Ethnic Conflict in California History,* ed. Charles Wollenberg, 1–22. Los Angeles: Tinnon Brown, 1970.

Bourdieu, Pierre. *Distinction: A Social Critique of the Judgement of Taste.* Cambridge: Harvard University Press, 1984.

Bowen, Ezra. *The High Sierra: The American Wilderness.* Time-Life Books. Washington, D.C.: Time, Inc., 1972.

Bratton, Susan P. *Christianity, Wilderness, and Wildlife: The Original Desert Solitaire.* Scranton: University of Scranton Press; London: Associated University Presses, 1993.

Bredahl, A. Carl, Jr. *New Ground: Western American Narrative and the Literary Canon.* Chapel Hill: University of North Carolina Press, 1989.

Brooks, Paul. *Speaking for Nature: How Literary Naturalists from Henry Thoreau to Rachel Car-*

son Have Shaped America. Boston: Houghton Mifflin, 1980.

Buell, Lawrence. *The Environmental Imagination: Thoreau, Nature Writing, and the Formation of American Culture.* Cambridge: Harvard University Press, 1995.

——. "The Thoreauvian Pilgrimage: The Structure of an American Cult." *American Literature* 61.2 (1989): 175–99.

Burroughs, John. "The Literary Treatment of Nature." *Atlantic Monthly* 94 (1904): 38–43.

Butler, Judith. *Gender Trouble: Feminism and the Subversion of Identity.* New York: Routledge, 1990.

Cahan, Abraham. *The Rise of David Levinsky.* 1917. Reprint. New York: Harper Torchbooks, 1960.

Castro, Michael. *Interpreting the Indian: Twentieth-Century Poets and Native Americans.* Albuquerque: University of New Mexico Press, 1983.

Cather, Willa. *O Pioneers!* 1913. Reprint. New York: Penguin Books, 1989.

——. *The Song of the Lark.* 1915. Reprint. Boston: Houghton Mifflin, 1988.

Chandler, Alfred D. *The Visible Hand: The Managerial Revolution in American Business.* Cambridge: Harvard University Press, 1977.

Chapman, Robert H. "The Deserts of Nevada and the Death Valley: U.S. Geological Survey." *National Geographic* 17 (1906): 482–97.

Chase, J. Smeaton. *Our Araby: Palm Springs and the Garden of the Sun.* New York: Little, 1923.

Cheyfitz, Eric. *The Poetics of Imperialism: Translation and Colonization from "The Tempest" to "Tarzan."* New York: Oxford University Press, 1991.

——. "Savage Law: The Plot against American Indians in *Johnson and Graham's Lesee v. M'Intosh* and *The Pioneers.*" In *Cultures of United States Imperialism,* ed. Amy Kaplan and Donald E. Pease, 109–28. Durham: Duke University Press, 1993.

Church, Peggy Pond. *Wind's Trail: The Early Life of Mary Austin.* Santa Fe: Museum of New Mexico, 1990.

Cixous, Hélène. "The Laugh of the Medusa." In *Feminisms: An Anthology of Literary Theory and Criticism,* ed. Robyn Warhol and Diane Price Herndl, 34–49. New Brunswick: Rutgers University Press, 1991.

Cohen, Felix. *Handbook of Federal Indian Law.* Washington, D.C.: Government Printing Office, 1942.

Commissioner of Indian Affairs. *Annual Report.* Washington, D.C.: Government Printing Office, 1934.

Congressional Record. 62.12 (11 September 1922). 67th Cong., 2d Session. Washington, D.C.: Government Printing Office, 1922.

Cott, Nancy F. *The Grounding of Modern Feminism.* New Haven: Yale University Press, 1987.

Cronon, William. *Nature's Metropolis: Chicago and the Great West.* New York: Norton, 1991.

——, ed. *Uncommon Ground: Rethinking the Human Place in Nature.* New York: Norton, 1996.

Cummins, Marjorie. *The Tache-Yokuts: Indians of the San Joaquin Valley.* Fresno: Pioneer, 1978.

Davis, Tracy C. *Actresses as Working Women: Their Social Identity in Victorian Culture.* London: Routledge, 1991.

d'Azevedo, Warren L., ed. *Great Basin.* Vol. 11 of *Handbook of North American Indians.* Washington, D.C.: Smithsonian Institution Press, 1986.

Denning, Michael. *Mechanic Accents: Dime Novels and Working-Class Culture in America.* New York: Verso, 1987.

Diamond, Irene, and Gloria Feman Orenstein, eds. *Reweaving the World: The Emergence of Ecofeminism.* San Francisco: Sierra Club, 1990.

Dizard, Jan E. *Going Wild: Hunting, Animal Rights, and the Contested Meaning of Nature.* Amherst: University of Massachusetts Press, 1994.

Donovan, Josephine. *Feminist Theory.* New York: Continuum, 1993.

Douglas, Mary, and Baron Isherwood. *The World of Goods: Towards an Anthropology of Consumption.* New York: Norton, 1978.

Doyle, Helen MacKnight. *Mary Austin: Woman of Genius.* New York: Gotham House, 1939.

Dredd, Firmin. "The Extinction of the Dime Novel." *Bookman* (March 1900): 46-48.

Dreiser, Theodore. *Sister Carrie.* 1907. Reprint. New York: Bantam Books, 1992.

Dudden, Faye E. *Women in the American Theater: Actresses and Audiences, 1790-1870.* New Haven: Yale University Press, 1994.

Duvert, Elizabeth. "With Stone, Star and Earth: The Presence of the Archaic in the Landscape Visions of Georgia O'Keeffe, Nancy Holt, and Michelle Stuart." In *The Desert Is No Lady: Southwestern Landscapes in Women's Writing and Art,* ed. Vera Norwood and Janice Monk, 197-222. New Haven: Yale University Press, 1987.

Dyer, Richard. "White." *Screen* 29.4 (1988): 44-64.

Eby, Clare Virginia. "*The Octopus:* Big Business as Art." *American Literary Realism* 26 (1994): 33-51.

Eliot, T. S. "Burnt Norton." In *Four Quartets: The Centenary Edition.* San Diego: Harcourt Brace Jovanovich, 1988.

Ellis, Reuben J. Introduction to *Beyond Borders: The Selected Essays of Mary Austin,* 1-21. Carbondale: Southern Illinois University Press, 1996.

Emerson, Ralph Waldo. "Experience." 1844. In *The Oxford Authors: Ralph Waldo Emerson.* Ed. Richard Poirier, 216-34. Oxford: Oxford University Press, 1990.

——. "Nature." 1836. In *The Oxford Authors: Ralph Waldo Emerson.* Ed. Richard Poirier, 2-36. Oxford: Oxford University Press, 1990.

——. "Self-Reliance." 1841. In *The Oxford Authors: Ralph Waldo Emerson.* Ed. Richard Poirier, 131-51. Oxford: Oxford University Press, 1990.

——. "The Young American." 1844. In *Collected Works,* 2:363-95. Boston: Houghton Mifflin, 1921.

Ernst, Eldon G. "American Religious History from a Pacific Coast Perspective." In *Religion and Society in the American West: Historical Essays,* ed. Carl Guarneri and David Alvarez, 3-39. New York: University Press of America, 1987.

Fergusson, Erna. "Crusade from Santa Fé." *North American Review* 242 (1937): 377-79.

Fink, Augusta. *I-Mary: A Biography of Mary Austin.* Tucson: University of Arizona Press, 1983.

Flaceliere, Robert. *Greek Oracles.* Trans. Douglas Garman. New York: Norton, 1965.

Foote, Mary Hallock. "The Fate of a Voice." In *The Last Assembly Ball.* Boston: Houghton Mifflin, 1889.

Foucault, Michel. "The Order of Discourse." In *Untying the Text: A Poststructuralist Reader,* ed. Robert Young, 48-78. New York: Routledge, 1990.

Franchot, Jenny. *Roads to Rome: The Antebellum Protestant Encounter with Catholicism.* Berkeley: University of California Press, 1994.

Frost, Richard. "The Romantic Inflation of Pueblo Culture." *American West* (January-February 1980): 5-9, 56-60.

Fryer, Judith. "Desert, Rock, Shelter, Legend: Willa Cather's Novels of the Southwest." In *The Desert Is No Lady: Southwestern Landscapes in Women's Writing and Art,* ed. Vera Norwood and Janice Monk, 27-46. New Haven: Yale University Press, 1987.

Fuss, Diane. "Reading Like a Feminist." *Differences* 1 (Summer 1998): 77-92.

Garber, Marjorie. *Vested Interests: Cross-Dressing and Cultural Anxiety.* New York: Routledge, 1992.

Gelfant, Blanche. "What More Can Carrie Want? Naturalistic Ways of Consuming Women." *Prospects: An Annual of American Cultural Studies* 19 (1994): 389-405.

Gilbert, Sandra M. "Costumes of the Mind: Transvestism as Metaphor in Modern Literature." *Critical Inquiry* (Winter 1980): 391-417.

Gilbert, Sandra M., and Susan Gubar. *No Man's Land: The Place of the Woman Writer in the 20th Century.* 2 vols. Vol. 1: *War of the Words.* Vol. 2: *Sexchanges.* New Haven: Yale University Press, 1988, 1989.

Gilot, Françoise, and Carlton Lake. *Life with Picasso.* New York: Anchor Books, 1989.

Glimp, Hudson A., Donald G. Ely, James Gerrish, Ed Houston, Rodney Knott, Dan Morrical, Bok Sowell, Charles Taylor, and Robert Van Keuren. "Rangelands, Pasture and Forage Crops." In *Sheep Production Handbook.* Englewood, Calif.: American Sheep Industry Association, forthcoming.

Glotfelty, Cheryll, and Harold Fromm, eds. *The Ecocriticism Reader: Landmarks in Literary Ecology.* Athens: University of Georgia Press, 1996.

Grant, Campbell. "Interior Chumash." In *California,* ed. Robert F. Heizer, 530-37. Vol. 8 of *Handbook of North American Indians.* Washington, D.C.: Smithsonian Institution Press, 1978.

Graulich, Melody. "A Book You Could Walk around In." Afterword to *Earth Horizon,* by Mary Austin. Albuquerque: University of New Mexico Press, 1991.

———. Afterword to *Cactus Thorn,* by Mary Austin. Reno: University of Nevada Press, 1988.

———. Introduction to and biography in *Western Trails: A Collection of Short Stories by Mary Austin.* Ed. Melody Graulich, 1-18. Reno: University of Nevada Press, 1987.

———. Introduction to *The Trail Book,* by Mary Austin. 1918. Reprint. Reno: University of Nevada Press, forthcoming.

———. "'I Thought at First She Was Talking about Herself': Mary Austin on Charlotte Perkins Gilman." *Jack London Journal* 1.1 (1994): 148-58.

———. "Mary, Mary, Quite Contrary." Review of *I-Mary,* by Augusta Fink. *Women's Review of Books* (January 1984): 16-17.

———. "'O Beautiful for Spacious Guys': An Essay on 'the Legitimate Inclinations of the Sexes.'" In *The Frontier Experience and the American Dream,* ed. David Mogen, Paul Bryant, and Mark Busby, 186-201. College Station: Texas A&M University Press, 1989.

Green, Rayna. "The Tribe Called Wannabee." *Folklore* 99 (1988): 30-55.

Griffin, Susan. "Curves along the Road." In *Reweaving the World: The Emergence of Ecofeminism,* ed. Irene Diamond and Gloria Feman Orenstein, 87-99. San Francisco: Sierra Club, 1990.

———. "Split Culture." In *Healing the Wounds: The Promise of Ecofeminism,* ed. Judith Plant, 7-17. Philadelphia: New Society, 1989.

Grinnell, George Bird. "Little Friend Coyote." *Harper's Monthly* (1902): 102.

Guarneri, Carl, and David Alvarez, eds. *Religion and Society in the American West: Historical Es-*

says. Lanham, Md.: University Press of America, 1987.

Guest, Francis F. "The Franciscan World View." In *New Directions in California History: A Book of Readings,* ed. James J. Rawls, 26-33. New York: McGraw-Hill, 1988.

H.D. [Hilda Doolittle]. *Selected Poems.* Ed. Louis L. Martz. New York: New Directions, 1988.

Halttunen, Karen. "From Parlor to Living Room: Domestic Taste, Interior Decoration and the Culture of Personality." In *Consuming Visions,* ed. Simon J. Bronner, 157-89. New York: Norton, 1989.

Haraway, Donna. "The Actors Are Cyborg, Nature Is Coyote, and the Geography Is Elsewhere: Postscript to 'Cyborgs at Large.'" In *Technoculture,* ed. Constance Penley and Andrew Ross. Cultural Politics 3. Minneapolis: University of Minnesota Press, 1991.

———. *Simians, Cyborgs, and Women: The Reinvention of Nature.* New York: Routledge, 1991.

Harding, Sandra. "Reinventing Ourselves as Other: More New Agents of History and Knowledge." In *American Feminist Thought at Century's End,* ed. Linda S. Kauffman, 140-64. Cambridge, Mass.: Blackwell Press, 1993.

Hart, Lynda. "'Til Death Do Us Part: Impossible Spaces in *Thelma and Louise*." *Journal of the History of Sexuality* 4.3 (1994): 430-46.

Harvey, Charles M. "The Indian of To-day and To-morrow." *American Review of Reviews* (June 1906): 697. Reprinted in *The Vanishing American: White Attitudes and U.S. Indian Policy,* by Brian Dippie, 97-98. Middletown: Wesleyan University Press, 1982.

Harvey, David. *Justice, Nature and the Geography of Difference.* Cambridge, Mass.: Blackwell, 1996.

Hays, Samuel P. *Conservation and the Gospel of Efficiency: The Progressive Conservation Movement, 1890-1920.* Cambridge: Harvard University Press, 1959.

Heizer, Robert F., ed. *California.* Vol. 8 of *Handbook of the North American Indians.* Washington, D.C.: Smithsonian Institution Press, 1978.

Hennesey, James. "Roman Catholics and American Politics, 1900-1960." In *Religion and American Politics from the Colonial Period to the 1980s,* ed. Mark A. Noll, 302-21. New York: Oxford University Press, 1990.

Hirsch, Marianne. *The Mother-Daughter Plot: Narrative, Psychoanalysis, Feminism.* Bloomington: Indiana University Press, 1989.

Hodge, Frederick Webb, ed. *Handbook of American Indians North of Mexico.* Bureau of American Ethnology Bulletin 30. Washington, D.C.: Government Printing Office, 1907.

Holder, Charles F. "The Heart of the Desert." *Outing* 45 (1904): 417-23.

Horwitz, Howard. *By the Law of Nature: Form and Value in Nineteenth-Century America.* New York: Oxford University Press, 1991.

Howe, Marie Jenney. Letter to Mary Austin, 22 May 1918. Box 12, Mary Austin Collection, Huntington Library, San Marino, California.

Hoyer, Mark T. *Dancing Ghosts: Native American and Christian Syncretism in Mary Austin's Work.* Reno: University of Nevada Press, 1998.

———. "Prophecy in a New West: Mary Austin and the Ghost Dance Religion." *Western American Literature* 30.3 (1995): 237-57.

———. "'To Bring the World into Divine Focus': *The Land of Little Rain* as Syncretic Prophecy." *Western American Literature* 31.1 (1996): 3-31.

———. "Weaving the Story: Northern Paiute Myth and Mary Austin's *The Basket Woman*." *American Indian Culture and Research Journal* 19.1 (1995): 133-51.

Hulse, Frederick. SERA-Inyo: Owens Valley Fieldnotes (1935). Ethnological Documents Collection, University Archives, Bancroft Library, University of California, Berkeley. CU-23.1.

Ingersoll, Ernest. "Plant Life in the Desert." *Harper's Monthly* 110 (1905): 576-91.

Janmohamed, Abdul. "The Economy of Manichean Allegory." In *The Post-Colonial Studies Reader,* ed. Bill Ashcroft, Gareth Griffiths, and Helen Tiffin, 18-23. New York: Routledge, 1995.

Jaycox, Faith. "Regeneration through Liberation: Mary Austin's 'The Walking Woman' and Western Narrative Formula." *Legacy: A Journal of Nineteenth-Century American Women Writers* 6.1 (1989): 5-12.

Jones, Carter. *Hope for the Race of Man: Indians, Intellectuals and the Regeneration of America, 1917-1934.* Ph.D. diss., Brown University, 1991. Ann Arbor, Mich.: University Microfilms, 1992.

Jones, Holway R. *John Muir and the Sierra Club: The Battle for Yosemite.* San Francisco: Sierra Club, 1965.

Kahrl, William L. *Water and Power: The Conflict over Los Angeles' Water Supply in the Owens Valley.* Berkeley: University of California Press, 1982.

Kaplan, Caren. "Resisting Autobiography: Out-Law Genres and Transnational Feminist Subjects." In *De/Colonizing the Subject: The Politics of Gender in Women's Autobiography,* ed. Sidonie Smith and Julia Watson, 115-38. Minneapolis: University of Minnesota Press, 1992.

Karell, Linda. "*Lost Borders* and Blurred Boundaries: Mary Austin as Storyteller." In *American Women Short Story Writers: A Collection of Critical Essays,* ed. Julie Brown, 153-66. New York: Garland, 1995.

Kimes, William F. *John Muir: A Reading Bibliography.* Palo Alto, Calif.: Wreden, 1977.

King, Ynestra. "The Ecology of Feminism and the Feminism of Ecology." In *Healing the Wounds: The Promise of Ecofeminism,* ed. Judith Plant, 18-28. Philadelphia: New Society, 1989.

———. "Healing the Wounds: Feminism, Ecology, and the Nature/Culture Dualism." In *Reweaving the World: The Emergence of Ecofeminism,* ed. Irene Diamond and Gloria Feman Orenstein, 106-21. San Francisco: Sierra Club, 1990.

Klimasmith, Betsy. "Storytellers, Story-Sellers: Artists, Muses, and Exploitation in the Work of Mary Austin." *Southwestern American Literature* 20.2 (1995): 21-33.

Kolodny, Annette. *The Lay of the Land: Metaphor as Experience and History in American Life and Letters.* Chapel Hill: University of North Carolina Press, 1975.

Kristeva, Julia. *Desire in Language: A Semiotic Approach to Literature and Art.* Ed. Leon S. Roudiez. Trans. Thomas Gora, Alice Jardine, and Leon S. Roudiez. New York: Columbia University Press, 1980.

Krupat, Arnold. "An Approach to Native American Texts." In *Critical Essays on Native American Literature,* ed. Andrew Widget, 116-31. Boston: Hall, 1985.

Laird, Carobeth. "Behavioral Patterns in Chemehuevi Myths." In *Flowers of the Wind: Papers on Ritual, Myth, and Symbolism in California and the Southwest,* ed. Thomas C. Blackburn, 97-103. Socorro, N.M.: Ballena Press, 1977.

Lamar, Howard R., ed. *The Reader's Encyclopedia of the American West.* New York: Harper and Row, 1977.

Lane, Franklin K. Letter to Mary Austin, 3 February 1919. Box 14, Mary Austin Collection, Huntington Library, San Marino, California.

Langlois, Karen. "Mary Austin and Houghton Mifflin Company: A Case Study in the Marketing of a Western Writer." *Western American Literature* 23.1 (1988): 31-42.

——. "Mary Austin and the New Theatre: The 1911 Production of *The Arrow Maker." Theatre History Studies* 8 (1988): 71-87.

Lanigan, Esther. *Mary Austin: Song of a Maverick.* New Haven: Yale University Press, 1989.

Lanser, Susan Sniader. *Fictions of Authority: Women Writers and Narrative Voice.* Ithaca: Cornell University Press, 1992.

Latta, Frank F. *Saga of Rancho El Tejon.* Santa Cruz, Calif.: Bear State Books, 1976.

Laut, Agnes. "The Indian's Idea of Fine Arts." *Outing* 46 (1905): 355-63.

Lears, T. J. Jackson. "From Starvation to Self-Realization: Advertising and the Therapeutic Roots of the Consumer Culture, 1880-1930." In *The Culture of Consumption,* ed. Richard Wightman Fox and T. J. Jackson Lears, 1-38. New York: Pantheon Books, 1983.

LeGuin, Ursula K. *Dancing at the Edge of the World.* New York: Harper and Row, 1989.

Leverenz, David. "The Last Real Man in America: From Natty Bumppo to Batman." In *The American Literary History Reader,* ed. Gordon Hutner, 262-90. New York: Oxford University Press, 1995.

Liljeblad, Sven. "Oral Tradition: Content and Style of Verbal Arts." In *Great Basin,* ed. Warren L. d'Azevedo, 641-59. Vol. 11 of *Handbook of the North American Indians.* Washington, D.C.: Smithsonian Institution Press, 1986.

Limbaugh, Ronald H., and Kirsten E. Lewis, eds. The John Muir Papers, 1858-1957 (Microform). Alexandria, Va.: Chadwyck-Healey, 1986.

Lindsay, Vachel. *Going-to-the-Stars.* New York: D. Appleton and Company, 1927.

Long, William J. "The Modern School of Nature-Study and Its Critics." *North American Review* 176 (1903): 688-98.

Luhan, Mabel Dodge. *Edge of Taos Desert: Escape to Reality, Intimate Memories.* Vol. 4. New York: Harcourt, Brace, 1937.

——. "The Indian Speaks." Manuscript in the Mabel Dodge Luhan Papers, Beinecke Library, Yale University, New Haven, Connecticut.

——. Letter to Mary Austin, n.d. Box 14, Mary Austin Collection, Huntington Library, San Marino, California.

——. Letter to John Collier, 21 November 1922. Collier Collection, Sterling Library, Yale University.

——. Letter to the Pueblos, 3 November 1922. Mabel Dodge Luhan Papers, Beinecke Library, Yale University, New Haven, Connecticut.

——. "Mary Austin: A Woman." In *Mary Austin: A Memorial,* ed. Willard Hoagland, 19-22. Santa Fe: Laboratory of Anthropology, 1944.

Lyon, Thomas J. *John Muir.* Boise: Boise State College, 1972.

Lyons, Mary E. "Peter C. Yorke: Advocate of the Irish from the Pulpit to the Podium." In *Religion and Society in the American West: Historical Essays,* ed. Carl Guarneri and David Alvarez, 401-22. Lanham, Md.: University Press of America, 1987.

Marcus, Alan I. *Agricultural Science and the Quest for Legitimacy: Farmers, Agricultural Colleges, and Experiment Stations, 1870-1890.* Ames: Iowa State University Press, 1985.

Marx, Leo. *Machine in the Garden: Technology and the Pastoral Ideal in America.* New York: Oxford University Press, 1967.

"Mary (Hunter) Austin 1868-1934." In *Twentieth-Century Literary Criticism,* 25:15-46. Detroit: Gale, 1988.

Masson, J. Moussaieff, and Susan McCarthy. *When Elephants Weep: The Emotional Lives of Animals.* New York: Delacorte Press, 1995.

Mazel, David. "American Literary Environmentalism as Domestic Orientalism." In *The Ecocriticism Reader: Landmarks in Literary Ecology,* ed. Cheryll Glotfelty and Harold Fromm, 137-46. Athens: University of Georgia Press, 1996.

McCracken, Grant. *Culture and Consumption.* Bloomington: Indiana University Press, 1988.

Melham, Tom. *John Muir's Wild America.* Washington, D.C.: National Geographic Society, 1976.

Merchant, Carolyn, ed. *Ecology.* Atlantic Highlands, N.J.: Humanities Press, 1994.

———. *Radical Ecology: The Search for a Livable World.* New York: Routledge, 1992.

Merriam, C. Hart. *Studies of the California Indians.* Berkeley: University of California Press, 1955.

Michael, William H. "'At the Plow and in the Harvest Field': Indian Conflict and Accommodation in the Owens Valley 1860-1880." Thesis, University of Oklahoma, 1993.

Michaels, Walter Benn. *The Gold Standard and the Logic of Naturalism: American Literature at the Turn of the Century.* Berkeley: University of California Press, 1987.

Mighetto, Lisa, ed. *Muir among the Animals: The Wildlife Writings of John Muir.* San Francisco: Sierra Club, 1986.

Miller, Nathan. *Theodore Roosevelt: A Life.* New York: William Morrow, 1992.

Minh-ha, Trinh T. *Woman Native Other: Writing Postcoloniality and Feminism.* Bloomington: Indiana University Press, 1989.

Mitchell, Lee. "White Slaves and Purple Sage: Plotting Sex in Zane Grey's West." *American Literary History* 6.2 (1994): 234-64.

Mooney, James. *The Ghost Dance Religion and the Sioux Outbreak of 1890.* Fourteenth Annual Report of the Bureau of American Ethnology to the Smithsonian Institution, 1892-1893, pt. 2. Washington, D.C.: Government Printing Office, 1896.

Morris, C. Patrick. "Heart and Feces: Symbols of Mortality in the Dying God Myth." In *Flowers of the Wind: Papers on Ritual, Myth, and Symbolism in California and the Southwest,* ed. Thomas C. Blackburn, 41-57. Socorro, N.M.: Ballena Press, 1977.

Morrow, Nancy. "The Artist as Heroine and Anti-Heroine in Mary Austin's *A Woman of Genius* and Anne Douglas Sedgewick's *Tante.*" *American Literary Realism, 1870-1910* 22.2 (1990): 17-29.

Mosse, George L. *Nationalism and Sexuality: Respectability and Abnormal Sexuality in Modern Europe.* New York: Fertig, 1985.

Muir, John. "Bears." (From *Our National Parks,* 1901.) In *Muir among the Animals: The Wildlife Writings of John Muir.* Ed. Lisa Mighetto, 161-75. San Francisco: Sierra Club, 1986.

———. Draft of "My First Summer." Pre-1911. In John Muir Papers, 1858-1957 (microform), ed. Ronald H. Limbaugh and Kirsten E. Lewis, reel 31. Alexandria, Va.: Chadwyck-Healey, 1986.

———. *John Muir: The Eight Wilderness Discovery Books.* Seattle: The Mountaineers, 1992.

———. *My First Summer in the Sierra.* 1911. Reprint. Ed. Edward Hoagland. New York: Penguin Books, 1987.

———. "Twenty Hill Hollow Journal." 1868. In John Muir Papers, 1858-1957 (microform), ed. Ronald H. Limbaugh and Kirsten E. Lewis, reel 23. Alexandria, Va.: Chadwyck-Healey, 1986.

———. "Wild Sheep." 1874. In John Muir: The Eight Wilderness Discovery Books, 419-28. Seattle: The Mountaineers, 1992.

———. "Wild Wool." 1875. In John Muir: The Eight Wilderness Discovery Books, 871-76. Seattle: The Mountaineers, 1992.

———. The Yosemite. 1912. Reprint. Garden City, N.Y.: Anchor-Doubleday, 1962.

Mumford, Lewis. Review of The American Rhythm, by Mary Austin. New Republic 35 (30 May 1923): 23-24.

Murphy, Patrick D. Literature, Nature, and Other: Ecofeminist Critiques. Albany: State University of New York Press, 1995.

———. "Voicing Another Nature." In A Dialogue of Voices: Feminist Literary Theory and Bakhtin, ed. Karen Hohne and Helen Wussow, 59-82. Minneapolis: University of Minnesota Press, 1994.

Nabhan, Gary Paul. "Cultural Parallax in Viewing North American Habitats." In Reinventing Nature? Responses to Postmodern Deconstruction, ed. Michael E. Soulé and Gary Lease, 87-101. Washington, D.C.: Island Press, 1995.

Nash, Catherine. "Remapping the Body/Land: New Cartographies of Identity, Gender and Landscape in Ireland." In Writing Women and Space: Colonial and Postcolonial Geographies, ed. Alison Blunt and Gillian Rose, 227-50. New York: Guilford Press, 1994.

Natches, Gilbert. "Northern Paiute Verbs." University of California Publications in American Anthropology and Ethnology 20 (December 1923): 245-59.

National Child Welfare Association. The Baby Book. New York: National Child Welfare Association, 1916.

Nelson, Barney. The Wild and the Domestic. Reno: University of Nevada Press, forthcoming.

Nochlin, Linda. Women, Art and Power: And Other Essays. New York: Harper and Row, 1988.

Norris, Frank. The Octopus. 1901. Reprint. New York: Signet, 1964; New York: Airmont, 1969.

Norwood, Vera. Made for This Earth: American Women and Nature. Chapel Hill: University of North Carolina Press, 1993.

———. "Mary Austin 1868-1934." In Heath Anthology of American Literature II. 2d ed., ed. Paul Lauter et al., 916-18. Lexington, Mass.: D. C. Heath, 1994.

———. "The Photographer and the Naturalist: Laura Gilpin and Mary Austin in the Southwest." 1982. In "Mary Austin 1868-1934." Twentieth-Century Literary Criticism, 25:39-41. Detroit: Gale, 1988.

O'Grady, John P. Pilgrims to the Wild: Everett Ruess, Henry David Thoreau, John Muir, Clarence King, Mary Austin. Salt Lake City: University of Utah Press, 1993.

O'Neill, Elizabeth Stone. Meadow in the Sky: A History of Yosemite's Tuolumne Meadows Region. Fresno: Panorama West Books, 1983.

Ortiz, Alphonso. The Tewa World. Chicago: University of Chicago Press, 1969.

Page, Jake. "A Charged Particle among the Force Fields of Her Times." Smithsonian 22 (June 1991): 122-36.

Parini, Jay. "The Greening of the Humanities." New York Times Magazine, 29 October 1995, 52-53.

Parker, Andrew, et al., eds. *Nationalisms and Sexualities.* New York: Routledge, 1992.

Patee, Fred Lewis. *The Development of the American Short Story: An Historical Survey.* New York: Harper and Brothers, 1923.

Patencio, Francisco. *Stories and Legends of the Palm Springs Indians, as Told to Margaret Boynton.* 2d ed. Palm Springs, Calif.: Desert Museum, 1970.

Payne, Darwin. *Owen Wister: Chronicler of the West, Gentleman of the East.* Dallas: Southern Methodist University Press, 1985.

Pearce, T. M., ed. *Literary America 1903-1934: The Mary Austin Letters.* Westport, Conn.: Greenwood Press, 1979.

——. *Mary Hunter Austin.* New York: Twayne, 1965.

Perrin, Noel. "Forever Virgin: The American View of America." In *On Nature: Nature, Landscape, and Natural History,* 13-22. San Francisco: North Point Press, 1987.

Phelps, Elizabeth Stuart. *The Story of Avis.* 1877. Reprint. New Brunswick: Rutgers University Press, 1992.

Pickens, Donald K. *Eugenics and the Progressives.* Nashville: Vanderbilt University Press, 1968.

Plant, Judith, ed. *Healing the Wounds: The Promise of Ecofeminism.* Philadelphia: New Society, 1989.

——. "Searching for Common Ground: Ecofeminism and Bioregionalism." In *Healing the Wounds: The Promise of Ecofeminism,* ed. Judith Plant, 155-61. Philadelphia: New Society, 1989.

Plumwood, Val. *Feminism and the Mastery of Nature.* New York: Routledge, 1993.

Poirier, Suzanne. "The Weir Mitchell Rest Cure: Doctor and Patients." *Women's Studies* 10 (1983): 15-40.

Porter, Nancy. Afterword to *A Woman of Genius,* by Mary Austin, 296-321. Old Westbury, N.Y.: Feminist Press, 1985.

Powell, John Wesley. "Institutions for the Arid Lands." 1890. In *Selected Prose.* Ed. George Crossette, 41-52. Boston: David Godine, 1970.

——. *Surveys of the Territories. Letter from the Acting President of the National Academy of Sciences Transmitting a Report of the Territories* (3 December 1878). 45th Cong., 3d sess. H. Misc. Doc. 5. Washington, D.C.: Government Printing Office, 1878.

Powell, Lawrence Clark. "Mary Austin: *The Land of Little Rain.*" In *California Classics: The Creative Literature of the Golden State,* 44-52. 1971. Reprint. Santa Barbara: Capra Press, 1982.

Pratt, Mary Louise. *Imperial Eyes: Travel Writing and Transculturation.* New York: Routledge, 1992.

Pryse, Marjorie, ed. Introduction to *Stories from the Country of Lost Borders,* by Mary Austin, vii-xxxv. New Brunswick: Rutgers University Press, 1987.

Rawls, James J., ed. *New Directions in California History: A Book of Readings.* New York: McGraw-Hill, 1988.

Reisner, Marc. *Cadillac Desert: The American West and Its Disappearing Water.* New York: Viking, 1986. Reprint. New York: Penguin Books, 1987.

Robinson, Marilynne. *Housekeeping.* New York: Farrar, Straus and Giroux, 1980.

Rotundo, E. Anthony. *American Manhood: Transformations in Masculinity from the Revolution to the Modern Era.* New York: Basic Books, 1993.

Rowell, Galen. "Along the High, Wild Sierra: The John Muir Trail." *National Geographic*

(April 1989): 466–93.

Rudnick, Lois P. "Mabel Dodge Luhan and the Myth of the Southwest." *Southwest Review* 68.3 (1983): 205–21.

——. *Mabel Dodge Luhan: New Woman, New Worlds.* Albuquerque: University of New Mexico Press, 1984.

——. "Re-Naming the Land: Anglo Expatriate Women in the Southwest." In *The Desert Is No Lady: Southwestern Landscapes in Women's Writing and Art,* ed. Vera Norwood and Janice Monk, 10–26. New Haven: Yale University Press, 1987.

——. *Utopian Vistas: The Mabel Dodge Luhan House and the American Counterculture.* Albuquerque: University of New Mexico Press, 1996.

Ruppert, James. "Discovering America: Mary Austin and Imagism." In *Studies in American Indian Literature: Critical Essays and Course Designs,* ed. Paula Gunn Allen, 243–58. New York: MLA, 1983.

——. "Mary Austin's Landscape Line in Native American Literature." *Southwest Review* 68 (1983): 376–90.

Sauder, Robert A. *The Lost Frontier: Water Diversion in the Growth and Destruction of Owens Valley Agriculture.* Tucson: University of Arizona Press, 1994.

Scheick, William J. "Mary Austin's Disfigurement of the Southwest in *The Land of Little Rain.*" *Western American Literature* 27 (1992): 37–46.

Schlesinger, Arthur M., Sr. "A Critical Period in American Religion, 1875–1900." In *Religion in American History: Interpretive Essays,* ed. John M. Mulder and John F. Wilson, 302–17. Englewood Cliffs, N.J.: Prentice-Hall, 1978.

Schultz, James Willard. *Apauk, Caller of Buffalo.* Boston: Houghton Mifflin, 1916.

Schwartz, Judith. *Radical Feminists of Heterodoxy.* New Lebanon, N.H.: New Victoria Publishers, 1982.

Seltzer, Mark. *Bodies and Machines.* New York: Routledge, 1992.

Showalter, Elaine, ed. Introduction to "Woman Alone." In *These Modern Women: Autobiographical Essays from the Twenties.* Old Westbury, N.Y.: Feminist Press, 1987.

Smith, Shawn. "Superficial Depths: Visions of Identity in the Age of Mechanical Reproduction, 1839–1900." Ph.D. diss., University of California San Diego, 1994.

Smith, Sidonie. "Construing Truths in Lying Mouths: Truthtelling in Women's Autobiography." *Studies in the Literary Imagination* 23.2 (1990): 145–63.

——. "Resisting the Gaze of Embodiment: Women's Autobiography in the Nineteenth Century." In *American Women's Autobiography: Fea(s)ts of Memory,* ed. Margo Culley, 75–110. Madison: University of Wisconsin Press, 1992.

Snyder, Gary. *The Practice of the Wild.* San Francisco: North Point Press, 1990.

Soja, Edward M. *Postmodern Geographies: The Reassertion of Space in Critical Social Theory.* London: Verso, 1989.

Sollors, Werner. *Beyond Ethnicity: Consent and Descent in American Culture.* New York: Oxford University Press, 1986.

Solnit, Rebecca. *Savage Dreams: A Journey into the Landscape Wars of the American West.* New York: Vintage Books, 1994.

Spench, Hazelton. Review of *Going-to-the-Stars,* by Vachel Lindsay. *New Republic,* 31 August 1927, 52.

Spretnak, Charlene. "Ecofeminism: Our Roots and Flowering." In *Reweaving the World: The*

Emergence of Ecofeminism, ed. Irene Diamond and Gloria Feman Orenstein, 3-14. San Francisco: Sierra Club, 1990.

Starr, Kevin. *Americans and the California Dream, 1850-1915.* New York: Oxford University Press, 1973.

———. *Inventing the Dream: California through the Progressive Era.* New York: Oxford University Press, 1985.

———. "Mary Austin: Mystic, Writer, Conservationist." *Sierra Bulletin* 61 (November-December 1976): 34.

———. "A Myth for Southern California." In *New Directions in California History: A Book of Readings,* ed. James J. Rawls, 205-12. New York: McGraw-Hill, 1988.

Stegner, Wallace. *Beyond the Hundredth Meridian: John Wesley Powell and the Second Opening of the West.* New York: Penguin Books, 1953.

———. *Where the Bluebird Sings to the Lemonade Springs: Living and Writing in the West.* New York: Penguin Books, 1992.

Stein, Gertrude. "Composition as Explanation." c. 1926. In *Selected Writings of Gertrude Stein.* Ed. Carl Van Vechten, 513-23. New York: Modern Library, 1962.

Stewart, Frank. *A Natural History of Nature Writing.* Washington, D.C.: Island Press, 1995.

Stewart, Grace. *A New Mythos: The Novel of the Artist as Heroine 1877-1977.* Montreal: Eden Women's Press, 1979.

Stineman, Esther Lanigan. *Mary Austin: Song of a Maverick.* New Haven: Yale University Press, 1989.

Sturtevant, William C., gen. ed. *Handbook of the North American Indians.* 15 vols. Washington, D.C.: Smithsonian Institution Press, 1984.

Szynkiewicz, Slawoj. "Sheep Bone as a Sign of Human Descent: Tibia Symbolism among the Mongols." In *Signifying Animals: Human Meaning in the Natural World,* ed. Roy Willis, 74-84. London: Routledge, 1990.

Tedlock, Dennis, and Barbara Tedlock, eds. *Teachings from the American Earth.* New York: Liveright, 1975.

Terrell, John Upton. *The Man Who Rediscovered America: A Biography of John Wesley Powell.* New York: Weybright and Talley, 1969.

Thelma and Louise. Screenplay by Callie Khouri. Directed by Ridley Scott. Culver City, Calif.: MGM/UA Home Video, 1992, c. 1991.

Tompkins, Jane. *West of Everything: The Inner Life of Westerns.* New York: Oxford University Press, 1992.

Trachtenberg, Alan. *The Incorporation of America: Culture and Society in the Gilded Age.* New York: Hill and Wang, 1982.

———. "Who Narrates? Dreiser's Presence in Sister Carrie." In *New Essays on Sister Carrie,* ed. Donald Pizer, 87-122. Cambridge: Cambridge University Press, 1991.

Tracy, Henry Chester. "Mary Austin." 1930. In "Mary Austin 1868-1934." *Twentieth-Century Literary Criticism,* 25:24-25. Detroit: Gale, 1988.

Tuan, Yi-Fu. *Dominance & Affection: The Making of Pets.* New Haven: Yale University Press, 1984.

———. *Topophilia: A Study of Environmental Perception, Attitudes, and Values.* 1974. Reprint. New York: Columbia University Press, 1990.

Turner, Frederick Jackson. "The Significance of the Frontier in American History." 1893. In

The Turner Thesis: Concerning the Role of the Frontier in American History, ed. George Rogers Taylor, 1-18. Boston: D. C. Heath, 1949.

Turner, Victor. *The Ritual Process.* Ithaca: Cornell University Press, 1969.

United States Senate. Hearings on S. 3865 and S. 4223. 67th Cong., 4th sess. Washington, D.C.: Government Printing Office, 1923.

United States Statutes 43.1: 639-42.

Van Doren, Mark. Review of *The American Rhythm,* by Mary Austin. *Nation,* 18 April 1923, 472.

Veblen, Thorstein. *The Theory of the Leisure Class.* 1899. Reprint. New York: Modern Library, 1934; New York: Penguin Books, 1994.

Walker, Francis Amasu. "The Indian Question." *Outlander* 75 (1874): 13-22.

Watterson, Isabel. Letter to Mary Austin, 2 June 1907. Mary Austin Collection, Huntington Library, San Marino, California.

Weber, David J. "The Collapse of the Missions." In *New Directions in California History: A Book of Readings,* ed. James J. Rawls, 48-59. New York: McGraw-Hill, 1988.

Weigle, Marta, and Kyle Fiore. *Santa Fe and Taos: The Writer's Era 1916-1941.* Santa Fe: Ancient City Press, 1994.

Welter, Barbara. *Dimity Convictions.* Athens: Ohio University Press, 1976.

———. "From Maria Monk to Paul Blanshard: A Century of Protestant Anti-Catholicism." In *Uncivil Religion: Interreligious Hostility in America,* ed. Robert N. Bellah and Frederick E. Greenspahn, 43-71. New York: Crossroad, 1987.

West, Cornell. "Prophetic Pragmatism." 1989. In *Pragmatism: A Reader,* ed. Louis Menand, 403-16. New York: Vintage-Random House, 1997.

West, Neil. "Biodiversity of Rangelands." *Journal of Range Management* 46 (1993): 2-13.

Wharton, Edith. *The House of Mirth.* 1905. Reprint. Ed. Elizabeth Ammons. New York: Norton, 1990.

White, Richard. "'Are You an Environmentalist or Do You Work for a Living?': Work and Nature." In *Uncommon Ground: Rethinking the Human Place in Nature,* ed. William Cronon, 171-85. New York: Norton, 1996.

———. *The Organic Machine.* New York: Hill and Wang, 1995.

Woodmansee, Martha. "On the Author Effect: Recovering Collectivity." *Cardozo Arts and Entertainment Law Journal* 10 (1992): 279-92.

Woolf, Virginia. *A Room of One's Own.* 1929. Reprint. New York: Harcourt Brace Jovanovich, 1981.

Wyatt, David. "Mary Austin: Nature and Nurturance." In *The Fall into Eden: Landscape and Imagination in California,* 67-95. New York: Cambridge University Press, 1986.

Yezierska, Anzia. *Bread Givers.* 1925. Reprint. New York: Persea Books, 1975.

Young, Robert, ed. *Untying the Text: A Poststructuralist Reader.* New York: Routledge, 1990.

Young, Vernon. "Mary Austin and the Earth Performance." 1950. In "Mary (Hunter) Austin 1868-1934." *Twentieth-Century Literary Criticism,* 25:29-32. Detroit: Gale, 1988.

Contributors

ANNA CAREW-MILLER

Anna Carew-Miller completed her Ph.D. at the University of New Mexico in 1994 with a dissertation entitled "'Telling the Truth about Herself': Mary Austin and the Autobiographical Voice of Feminist Theory." She has published articles on early American literature, Native American literature, and critical theory and is interested in the theory of cultural constructions of self and nature. She currently heads the English Department at The Gunnery, an independent school in Connecticut, and continues to write on natural history subjects and Mary Austin.

KATHRYN DEZUR

Kathryn DeZur is a Ph.D. candidate in English at the Claremont Graduate University. Her dissertation focuses on late medieval and early modern English and Italian literature, and she has a sustained interest in colonialism/imperialism and women writers. She has been the associate editor of *Women's Studies: An Interdisciplinary Journal* for four years.

MELODY GRAULICH

After teaching American studies and women's studies for eighteen years at the University of New Hampshire, where she edited three of Mary Austin's books, Melody Graulich has moved much closer to Austin country. She now lives in Cache Valley, Utah, where she edits *Western American Literature* and teaches at Utah State University. She can now drive to the Owens Valley, where she plans to spend some time rethinking borders as she begins work on a new project on Japanese American internment camps.

TARA HART

Tara Hart lives in Baltimore and teaches literature and composition at Howard Community College in Columbia, Maryland. "Serving Suspended Sentences" is part of her doctoral dissertation ("Tender Horizons: The American Landscapes of Austin and Stein"), which received the 1996 Carl Bode Prize for the Best Graduate Dissertation in American Literature at the University of Maryland at College Park.

MARK HOYER

Currently an independent scholar working from his home in the Central Valley of California, Mark Hoyer has taught at the University of South Dakota and the University of California, Davis. His book *Dancing Ghosts: Native American and Christian Syncretism in Mary Austin's Work* (University of Nevada Press, 1998) explores the influences of native Great Basin and California cultures on Mary Austin in the first half of her writing career. He is currently working on a bioregional and multicultural literary study of the Klamath River in northwestern California. Other articles dealing with Mary Austin's use of Northern Paiute and Shoshone oral traditions have appeared in *Western American Literature* and the *American Indian Culture and Research Journal*.

LINDA K. KARELL

Linda Karell is an assistant professor at Montana State University, where she teaches literature of the American West and American literature. Her current project is a book-length study of collaboration in western American literature.

ELIZABETH KLIMASMITH

Elizabeth Klimasmith is a Ph.D. candidate in American literature at the University of Washington, where she serves as assistant director of the Expository Writing Program. Her essay on *A Woman of Genius* is part of a larger project on gender, class, and popular culture in the American urban landscape. She has also published essays in *ATQ* and *Southwestern American Literature*.

DALE METCALFE

Dale Metcalfe abandoned a career in corporate communications for a Ph.D. in American literature, which she earned at the University of California, Davis. Mary Hunter Austin, whose feminism and fascination with American Indian cultures mirrored her own interests, became the center of her studies. She is an associate professor of writing and literature at Prince George's Community College in Largo, Maryland. She continues to explore Austin's work and thought and to be inspired by her vision and audacity.

BARNEY (BARBARA) NELSON

A fifteenth-generation rural American, Barney Nelson has lived most of her life on farms and ranches in Iowa, Arizona, and Texas. She has authored more than three hundred magazine articles and four books (*The Last Campfire: The Life Story of Ted Gray, a West Texas Rancher* [Texas A&M Press, 1984], *Voices and Visions of the American West* [Texas Monthly Press, 1986], *Here's to the Vinegarroon!* [Territorial Printer, 1989], and *The Wild Domestic* [University of Nevada Press, forthcoming]), and her photographs have appeared as covers for most U.S. livestock magazines. She currently serves as environmental editor for *Range* magazine. She received a Ph.D. from the University of Nevada, Reno, in 1997 and is currently an assistant professor of English at Sul Ross State University in Alpine, Texas, where she specializes in classes dealing with the contemporary rural West, rural women, nature writers, and creative nonfiction writing.

ANNE RAINE

Anne Raine holds a master's degree in feminism and the visual arts from the University of Leeds and is now pursuing a Ph.D. in American literature at the University of Washington, Seattle. Her current research explores the intersections of American modernist aesthetics and socioecological theory and practice, focusing on landscape, artifacts, and human–nonhuman relations in writings by early twentieth-century women writers.

MARK SCHLENZ

Mark Schlenz received his doctorate from the University of California at Santa Barbara, where he now teaches preprofessional writing courses for environmental studies majors. His dissertation examines bioregional perspectives in the works of Mary Austin and Willa Cather. He recently published an environmental history essay on Mono Lake and has prepared an introduction for an edition of Mary Austin's *The Basket Woman* to be issued by the University of Nevada Press.

JUDY NOLTE TEMPLE

Judy Nolte Temple is an associate professor of women's studies and English at the University of Arizona. Under her previous name of Lensink she published an interdisciplinary study of a thirty-year-long pioneer diary, *"A Secret to be Burried"* (Iowa, 1989). She is currently working on a book-length study of the legend and private writings of Colorado's "Baby Doe" Tabor. She still becomes Mary Austin on occasion for humanities audiences throughout the West. Reading and portraying Austin combines her interests in auto/biography with those in southwestern culture, about which she has published two collections: *Old Southwest/New Southwest* (under Lensink) and *Open Spaces, City Places.*

NICOLE TONKOVICH

Nicole Tonkovich is an associate professor of U.S. literature at the University of California, San Diego, and the author of *Domesticity with a Difference: The Nonfiction of Catharine Beecher, Sarah J. Hale, Fanny Fern, and Margaret Fuller.*

MICHELLE CAMPBELL TOOHEY

Michelle Campbell Toohey is an assistant professor of English at Westmoreland County Community College. She recently received a Ph.D. from Indiana University of Pennsylvania in English with an emphasis on ecofeminist criticism and dissent literature. She has published papers in *ISLE* and *Studies in the Humanities,* and her current research interrogates women's political discourse.

Index

Abbey, Edward, xiv, 156, 166*n*8

"Aboriginal American Literature" (Austin), xxi

Actresses, 130-35, 140-46, 148*n*7

Adams, Ansel, xi, xii, xviii, xxi

Addams, Jane, 270

Agriculture, 249-53, 265*n*33, 265*n*38

"Agua Dulce" (Austin), 33

Allen, Paul Gunn, 78-79

"American Form of the Novel" (Austin), 244

American Indian Poetry (Cronyn), 83

American Indians. *See* Native Americans

American Rhythm (Austin), 34*n*4, 42, 66, 67, 70, 71, 74, 79, 81, 83, 83*n*1, 161, 164, 180, 263*n*5

Ammons, Elizabeth, xiv, xvi-xvii, xxiii*n*13, 105, 108, 109-10, 125*n*11, 134, 148*n*10

Androgyny, 105, 106

Arrow-Maker (Austin): authority over language production and dissemination in, 48-49; biblical and Native American motifs in, 46, 50-51; Chisera figure in, 46-51, 57, 69-70, 113-15, 117; dilemma of woman artist in, 106, 108; as drama of spiritual journey generally, 42-43; ending of, 51, 56, 62*n*26; feminist reading of, xv, 48; plot summary of, 46-48; publication of, 51; race and gender in, 44-51, 113-15; revisions of, 164; theatrical productions of, 62*n*31, 69, 113-14; theme of, 48

Ashcroft, Bill, 29

Auster, Albert, 130, 145-46

Austin, Mary: ancestors of, 168-69; biographies of, xiv; and cancer recovery, 17-18; and Carmel artists' colony, 16; and Catholicism, 17-18; on Chautauquas, 153; childhood of, 40-41, 66, 134, 148*n*11, 153, 175-76; critical responses to, xi-xxii; daughter of, 10-11, 124, 134, 148*n*11, 155-56, 160, 161, 169; drama as interest of, 40-43; economies of style of, 92-94; emotional "breakdown" of, 269-70; financial pressures on, 112, 124; in-print works of, xi; in Italy, 17; marriage of, 15-16, 21, 124; on "matrix" of own creativity, xiii; metaphors for creative territories of, xvii; in Mexico, 281*n*26; mother of, 10, 169-70; move to California, 21; nonconformity of, 16, 109, 115; personality of, xiv, xxiii*n*9; placement of ashes of, 158; poetry of, 65-83; politics of, 231; and Protestantism, 41, 177-78; Santa Fe home of, 124, 164; separation from husband by, 15-16, 116, 124, 189; style of, xiv-xv, 87-92, 223; on successful novels, 244;

303